KU-710-635

Families in
Multicultural Perspective

PERSPECTIVES ON MARRIAGE AND THE FAMILY
Bert N. Adams and David M. Klein, Editors

WIFE BATTERING: A SYSTEMS THEORY APPROACH
Jean Giles-Sim

COMMUTER MARRIAGE: A STUDY OF WORK AND FAMILY
Naomi Gerstel and Harriet Gross

HELPING THE ELDERLY: THE COMPLEMENTARY ROLES OF
INFORMAL NETWORKS AND FORMAL SYSTEMS
Eugene Litwak

REMARRIAGE AND STEPPARENTING:
CURRENT RESEARCH AND THEORY
Kay Pasley and Marilyn Ihinger-Tallman (Eds.)

FEMINISM, CHILDREN, AND THE NEW FAMILIES
Sanford M. Dornbusch and Myra F. Strober (Eds.)

DYNAMICS OF FAMILY DEVELOPMENT:
A THEORETICAL PERSPECTIVE
James M. White

PORTRAIT OF DIVORCE:
ADJUSTMENT TO MARITAL BREAKDOWN
Gay C. Kitson with William M. Holmes

WOMEN AND FAMILIES: FEMINIST RECONSTRUCTIONS
Kristine M. Baber and Katherine R. Allen

CHILDREN'S STRESS AND COPING: A FAMILY PERSPECTIVE
Elaine Shaw Sorensen

WHEN LOVE DIES: THE PROCESS OF MARITAL DISAFFECTION
Karen Kayser

FAMILIES BEFORE AND AFTER *PERESTROIKA*:
RUSSIAN AND U.S. PERSPECTIVES
James W. Maddock, M. Janice Hogan,
Anatolyi I. Antonov, and Mikhail S. Matskovsky (Eds.)

METAPHORS OF FAMILY SYSTEMS THEORY:
TOWARD NEW CONSTRUCTIONS
Paul C. Rosenblatt

FAMILIES IN MULTICULTURAL PERSPECTIVE
Bron B. Ingoldsby and Suzanna Smith (Eds.)

THE UNIVERSITY OF
WINCHESTER

Martial Rose Library
Tel: 01962 827306

1 7 JUN 2011

1 1 NOV 2011

2 9 MAR 2012

- 5 APR 2012

- 3 APR 2013

To be returned on or before the day marked above, subject to recall.

WITHDRAWN FROM
THE LIBRARY
UNIVERSITY OF
WINCHESTER

KA 0231407 X

FAMILIES IN MULTICULTURAL PERSPECTIVE

Edited by

BRON B. INGOLDSBY
SUZANNA SMITH

THE GUILFORD PRESS
New York   London

To our spouses and children
for the support and joy they bring us:
Valerie Percevault Ingoldsby, Marie and Hilary Ingoldsby,
Gary Appelson, and Jesse Smith-Appelson

© 1995 The Guilford Press
A Division of Guilford Publications, Inc.
72 Spring Street, New York, NY 10012

All rights reserved

No part of this book may be reproduced, stored in a retrieval
system, or transmitted, in any form or by any means, electronic,
mechanical, photocopying, microfilming, recording, or otherwise,
without written permission from the Publisher.

Printed in the United States of America

This book is printed on acid-free paper.

Last digit is print number: 9 8 7 6 5 4 3 2

Library of Congress Cataloging-in-Publication Data

Families in multicultural perspective / edited by Bron B. Ingoldsby,
  Suzanna Smith.
      p.   cm.
  Includes bibliographical references (p.   ) and index.
  ISBN 0-89862-307-3
  1. Family—Cross-cultural studies. 2. Kinship—Cross-cultural
studies. 3. Marriage customs and rites—Cross-cultural studies.
4. Sex role—Cross-cultural studies. 5. Home economics—Cross-
cultural studies. 6. Multiculturalism. I. Ingoldsby, Bron B.
II. Smith, Suzanna D.
GN480.F35   1995
306.85—dc20   94-33457
                                                                CIP

KING ALFRED'S COLLEGE
WINCHESTER

306.85 ING. 023140 7X

Contributors

Douglas A. Abbott, Associate Professor of Family and Consumer Sciences, University of Nebraska, Lincoln, Nebraska

Jack O. Balswick, Professor of Sociology and Family Development, Fuller Theological Seminary, Pasadena, California

Judith K. Balswick, Associate Professor of Family Therapy, Fuller Theological Seminary, Pasadena, California

Norma J. Burgess, Associate Professor of Child and Family Studies, Syracuse University, Syracuse, New York

Linda L. Haas, Associate Professor of Sociology, Indiana University, Indianapolis, Indiana

D. Terri Heath, Assistant Professor of Sociology, Linfield College, McMinnville, Oregon

Bron B. Ingoldsby, Professor of Family Science, Ricks College, Rexburg, Idaho

Gary R. Lee, Professor of Sociology, University of Florida, Gainesville, Florida

Patrick C. McKenry, Professor of Family Relations and Human Development and Black Studies, Ohio State University, Columbus, Ohio

William H. Meredith, Professor of Family and Consumer Sciences, University of Nebraska, Lincoln, Nebraska

Rosalie Huisinga Norem, Advisor for Natural Resources and the Environment, Coordinator of Latin American Programs, Agency for International Development, Office for Women in Development, Washington, DC

Sharon J. Price, Professor of Child and Family Development and Sociology, University of Georgia, Athens, Georgia

Suzanna Smith, Associate Professor of Human Development, University of Florida, Gainesville, Florida

Max E. Stanton, Professor of Sociology and Anthropology, Brigham Young University, Laie, Hawaii

Acknowledgments

We organized and edited this text with the assistance and support of a number of people. We particularly want to thank the scholars who contributed chapters in their areas of expertise. Most of them have already published extensively on the topics they cover, and we felt that the reader would benefit greatly from their knowledge. Working with each of the chapter authors made this project all the more enjoyable, and we very much appreciate their participation.

We want to thank Sharon Panulla, the Guilford editor in charge of this project, for her ongoing support. A special thanks goes to the series editors of Perspectives on Marriage and the Family, Bert Adams and David Klein, for their careful guidance and thoughtful encouragement throughout the book's production.

Preface

Families in Multicultural Perspective travels across geographic, cultural, and historical boundaries to explore the diversity of the world's families. The key word is *diversity*—in family structure, processes, history, and social and environmental contexts.

In writing this text, we had three major goals, discussed in more detail in the following sections:

- Increase students' recognition of and respect for cultural diversity as it influences family life.
- Meet educators' needs for a comparative family text.
- Contribute to the development of new ways of thinking about families by examining diversity in families.

FAMILIES AND CULTURAL DIVERSITY

We live in an age of continuous change and ever-increasing interdependence. We are currently witnessing the integration of nations into a global political and economic system. In addition, the United States is becoming an increasingly diverse nation as the African American, Hispanic, and Asian segments of the population consistently grow.

Many U.S. citizens are often accused of being ignorant of and insensitive to the customs and life-styles of other cultures. We rarely learn foreign languages, although this would open up new relationships and cultural experiences. When we visit foreign countries, we seldom seek out nationals to better understand their society. Even in our own country, one of the most diverse in the world, we surround ourselves with those like us and often know little about others.

This is indicative of the ethnocentrism that is firmly rooted in our consciousness and behavior. We tend to see the world only through our own eyes. We impose our own values on others, judging their behaviors and beliefs as strange or inferior instead of different and valuable.

The internationalization of economies, governments, and cultures creates new opportunities for examining diversity of social structures and processes, including family life. As the reader will discover, throughout history and across the planet, there have been many approaches for organizing and managing the business of families, such as finding a mate, producing offspring, relating to family members, and earning a living. We find that families are central to life in every society, no matter what their structure. Typically, families adapt to a multitude of environmental, economic, and political pressures and survive.

Increasingly, the importance of families is being recognized by the international community. For instance, 1994 marked the celebration of the United Nations International Year of the Family (IYF). The overarching goal of the IYF was to stimulate local, national, and international actions that are part of a sustained effort to promote awareness of family diversity, family needs, and gender-based inequality within families. In addition, the IYF encouraged the development of "family-sensitive" policies and services. Although individuals may disagree with any of the IYF's specific principles, we applaud the efforts of the international community to recognize the importance of families in all their various forms and to promote awareness of family diversity.

A COMPARATIVE FAMILY TEXT

Our second objective was to write a book that would meet educators' needs for a comparative family text. Using a mail survey, we asked a selected group of college and university instructors to choose, from a fairly comprehensive list, those topics they considered most important for a comparative family text. The chapters we have included in this book were chosen on the basis of the priority areas these educators identified. (See Smith & Ingoldsby, 1992, for a complete report of our findings.)

Our findings revealed that educators highly valued the traditional approaches to comparative family studies. Those who responded to our survey said it was important for a text to address what we might consider the foundations of comparative and multicultural family studies. These are family origin and universality, family functions, marital structure, kinship rules, and comparative research methods. We discuss these topics in the first two sections of this text, "Foundations of Comparative Family Studies" and "Family Variation."

Educators participating in the survey also placed a priority on topics pertaining to family development, particularly mate selection, marriage adjustment, parenting, divorce, and aging. These topics form the third section of this volume, "Family Development."

In addition, we found that educators were looking for a text that offered a closer look at contemporary concerns and particular cultural groups. Educators believed that students need to be informed about family life in certain contemporary societies, particularly the United States, Asia, Africa, and Latin America. In the text, examples from Third World regions are integrated into the chapters, as well as highlighted for themes they illustrate well, such as China for treatment of the elderly and Latin America for a discussion of patriarchy.

Finally, educators gave the highest ratings of importance to a group of topics seldom included in comparative family texts: social inequality, as manifested in gender stratification, class structure, racial discrimination, and poverty. In fact, 96% of those surveyed viewed the topic of gender roles as very important. We dedicated the section "Gender and Family Relations" to this subject. In the final section, "Social Inequality in the Contemporary World," we address other aspects of social inequality related to racism, patriarchy, and poverty.

We have attempted to be as comprehensive as possible in addressing each of the historical periods, world geographical regions, and major ideological viewpoints that have shaped human families. In this, we have been restricted by the availability of data and the interest areas that emerged from our study. Regarding historical periods, Chapters 2, 4, and 7 have drawn on material from ancient and pre-Renaissance history, but the text as a whole is strongest in detailing events from 1500 A.D. to the present day. As for world regions, our coverage of the Americas, Europe, Africa, and Asia is extensive but is weaker for the Middle East and Pacific regions. Finally, we discuss Judaic and Christian influences on families but are limited in our attention to Muslim, Eastern, and aboriginal philosophies. Although no text can include everything, we regret these losses.

One of the ways we have sought to increase student awareness and appreciation of diversity is with the inclusion of a "Student Exercise Bank," which is accompanied by "Exercise Guidelines for the Instructor." This collection of exercises, found at the back of the text, offers two exercises for each section of the text. The bank is designed to accomplish the following:

- Develop students' awareness of their own perspectives and biases regarding the major topics included in the text.
- Help students to better understand the major concepts presented.
- Give students an opportunity to apply these concepts.

In the Appendix at the end of the text, we present tables that provide detailed information about worldwide diversity in family formation, dissolution, and living conditions. These tables demonstrate global similarities and differences in family experiences and can be used to highlight or supplement information presented in some chapters.

NEW WAYS OF THINKING ABOUT FAMILIES

Our third goal for this text was to contribute to new ways of thinking about families. This is very natural for a text about family diversity, but it moves us into areas of theory and research not traditionally addressed in comparative family studies.

A theory is a way of seeing things that allows us to organize and understand all the data we collect. Good theories provide explanations for our observations and allow us to predict what we should be able to find, given our theory's constructs and assumptions. Just as there is diversity in families, there are various theoretical frameworks for understanding family structure and interaction, each one providing certain insights and obscuring others.

Much of the germinal work in comparative family studies was rooted in theories that emphasized family structure and function. These theories presented a sometimes narrow view of the world that was based on Western constructions of family life but provided important, basic concepts and the impetus for considerable research. New approaches emerging in the 1960s and 1970s placed a specific emphasis on multiculturalism and, consequently, offered different ways of looking at and studying families. In the structure and content of this book, we incorporate both traditional and emerging approaches.

As we review the early ethnographic work in Part II, we see the family from the perspective of *structural–functional theory*. This approach, which focused on the marital and kinship structures and family members' functional roles, has been used extensively by social scientists to organize and to explain research study results.

Later, family sociologists relied on *developmental theory*, which presumes that families can best be understood by knowing their stage of development in the "family life cycle." We follow such a perspective in Part III.

More recently, *feminist theory* has focused attention on the construction of family lives based on socialized gender roles, gender differences in power and communication, and the systematic oppression of women in cross-gender interactions. This approach has coincided with the development of other oppression-sensitive models centered around the social construction of racial, ethnic, and class-based inequalities and their impacts on families. These perspectives provide the theoretical grounding for Parts IV and V.

In closing, this book was written as a celebration of the diversity of family forms, processes, and experiences throughout the world. We approach this topic from the perspective that understanding differences in cultures, societies, and families helps to broaden and deepen our knowledge and appreciation of all families, and can also help us to learn more about our own societies. We hope that readers will join us in this celebration.

BRON B. INGOLDSBY
SUZANNA SMITH

REFERENCE

Smith, S., & Ingoldsby, B. (1992). Multicultural family studies: Educating students for diversity. *Family Relations*, *41*, 25–30.

Contents

PART ONE

FOUNDATIONS OF COMPARATIVE FAMILY STUDIES

Courtesy Robert Thorpe.

Introduction

Part I of this text provides the foundations necessary for the study of families from a comparative perspective. This includes an overview of family theories that guide our thinking about family life, a historical perspective on families, and a summary of the research methods used to conduct research on families in different societies. Together, these provide the bases for understanding the ways family scholars look at and study families in different societies.

In Chapter 1, "Family Theory and Multicultural Family Studies," Suzanna Smith briefly highlights the diversity of the world's families and asks how we can begin to understand such diversity. Smith suggests that theoretical perspectives help us to comprehend various family forms, processes, and experiences. She reviews major family theories and examines their existing and potential contributions to a multicultural perspective.

Chapter 2, "The Family in Western History," examines the historical roots of many U.S. families from ancient times through the colonial period and up to the present. Bron B. Ingoldsby pays particular attention to the role of ideology regarding gender and power in shaping the marital and parent–child relationships of white families. Throughout the chapter, the reader traces the continued subordination of women and children to men within the family structure of the period. (Chapter 14 presents an analysis of the history of African American families in the United States.)

In Chapter 3, "Comparative Research Methodology," Gary R. Lee provides an overview of the research methodologies that guide us in making comparisons about human behavior across cultures. Lee reviews the major types of comparative family research, including cross-cultural, cross-societal, and cross-national. He emphasizes the methodological issues in comparative research that make it difficult for scholars to draw conclusions about differences and similarities across cultures. Lee also underscores the important interplay between theory and research, pointing out that theory gives us the guide to our research whereas comparative research enables us to test theories about how societies affect human behavior.

CHAPTER ONE

Family Theory and Multicultural Family Studies

SUZANNA SMITH

Major demographic changes are reshaping our globe. World population has doubled in the last 40 years and within the next 30 to 40 years another 3 billion people will be added, most of them in Third World regions (Population Reference Bureau, 1989). Currently, 77% of the world's population lives in the Third World (Encyclopedia Britannica, 1992). By 2025, five out of six people will live in Latin America, Africa, Asia, and the Middle East. In contrast, only one in six persons will live in the industrialized nations, including all of Europe, the United States, Canada, Australia, New Zealand, Russia, and Japan (Population Reference Bureau, 1989). These trends indicate that Third World populations will become an increasingly visible and important part of the world system whose needs must be recognized.

There are vast differences in the population structures of the more and less industrialized countries that affect families and societies. Whereas families in industrialized nations typically are smaller and older, those in the Third World are larger and younger. All industrialized countries are facing the challenges associated with the aging of their populations due to low birth rates and increased life expectancy. Currently, 12% of the population in the most industrialized nations is age 65 and older; this rate will be 20% or more by the year 2030 (Encyclopedia Britannica, 1992; Population Reference Bureau, 1989). In contrast, in Third World countries higher mortality rates and birth rates than in industrialized nations create a younger age structure (United Nations, 1991). About 36% of the population of Third World countries is younger than age 15, compared to 21% in industrialized nations (Population Reference Bureau, 1989; Encyclopedia Britannica, 1992).

Differences among the world's nations in demographic, economic, and household conditions often have profound effects on family formation and

5

development. For example, in industrialized nations, longer life-spans, lower infant mortality rates, higher literacy levels, and the growth in demand for female labor in certain jobs have meant that women no longer need to be defined solely by their family role, and many postpone marriage and child-bearing. Also, the increased availability of contraception has increased women's ability to limit the number of children they have, which has resulted in lower fertility rates and smaller household sizes (Goldscheider & Waite, 1991; Hutter, 1981). In contrast, a shorter life expectancy, higher infant mortality, lower literacy levels, an agriculturally based economy, and earlier age of marriage for many Third World women mean that their lives tend to be defined by marriage and childrearing; other options are limited (United Nations, 1991).

Most of the world's economically developed countries have maintained sufficiently reliable information about their populations so that changes over time in a few family-relevant characteristics can be observed. In the past few decades, marriage rates and married couple families with children have de-clined in many industrialized nations, while divorce and nonmarital childbearing have increased (Encyclopedia Britannica, 1993; U.S. Bureau of the Census, 1992).

There seems to be considerable diversity in family life worldwide, not a standardization of family forms and no prototypical contemporary family (Tepperman & Wilson, 1993). Indeed, due to the diversity of living condi-tions, social forces, and cultures worldwide, "the only common feature . . . of family life patterns . . . is *convergence to diversity*" (Boh, 1989, cited in Cheal, 1991, p. 175; emphasis in original). (For more detailed information about international diversity, see the Appendix at the end of the text.)

WHAT IS FAMILY?

This variety raises certain questions for us as students of the family. How are we to understand the diversity and complexity of family life within and across cultures? To begin, we might search for definitions of "the family." Some family scholars define family as a group of related persons in differ-entiated family positions, such as husband and wife, parent and child, or aunt and niece, who fulfill the functions necessary to ensure family sur-vival, such as reproduction, child socialization, and emotional gratifica-tion (Winch, 1979). This definition is often interpreted as establishing the heterosexual nuclear family—a legally married couple living together with their offspring—as the norm. Some accept that there may be a single adult heading the household but require that a dependent child or adult be present (Popenoe, 1993).

Other scholars advise that we need to explore the roots of family variations in a multitude of ethnic, racial, and cultural identities (Cheal, 1991; Thomas & Wilcox, 1987). Some argue that we have not yet understood variations in family structure, function, and interaction because we have viewed all families in comparison with a white middle-class nuclear family model, rather than on their own terms and in a particular sociohistorical context (Gubrium & Holstein, 1990; Stacey, 1990, 1993; Thorne, 1992). Some family scholars argue that we have tended to see families that do not conform to the standard nuclear family as "deviant" (Burgess, Chapter 14, this volume; Cheal, 1991; Hutter, 1981; Smith, 1993). Still others suggest that family is defined by individual experiences rather than according to a particular structure, and that no single family form is right for all people at all times (Gubrium & Holstein, 1990).

Some family scholars argue that changes in U.S. families, such as increased divorce and nonmarital cohabitation, signal the weakening or even death of marriage and the family (Bellah, Madsden, Sullivan, Swidler, & Tipton, 1985; Cheal, 1991; Popenoe, 1988, 1993). Others suggest that a portrait of family as a unified and harmonious whole conceals internal inequities and coercion, based on gender and age hierarchies, that give adult men greater authority and power in the home and may actually be detrimental to women and children (Balswick & Balswick, Chapter 13, this volume; Cheal, 1991; Smith, 1987).

Considering these controversial debates, what are we to conclude is the "truth" about families? In this book, we suggest that there is no single, correct definition of family (Sprey, 1988, 1990). Rather, there are multiple definitions formulated from a particular theoretical perspective (Doherty, Boss, LaRossa, Schumm, & Steinmetz, 1993). In other words, theory shapes our definitions and expectations of family life. How we answer the question, "What is family?" depends in part on how we *think* about families, their similarities, and their differences. Similarly, what we *know* about families is also based on theories that guide our research because our theory determines what questions we will study (the importance of theory for comparative research is discussed by Lee in Chapter 3, this volume). In addition, the theoretical perspective one adopts is influenced by historical developments of the time, ideological beliefs, and personal experiences (Levin & Trost, 1992; Stacey, 1993). Consequently, no one theory could satisfactorily represent "the" truth. But the *many* ways we look at families can help us to better understand them.

This chapter provides an overview of major family theories that have shaped our understanding of family life. Some of these theories view the family as a nuclear unit with certain functions. Historically, these theories dominated the comparative study of families and contributed basic theoretical constructs regarding family organization. Other more recent theories interpreted family as based on personal experience and subjective definitions. These emerging theories often emphasize diversity and the social influences such as gender, race, and ethnicity that structure different experiences of family and society. All family theories have contributed in different ways to our understanding of family diversity precisely because they offer differing perspectives. I do not confine the discussion to theories that have explicitly addressed diversity or have been used to study families cross-culturally. Instead, I examine each theory's major concepts, as well as the theory's use—or potential use—in multicultural family studies.

WHAT IS FAMILY THEORY?

The word "theory" is rooted in a Greek word that means "to look at, view, or contemplate" (Osmond & Thorne, 1993, p. 591). A theory is a set of interconnected ideas that frames the world in a certain way and guides how we observe and explain phenomena. Family theories are concerned with explaining general patterns of behavior across families. For example, a family theory might explain the conditions that lead couples to divorce, or the process families use to recover from a major financial loss. However, family theories are *not* concerned with *specific* family or individual behaviors, such as why a certain couple divorced (Doherty et al., 1993).

Family theories structure how we think about families, what we observe, how we interpret this knowledge, and how we use the information in programs and policies that affect family life. Consequently, theories have a profound effect on what we know about families. Yet a theory presents a certain, limited view based on its particular vocabulary, ideas, and interpretations of family life (Sprey, 1990). To a large extent, theorists conceive their questions and answers in a unique and time-bound sociocultural setting (Sprey, 1988). Thus, family theories reflect the changes in, and concerns regarding, family life of the times (Berardo & Shehan, 1984). Certain themes emerge, depending on the historical period in which the theory was developed.

In this chapter, I group theories according to their major themes. "Structure and Function" emphasizes family composition, roles, and functions in society. "Systems Theories" focuses on three theories that emphasize family interaction and stability. "Individualism and Interaction" brings into focus the centrality of the concept of individualism and autonomy in social interactions. "Difference and Diversity" reviews theories that emphasize the importance of understanding differences within and among families based on social structural conditions such as gender, class, race, and ethnicity. The chapter concludes with a discussion of "Implications for Multicultural Family Studies."

STRUCTURE AND FUNCTION

Structural–functional theory has been a major influential approach to the study of the family for more than 30 years (Broderick, 1993). Technically, structural–functional theory is one type of systems theory. I cover it separately here because of its distinct importance to comparative family studies and its differences from other systems theories discussed in the next section. Those focus more on family process rather than structure.

This perspective views society as an organism that strives to resist change and maintain itself in some sort of balance or equilibrium (Broderick, 1993; Hutter, 1981). Stability and order are considered natural and desirable, whereas conflict and disorder are evidence of deviance and dysfunction in the system. The theory is concerned with the functional connections among the various parts of the system, that is, how each part supports or detracts from the system's functioning (Broderick, 1993; Hutter, 1981; Kingsbury & Scanzoni, 1993).

The social patterns that maintain the larger social system are *functional requisites*. Every society must meet these in some way if it is to survive. For example, every society must find a way to meet its members' physical needs. The members might hunt and gather, grow crops, or sell their labor for cash to purchase food, but if they do not find some way to successfully perform this function they will not survive (Broderick, 1993).

In every society, some arrangement of biologically related persons, that is, "the family," has had the primary function of recruiting new members through reproduction and socialization. The structure of the family—the number and designation of familial positions such as spouse, parent, child, and other kin—might vary considerably. Yet certain functions are universally met by families to satisfy members' physical and psychological needs and to meet the survival and maintenance needs of society (Broderick, 1993; Kingsbury & Scanzoni, 1993). Because of the importance of these concepts to multicultural family studies, they are discussed in detail by Ingoldsby (Chapters 4 and 6, this volume).

Probably the most well-known scholar associated with the structural–functional perspective on families was Talcott Parsons.[1] Writing in the 1950s, Parsons proposed that, like all other social systems, if the family were to survive, it had to develop the mechanisms to meet certain functions. Parsons gave considerable attention to the "instrumental and expressive functions"— instrumental involving survival and expressive pertaining to maintenance of morale and cooperation (Broderick, 1993).

Parsons observed that in industrial societies, the ideal family structure to carry out these societal functions and to satisfy the physical and psychological needs of family members is the nuclear family (Clayton, 1979; Kingsbury & Scanzoni, 1993). According to Parsons, the family unit must have a particular arrangement of roles within the social system to be successful at meeting its functions. Instrumental activities are assigned to the husband/father, who specializes in being the breadwinner and family chief. Expressive activities are assigned to the wife/mother, who specializes in nurturing family members and building family relationships (Kingsbury & Scanzoni, 1993). According to the theory, this gender-role specialization maintains family equilibrium while enabling families to reproduce and socialize children, thereby reinforcing societal equilibrium (Kingsbury & Scanzoni, 1993).

While Parsons focused his attention on systems stability, other scholars in this tradition were interested in the social conditions associated with family change. Three separate investigations (Goode, 1968; Nimkoff & Middleton, 1960; Winch & Blumberg, 1968) found that family structure, function, and societal complexity are related. Simpler, preindustrial societies (hunting and gathering) and more advanced industrial societies have smaller family structures, whereas agricultural societies are characterized by extended families. Also, families of all structures perform certain functions in society not met by other institutions. As societies move toward modernization, industrialization, and urbanization, traditional family forms shift from the extended family to the "conjugal" family (Clayton, 1979). Basically, families become smaller and based on the nuclear structure, free choice of marital partner is possible, relationships between spouses are more equal, and parents have less authority over children (Goode, 1968).

These concepts continue to influence contemporary studies of the relations between social change and family structure (e.g., Brydon & Chant, 1989, pp. 134–160). In addition, these studies demonstrated that although the economy is an important determinant of family structure and function (Winch, 1979), family patterns cannot be predicted on the basis of economic and technological change alone. Families are also influenced by ideological and cultural changes pertaining to individualism, autonomy, and family and gender roles (Hutter, 1981). Thus, the social, cultural, and historical context are vitally important to understanding family arrangements and interactions.

In conclusion, structural–functional theory made significant contributions to the family field in general and to comparative family studies in particular. The theory prompted social scientists to construct important cross-cultural data sets of studies of societies worldwide that allowed them to test their ideas about major theoretical issues (these data sets are discussed by Lee, Chapter 3, this volume). The theory provided one of the first formulations of several important "systems" concepts that have been extensively adopted by other theories, notably family systems, human ecology, and symbolic interactionism, which are discussed in more detail later in this chapter. Structural–functional theory also provided some of the conceptual building blocks for comparative family studies, particularly kinship and marital structure, and universal family functions (see Ingoldsby, Chapters 4 and 6, this volume). One of the most criticized aspects of the theory has been its "rigid" conceptualization of gender roles and the tendency to present the nuclear family form as the ideal model for Western families, without regard to the viability of other family forms (Broderick, 1993; Epstein, 1988; Thorne, 1992). Indeed, as we will see in the discussion of other theories, many that came after structural–functionalism attempted to overcome some of its problems (e.g., family systems) or to challenge its basic assumptions (e.g., feminism and phenomenology).

SYSTEMS THEORIES

This section includes family theories that are based on systems concepts—family systems, human ecology, and family development. Because the basic concepts of these theories are similar, I review them here and then discuss their unique contributions in subsequent sections.

The basic systems concept is that the family is an organic system striving to maintain balance as it confronts external pressures (Hill & Rodgers, 1964). Following are the processes by which family systems operate (Broderick, 1993; Bubolz & Sontag, 1993; Mattessich & Hill, 1987).

1. Family members are considered interdependent parts of a larger whole; each family member's behavior affects all other family members.
2. To adapt, human systems take in information, make decisions about alternatives, try out a response, get feedback about its success, and modify behavior as needed.
3. Families maintain permeable boundaries that establish them as distinct from other social groups, such as separate residences, family rituals, and "inside" jokes.
4. Like other social organizations, families must accomplish certain tasks in order to survive, such as physical sustenance, economic maintenance, reproduction (through birth or adoption) of family members, socialization for family and work roles, and emotional nurturance. This task performance is functional not only for families but for the larger society (Broderick, 1993; Bubolz & Sontag, 1993; Mattessich & Hill, 1987).

Family Systems Theory

Family systems theory is based on general systems theory, an interdisciplinary theory that originated after World War II in the physical sciences

(Broderick, 1993; Cheal, 1991). According to general systems theory, a system is a "set of elements [the elements being the parts of the system] standing in interaction among themselves and with the environment" (Von Bertalanffy, 1975, cited in Whitechurch & Constantine, 1993, p. 332). Basically, the theory proposed that living systems exchange information with the environment and use energy or feedback from the environment to grow, differentiate, or modify or correct a course of action (Broderick, 1993).

Family systems theory emphasizes the whole family rather than the individual within the system. The family has qualities that can only be described from the combined characteristics of its members, that is, the relationships among them. This system strives to maintain equilibrium (also called homeostasis) and to adapt to changes in the environment through a complex communication process of information exchange (Broderick, 1990; Whitechurch & Constantine, 1993).

The family systems approach is unique from other systems models in that it examines the communication processes family members use to develop cohesion and resolve conflict. The theory emphasizes *family transactional patterns*—recurring sequences of behavior among family members that can be observed over long periods of time. The theory looks at the reciprocal impacts of individuals' behavior on others in the system and of everyone's action on the entire system (Broderick, 1990; Whitechurch & Constantine, 1993). Many of the same questions about transactions among individuals are also asked about the subsystems—the adult couple, parent–child dyads, and siblings. For example, we might ask how various subsystems communicate or conflict with each other (Whitechurch & Constantine, 1993).

Family systems are connected with larger systems, or *suprasystems*. These include extended family networks, workplaces, neighborhoods, and schools. Suprasystems also include racial, ethnic, and regional subcultures. Family systems maintain separateness from other systems through *boundaries*. The boundary defines the system and represents the point of contact with the environment—other systems external to but in transaction with the family.

Because families and their members must interact with other institutions to get the resources they need, family boundaries are always at least somewhat permeable to allow inputs from other systems such as information, goods and services, and elements for survival such as food and clothing. Families may be described as more or less *closed or open systems*, depending on the degree to which they admit environmental inputs (Broderick, 1993; Cheal, 1991).

Family systems theory has been used extensively as a framework for therapeutic intervention because of its usefulness in conceptualizing family problems and possible ways to restore order. Due to this emphasis on internal family processes, most family systems scholars have paid less attention to the integration of family members and units into the larger community and culture. However, some early studies showed an association between social class, ethnicity, and family process. Other more recent work has found that physical and mental health and security in the community are associated with social structural conditions such as immigrant status and social network ties. Community-based supports or constraints may actually be more important than internal family problems to adjustment (Broderick, 1990). These studies suggest that transactions between families and other systems may be a particularly important but underrecognized dimension of family process.

Family systems theory has important concepts to offer to multicultural family studies. Much of the current international development literature on Third World households provides useful information about family structure, gender roles, and rational decision making involved in household functioning but neglects the psychosocial processes at the heart of families. Systems theory could be adopted to describe the interactional process among family members and the outcome of this communication, in any cultural setting. The theory's emphasis on the communication process as an adaptive response to pressures on the system could be particularly important to understanding family adjustment to economic change, poverty, and environmental degradation.

Human Ecology Theory

The previous discussion of family systems theory noted that its attention to transactions between individuals, families, and external social systems was generally unexplored. A theoretical approach that *focuses* on human–environment linkages is human ecology (Bronfenbrenner, 1979, 1986; Bubolz & Sontag, 1993).

Human ecology emerged in the late 19th century and reemerged in the 1960s. The theory is built on the concept of ecology, defined as the "study of interrelationships between organisms . . . and the environment, both organic and inorganic" (Bubolz & Sontag, 1993, p. 419). Family ecology, which developed out of home economics, focuses on the relations between families and their various environments. The family is conceived as a life-support system dependent on the natural environment for physical sustenance and on the social environment for human contact and meaning (Hook & Paolucci, 1970). A premise of family ecology theory that differs from other systems theories of families is that all human populations are interdependent with the earth's resources, so human quality of life cannot be considered apart from the health of the world's ecosystem (Bubolz & Sontag, 1993).

The human ecosystem is composed of the following environments: the *natural physical–biological environment*, including climate, animals, social, water, and plants; the *social–cultural environment*, encompassing social networks of humans (e.g., neighbors and community), cultural constructions (e.g., laws, values, and norms), and social and economic institutions; and the *human-built environment*, including roads, farms, and cities. A *family ecosystem* comprises these environments with which a family interacts. Each of these systems is connected so that they mutually influence the other (Bubolz & Sontag, 1993). If we were to use an ecological perspective to study families, we would be interested in the interactions of family members with their environment.

To summarize, family ecology theory assumes that families, regardless of their structure, ethnic or national origin, social class, or life stage, take in energy and information and make necessary adaptations to the environment. They do this not only through communication and decision making but through managing the physical and material resources and technologies available to them as they carry out their daily activities. Human development takes place in the family context and is influenced by the reciprocal interactions with the other three types of environments.

Previous applications of the ecosystem approach have demonstrated its usefulness. For example, this theory has been used to compare black South African children's development in three different rural environments and found that children in dry, unproductive resettlement areas scored lowest on measures of self-concept, cognitive development, and physical growth. Other studies have focused on the relationships between environmental factors, youth behaviors, and educational outcomes for U.S. African American and Hispanic students (for a review, see Bubolz & Sontag, 1993). Further comparative research is need to demonstrate how transactions between complex, interdependent systems can be measured and interpreted.

Human ecology theory has the capacity to be a useful framework for multicultural family studies for the following reasons. First, it accepts diverse family structures and inclusive definitions of family to encompass not only those related by blood, marriage, or adoption but others who share common resources, goals, and commitment to maintaining a family-like relationship over time. Second, it assumes that cultural diversity may affect family interaction and human development. Third, human ecology theory presents individual and family problems in relation to the larger society. Thus, family problems in education, employment, or housing are related to structural factors such as discrimination and poverty, not to individual pathology or dysfunctional family communication (for a similar point, see Broderick, 1990). Fourth, the theory's emphasis on environmental resources makes it particularly applicable to studies of rural families in developing countries that depend on natural resources for survival.

Human ecology theory is unlike most other family theories in that it places a responsibility on scholars to study and assist groups that lack resources, social power, and control over their lives, such as the poor, elderly, disabled, and women. It emphasizes "human betterment" (Bubolz & Sontag, 1993, p. 426) in terms of economic adequacy, justice, freedom, and peace. These ideas are explicitly international—the needs of the "have-nots" in the developing world must be addressed. Because of its commitment to action, the theory might be utilized as a framework for analyzing the interactions between human development and social conditions such as poverty at all eco-systems levels, including the individual, family, community, and society. This could result in public policies, institutional programs, and community action plans at each level to alleviate such problems.

Family Development Theory

Family development theory emerged during the optimistic period of social reconstruction after World War II (Duvall, 1988). This theory placed the nuclear family and its regular patterns of expansion, transition, and contraction at the forefront of considerable theory building, research, and clinical practice. Family development theory pioneered the understanding of the processes of change in families (Broderick, 1990; Mattessich & Hill, 1987).

According to the theory, families go through a predictable sequence of *family life-cycle stages* that are precipitated by family members' biological, social, and psychological needs, such as such as the birth of a first child or retirement (Rodgers & White, 1993). The theory also recognizes that the social and historical context is important for family development. Transitions to another stage are caused not only by individual and family processes but by society's norms, historical events, and ecological conditions (e.g., retirement is expected to occur at a certain age but may be delayed due to economic strains during a recession) (Mattessich & Hill, 1987). Mattessich and Hill (1987, p. 445) present the sequence of family life-cycle stages that most families experience as follows:

1. Newly established couple (childless)
2. Childbearing families (infants and preschoolers)
3. Families with school children (one or more of school age)
4. Families with secondary school children (one or more in adolescence)
5. Families with young adults (one or more over 18)
6. Families in middle years (children launched)
7. Aging families (parents in retirement)

At each stage, *family developmental tasks* must be accomplished if families are to move on successfully to the next stage and to maintain balance in the family (Cheal, 1991; Hill & Rodgers, 1964; Rodgers & White, 1993). Family roles emerge and change to help families make the transition to new stages and to meet their needs at each stage. For example, the birth of a first child introduces the need for a father to develop nurturing competencies to care for a newborn (Mattessich & Hill, 1987).

Family changes that result from developmental transitions may create a crisis because these changes require significant role alterations and family reorganization (Mattessich & Hill, 1987). The periods of disorder that accompany these role changes are called *normal crises of transition.* For example, the first few months after a child's birth are often chaotic because a couple is adjusting to the addition of a new family member, changes in sleep patterns, unfamiliar roles, and new ways of interacting.

Since 1950, the family development model has been an important theoretical orientation for teaching, research, and clinical practice (Broderick, 1990; Mattessich & Hill, 1987). Although mainly applied to U.S. families, the family development perspective has been used to a limited extent in comparative research. For example, studies of several European counties and the United States revealed a decline in marital satisfaction, and in shared power and decision making between men and women over the course of the couple's marital career. Other, country-specific studies have demonstrated the applicability of family development concepts across cultures (for examples, see Heath, Chapter 8, this volume; and McKenry & Price, Chapter 9, this volume).

Despite the theory's contributions, it has been criticized for presenting a "modal" course of family development. According to critics, the model of a two-parent childrearing family does not capture the enormous variation in family structures and experiences that have resulted from contemporary demographic and social changes in the United States, such as increases in divorce, remarriage, and single parenthood (Broderick, 1993). In addition, the theory may not be able to accommodate the multiple variations in family development due to variations in the values, practices, and goals of different racial and cultural groups.

However, proponents of the theory (Mattessich & Hill, 1987) refute this criticism. They present cross-cultural evidence that the ordering and sequencing of family development are universal, whereas the content of family roles and social expectations of families may vary culturally and historically. They suggest that the general outline of family development could be applied to families in various cultures while also taking into account their unique goals, aspirations, and activities defined in relation to their culture.

According to Mattessich and Hill (1987), the solution is not to reject the theory but to come up with the developmental patterns for these other family structures. The difficulty would be in defining phenomenologically equivalent life stages and developmental tasks that could be tested for different cultural groups. Whether or not these conceptual and methodological difficulties can be addressed depends in large part on the success of future research in testing models of family development that apply to other cultures (Mattessich & Hill, 1987; Rodgers & White, 1993).

INDIVIDUALISM AND INTERACTION

Individualism and personal autonomy, choice, and identity have become prominent concerns in social science literature. Applied to families, the acceptance of individualism as a social norm means greater freedom to shape intimate relationships to personal needs and desires (Cheal, 1991). The following sections discuss the major family theories that are organized around individuals and their interactions, symbolic interactionism, and exchange. Although both are popular frameworks for analyzing the white nuclear family in the United States, neither of these has been used extensively in multicultural studies.

Symbolic Interactionism

Symbolic interactionism was the principal theoretical orientation of the 1920s and 1930s and is one of the most popular family perspectives today, possibly because the theory is able to accommodate an interest in the individual in the context of family (LaRossa & Reitzes, 1993). The theory defines family as "a unit of interacting personalities." This means that family life is constituted by dyadic and family interactions that maintain marital and parent–child relationships (Hutter, 1981).

Symbolic interactionism proposes that humans create symbolic worlds through their interactions and that these in turn shape human behavior. Humans act toward things (including other people) on the basis of the meanings these things have for them. Meanings are based on cultural symbols and social values, which are communicated through verbal and nonverbal interactions. Individuals consciously use verbal and nonverbal behaviors to "perform" a role and identity. At the same time, they interpret and assign meaning to others' responses. Through these social interactions, individuals gauge the appropriateness of their behavior in particular settings and "align" themselves with cultural expectations communicated by the other person. This process of "aligning actions" helps to explain how cultural values are understood and responded to at the individual level (LaRossa & Reitzes, 1993).

Each person's sense of identity is derived from social interactions (LaRossa & Reitzes, 1993). That is, how we think of ourselves emerges from our communication with others. One important concept is that of *salience of identity*. This refers to the probability of an identity being invoked in a given situation or a variety of situations based on its relative importance to the individual. The more prominent the identity, the more motivated an individual is to perform and excel in associated role-related behaviors. For example, an employed woman's tendency to spend more hours than her employed husband in child care may be explained by the salience of the parenting role. This is determined not only by her personal desires but by social norms that women should value parenting more than men do and motherhood more than their other identities (LaRossa & Reitzes, 1993).

Roles refer to shared norms about how individuals who occupy certain social positions should behave. Roles specify the knowledge, ability, and emotions that are expected of individuals in their interactions. For example, the norms associated with parenthood in industrial societies include prescriptions about the quality and quantity of what parents should know, what skills they should possess, how motivated they should be, and the emotional energy they should give to their children (LaRossa & Reitzes, 1993). Roles change over time, based on changing interactions, contexts, and past experiences. For instance, becoming a parent of a second child will be different due to the accumulation of knowledge, skills, and experience from the firstborn child.

In summary, symbolic interactionism focuses on the individual and the development of his/her identity through social interactions, particularly in the family. The theory's emphasis on meanings individuals assign to interactions can enhance our understanding of family life by adding a phenomenological dimension to our awareness of family structure.

The theory's drawbacks for adding to a multicultural perspective come in large part from a history of being applied almost exclusively to the study of middle-class white families in the United States, and the theory's failure to situate individuals and families in a particular social, economic, cultural, or historical context (Hutter, 1981). Consequently, we may be unable to see the repercussions of events external to the family for the organization and functioning of family life. For example, losing a job symbolizes failure to a man who derives his primary identity from the breadwinner role, but unemployment also places a significant financial burden on the man's family; this event can be understood in economic as well as symbolic terms.

In addition, the focus on symbolic interactions may overlook socially sanctioned, hierarchical structures within families and society and the impacts of these structures on the meanings family members assign to their interactions. In many societies, men have the capacity to impose *their definitions of reality* on women due to men's legitimized power in virtually all social institutions. For example, in rural African households men usually have greater control and influence over women's work because of men's greater access to resources such as land, money, agricultural inputs, and material goods, as well as greater power and prestige (Blumberg, 1991). It is fair to say that couples' interactions are driven by men's individual and social resources and legitimized power, rather than by the symbolic meanings individuals give to their personal interactions (Cheal, 1991).

Nevertheless, symbolic interactionism may have the potential to examine how social factors such as gender, race, ethnicity, social class, and age operate through individuals' interactions, as persons interpret symbols and shared social meanings communicated in their interactions. The theory could, for example, guide research that would define the symbolic processes operating in African American families and how these differ from European American families (LaRossa & Reitzes, 1993). Or, symbolic interaction could be used as a framework for a comparison of the salience of the mother role for working-class women in the United States and Brazil, and the impacts of the interpretation of motherhood on these women's view of the feminist movement (see, e.g., Enloe, 1989).

Such applications of the theory have yet to be tested. However, if further research demonstrates the effectiveness of the theory in tapping the development of identity and meaning in particular social and cultural contexts, while taking into account the impacts of power and inequality on social interactions, it could be useful for multicultural studies.

Exchange and Resource Theories

Exchange theory, a popular framework in family studies, is based on an economic metaphor that uses a profit motive as a basis of social interaction (Cheal, 1991). Social relationships are considered "markets" in which individuals "act out of self-interest with the goal of maximizing profits" (Sabatelli & Shehan, 1993, p. 385). (For further discussions and applications of exchange principles, see Ingoldsby, Chapter 7, this volume; and Balswick & Balswick, Chapter 13, this volume.)

Contemporary exchange theories use the concepts of rewards, resources, and costs as the foundation of interpersonal exchanges. *Rewards* include personal attraction, social acceptance, social approval, instrumental services, prestige, and power. When individuals receive rewards from participating in a relationship, they are more likely to engage in the interaction with the rewarding individual again. *Resources* are any "commodity," such as "love, status, services, goods, information, and money" (Sabatelli & Shehan, 1993, p. 398), that can be transferred interpersonally, enabling one person to reward another. *Costs* include punishments experienced as a result of a certain exchange, or rewards that have been forgone due to engaging in one behavior or course of action rather than another. There are three types of costs: Direct costs are the resources given to others in an exchange. Investment costs include the time people spend acquiring skills to reward others. Opportunity costs are rewards that are given up at least temporarily as a result of participating in a relationship (Sabatelli & Shehan, 1993).

When assessing the value of the relationship, individuals evaluate its outcomes in comparison with certain standards, such as social norms of physical attractiveness and "style," and personal preferences and aspirations regarding appearance, intelligence, personality, and friendship networks. This *Comparison Level* (CL) serves as a standard for evaluating the rewards and costs of a relationship in relation to what people feel they deserve or can obtain. Relationships that fall above the CL are evaluated as satisfying; those below the CL would be considered unsatisfying (Sabatelli & Shehan, 1993). When expectations regarding some highly valued aspect of the relationship are not met, the general assessment of the relationship will be low (Sabetelli & Shehan, 1993).

Even high levels of rewards do not ensure that a relationship will continue. Individuals compare available alternatives with their present relationship and these comparisons help the individual to decide whether to remain in or leave the relationship. The lowest acceptable level of outcomes relative to available alternatives is called *Comparison Level of Alternatives*. This does not mean that a better alternative actually exists. Rather, the person *believes* a more rewarding relationship can be found and can overcome barriers to leaving, such as emotional and financial dependence, religious or family pressures to stay together, and continued feelings of love and attraction. This individual is more likely to leave an unsatisfying relationship than is someone who believes that he/she will not find a better relationship (Sabatelli & Shehan, 1993).

Relationships are generally viewed as satisfying when partners make about equal contributions and receive about equal positive outcomes. Under these conditions, a relationship meets expectations of *fairness*. When individuals do not believe the relationship outcomes are fair, they can reduce their "investments" in the relationship or try to increase their "profits" by attempting to change the other person's behavior. Another major consideration is whether exchanges are considered mutually responsive, or "reciprocal." *Reciprocity* refers to conditions in which individuals negotiate exchanges that not only benefit themselves but are mutually rewarding and take each others' needs into account.

In summary, exchange theory gives us basic concepts with which to analyze the cognitive factors involved in the development, maintenance, and change of intimate relationships. In close relationships, the *relative* levels of partners' resources, dependence, and attraction impact the interaction, including intimacy, satisfaction, and stability.

Exchange theorists have devoted considerable attention to the dynamics of power and exchange in relationships. According to the theory, *power* refers to the control of another's behavior by resisting compliance or extracting it from the other person. An individual is able to extract compliance when he/she controls resources that are needed by the other person or in the relationship. The relationship is considered *asymmetrical* when one partner has fewer resources, is more dependent, and is more attracted to the relationship. Asymmetrical relationships are not mutually satisfying and rewarding. Based on these principles, exchange theory has made a particular contribution to the analysis of the inequitable distribution of resources based on gender and the impacts of this asymmetry on marital decision-making power and control (Sabatelli & Shehan, 1993)

Economists have used exchange principles to identify the use of resources in marital interactions in Third World settings. For example, Jones (1986) studied changes in household labor allocation to farming when cash crops were introduced to an area of Cameroon (Jones, 1986). Results indicated that women were obligated by tradition to shift some of their time to their husbands' cash-crop fields, at the expense of food production for their families. A woman could expect to be compensated by her husband in cash, which offset the costs of lost time for food-crop production for their families. When women received a lower level of cash returns for their work than expected, they altered their behavior to increase their benefits and to restore greater symmetry to the relationship—they reduced their time in their husbands' fields, refused to prepare their husbands' food, or stopped working at critical points in the production cycle. Nevertheless, they could not go "too far" in negotiating a more equitable relationship for fear of being beaten by their husbands in reprisal.

Early presentations of the theory formulated by anthropologists also demonstrated its applicability in various cultural contexts. Lévi-Strauss (1969) emphasized that exchange behavior is regulated by social norms and values; thus, exchange interactions are not restricted to direct interaction among individuals but include "complex networks of indirect exchange among various social groups" (Sabatelli & Shehan, 1993, p. 388).

However, the theory's contemporary individualistic orientation may not adequately capture the complex sets of relationships embedded in local kinship ties, cultural beliefs, and social structure. Indeed, exchange theory can be criticized for simplifying complex human interactions as a calculated give and take between individuals. The theory assumes that a rational, cost–benefit analysis drives their exchanges; rich, complicated, and varied social and cultural influences tend to be reduced to a cognitive process "mediated" by culture, race, class, and gender (see Sabatelli & Shehan, 1993, p. 404).

For instance, exchange theory assumes that people enter and exit exchanges voluntarily (e.g., courtship and marriage). Yet culturally defined social obligations may limit individuals' abilities to seek their own rewards (Osmond & Thorne, 1993). Because women in many societies lack individual resources and social status, they are at a disadvantage in any exchange relationship. For example, a young, lower-class woman in Bangladesh has little say as to whether or not she will be betrothed to a potential mate. A complex system of obligations based on social customs and responsibilities to benefactors determines the woman's future, not her personal preferences (White, 1992). Thus, to be appropriate to this situation, exchange theory would need to present a broad picture of multiple exchange networks and to account for gender-based inequalities throughout this system. (For further discussion of the limitations of this approach to understanding the complexities of marital interactions, see Balswick & Balswick, Chapter 13, this volume.)

DIFFERENCE AND DIVERSITY

The social movements of the 1960s and 1970s—civil rights, antiwar, and feminist—provided the backdrop for a new wave of theory development that focused on diversity, the inventiveness of individual actors, and participatory democracy (Gubrium & Holstein, 1993). In this section, I describe two theoretical approaches, feminism and phenomenology.

Feminist Theories

There is a wide range of feminist perspectives rather than a singular feminist theory, but these approaches share one overarching viewpoint as well as several themes (Osmond & Thorne, 1993). In general, feminist theories combine a focus on women and their subordination in society *and* a commitment to ending that subordination. Existing gender relations in family and society are considered unacceptable and in need of correction through social change and political action.

The concept of *gender* has been considered by some to be the most important advance in feminist theory because it brings into focus the social construction of differences between men and women. For years scientists assumed that differences in men's and women's behavior were a reflection of biological traits. Feminist scholars argued that culture, not nature, constructs dichotomous role categories such as masculine–feminine and woman–man (Osmond & Thorne, 1993; West & Zimmerman, 1987). Society exerts control over behavior through the socialization of men and women into different social roles that define what behavior is considered appropriate and "natural" for each gender (e.g., independence and aggressiveness are associated with masculinity). The process of identification with masculinity or femininity begins in childhood but continues throughout life as people "do" gender, that is, carry out expected gender behaviors in their interactions at home and outside the family (Osmond & Thorne, 1993; West & Zimmerman, 1987).

Within feminism, there are various theoretical perspectives that differ in their focus, as described next. Recall that feminist theory includes an explanation of women's subordination as well as a commitment to end it. Thus, each theory has a particular perspective on the source of women's subordination and each assumes a specific course of action to free women from oppression.

According to *liberal feminism*, women and men have the same rational and spiritual capabilities and equality can be obtained if they have the same educational, economic, and political opportunities. Liberal feminists believe that social and legal reforms will create these opportunities for women by ending sex discrimination and stereotyping and improving educational and employment opportunities (Osmond & Thorne, 1993).

Radical feminism focuses on patriarchy as the source of women's oppression and proposes that patriarchy must be eliminated to change men's power over women. One branch of radical feminism challenges men's control over women's sexuality and reproduction in various forms, including pornography, prostitution, and rape, as well as reproductive technologies and access to legalized abortion. A second branch of radical feminism celebrates women's cultural, spiritual, and sexual experiences, such as women's nurturance of others, their physical beauty in all its shapes and sizes, and their unique capacity to bear children (Osmond & Thorne, 1993).

Socialist or materialist feminism, which is based on Marxism, emphasizes the "material" base of women's subordination in capitalism as well as patriarchy (Osmond & Thorne, 1993). The emphasis is on the "underlying economic relations that structure social interactions between men, women, and children," including family relations (Cheal, 1991, p. 93), and privilege men and while devaluing women's work. Feminists argue that equality is not possible in a class-based society and that radical social change, rather than reform, is necessary to overcome oppression. They focus on changing the economic and political aspects of women's work, such as their concentration in lower-paid sectors of the labor force and uncompensated responsibility for supplying most household labor (Hartmann, 1981).

Feminists who look at the nature of personal experience and everyday life have used and modified symbolic interactionism, phenomenology, and ethnomethodology in *feminist interpretive approaches* (Osmond & Thorne, 1993). These approaches focus on how gender is constructed in interactions, how men use power in their interactions to dominate women, and how women and men have conflicting views of their experiences that may impact communication (Tannen, 1990). Interpretive approaches make women's subordination "real" by describing how it is played out in everyday interactions. Interactionists expect that this understanding enables us to begin to change our gender-based interactions (Osmond & Thorne, 1993).

Many feminists have criticized Freud's model of psychosexual development, his premise that biology is destiny, and the sexism in his practice. *Feminist psychoanalytic approaches* have attempted to eliminate these male-centered and sexist assumptions. These feminist perspectives have focused on, for example, the centrality of mothering to children's development and women's interpretation of morality as based in caring and compassion for others. Feminist psychoanalysts observe that the social world is connected to internal psychic worlds. However, they also believe that unconscious patterns of dominance can be changed, and that equality is possible with basic transformations in men's and women's psyches (Osmond & Thorne, 1993).

All feminists view gender relations as being at the core of family life and that it is almost universally true that women have the primary responsibility for family matters (Abel, 1986; Ferree, 1990; Osmond & Thorne, 1993; Robinson, 1988). Cultural ideologies that associate women with motherhood and care giving often constrain women's participation in other arenas, not only because women are socialized for family roles but because assumptions about what is "appropriate" for women to do limit their opportunities in the workplace. Thus, the family is considered not just a site of loving family relations but also a locus of women's subordination and control (Hartmann, 1981).

Feminism has made a particular contribution by challenging the view of "the family," arguing that it is a monolithic construct that does not accurately represent the diversity of household forms, kinship arrangements, and sexual relationships that are part of social life (Osmond & Thorne, 1993; Thorne & Yalom, 1992). Feminists have exposed these biases toward the everyday realities and varieties of family life by examining the experiences of working single mothers, complex extended kin groups formed through divorces and remarriages, and gay adoptive couples (Stacey, 1990). Black feminists have played a major role in reconceptualizing the family by rejecting the middle-class nuclear family as the norm for all families (Burgess, Chapter 14, this volume; Dilworth-Anderson, Burton, & Johnson, 1993; Osmond & Thorne, 1993).

This means that the conceptualization of the family as a unified interest group is incorrect. Individuals within families have different interests and activities, which often come into conflict with each other, and different resources to influence other family members (Hartmann, 1981). Feminist scholars have suggested that rather than studying the family as a unit we should focus attention on the underlying gender system that structures differences between men and women in their work and family activities and in their power in decision making (Cheal, 1991; Thorne, 1992). They have also proposed that we should view family as a construct of meanings and relationships distinguishable from the household as a residential and economic unit. This is an important shift from a focus on family *structure* to families as "units of *experience*" (Osmond & Thorne, 1993, p. 617; emphasis added).

As I have pointed out in previous sections, early comparative family work examined the family as an isolated unit while neglecting its integration into larger economic and governmental systems that affected family life. In contrast, feminist scholarship recognizes that gender is a basic structural feature not only of families but of all other institutions, including work, religion, medicine, and education. By placing women at the center of analysis, feminism focuses our attention not only on the work women do in the family but also on basic issues of inequality in all institutions across all societies (Osmond & Thorne, 1993). Substantial documentation of indicators of women's worldwide subordination now exists (United Nations, 1991).

However, feminist theory's emphasis on social context also guides us to examine how interpretations of women's place in society vary from one culture to another and from one historical period to the next. For example, in the United States in the 19th century, men were glorified as "good providers" (Osmond & Thorne, 1993). In the 1980s, "real men" ate beef but certainly not quiche. In the 1990s, this image of masculinity is giving way for some men to the "sensitive new age guy" who avoids eating red meat, likes to talk about his feelings, is constantly expanding his consciousness, and is concerned about his partner's and children's well-being (e.g., Lavin, 1991). It is important to note that because gender differences are part of specific sociocultural contexts, we cannot assume that the norms regarding gender are the same in Argentina as they are in Arkansas, or that Cuba's upper class creates gender in the same ways as the country's working poor (Fenstermaker, West, & Zimmerman, 1991).

In addition, feminist theory forces us to go beyond a primary focus on kinship structure to look at the *dynamics* of structural influences on family life. It shifts our focus from defining who is in or out of the family to questions about how cultural ideology, social norms, religious beliefs, and cultural practices determine acceptable gender and age-related behavior, limit women's life options, and perpetuate the traditional social order.

Finally, feminist theory suggests that family scholarship should be used to benefit women through direct intervention (e.g., helping battered women), social action, and legal and policy changes that ultimately empower women in their families and society. These changes can be expected to be met with resistance, sometimes by those in positions of power, sometimes by women themselves who have different interpretations of women's roles than do feminist scholars. Thus, feminist theory poses challenges to feminist scholars who work directly with men, women, and communities on research projects and assistance programs for women.

This summary of feminist theory suggests that it is particularly useful for multicultural family studies because it emphasizes the cultural, social, and historical influences on women's and men's family and work roles, decision making, and intrafamilial communication. (For in-depth discussions of feminist principles as applied in multicultural settings, see Smith, Chapter 11, this volume; Haas, Chapter 12, this volume; and Balswick & Balswick, Chapter 13, this volume.)

Phenomenology

Phenomenology provides a dramatically different approach by focusing on the meaning of everyday life to social actors. (Phenomenology is indebted to symbolic interactionism for this concept.) The meanings people use to organize and interpret the world in understandable terms can be called culture.

In their recent review, Gubrium and Holstein (1993) call family "a way of attaching meaning to interpersonal relations" in social interaction (p. 654). In other words, family is not so much a "thing"—a concrete entity—but a way of interpreting interpersonal ties. Phenomenology assumes that because people construct their own social worlds, things, including families, can have a *variety* of meanings, depending on the observer. Thus, definitions of family can vary from person to person. Some may think of family as father–mother–children. Others define family by feelings of caring, belonging, and commitment, regardless of the kinship status of loved ones (Gubrium & Holstein, 1990; Lindsey, 1981). Thus, we could use the term "being family" to describe the underlying sense of trust and commitment in certain social relationships rather than to focus only on kinship ties and family structure (Gubrium & Holstein, 1990).

Phenomenology emphasizes what is termed "family discourse"—the talk and practical reasoning about families. The focus of this work is *interpretations people make about families*, not the family structure as an entity. The theoretical concern is less about defining who is part of "the" family and more on how people use family as an idea to specify their relations with others (Gubrium & Holstein, 1990).

For example, according to the theory, marriage is not just a legal and ceremonial institution; it is the continuing construction of a relationship through conversation about concrete realities that establish partners as a unit larger than husband and wife (Gubrium & Holstein, 1993). Similarly, families, not just couples, construct a reality from members' *shared* assumptions about how the world is organized and how they should manage it (Reiss, 1981). Thus, family is a "project" that family members engage in through their discourse.

As indicated earlier, the focus of phenomenology is on the social construction of everyday life. The concept of *life world* refers to our *experience* of life, which we take for granted. We assume our life world has a certain definable physical and temporal reality, but what we believe to be reality is actually shaped from everyday, subjective experience (Gubrium & Holstein, 1990, 1993). This means that "objects," including families, cannot be viewed as separate from the "subjects" that view them and cannot be described apart from the meaning these subjects ascribe to the objects.

In the everyday life world, "we take for granted that some interpersonal linkages are familial and others are not" (Gubrium & Holstein, 1993, p. 656). "Family" matters can be defined on the basis of the following charactersitics: *affectional*, which refers to the quality of the relationship, particularly the love and attention given by one person to another; *custodial*, the ties or bonds that link persons in caregiving relationships; and *durational*, a sense of history of the relationships and of ongoing commitment to support through a family connection (Gubrium & Holstein, 1990).

Our interpretation of home life is based on our *stock of knowledge* about the life world. This includes our images, theories, values, attitudes, and ideas about what constitutes family. In other words, the stock of knowledge is a way of assigning meaning to experience (Gubrium & Holstein, 1993). The stock of knowledge is dynamic. It expands and shrinks as we interact with the world, develop theories about our experiences, and add personal experiences of family to the stock. The result is different interpretations of reality. An example is the conflicting definitions of family. According to the phenomenological perspective, such definitions represent different ways of interpreting interpersonal relations, based on the relevant stock of knowledge and individual perspective.

One of the mistaken criticisms of phenomenology is that, by allowing individuals to define their own family boundaries, *anyone* can be included as a family member. The theory does interpret family as those who share ideas about who family is and have collective representations about house, home, family, caring, and other aspects of family life. However, not just anyone can be considered family. Descriptions must make sense and must "convince the . . . observer of the organized character of the setting in question." Thus, the definition of family is not based on just one individual's interpretations but must relate to "what everyone knows" about family (Gubrium & Holstein, 1993, p. 662). I add a word of caution here to note that "what everyone knows" must be considered in reference to the cultural context. As indicated earlier, shared knowledge about the nuclear family may tell us little about the organized character of polygamous African families.

To summarize, phenomenology emphasizes the social construction and contents of daily life. The theory proposes that by looking at the practical interpretations of everyday life to those who live it, we can better understand cultural belief systems and how these organize people's domestic realities (Gubrium & Holstein, 1993).

Phenomenology has already demonstrated its usefulness in identifying the meaning of families in cultural context. By emphasizing how individuals use familial "labels," such as mother, father, sister, brother, to include nonbiological kin as a part of family linkages, phenomenology allows people themselves to define family on their own terms and in the context of their everyday realities. For example, in African households someone called brother may or may not be related by blood or even live in the same household. Phenomenology instructs us that we learn much more about African households by understanding the meaning of brother in family discourse, who uses it, to whom the term is applied, and how this interpretation fits with everyday life, than by recognizing only biological kin as brothers.

Similarly, Stack's (1974) famous study of an urban black community illustrates how U.S. cultures also use expansive definitions of family. Some study participants indicated that their own blood ties, including parents, had little to do with rearing them or supporting them in their daily lives. "Substitute" parents and kin were responsible for childrearing and providing instrumental and emotional support and were the ones who were considered kinfolk.

The phenomenological approach shifts the focus of study from quantification of "objective" aspects of family life to how families use the "vocabulary of family" to describe their lives (Gubrium & Holstein, 1993). Thus, the approach should be chosen when the goal is to better understand interpretations of family within and across various cultural and social settings.

IMPLICATIONS FOR MULTICULTURAL FAMILY STUDIES

In this chapter, I reviewed major family theories and discussed their contributions, potential usefulness, and possible problems as frameworks for multicultural family studies. Table 1.1 presents an overview of the findings.

The first column shows the varying definitions of family from the particular theoretical perspective. As I discussed earlier, each theory's definition focuses our attention on certain aspects of family life. The second column shows how each theory already makes a unique contribution to our understanding of family diversity, depending on its particular focus, such as family structure, process, development, ideology, and so on. The third column summarizes key potential uses of the theory for multicultural family studies. Each theory could make a certain contribution, depending on its focus and the aspect of family life being studied. The last column presents some possible problems with each theory; again these limitations are a result of the theory's focus rather than a problem that means the theory should be rejected. Family scholars might overcome some of these constraints by selecting theories that appear most appropriate to guide investigations of certain topics (e.g., family systems theory to study family interactional processes related to mate selection in Bangladesh). Thus, no one theory would be appropriate for all situations, but one could be selected that would provide the best "fit" between the theory's concepts and the family phenomena under study.

Despite these theoretical contributions, family theories as a whole place some limitations on our understanding of family diversity.

1. The concentrated theoretical and empirical focus on white, Western, two-parent families has limited our understanding of other families and has resulted in an implicit or explicit model of comparison for all families, regardless of cultural, ethnic, racial, or class differences. As a result, diverse family patterns are overlooked, misunderstood, judged as deviant, or assumed to be on the same assimilative path to the nuclear family form (Gubrium & Holstein, 1990; Thorne, 1992).

2. The focus on the family *unit* as a cooperative, homeostatic group overlooks differences *within the family*, in individual interests, personal concerns, and access to resources. Due to the stratification of most societies and families along gender and generational lines, the unequal distribution of resources and power tends to favor the interests of men over those of women and children (Hare-Mustin, 1988; Whitechurch & Constantine, 1993).

3. A conceptual focus on individual processes and intrafamilial interactions tends to isolate families from the social context and limits our understanding of the influences of diverse social, cultural, and historical forces that affect family processes (Broderick, 1993).

To overcome these limitations and make a significant contribution to emerging global and multicultural studies, family scholars could examine and modify existing theoretical biases that limit our understanding of diversity. This would require situating and interpreting family lives in their social, cultural, and historical contexts and recognizing the impacts of oppression on families and their members (Burgess, Chapter 14, this volume; Dilworth-Anderson et al., 1993). From a practical standpoint, families of various structures and backgrounds would need to be included in further research and theory-building efforts and a priority placed on understanding the topic of study from the standpoints of families of different cultures. Such an approach would direct us to Third World women, men, and children; to ethnic and

TABLE 1.1. Contributions of Family Theories to Multicultural Family Studies

Theory	Definition of family	Contributions to multicultural studies	Potential use in multicultural studies	Possible problems
Structural–functionalism	A structure that satisfies members' needs and operates for the survival and maintenance of society	Basic systems concepts Basic comparative family concepts Cross-cultural data sets Studies of family structure, function, and social change	Descriptions and explanations of marital and family structure and family functions cross-culturally	Rigid interpretation of gender roles Overemphasis on stability versus change
Family systems	An organic system striving to maintain a balance as it confronts external pressures	Studies of impacts of social structural factors on family well-being	Descriptions and explanations of interactional processes in multicultural settings	Neglect of: • Family interactions with other social systems • Hierarchies within families
Human ecology	A life-support system dependent on the natural and social environments	Acceptance of family and cultural diversity Studies of impacts of environment on human development	Description of relations of family with other environmental systems Advocacy for human betterment	Difficulty operationalizing transactional processes between families and environment
Family development	An intergenerational social group, governed by social norms pertaining to marriage and family, striving to maintain a balance as it changes over the course of the family life cycle	Evidence of similar family development patterns in different cultures	Identification of predictable variations in sequences of family life cycle for diverse cultural groups	Modal pattern of family development may not apply to diverse families and cultures
Symbolic interactionism	A unit of interacting personalities	Concept that cultural symbols and social norms affect interactions, through individual interpretations of the meaning of those interactions	Identification of processes whereby social and cultural variables affect identity and interactions	Neglect of social influences on individual perceptions and interactions

Theory	View of Family	Contributions	Applications	Limitations
Exchange	A set of relationships where individuals act to maximize profits	Studies of marital negotiation and power	Identification of decision-making and negotiation processes between husbands and wives in various cultures	Emphasis on individual interactions without recognition of the influence of: • Gender-based power differences • Cultural factors • Complex social networks
Feminist	A site of oppression and conflict due to women's subordination A source of strength, solidarity, and ability to survive Units of experience	Documentation of women's subordination in societies worldwide Studies of gender roles in families and other institutions cross-culturally Increased information on cultural and social impacts on gender and families Advocacy for women of various racial, ethnic, cultural, and class backgrounds	Framework for comparative studies of: • Women's subordination and strength in families • Process of empowerment in families and communities • Meaning of family life for women Framework guiding interventions to empower women	Cultural resistance to feminist principles and reforms Cultural conflicts over meaning of motherhood and family
Phenomenology	A way of attaching meaning to interpersonal relations	Expansion of understanding of diversity of meanings of what constitutes "family"	Increased understanding of interpretations of family in various cultures Focus on everyday life and impacts of family beliefs on domestic life	Difficulty of First World scholars in understanding and studying complex family organizations in Third World settings Limited to studies of personal interpretations of families rather than of family process, development, etc.

racial minority groups in the United States and Europe; and to other populations underrepresented in the family literature to more fully explain family life in its cultural context.[2] The result would be an improved understanding, not only of the particular family phenomena under investigation but of the usefulness of various theoretical approaches.

NOTES

1. Space limitations precluded a discussion of Parsons's predecessors. For a useful summary of Zimmerman, Ogburn, and others, see Clayton (1979).

2. I recognize that the omission of Third World scholars' voices from this chapter limits our views of family theory. I hope that in the future their views will become more integrated and accessible in the family literature.

REFERENCES

Abel, E. (1986). Adult daughters and care to the elderly. *Feminist Studies, 12,* 479–497.

Bellah, R. N., Madsden, R., Sullivan, W. M., Swidler, A., & Tipton, S. M. (1985). *Habits of the heart: Individualism and commitment in American life.* Berkeley: University of California Press.

Berardo, F. M., & Shehan, C. L. (1984). Family scholarship: Reflection of the changing family? *Journal of Family Issues, 5,* 577–598.

Blumberg, R. L. (1991). *Gender, family, and economy.* Newbury Park, CA: Sage.

Broderick, C. B. (1990). Family process theory. In J. Sprey (Ed.), *Fashioning family theory: New approaches* (pp. 171–206). Newbury Park, CA: Sage.

Broderick, C. B. (1993). *Understanding family process.* Newbury Park, CA: Sage.

Bronfenbrenner, U. (1979). *The ecology of human development: Experiments by nature and design.* Cambridge, MA: Harvard University Press.

Bronfenbrenner, U. (1986). Ecology of the family as a context for human development: Research perspectives. *Developmental Psychology, 22,* 723–742.

Brydon, L., & Chant, S. (1989). *Women in the Third World.* New Brunswick, NJ: Rutgers University Press.

Bubolz, M. M., & Sontag, M. S. (1993). Human ecology theory. In P. G. Boss, W. J. Doherty, R. LaRossa, W. R. Schumm, & S. K. Steinmetz, *Sourcebook of family theories and methods* (pp. 419–448). New York: Plenum Press.

Cheal, D. (1991). *Family and the state of theory.* Toronto: University of Toronto Press.

Clayton, R. R. (1979). *The family, marriage, and social change* (2nd ed.). Lexington, MA: D. C. Heath.

Dilworth-Anderson, P., Burton, L. M., & Johnson, L. B. (1993). Reframing theories for understanding race, ethnicity, and families. In P. G. Boss, W. J. Doherty, R. LaRossa, W. R. Schumm, & S. K. Steinmetz (Eds.), *Sourcebook of family theories and methods* (pp. 627–645). New York: Plenum Press.

Doherty, W. J., Boss, P. G., La Rossa, R., Schumm, W. R., & Steinmetz, S. K. (1993). Family theories and methods: A contextual approach. In P. G. Boss, W. J. Doherty, R. LaRossa, W. R. Schumm, & S. K. Steinmetz (Eds.), *Sourcebook of family theories and methods* (pp. 3–30). New York: Plenum Press.

Duvall, E. M. (1988). Family development's first forty years. *Family Relations, 37,* 127–134.

Encyclopedia Britannica. (1992). *1992 Britannica Book of the Year.* Chicago: Author.

Encyclopedia Britannica. (1993). *1993 Britannica Book of the Year.* Chicago: Author.

Enloe, C. (1989). *Bananas, beaches, and bases.* Berkeley: University of California Press.

Epstein, C. F. (1988). *Deceptive distinctions: Sex, gender, and the social order.* New Haven: Yale University Press.

Fenstermaker, S., West, C., & Zimmerman, D. H. (1991). Gender inequality: New conceptual terrain. In R. L. Blumberg (Ed.), *Gender, family, and economy* (pp. 289–307). Newbury Park, CA: Sage.

Ferree, M. M. (1990). Beyond separate spheres: Feminism and family research. *Journal of Marriage and the Family, 52,* 866–884.

Goldscheider, F. K., & Waite, L. J. (1991). *New families, no families?* Berkeley: University of California Press.

Goode, W. J. (1968). The role of the family in industrialization. In R. F. Winch & L. W. Goodman (Eds.), *Selected studies in marriage and the family* (pp. 64–70). New York: Holt, Rinehart & Winston.

Gubrium, J. F., & Holstein, J. A. (1990). *What is family?* Mountain View, CA: Mayfield.

Gubrium, J. F., & Holstein, J. A. (1993). Phenomenology, ethnomethodology, and family discourse. In P. G. Boss, W. J. Doherty, R. LaRossa, W. R. Schumm, & S. K. Steinmetz (Eds.), *Sourcebook of family theories and methods* (pp. 651–672). New York: Plenum Press.

Hare-Mustin, R. (1988). Family change and gender differences. *Family Relations, 37,* 36–41.

Hartmann, H. I. (1981). The family as the locus of gender, class, and political struggle: The example of housework. *Signs, Journal of Women in Culture and Society, 6,* 366–394.

Hill, R., & Rodgers, R. (1964). The developmental approach. In H. Christensen (Ed.), *Handbook of marriage and the family* (pp. 171–211). Chicago: Rand-McNally.

Hook, N., & Paolucci, B. (1970). The family as an ecosystem. *Journal of Home Economics, 62,* 315–318.

Hutter, M. (1981). *The changing family: Comparative perspectives.* New York: Wiley.

Jones, C. (1986). Intra-household bargaining in response to the introduction of new crops: A case study from Cameroon. In J. D. Moock (Ed.), *Understanding Africa's rural households and farming systems.* Boulder, CO: Westview Press.

Kingsbury, N., & Scanzoni, J. (1993). Structural–functionalism. In P. G. Boss, W. J. Doherty, R. LaRossa, W. R. Schumm, & S. K. Steinmetz (Eds.), *Sourcebook of family theories and methods* (pp. 195-217). New York: Plenum Press.

LaRossa, R., & Reitzes, D. C. (1993). Symbolic interactionism and family studies. In P. G. Boss, W. J. Doherty, R. LaRossa, W. R. Schumm, & S. K. Steinmetz (Eds.), *Sourcebook of family theories and methods* (pp. 135–162). New York: Plenum Press.

Lavin, C. (Performer). (1991). Sensitive new age guys. *Christine Lavin, Patty Larkin, Megon McDonough, Sally Fingeret: Live at the Birchmore* [cassette recording]. Cambridge, MA: Rounder Corp.

Lévi-Strauss, C. (1969). *The elementary structures of kinship*. Boston: Beacon Press.

Levin, I., & Trost, J. (1992). Understanding the concept of family. *Family Relations, 41,* 348–351.

Lindsey, K. (1981). *Friends as family*. Boston: Beacon Press.

Mattessich, P. & Hill, R. (1987). Life cycle and family development. In M. B. Sussman & S. K. Steinmetz (Eds.), *Handbook of marriage and the family* (pp. 437–469). New York: Plenum Press.

Nimkoff, M. F., & Middleton, R. (1960). Types of family and types of economy. *American Journal of Sociology, 66,* 215–225.

Osmond, M., & Thorne, B. (1993). Feminist theories: The social construction of gender in families and society. In P. G. Boss, W. J. Doherty, R. LaRossa, W. R. Schumm, & S. K. Steinmetz (Eds.), *Sourcebook of family theories and methods* (pp. 591–622). New York: Plenum Press.

Popenoe, D. (1988). *Disturbing the nest: Family change and decline in modern societies*. New York: Aldine de Gruyter.

Popenoe, D. (1993). American family decline, 1960–1990: A review and appraisal. *Journal of Marriage and the Family, 55,* 527–541.

Population Reference Bureau. (1989). *America in the twenty-first century: A demographic overview*. Washington, DC: Author.

Reiss, D. (1981). *The family's construction of reality*. Cambridge, MA: Harvard University Press.

Robinson, J. P. (1988). Who's doing the housework? *American Demographics, 10*(12), 24–28, 63.

Rodgers, R. H., & White, J. M. (1993). Family development theory. In P. G. Boss, W. J. Doherty, R. LaRossa, W. R. Schumm, & S. K. Steinmetz (Eds.), *Sourcebook of family theories and methods* (pp. 225–254). New York: Plenum Press.

Sabatelli, R., & Shehan, C. L. (1993). Exchange and resource theories. In P. G. Boss, W. J. Doherty, R. LaRossa, W. R. Schumm, & S. K. Steinmetz (Eds.), *Sourcebook of family theories and methods* (pp. 384–411). New York: Plenum Press.

Smith, D. E. (1987). *The everyday work as problematic*. Boston: Northeastern University Press.

Smith, D. E. (1993). The standard North American family. *Journal of Family Issues, 14,* 50–65.

Sprey, J. (1988). Current theorizing on the family: An appraisal. *Journal of Marriage and the Family, 50,* 875–890.

Sprey, J. (1990). Theoretical practice in family studies. In J. Sprey (Ed.), *Fashioning family theory* (pp. 9–33). Newbury Park, CA: Sage.

Stacey, J. (1990). *Brave new families: Stories of domestic upheaval in late twentieth century America*. New York: Basic Books.

Stacey, J. (1993). Good riddance to "The Family": A response to David Popenoe. *Journal of Marriage and the Family, 55,* 545–547.

Stack, C. (1974). *All our kin.* New York: Harper & Row.

Tannen, D. (1990). *You just don't understand.* New York: Ballantine Books.

Tepperman, L., & Wilson, S. (Eds.). (1993). *Next of kin.* Englewood Cliffs, NJ: Prentice Hall.

Thomas, D. L., & Wilcox, J. E. (1987). The rise of family theory: A historical and critical analysis. In M. B. Sussman & S. K. Steinmetz (Eds.), *Handbook of marriage and the family* (pp. 81–102). New York: Plenum Press.

Thorne, B. (1992). Feminism and the family: Two decades of thought. In B. Thorne & M. Yalom (Eds.), *Rethinking the family* (rev. ed., pp. 3–30). Boston: Northeastern University Press.

Thorne, B., & Yalom, M. (Eds.). (1992). *Rethinking the family* (rev. ed.). Boston: Northeastern University Press.

United Nations. (1991). *The world's women 1970–1990.* New York: Author.

U.S. Bureau of the Census. (1992). *Statistical abstract of the United States 1992.* Washington, DC: U.S. Government Printing Office.

West, C., & Zimmerman, D. H. (1987). Doing gender. *Gender and Society, 1,* 125–151.

White, S. (1992). *Arguing with the crocodile: Gender and class in Bangladesh.* London: Zed Books.

Whitechurch, G., & Constantine, L. (1993). Systems theory. In P. G. Boss, W. J. Doherty, R. LaRossa, W. R. Schumm, and S. K. Steinmetz (Eds.), *Sourcebook of family theories and methods* (pp. 325–352). New York: Plenum Press.

Winch, R. F. (1979). Toward a model of familial organization. In W. R. Burr, R. Hill, F. I. Nye, & I. R. Reiss (Eds.), *Contemporary theories about the family* (Vol. 1, pp. 162–179). New York: Free Press.

Winch, R. F., & Blumberg, R. L. (1968). Societal complexity and familial organization. In R. F. Winch & L. W. Goodman (Eds.), *Selected studies in marriage and the family* (pp. 70–92). New York: Holt, Rinehart & Winston.

CHAPTER TWO

The Family in Western History

BRON B. INGOLDSBY

This chapter gives the reader an understanding of how the modern white North American family came to be what it is. I trace certain aspects of family interaction from the time of the ancient Hebrews through their European and colonial evolutions. This perspective helps us to understand how things came to be as they are today, in both their generalities and their diversity. Cultural changes across time supply part of the historical perspective within which we can understand family practices in the modern world.

I say *part* of the perspective because many millions of peoples do not share the white Christian heritage. It is not possible, however, to give even an overview of the historical antecedents for the family of all the races and cultures of the world. Historians have thus far given us much more information on European family life, due to the political dominance of the West in recent centuries. So, with some reluctance, but in order to provide a coherent picture, I am forced to narrow my focus to this particular group, as most family historians before me have done. However, this volume provides some historical background for minority groups in other chapters.

I also ignore certain aspects of family life that are explained in historical perspective in other chapters, such as mate selection and marital structure. Instead, my focus is on two often interrelated topics: sexuality and power. Much of Western history has been characterized by husband dominance over wives and parental dominance over children, and sex has been much of the rationale for that dominance.

The historical record provides us with much more information on what people were taught as to proper family behavior than it does on what people actually did. It also gives us more information about the wealthy and powerful than it does about the common people. The problem of norms versus actual behavior can be a thorny one, but we can assume that there is some correlation between what is written and what is practiced (Brady, 1991). In each case, I try to clarify when I am talking about proscriptions for behavior and when I am talking about empirical behavior itself.

Finally, much of the historical literature about gender and family relations is religious in nature. It is precisely because so many Western norms have religious sanction that institutions such as patriarchy have been so impervious to change until recent times. With these limitations in mind, I now divide our look at the family into eight historical periods. Each builds on and alters its predecessor in various ways, leading eventually to today's family.

THE HEBREWS

The Hebrew nomads began to take possession of Canaan around the middle of the 12th century B.C. Tribal life evolved into a nation with a capital and temple in Jerusalem. In the sixth century B.C. the kingdom of Judah was overthrown by the Babylonians, and the Jews remained under the control of various foreign powers until 70 A.D., when they were scattered as a people by the Romans. Their great legislator, Moses, was reared in Egypt, and much of their code seems to be borrowed from that civilization (Bardis, 1966).

The society of the Old Testament Israelites was clearly patriarchal. Wives were expected to be submissive to their husbands, and were often viewed as little more than property. For instance, in the Ten Commandments of Exodus, chapter 20, wives are listed with other domestic property as things not to be coveted when belonging to one's neighbor.

Marriages were simple affairs, arranged between families. A girl belonged to her father until she was sold (brideprice) to her husband. Typically, betrothals were arranged at about the time of puberty (Kephart & Jedlicka, 1991). Although there is evidence of loving husband–wife relationships, love was not the key purpose of marriage. It was a responsibility expected of everyone, in order to ensure the continuation of family lines through childbearing. The commandment to multiply and replenish the earth was taken seriously, and large families were seen as a sign of God's blessing. There was strong endogamous pressure to preserve cultural identity (Queen, Habenstein, & Quadagno, 1985).

The area of reproduction provides one piece of evidence of beliefs about female inferiority. The Hebrews shared the almost universal tendency of primitive societies to label women as unclean, due to menstruation and childbirth, and to require purification (Fielding, 1942). Banishment was the penalty for a couple's having intercourse during the woman's period (Leviticus 20:18), and menstruating women were to separate themselves from the rest of the community. When giving birth to a boy, the mother was considered unclean for 7 days and experienced a purification period lasting an additional 33 days. If she had a girl, the purification period was doubled (Leviticus 12:1–5).

However, the differential in gender status was nowhere more apparent than in the area of sexuality. The "double standard," where sexual activity is condemned for women but acceptable for men, seems to come from the Hebrews and other Middle Eastern groups. Although it was rarely enforced, women could be put to death for adultery and suffer other serious penalties for fornication. Men were not to have intercourse with another man's wife, not because of the effect on the marital relationship but because to do so would be a violation of the other man's property rights and a confusion of blood lines. The importance of genealogy is seen in Deuteronomy 23:2 where illegitimate children and their offspring could not be part of the congregation for 10 generations.

Men were allowed to have as many wives and concubines (secondary wives whose children did not have the same inheritance status) as they could support. Sex-ratio constraints limited this practice to the wealthy, and it therefore was experienced by only a small minority. And although penalties existed for nonmarital sex, they were often minor. For instance, intercourse with a slave girl betrothed to another resulted in her being scourged, but the man was forgiven if he brought a ram as an offering to the priest (Leviticus 19:20–22).

Leviticus, chapter 18, focuses on forbidden marital or sexual relationships and is the basis for subsequent Western law on incest and related prohibitions. Intercourse with one's parents, siblings, and children is forbidden, as well as with aunts, uncles, and various in-law relations. Chapter 20 proscribes the death penalty for certain sexual relations including adultery, some forms of incest, homosexuality, and bestiality. If a wife were accused of adultery, an ordeal was designed (Numbers, chapter 5) to test her claim of innocence. She would drink holy water and if guilty, her belly would swell and her thigh would rot.

Today's high divorce rate concerns many, and it is often believed that divorce is a relatively new phenomenon invented by a decadent society. In fact, the termination of marriages has always been allowed under certain circumstances, even in societies that highly value marital stability. Hebrew men could divorce their wives for practically any reason, although Hebrew women had no such recourse. Adultery and incompatibility were considered plausible grounds, but infertility (presumed to be the woman's fault) was the most common reason. Husbands, however, were subject to severe social disapproval if they divorced their wives for frivolous reasons, and under certain conditions they were never allowed to divorce. These conditions were present when the husband and wife had had premarital intercourse or if the wife was taken into captivity or insane (Bardis, 1963).

Children are always highly valued in agricultural societies as workers, and Old Testament stories give the impression of considerable love and devotion between parent and child. This does not mean that they were treated with the kindness and dignity that is expected today, however. Children were expected to be obedient, and severe punishment followed wrongdoing. Solomon stated, "He that spareth his rod hateth his son: but he that loveth him chasteneth him betimes" (Proverbs 13:24).

Beatings met with social approval, and it was possible (although apparently rare) to go further to curb disobedience. The law of Moses permitted parents to kill any child who struck or cursed them (Exodus 21:15–17). Parental authority was virtually absolute. The practice of primogeniture, where the eldest son inherits most of the family property, often resulted in sibling rivalry, especially if it was disregarded. The stories of Joseph and his brothers and Jacob and Esau are prime examples. Daughters were seldom considered important enough even to be mentioned.

We have inherited a number of notions and practices from the Judaic codes. They include male dominance in marital and family relationships, the sexual double standard, and the justification of the mistreatment of children. Family life was private, and its members were the property of the husband, who could do basically as he saw fit.

THE GREEKS

Although there is some evidence of a matriarchal system in prehistoric Greece, by the time of the "golden age of civilization" it was very much a man's world. Female subservience in Hebrew culture seems benign when compared to the Greeks. Marriage was for social reasons, chiefly seen as necessary for securing an heir. As this quote from Demosthenes demonstrates, men went elsewhere for companionship: "We marry women to have legitimate children and to have faithful guardians of our homes. We maintain concubines for our daily service and comfort, and courtesans for the enjoyment of love" (Fielding, 1942, p. 204).

Now-famous Greek thinkers did not hesitate to speculate on proper family life. Plato, for instance, felt that common possession of wives, for the upper classes at least, would be better than monogamy, and that weak children should be allowed to die by exposure (Adams & Steinmetz, 1993).

Greek men were interested in intellectual qualities and did not see women as rational. In Athens, a wife's position was quite menial: She was not educated and could not leave the house without her husband's permission. If she did leave, she had to be veiled (so as not to arouse the desires of other men) and chaperoned (Fielding, 1942). She typically stayed in her own quarters and only joined her husband at mealtimes. Even this, however, was not permitted if there were guests for dinner. The Greeks invented the chastity belt, as they felt that any man could talk any woman into having sex with him, due to the woman's low reasoning skills.

There is considerable evidence that men considered women to be inferior to them. Pericles held that the best reputation a woman could have was not to be spoken of among men for good or evil, and Aristotle regarded slavish obedience as the highest virtue for an uneducated wife. Spartan husbands could even arrange extramarital affairs for their wives in the interest of eugenics, so obsessed was this military society with producing physically superior children. The laws of Lycurgus permitted a "man of character" who had a passion for a modest and beautiful woman to ask her husband if he might mate with her in order to produce more excellent children. The husband could permit this, but Greek law also permitted a husband to kill an adulterer. In general, however, Spartan women had much more freedom than did their counterparts in the city state of Athens (Bardis, 1964a).

Many of the beliefs still held by some about gender differences seem to come straight out of the literature of the Greeks. In Xenophon's *Oeconomicus*, these words come from a discussion with Socrates:

> God from the beginning made the woman's nature for the indoor and the man's for the outdoor tasks and cares. . . . Knowing that to the woman's nature he gave and assigned the rearing of infants, he gave to her more affection for babies than to the man . . . he gave him a larger share of courage. . . . So it is better for the woman to stay at home than to abide in the fields, but it is more disgraceful for the man to stay at home. (Bardis, 1964a, pp. 164–165)

In Homer's *Odyssey* we see further evidence of male dominance: "But go now to the home, and attend to thy household affairs; To the spinning wheel and the loom, and bid thy maids be assiduous At the tasks that to them were allotted. To speak is the privilege of men." Prostitution was also developed as a public service by the famous Athenian lawmaker Solon. "Solon, be praised! For thou didst purchase public women for the welfare of the city, to preserve the morals of the city that is full of strong, young men, who, without thy wise institution, would indulge in the annoying pursuit of better-class women" (Fielding, 1942, pp. 202, 204).

The better-class women referred to may have been the *hetairae*, a special class of mistresses trained to be women of beauty, charm, and intellect. These temple prostitutes had a life much freer than that of wives and often obtained considerable power and wealth. Men sought them out for sexual and intellectual companionship, and they enjoyed the highest status for women in Greek society (Bardis, 1964a).

In relation to the treatment of children, adoption was common when a couple had no sons. Only sons inherited, with the bulk of the family estate going to the eldest. The wife could not inherit her husband's property, and if a man had only daughters, one of them might be forced to marry a close relative, who would then be the recipient (Bardis, 1964a).

The double standard was quite exaggerated under the Greeks. For men, the social ideal seemed to be the full expression of sensuality with a minimum of restraints, whereas for women adultery was a criminal act, grounds for divorce and justification for being put to death. A woman could sue her husband for divorce, but only with his consent, or if she could prove cruelty (Bardis, 1964a).

Finally, the opinion of Greek women was so low that it formed part of the cultural approval of homosexuality. The actual incidence is unknown, but household illustrations portrayed homosexual relations, and Greek writers were open on the subject. Men turned to each other for intellectual and emotional support and this frequent interaction and dependence are believed by some (see Kephart & Jedlicka, 1991) to be responsible. Actually, homosexuality does not seem to have been seen as abnormal by either the ancient Greeks or the Romans. Passive or "feminine" behavior or positions were criticized in males, but as long as a man assumed the active role, the object of his passion did not seem to be important (Veyne, 1985).

Ancient Greece, then, represents the nadir for female status in family and general relations. Their subjugation was complete, with courtesans more valued than wives and all men more valued than any woman.

THE ROMANS

Like the ancient Hebrew and Greek families, the Romans were patriarchal. In contrast, they were, however, monogamous and did not approve of polygyny or concubinage. The early Romans were very much male centered, being patrilocal and patrilineal as well as patriarchal.

The Roman *familia*, or household, included everyone under the authority of the male head of the family, or *paterfamilia*: typically, the man's wife, unmarried daughters, sons, and their spouses and children. Everyone in the male line was under the control of the *paterfamilia* until that person died, at which time each adult married male could start his own household.

In upper-class families, the girl's family provided a dowry, which became the property of the husband, or of his *paterfamilia*. Lower-class weddings were often without ceremony or official witnesses, and the couple's cohabitation was recognized as a common-law marriage. This validation of the private decision of the couple continues in many parts of the world today. Upper-class ceremonies included a contract and a procession (Bardis, 1963b).

As with the Hebrews, children, especially boys, were desired. The father had the right to reject children and would occasionally leave them to die or sell them. This was more likely to occur with deformed or female children. Most children were accepted into the household and received their education by observing and working with their same-sex parent.

Men could divorce their wives for practically any reason but were restricted by social expectation to the causes of adultery, making poison, drinking wine, and counterfeiting house keys. The power of the *paterfamilia* was so great that he could not only divorce his own wife but force a son to divorce, if he wanted him to, as well. When she married, a daughter became a member of her husband's family (Bardis, 1963b).

In the second century B.C., Rome and Carthage were engaged in a long series of wars with each other. Major wars often serve as a turning point for societal customs, and the Punic wars are perhaps the best historical example of how war can enhance the status of women. As the men were away from home, on occasion for years at a time, their wives of necessity took over many of the household responsibilities.

Roman women were already better off than their Greek counterparts in that they were not confined to family quarters and they controlled childrearing to a certain degree. After the war, they became more independent. In many marriages, for instance, a wife remained under her father's authority, instead of being transferred to the *manus* (control) of her husband. Because the fathers rarely exercised power over these adult daughters, the daughters were able to gain some freedom and wealth (Bardis, 1963b).

According to Queen et al. (1985), divorce became easier to obtain and therefore more frequent. Women were able to secure divorces, and some upper-class Romans remarried frequently. Enough women became independently wealthy due to inheritances from their father or husband that laws were passed to discourage it. In essence, the status of the sexes became more equalitarian.

Many historians have also noted a change in sexual mores after Rome became an empire. People began to live sexually freer lives, with such activities as adultery and abortion becoming more common. Serious legal penalties were designed for adulterers—such as loss of property and even death—but enforcement was not regular. Prostitution became more acceptable, and statesmen decried the decaying moral values of the time (Bardis, 1963b).

To summarize, until the Punic wars, the Roman household was the religious, educational, economic, and legal center of society. The father exercised considerable control over the lives of all family members. This power was gradually reduced, especially after the wars with Carthage. Many young people ceased to regard marriage as an obligation and assumed more personal control over the process. The legal and social status of both women and children improved. Men tended to view these trends with alarm and attributed moral degeneracy to these changes.

EARLY CHRISTIANITY

In the first century after the life of Jesus Christ, domestic mores were not distinctly Christian but were, rather, a mix of Jewish, Greek, and Roman customs. Gradually, however, a fairly homogeneous doctrine developed for marriage, sex, and family life. While partially based on New Testament ideas, they also reflected a repulsion of the life-style of upper-class Romans and an acceptance of the Persian notion of duality, where the body and spirit are opposed to each other (see Queen et al., 1985).

Although Rome was sacked in 410 A.D., its era had ended almost a century earlier when the Emperor Constantine allied the government with the Christian church. A persecuted cult became the state religion and eventually the legal as well as social and moral successor to the empire in Europe (Tannahill, 1980). Indeed, no force has had greater influence in shaping Western thought concerning the relation between the sexes than has had Christianity.

In addition to the history of Jesus and the writings of Paul, our major source of information is the writings of influential early church fathers, such as St. Jerome, St. Augustine, and Tertullian. In a time of general illiteracy, reading and writing belonged to the monasteries, and they only saved information that supported the church positions. As a result, the conclusions of these men were not seriously debated or modified and ended up having tremendous long-term impact (Tannahill, 1980).

It appears that Jesus taught that it was intended for adult men and women to leave their parents and marry, and that the only acceptable reason for divorce was adultery. He also loved children, and consistently treated women with dignity and respect. However, loyalty to his gospel was more important than family relationships (see Matthew, chapter 19).

St. Paul expands on these concepts and provides the basis for the ultimate devaluation of marriage and of women, which develops in the early Christian church. In his first letter to the Corinthians (chapter 7) he explains that although marriage is acceptable, it distracts disciples from their religious devotion (7:33–38), and that therefore it is better to remain single if you can resist sexual temptation (7:8–9). However, there is nothing dishonorable about marital sex (see Hebrews 13:4).

St. Paul repeatedly makes it clear, however, that women are to be subject to men. They were not to speak in church but to learn from their husbands instead (1 Corinthians 14:34–35). In his first letter to Timothy (2:9–14), Paul explains that women are to be modest and subject to men because Eve was the one who transgressed in the Garden of Eden. A cruel patriarchy was not condoned, however. Even though wives were to submit themselves to their husbands, and children were to obey their parents, husbands were commanded to love their wives and not abuse their children (Colossians 3:18–21).

Paul may have been reacting to the "excesses" of Rome in wishing for the good old days of a clear hierarchy, but he provided justification for the subordination of women.

In the first few centuries A.D., there was considerable ambivalence on the part of church leaders toward such subjects as marriage, women, and sexuality. The Christian standards of monogamy, nonmarital chastity, and marital fidelity strengthened the nuclear family and attacked the double standard. However, according to Queen et al. (1985), even as the Roman emperors were penalizing citizens who refused to marry, the church fathers were praising them and according higher status to virgins and widows than to married couples.

Women were valued members of the church and were often idealized as charitable reflections of Mary. On the other hand, like Eve, they tempted men into sin and away from devotion. And while sex was necessary for procreation (the making of more Christians and virgins), it was also the original sin that had to be overcome in subjecting the body to the spirit (Tannahill, 1980).

In the end, the church adopted a negative view on each of these issues. It came down to a rejection of physical pleasure, and therefore those things connected with it (from the male view, women and marriage).

A few quotes from early church leaders convey the inferior status of women. Tertullian said: "You are the devil's gateway: You are the unsealer of that forbidden tree: You are the first deserter of the divine law: You are she who persuaded him whom the devil was not valiant enough to attack." Chrysostom declared that women are "a necessary evil, a natural temptation, a desirable calamity, a domestic peril, a deadly fascination and a painted ill" (Queen et al., 1985, p. 138).

Clement of Alexandria wrote that "every woman ought to be filled with shame at the thought that she is a woman." This was more than just hyperbole; in 585, the Council of Macon seriously debated whether or not women had souls. The bishops decided that they do, but only by a one-vote majority (Bardis, 1964b).

That women were not to go to any effort to enhance their beauty was made clear in a letter from St. Jerome to a wealthy woman in 403. It contained advice on how to rear her daughter and included the following:

> Her very dress and outward appearance should remind her of Him to whom she is promised. Do not pierce her ears, or paint with white lead and rouge the cheeks that are consecrated to Christ, Do not load her neck with pearls and gold, do not weigh down her head with jewels, do not dye her hair red and thereby presage her for the fires of hell. . . . I know some people have laid down the rule that a Christian virgin should not bathe along with eunuchs or with married women, inasmuch as eunuchs are still men at heart, and women big with child are a revolting sight. For

myself I disapprove altogether of baths in the case of a full-grown virgin. She ought to blush at herself and be unable to look at her own nakedness. (Queen et al., 1985, pp. 142–143)

The condemnation of sexual pleasure itself was just as strong. The sole purpose of coitus was for procreation; anything else was lustful, and therefore sinful. Any form of contraception was condemned, as were all "unnatural" acts such as anal and oral intercourse, homosexuality, and bestiality. Such crimes could result in a penance of fasting from all but bread and water for years; even a nocturnal emission demanded a few days of fasting or the reciting of psalms (Tannahill, 1980).

Probably no other culture has had such a stern code: All suggestive books, songs, and dances were forbidden as well. The Christian custom of kissing each other as a greeting became suspect, and second kisses were considered sinful. At least one church father, Origen, castrated himself in order to escape sexual desire. In 398, the Council of Carthage declared that out of respect for the sacred nature of the wedding benediction, newlyweds should not have intercourse on their wedding night. This rule was later extended to three nights but could be avoided by paying a fee to the church (Queen et al., 1985).

Some saints tried to prove their superiority to the temptations of the flesh by marrying but staying celibate. But such repression of natural urges can lead to obsessing on it. Jerome, who shunned even eating and washing as invitations to lust, was plagued with visions of dancing girls and inflamed with lust as he fasted in the desert. Other monks and nuns complained of the devil tempting them to indecent acts in their dreams and believed in succubi, or erotic demons (Bardis, 1964b).

Over time, the church established control over marriage itself. In 305, the Council of Elvira forbade women to marry non-Catholics. Couples were encouraged to have the approval of the bishop, and by the sixth century, relatives within the seventh degree (including affinal relations and godparents) were forbidden to marry. This means that no one more closely related than third cousins could marry. To make sure that no one violated these restrictions, banns announcing a couple's intent to marry had to be posted in the church before the wedding so that anyone who thought they were too closely related could object to the marriage. These restrictions posed quite a burden in small towns, where almost everyone was related to some degree. After some ambivalence, marriages were declared indissoluble in 407, and remarriages could result in excommunication even if the spouse had been guilty of adultery (Queen et al., 1985).

Celibacy for church officials was encouraged from 398 on and was made mandatory in the 11th century. For the layman, however, interacting with women remained a dangerous necessity. To summarize, the status of women and of marriage declined during the early Christian era. In fact, women and sexuality were associated with evil. However, monogamous marriage and fidelity were strengthened. Not a lot was written about children, but their status rose as abortion, infanticide, and child selling were all condemned. These practices continued at various levels, however.

THE MIDDLE AGES

The period in Europe from about 500 A.D. to 1500 A.D. is referred to as the Medieval Period, or the Dark Ages, as well as the Middle Ages. It is generally seen as a time of slowed progression and loss of knowledge coming between the classic and renaissance periods of history. I say little of the first half millennium here, as it overlaps with early Christianity.

By the year 1000, the church had gained considerable control over marriage and family life. Even the nobility had conformed to the rules of indissoluble monogamy and kinship restrictions. Admonitions against adultery and fornication had had less effect. The larger kinship group, or clan, still had influence, but it was beginning to wane. Individual households took over marriage arrangements, with parents in control (Gies & Gies, 1987).

Important changes occurred in the 11th century. Here we find the first appearance of the surname, passed down the father's line. Also, the rule of primogeniture became common. Both of these diminished the status of women and made things more difficult for noninheriting children. They could either leave home empty handed, or enter the church. Peasant girls did not have the option of the convent, so pressure to marry was great.

The focus of marriage shifted from family arrangement to the couple in the late 1100s, when church leaders established that mutual consent with affection was the heart of a valid marriage. Minimum ages of 14 for the groom and 12 for the bride were set, except for the child marriages arranged by nobility, which became valid once consummated. Marriage was delayed for noninheriting sons, and it was socially acceptable for a single male (including priests) to have a mistress (Gies & Gies, 1987).

Marriage became one of the seven sacraments in 1164, and marriages took place in the church and under the direction of clergy. In the mid-1500s, the Council of Trent distinguished between separation and annulment. The former could be granted for adultery, apostasy, or cruelty, but remarriage (never recommended anyway) was not allowed. An annulment declared that the marriage had not been valid from the beginning (usually for violating the incest restrictions, which had been relaxed to the fourth degree of kinship in 1215), in which case one could marry another person (Bardis, 1964b).

The Black Death, or Bubonic Plague, had tremendous impact on family life and society in general. The first outbreak was in Italy in 1347, and it returned in waves about every 10 years thereafter for the rest of the century.

It afflicted the young at a higher rate than it did adults, but the mortality rates were very high for all groups. In some British districts, as many as 65% of the inhabitants died, and in various cases entire villages were deserted (Gies & Gies, 1987). It is still the ultimate metaphor for calamity and remains with us even in children's games: "Ring around the rosie / Pockets full of posies / Ashes, ashes, we all fall down."

Its source is uncertain, but it is believed to have been carried by fleas on rats brought on boats from Turkey. Practice of sanitation was poor during these centuries (people rarely bathed and threw their trash into the streets) and people did not understand how diseases were transmitted. Education was limited and was often diverted into such philosophical puzzles as the following: What language does a deaf–mute hear in his heart? (Hebrew.) What is the worst sin one can commit? (Sodomy.) Moreover, although they understood such celestial things as rain and eclipses, other subjects closer to home were less clear. Many believed the fabulous tales for faraway lands: cyclopes, Amazons with tears of silver, snakes with jewels for eyes, and the Garden of Eden protected by a high wall. Fireflies were the souls of unbaptized dead infants, and alchemy was the most popular applied science (Tuchman, 1978).

Even though the plague was devastating at a personal level, it had positive consequences on society as a whole. It came at a time when overpopulation was resulting in a negative economic picture. Survivors were able to move onto vacated land, and improved agricultural techniques were developed. Later-born children were able to have land, and the average size of holdings doubled. Due to the surplus of land and shortage of workers, peasants were able to command higher wages and improve their living conditions.

Access to income allowed people to marry earlier. In Prato, Italy, the average age for marriage was 24 for men and 16 for women in 1371; it had been 40 and 25 before the plague. The lowered age of marriage resulted in higher birthrates, which peaked in connection with each outbreak of the disease (Gies & Gies, 1987).

Information about the relationships of ordinary people indicates that young single males often resorted to prostitutes or rape for sexual experience. In courtship, a good deal of petting behavior was culturally acceptable until about 1700. After that time we see a dramatic drop in the rate of prenuptial pregnancy, indicating that church teachings were having an effect (Flandrin, 1977). Legally and socially, women were inferior to men, but spouses tended to work together almost as equals, and love and affection often grew between them.

A great deal of literature has survived concerning the love and sex lives of the aristocracy, and it centers around the related concepts of chivalry and courtly love. Chivalry was a code of honor and behavior for knights, which grew out of the crusades and was designed to combine warfare with religiosity. Men were expected to have great physical strength, which they showed off at tournaments when real battles were not available. It included treating women with respect, even though they were still seen as wicked. For instance, there was believed to be a special place in hell for women who plucked their eyebrows, and of the seven deadly sins, that of ire was depicted as a woman (Tuchman, 1978).

Brought back from the crusades were the veneration of Mary, from the Eastern Church, and the exotic harem, from the Muslims. Traveling entertainers, the troubadours, combined these into a powerfully attractive concept for the upper classes. The poems told of great ladies who symbolized purity, and knights who were inspired to feats of heroism out of love for them. The lady would eventually return the feelings, but the relationship was never to be consummated as she was always already married to a nobleman. Such songs were appealing to lonely women who were running the family castle while their husbands were off fighting somewhere, and to traveling knights looking to go beyond the story line (Tannahill, 1980).

Courtly love, then, means the kind of love that went on at court. Essentially, the feeling was that only adulterous love could be true love because marriages tended to be arranged for political or wealth purposes. The stories of King Arthur's Court, which centered on this theme, became popular at this time. That romantic love could occur only outside marriage was directly opposed to church teachings and resulted in tension between culture and religion.

Whereas this would seem to do damage to the institution of marriage, and encourage the sexual exploitation of women, it also encouraged men to treat women with greater gentleness and politeness. In fact, "courtesy" is based on the word court and refers to the way women were treated in royal courts. This glorification of seduction brought men and women together for more than just economic reasons and therefore set the stage for eventual psychological intimacy between the sexes in marriage.

Finally, theories that children were seen as miniature adults who did not receive much affection from parents have been undermined by more recent research. Law and custom gave children special protections as minors. Descriptions of children's play is very similar to what one would read today, and careful instructions for infant care are found. Some of this advice was not good, such as recommendations for swaddling and pressing an infant's ears and limbs into desired shapes, but the concern was there. The infant death rate was high and parents mourned their loss, often consoling themselves with the belief that the child's soul would be reincarnated in a later child born to the family.

Peasant women nursed their own babies, but the wealthy tended to hire wet nurses, who not only fed but reared the children for them. A principal concern was the moral character of the wet nurse, as it was believed that bad traits could be passed to the baby via the breast milk. Infanticide persisted but at lower rates; one study found only two likely infanticides out of 4,000 recorded deaths. Neglect was often fatal, as it was common to leave babies alone in the house near the fire while everyone else worked outside. Some children were apprenticed out at early ages, but many stayed at home and did chores assigned to them by their parents. Discipline was harsh by today's standards, but some church leaders spoke out against corporal punishment and in favor of love and affection (Gies & Gies, 1987).

During this period, the view of women improved from negative to ambivalent, as they came to represent purity as well as inferiority. The courtly love complex encouraged men to treat women with more respect, and romance was introduced into sexual relationships. Childhood was recognized and protected to a greater degree than it had been in times past.

THE RENAISSANCE

The next two centuries are a short, but important period. The French term for rebirth refers to dramatic progress after centuries of stagnation. Some of this was brought about by the discovery of the New World, and part of it was a function of the Protestant Reformation. Luther, Calvin, and others spoke against the consanguinity rules, which restricted mate choice, liberalized grounds for divorce (adultery, desertion, and cruelty), and declared that marriage and family life were superior to chastity. Some theologians concluded that the woman's pleasure was important for conception and advised husbands on how to bring their wives to orgasm (Gies & Gies, 1987).

Family structure shifted from large family lineages to the nuclear family, as outside agencies took over many of the traditional family functions. At first, loyalty was shifted from the clan to the patriarch. The wife was considered to be, along with the children, the property of the husband, who was the only legal entity in the group (Queen et al., 1985).

A key aspect of the Renaissance was the creation of a middle class. With the rise of cities and commerce, other options besides agriculture became available. Nonnobles discovered that they could not only survive but become rich as middle men, engaged in the buying, transport, and selling of goods. The new economic situation lead to what Laslett (1977) has called the uniquely "Western" family: nuclear family form, a small age gap between spouses, relatively late childbearing, and the presence of servants in households. Extended families did not function well in a commerce-based economy and gradually gave way to the smaller, more private and efficient nuclear structure.

This business class was influenced by the ideas of romantic love, which had filtered down from the aristocracy. As a result, they developed the art of "courtship." Employing the vocabulary and behaviors of courtly love, middle-class men began to use them on the women to whom they had been betrothed through parental match making. During the time before their marriage, young men "courted" their future brides with adoring talk, gifts, and romantic poetry.

This kind of interaction led some to fall in love with each other, which called into question the idea that love and marriage could not coexist. This interaction gradually led to rebellion against parental mate choice, because young people discovered that it was more gratifying to marry for love and that they, rather than any others, were the most qualified to make the selection based on that criterion. The behaviors of adulterous courtly love actually reversed the concept and brought love and marriage together and eventually replaced arranged marriages with free-choice marriages. This shift was slow and did not find its culmination until the modern era.

COLONIAL AMERICA

This period stretches from the early 1600s, with the Puritan settling of New England, to the mid-1800s and the industrial revolution. The Puritans came to America with the protestant values of Europe. They believed strongly in marriage, strict childhood discipline, and paternal dominance. They felt that wives should be domestic and submissive, and, in fact, a woman could not engage in business without her husband's consent, and all that she had was owned by him.

However, life in the rugged New World modified patriarchy to some extent and shaped marriage in many ways. This was chiefly due to the shortage of women, which made them a scarce and valuable resource. Women served many economic functions and could choose their mates from a number of suitors. In addition to the making of clothes, food, and other household products, many women carried on income-producing activities outside the home, such as teaching, retailing, and newspaper publishing (Queen et al., 1985). This does not mean that they were liberated in the modern sense. Wives could work at anything as long as it was acceptable to their husbands and could be understood as something that helped the family as a whole (Caffrey, 1991).

Europeans discovered that Native American families also had sexual division of labor, but it was sometimes the reverse of what they were used to. Native American women were often the farmers. The Europeans tried to encourage them to make cloth while the men farmed, so as to fit their own sex-role stereotypes. Slaves came from African cultures built around extended families. Marriage remained important to African Americans, and free choice was generally permitted, but the masters could interfere (Caffrey, 1991). They also disapproved of Native American sexual practices, which were more permissive of premarital relations, polygamy, and homosexuality. White settlers often rationalized such perceived differences as justification for rape against not only Native American women but African slaves and lower-social-class European indentured servants as well (D'Emilio & Freedman, 1988).

Because marriage was important for a comfortable life, and the Puritans were strongly opposed to nonmarital sex, singlehood was viewed with suspicion and courtship was often brief. Remarriage was common for those widowed; in fact, the first marriage at Plymouth was between Edward Winslow and Susanna White, whose respective spouses had died only 7 and 12 weeks previously. In Connecticut, single males could not live alone without permission, and Hartford laid a tax on single men (Queen et al., 1985).

Typically, a young man had to receive the permission of the woman's father in order to begin courtship, and she could veto her parents' choice for her. Dowries seemed to be more important than love, but there were cases of young couples marrying in spite of parental objections. Marriage was a civil contract, but banns had to be posted for 2 weeks before the ceremony. Love was not expected before marriage, but it was hoped that it would develop as time went on.

Most important was chastity, as the Puritans opposed all sexual activity outside marriage. Public confession was part of the repentance process for fornication, and records indicate that up to one-third of couples engaged in premarital relations (Caffrey, 1991) in spite of the penalties attached, which included being fined, whipped, and forced to marry each other. Adultery could actually merit the death penalty, or at least the "scarlet letter," an "A" pinned to one's clothes or burned onto the face. The letter "I" was used for incest. To protect couples from themselves, young people were prohibited from riding off together with sinful intent, and "gynecandrical dancing" was condemned by church leaders (Queen et al., 1985).

Such views render the custom of "bundling" most interesting. Bundling was a courtship practice found to be common in the mid- to late 1700s. It meant that the courting couple would be in bed together but with their clothes on. With fuel at a premium, it was often difficult to keep a house warm in the evenings, which was when a man would be visiting his betrothed at her home. In order to keep warm, they would bundle in her bed together. A board might be placed in the middle to keep them separate, or the girl could be put in a bundling or duffle-like chastity bag. The girl's parents were usually in the room as well (Kephart & Jedlicka, 1991).

The word "puritanical" is often used to mean antisexual, but this is not an accurate understanding of this time. Drawing much of their philosophy from the Old Testament Hebrews, the Puritans did not worship virginity and felt that sex was good and meant to be enjoyed, but that it should be confined to marriage. In Morgan's (1942) classic study, he quotes from a sermon by John Cotton: "Women are creatures without which there is no comfortable Living for man. . . . They are a sort of Blasphemers then who despise and decry them, and call them a necessary Evil, for they are a necessary Good" (p. 592). Public displays of affection were not permitted, however, as evidenced by the case of a sea captain who was put in the stocks for 2 hours because he kissed his wife on their doorstep on a Sunday, upon his return from a 3-year sea voyage.

The situation was somewhat different in the southern colonies, which were more rural and included slavery. There was a chivalry much like that of the Middle Ages, in which upper-class white women were put on a pedestal. These women were treated with graciousness and respect and their sexual purity was closely guarded. They were expected to turn a blind eye, however, to their husbands' infidelities, which often included the exploitation of female slaves. Penalties for sex crimes were limited to fines (and to women) and common-law marriages were recognized, due in part to a lack of clergy to perform the ceremony (D'Emilio & Freedman, 1988). In both the New England and southern colonies, a first marriage usually occurred when the man could afford it, which was in his late 20s.

So we see some general overall progress in the treatment of women from previous times. The same was true with respect to the treatment of children. The Puritans regarded having children as a commandment from God, and they seemed to spend more time with their children and to be more emotionally attached to them than had been their European ancestors. There was a significant decline in such practices as swaddling, wet nursing, and sending children out at young ages as apprentices.

However, the Puritans did accept the Calvinistic idea that children are born sinful and must be forced to be good. The goal of discipline was to the break the will of the child. While this certainly included physical punishment, the focus was on internalized restraints. Children were taught that they were born evil, and that their slim chance for salvation lay in obedience to and respect for their parents and other adults. Such concepts were drilled into them in school, where they memorized such couplets as "In Adam's Fall / We sinned all," and "The Idle Fool / Is Whipt at school."

By the 1800s, this tradition of inherently sinful children was challenged as the values of society for children shifted from obedience to self-reliance, and the influence of philosophers such as John Locke and Jean-Jacques Rousseau increased. Locke said that children were born neither good nor bad but as "blank slates" to be written on by experience, and Rousseau took the opposite stand of the Puritans in claiming that children were born good.

THE MODERN NORTH AMERICAN FAMILY

The industrialization and urbanization of the 19th century brought with it important changes in the Western family. Before the time of factories and mass production, family members tended to spend their days together on their farms or in other commercial endeavors. Father, mother, and children worked with their animals, crops, and household chores, which included preserving food and making clothes. What education the children received they got from their parents.

With the advent of factory work, husbands, wives, and children went to work in the mills for wages. Eventually, child labor laws sent the younger children back home and into the public schools. The mothers stayed at home to care for the young children, and what many refer to as the "traditional" family was created. The literature of this time (see Queen et al., 1985) speaks of a sense of family disruption, which resulted in an idealization of the home as a refuge from the cruel outside world and of women as its domestic center.

It became unacceptable for middle-class women to work for money outside the home after marriage. As the United States struggled to adapt to democratic rather than hierarchical ways of thinking, the notion of separate spheres developed. Women were assigned the domestic sphere, where they were supposed to have authority. In reality, men were still the chief decision makers. Over time, both parental and male authority were undermined as the family wage economy of the colonial household was replaced by separate wages for individual workers (Caffrey, 1991).

According to Kephart and Jedlicka (1991), as young people moved to the cities for work they became less under the influence of their parents for mate selection. They did not have to worry about inheriting family land, and they were now interacting with prospective mates whom their parents had never even met. Love replaced parental permission and the use of dowries disappeared. This resulted in a change from a controlled courtship to the dating with which we are familiar today.

From about the mid-1800s until World War I was a time often referred to as the Victorian era, named after the queen who ruled England during much of this period. Once again, the roles for women were restricted, similar to the chivalry of the middle ages and the southern colonies. American and European society also experienced its most repressive attitude toward sexuality since the time of the early Christians.

Welter (1966/1978) discusses the "cult of true womanhood" which emerged in the 1800s. There were four qualities a good woman was expected to have, the first being piety. Men were cautioned to look for a mate who was religious, probably because religion did not tempt women away from their "proper sphere," which was the home. The second trait was purity, which I discuss in greater detail later. Essentially, women were to avoid arousing sexual feelings in men. This advice comes from a book, *The Young Lady's Friend*: "Sit not with another in a place that is too narrow; read not out of the same book; let not your eagerness to see anything induce you to place your head close to another person's" (Welter, 1966/1978, p. 315).

The third virtue of true womanhood was submission. Women were taught that they were weak and needed a husband as a protector. Being inferior to men (one physician said, "Woman has a head almost too small for intellect but just big enough for love"; see Welter, 1966/1978, p. 318), wives were admonished to obey their husbands and only give advice when it is asked for. The final and perhaps most important trait was domesticity. A woman's role in life was to maintain a cheerful home for her husband and sons. Housework and related tasks were extolled, and a truly patriotic woman was one who stayed at home rather than wanting to vote or do other "male" things.

The Victorians were very antisexual and considered any intercourse except for procreation to be excessive and degrading. Even in marriage it was embarrassing, and experts recommended limiting it to no more than once a month. Some foods common today were developed for the express purpose of lowering sexual desire in males. They include corn flakes and Dr. Sylvester Graham's crackers.

In reference to the quality of purity, female clothing was heavy and designed to hide a woman's natural form, so as to reduce the sexual appetite of men. Even the legs of pianos and other furniture were covered so that one's mind would not be drawn to inappropriate thoughts. The sexes were often separated for certain dangerous activities, such as swimming and looking at classical art. Ladies were always expected to act in a dignified and discreet manner and to never smoke, drink, or swear (Kephart & Jedlicka, 1991).

Medical experts supported the notions that sex could be unhealthy and that women were pure. The following example summarizes the popular view:

> There are many females who never feel any sexual excitement whatever.
> . . . The best mothers, wives and managers of households know little or
> nothing of the sexual pleasure. Love of home, children and domestic duties
> are the only passions they feel. As a rule, the modest woman submits to
> her husband, but only to please him; and, but for the desire of maternity,
> would far rather be relieved from his attentions. (Truitt, 1916, p. 162)

Too much sex could also be hard on the health of males. It was believed that the loss of semen sapped a man's strength, and that intercourse should therefore be infrequent. Many books noted how intercourse debilitated a man and could ruin his marriage as well (see, e.g., Macfadden, 1904).

It is small wonder that Freud found sexual trauma and guilt to be at the base of most neurotic disorders. Denied intimate relations with her husband, a woman's closest male relationships were often with her sons, which could partially explain such Oedipal-sounding songs as *I want a girl just like the girl who married dear old dad*. There is considerable evidence that the typical Victorian family was far from the fancied ideal, and that incest rates may have been fairly high, especially for the poor living in overcrowded conditions (Wohl, 1978). Men were considered to be weaker, so prostitution flourished as husbands spared their wives their animal nature.

The Victorian era was a time of transition and paradox. The private, middle-class family had been developing since the time of the Renaissance, and movement for equality within that unit conflicted with patriarchal tradition. For instance, women were in charge at home but under their husband's control; more permissive laws concerning such issues as abortion, divorce, and custody shifted power from husbands to male legislators and judges; intimacy and romance were valued, but the morally superior woman was to restrain her husband's lustful nature while meeting his needs; marriages were to be both passionate and sexless; fathers were to be the head of the home but children were reared almost exclusively by the mother; a woman was to rear sons to function in the outside world but was to know nothing about it herself (Brady, 1991). Such contradictions certainly resulted in much confusion as husbands, wives, and children sought to know and interact with each other.

By the 1920s, Americans were emerging from this romantic but conflicted sexuality and into today's commercial and erotic sexual culture in which sexual relations are expected to provide happiness and are not tied to reproduction. Since that time, sexuality for both males and females has come to be seen as a legitimate source of personal meaning and a necessary part of people's lives. With the acceptance of the erotic, the commercialization of sex has increased dramatically in recent decades. Since the 1960s and the decline of the baby boom, the demographics of the U.S. family have changed along with the new sexual standard. The typical U.S. couple now marries later, has fewer children, and is more likely to divorce than was the case before the shift toward sexual equality in the 1920s (D'Emilio & Freedman, 1988).

Meanwhile, after millennia of stagnation, women were finally making dramatic progress in the area of political rights. One watershed event was a women's rights convention held in Seneca Falls, New York, in 1848. The three declared goals were all achieved in later decades in the United States: to gain legal and property rights for women, to allow women into higher education, and to procure full political rights.

Women were admitted into Oberlin College in 1883, and others followed. Today, slightly more women than men enroll in U.S. colleges. The 19th amendment to the Constitution gave women the right to vote in 1920, and other equality rights have followed. Some issues still remain, but for the first time in history males do not have tremendous social and legal power over women. As did previous wars, the Civil War and World War I and World War II pushed women into the economic sphere and resulted in greater rights for women (Kephart & Jedlicka, 1991). Children also are protected from the arbitrary use of power as many abusive activities against children have become illegal and received media attention.

CONCLUSION

Power and sexuality have always been linked in Western history. The "status quo" from which we start is the Hebrew culture, which provided a religious rationale for patriarchy over women and children. As inferior beings, women and children were to be benevolently controlled by their husbands/fathers, and males were allowed more sexual expression than were women. This view was intensified by the Greeks, who added a "scientific" rationale for the inferiority of women.

Roman times saw the beginning of a system for bringing about gradual change, which is disruption and reaction. The Punic wars disrupted the economic system, which enhanced the status of women by forcing men to allow them into the world of work. Early Christianity reacted to the perceived dangers of female equality by reemphasizing women's inferiority by way of religious dogma. Women and sexuality became associated with evil. Church teachings, however, denounced the previously acceptable practices of killing or selling unwanted children.

The Middle Ages was a time of paradox as the now-standard view of women as inferior and dangerous coexisted with a view that women were morally superior to males and should be treated with romance and respect. Whereas much of this was simply a seduction technique, it did raise the view of women in the eyes of many men and opened the door to true intimacy.

The economic changes of the Renaissance became an important turning point. As commerce led to the private, nuclear middle-class family, couple relations became more intimate and therefore equalitarian. That is, as couples worked together disconnected from the extended family, they came to like and respect each other more. As they recognized the pleasures of sexual and psychological intimacy, it became harder for one to treat the other as property.

Colonial America still held onto the importance of marriage as an economic union but recognized the value of women in this endeavor. In addition, sexual pleasure was good for both sexes, but only if tied to family reproduction. Sex outside marriage was seen as a threat to the social order. This shift toward greater equality, brought about by democratic political ideals and sex ratio and economic conditions, led to a conflicted sexuality in the Victorian era as couples valued intimacy–equality but men still wanted to be in charge.

Ministers were replaced by physicians in the attempt to hold on to traditional ways of thinking. Doctors argued that menstruation diverted blood from the brain and made women irrational, indicating that they could not function in the public sphere. Scientists found that females had smaller brains than males (not taking into account differences in body size and weight) and argued that they were naturally inferior as a result (Caffrey, 1991).

Such efforts were insufficient to stem the tide in the direction of free mate choice based on love and the equality that such intimacy implied. World War I and World War II provided further disruptions to the economic and social order, resulting in more women in the work force, which gave them more equality in marriage and led to a greater acceptance of sexuality for men and women both in and out of marriage.

However, there are those today who argue that society has become too permissive and that the rise in divorce rates, dual-career families, and single-parent families, which have resulted in part from greater gender equality, has harmed the quality of childrearing (Popenoe, 1993).

Although it is clear that dramatic strides away from patriarchy and toward gender equality have occurred in the last 150 years, attitudes toward sexuality continue to shift. North American society is at present relatively permissive after a long tradition of either the double standard or sexual repression, but it is unclear what the future holds.

REFERENCES

Adams, B., & Steinmetz, S. (1993). Family theory and methods in the classics. In P. G. Boss, W. J. Doherty, R. LaRossa, W. R. Schumm, & S. K. Steinmetz (Eds.), *Sourcebook of family theories and methods: A contextual approach* (pp. 71–94). New York: Plenum Press.

Bardis, P. (1963a). Main features of the ancient Hebrew family. *Social Science, 38,* 168–183.

Bardis, P. (1963b). Main features of the ancient Roman family. *Social Science, 38,* 225–240.

Bardis, P. (1964a). The ancient Greek family. *Social Science, 39,* 156–175.

Bardis, P. (1964b). Early Christianity and the family. *Sociological Bulletin, 13,* 1–23.

Bardis, P. (1966). Marriage and family customs in ancient Egypt: An interdisciplinary study. *Social Science, 41,* 229–245.

Brady, M. (1991). The new model middle-class family (1815–1930). In J. Hawes & E. Nybakken (Eds.), *American families: A research guide and historical handbook* (pp. 83–117). New York: Greenwood Press.

Caffrey, M. (1991). Women and families. In J. Hawes & E. Nybakken (Eds.), *American families: A research guide and historical handbook* (pp. 223–254). New York: Greenwood Press.

D'Emilio, D., & Freedman, E. (1988). *Intimate matters: A history of sexuality in America.* New York: Harper & Row.

Fielding, W. (1942). *Strange customs of courtship and marriage*. New York: New Home Library.

Flandrin, J.-L. (1977). Repression and change in the sexual life of young people in medieval and early modern times. *Journal of Family History*, 2(Fall), 196–210.

Gies, F., & Gies, J. (1987). *Marriage and the family in the Middle Ages*. New York: Harper & Row.

The Holy Bible. King James Version.

Kephart, W., & Jedlicka, D. (1991). *The family, society, and the individual*. New York: HarperCollins.

Laslett, P. (1977). Characteristics of the Western family considered over time. *Journal of Family History*, 2(Summer), 89–115.

Macfadden, B. (1904). *Superb virility of manhood*. New York: Physical Culture.

Morgan, E. (1942). The Puritans and sex. *New England Quarterly*, 15(4), 591–607.

Popenoe, D. (1993). American family decline, 1960–1990: A review and appraisal. *Journal of Marriage and the Family*, 55(3) 527–542.

Queen, S., Habenstein, R., & Quadagno, J. (1985). *The family in various cultures*. New York: Harper & Row.

Tannahill, R. (1980). *Sex in history*. New York: Stein & Day.

Truitt, W. (1916). *Eugenics*. Marietta, OH: Mullikin.

Tuchman, B. (1978). *A distant mirror*. New York: Knopf.

Veyne, P. (1985). Homosexuality in ancient Rome. In P. Aries & A. Bejin (Eds.), *Western sexuality: Practice and precept in past and present times* (pp. 26–35). Oxford, England: Basil Blackwell.

Welter, B. (1966). The cult of true womanhood: 1820–1860. *American Quarterly*, 18, 151–174. Reprinted in M. Gordon (Ed.), *The American family in social-historical perspective* (2nd ed., pp. 313–333). New York: St. Martin's Press, 1978.

Wohl, A. (1978). *The Victorian family*. New York: St. Martin's Press.

CHAPTER THREE

Comparative Research Methodology

GARY R. LEE

Research on human behavior, like most other types of scientific research, is based on the logic of correlation. This means that we examine the ways in which things go together in patterns. The things we study—traits, characteristics, or behaviors of individuals or other units of analysis, such as organizations or political units—are called variables because they take different values in different cases. In other words, they vary. Correlation, in its generic usage, is another term for *covariation*, which means the way variables vary together. We know, for example, that people with more education typically have higher incomes than those with less education (a *positive* correlation, meaning that the two variables tend to have similar values in most cases). We also know that the faster one drives, the lower one's gas mileage (a *negative* correlation, meaning that the variables tend to have opposite values).

The objective of behavioral science is not simply to observe and catalogue correlations among variables involving human behavior but rather to *explain* why we observe the patterns or correlations we do instead of some other patterns or correlations. The body of knowledge developed to predict and explain patterns of relations among variables is termed "theory." The body of knowledge that guides us in the process of observing behavior and processing the information we obtain from those observations is termed "research methodology." Although the latter is the focus of this chapter, theory and methods are intimately connected.

This chapter is explicitly about *comparative* research methods. In a literal sense, all social research is comparative (Lee, 1982). When we say that "church attendance is negatively correlated with the probability of divorce," for example, we are saying that we have compared married persons who go to church frequently with those who go less frequently, and the latter were observed to have a higher probability of divorce. This is a comparative statement. In practice, however, comparative research has come to mean research in which two or more *societies* are compared in some way.

Comparing societies is the only way of observing variation in the characteristics of societies and ascertaining how these characteristics affect the behavior of their members. When conducting comparative research, we are able to observe multiple societies with varying characteristics and to look for the ways in which these characteristics "hang together" in patterns and covary with the behavior of individuals. We cannot do this without comparing societies because, within any single society, all characteristics of that society are "constants"—that is, they do not vary. Therefore, we cannot observe patterns of covariation among these characteristics or between these characteristics and the behavior of individuals. Studies conducted exclusively in the United States, for example, can tell us only how people in the United States behave. They cannot tell us whether the behavior we observe is similar to or different from the behavior of members of other societies, nor can they tell us whether this behavior is due to some particular characteristic(s) of the United States as a society.

For example, we know that in the United States the psychological well-being of older persons is positively related to the frequency with which they interact with their friends but unrelated to their frequency of interaction with their adult children or other kin (Lee & Ishii-Kuntz, 1987). Would this pattern also appear in other societies such as Japan or Korea, where the culture places a much stronger emphasis on the value of intergenerational relations and a correspondingly lower emphasis on the value of independence from kin? Without comparative research, we do not know whether this pattern is specific to the United States, or to societies like the United States, or a general feature of human societies. More important, if these correlations do appear in some societies but not others, without comparison we do not know what particular features of our society might produce these patterns. Comparative research could provide evidence that would allow us to explain why these relations are observed in the United States, by identifying the distinctive features of the societies in which these correlations appear.

Although comparative research is valuable, it is also difficult to do, and particularly difficult to do well. In this chapter I discuss some of the problems encountered in the conduct of comparative research and some of the ways in which researchers have attempted to resolve these problems. First, however, I describe the various types of comparative research. One type begins with descriptions of small, homogeneous societies by "ethnographers." A second type uses descriptive statistics on societies' populations, such as census data, as its raw material. The third type involves the conduct of separate but related surveys, experiments, or other studies in two or more societies, with the objective of comparing the results. Whereas all three types have in common a focus on comparing the characteristics of societies, they are quite different in what they can do and how they attempt to do it.[1]

TYPES OF COMPARATIVE RESEARCH

Cross-Cultural Research

One of the most common research methods used to gather information about other societies is the ethnographic method. Ethnography is concerned with the systematic, detailed description of the way of life of a group of people or a society. The ethnographer accomplishes this primarily by direct observation, which involves living with the people under study, examining their customs and behaviors, interviewing key informants, and using other strategies designed to allow the ethnographer to describe what it is like to be a member of this society.

One reason ethnographies are used so frequently is that researchers are able to provide rich, complex descriptions of single societies, or of communities within societies. For example, Middleton (1965) lived among and studied the Lugbara of Uganda and wrote an ethnography describing their stratification system, religion, familial and kinship systems, and political structure; such contents are typical of ethnographies. Smith (1970) described village life in China. Although he could not describe the entirety of Chinese society with the ethnographic method, he provided a thorough and detailed understanding of the way of life of people in rural villages typical of large segments of the population. Jacobs (1974) applied the ethnographic method to the study of a U.S. retirement community. Each of these studies gives the reader a coherent picture of what life is like in the societies and communities described, and what it might be like to be a member of the society or community.

However, according to my definition, research done in a single society (whether by ethnographic or other means) is not *comparative* because it cannot examine variation in the properties of societies. But ethnographic research, although not inherently comparative, may be employed for comparative purposes if multiple ethnographies are compared. This type of research has been termed "cross-cultural" (Lee, 1982).

Ethnographies are written descriptions of the way of life of a group of people. To compare ethnographies systematically, we must code and quantify the information they contain. In other words, the written descriptions—words—must be turned into values of variables—numbers—which are then recorded in a form suitable for analysis. This process is referred to as ethnology. Because the ethnography has been a cornerstone of anthropological research for many decades, extending well back into the 19th century, thousands of ethnographies exist. Comparisons of all these written descriptions of societies would be impossible without ethnology.

Fortunately, several data sets have been constructed, with codes assigned to a great many variables described in the texts of existing ethnographies. This makes it possible to compare literally hundreds of human societies in terms of the typical behaviors of their members and their characteristics as societies. Virtually all these data sets exist as a result of the work of the anthropologist George Peter Murdock. They include the Ethnographic Atlas (Murdock, 1967), the Standard Cross-Cultural Sample (Murdock & White, 1969; Barry & Schlegel, 1980), and the Atlas of World Cultures (Murdock, 1981). Ellis and Petersen (1992), for example, used a subset of the Standard Cross-Cultural Sample to discover that in societies in which parents tend to value conformity in children, they are more likely to use physical punishment, lecturing, and other control techniques as disciplinary strategies than are parents in societies in which self-reliance is highly valued in children.

The societies contained in these cross-cultural data sets are small and relatively homogeneous. Many of them no longer exist, at least in the forms in which they were described in the ethnographies. No modern, industrial societies are included because the ethnographic method is not appropriate for the study of such societies. The goal of ethnographic research is to describe the complete society, and the United States and similar complex societies are simply too large and diverse to be described in their entirety by observational methods.

We can conduct ethnographic research *within* large, complex societies such as the United States, but we cannot describe the entire society by doing so. For example, Salamon (1992) studied farmers in the American Midwest and their connections to family and community using ethnographic methods supplemented by some survey and other data. She provided a thorough description and analysis of the way of life of the people she studied, but, of course, her study pertains only to the "community" of farm families she observed rather than to the entirety of U.S. society. Wolf (1992) did a similar study of women employed in factories in Java, showing how industrialization in rural areas of a Third World country affects individual and family lives. As valuable as these studies are, they cannot describe the United States or Java as *societies* but only the specific communities and types of people within these societies that were actually observed. This is not a criticism; these studies were never intended to describe entire societies. If this were the intent, a different methodology would have been employed.

The purpose of using cross-cultural data sets such as the Ethnographic Atlas is not to describe the contemporary world, as many of the societies contained in these data banks no longer exist, or exist in a very different form.

However, cross-cultural data may be very valuable for testing theories about the relations among characteristics or properties of societies. I return to this issue later.

Cross-cultural research does not provide data on the behavior of individuals within societies. The ethnography gives descriptions of how people behave in common circumstances in their societies, but these descriptions of individuals cannot be retained in the process of ethnologic coding. Instead, the ethnologist codes the *typical* behavior of individuals or categories of individuals. For example, we might find that older persons in Society A typically have high status, whereas those in Society B have low status. We cannot compare high- and low-status elders within the same society by cross-cultural research, but we might find that societies in which elders have high status are more likely to have agricultural economies, whereas those in which elders have low status are more likely to have hunting-and-gathering economies (Balkwell & Balswick, 1981; Ishii-Kuntz & Lee, 1987). When we do this for a large number of societies, we are treating each society as a case in a cross-cultural survey, much as we treat individuals as cases in surveys within our own society. Using the cross-cultural method, we can learn about the correlations among the characteristics of societies but not about how these characteristics are related to the behavior of individuals within those societies.

Cross-Societal Research

As noted earlier, cross-cultural research is useful for smaller, relatively homogeneous societies because their populations may be observed directly and behavior is fairly uniform within the group. But large, complex societies cannot be described in full by the ethnographic method and, thus, are not included in cross-cultural data banks. However, there are many compilations of statistics on the populations of contemporary societies that provide information on the aggregate behaviors of members of these societies (e.g., average ages at marriage, divorce rates, or gross domestic product). These may be considered statistical counterparts of the ethnographic observations used in cross-cultural research. Comparative research based on aggregate statistical descriptions of multiple societies is termed "cross-societal."

Again, cross-societal research does not allow the study of individuals within societies. The behavior of populations as aggregates is the focus of this type of research. We may discover through cross-societal research that divorce rates are higher in societies with higher rates of labor force participation by adult women (Trent & South, 1989). However, we cannot determine whether women who are employed are more or less likely to divorce than women who are not employed.

Statistical data on contemporary societies are available through a great variety of sources. One of the richest is the United Nations *Demographic Yearbook* (e.g., United Nations, 1992), which publishes data on many social and demographic characteristics of societies each year. This is only one example, however; there are literally hundreds of possible sources of data on the world's societies. Consequently, a major component of the cross-societal researcher's task is to assemble data from various appropriate sources that are relevant to the objectives of the research. Unlike cross-cultural research, there are few preexisting data sets (such as the Ethnographic Atlas) available in ready-to-analyze form. However, transcribing statistical data from published sources is not nearly as difficult or time-consuming a task as is content-analyzing and coding written ethnographic descriptions of cultures.

Cross-societal research is becoming increasingly common, and the method has been employed to study a great variety of family phenomena. For example, Trent and South (1989) were interested in the effects of certain structural properties of societies on the divorce rate. They obtained estimates of the crude divorce rates (number of divorces per thousand population) from the United Nations *Demographic Yearbook* for 66 societies from around the world, and they constructed measures of several potential predictors of the divorce rate from a variety of sources. The predictors included societal modernization, the rate of labor force participation among adult women, and the sex ratio (number of males per 100 females). Their theory led them to expect that the more modern societies, those with higher rates of female labor force participation, and those with lower sex ratios (fewer men than women) would have higher divorce rates, and this is basically what they found. Their analysis showed that divorce covaries strongly with several dimensions of social structure and population composition.

Both cross-cultural and cross-societal research analyze data *on* societies but not data *in* societies. That is, each provides one observation per variable per society, regardless of the number of individuals in each society who were observed in the collection of the original data. Cross-national research, to which we now turn, involves the analysis of data collected *within* multiple societies.

Cross-National Research

Research conducted *within* two or more societies, either simultaneously or sequentially, may be termed "cross-national." The objective is to obtain comparable data on some set of issues from samples of individuals or other units of analysis (e.g., organizations or political subunits) in all societies included in the research. Analyses are then conducted within each society in the study, and results are compared to determine whether relations among relevant variables are similar or different across the various societies in the sample.

Cross-national research is, in most respects, the most powerful of the various forms of comparative research because it involves analyses on both the individual and societal levels (Kohn, 1987, 1989). It is the clearest way of ascertaining whether the characteristics of the societies in which they live affect the behaviors of individuals. However, it is also the most difficult and expensive form of comparative research because it requires the collection of original data in multiple societies; one does not have banks of cross-national data to rely on. Because of this, and because of the complexity of comparisons at multiple levels of analysis (individual as well as societal), it is virtually always the case that cross-national studies involve very small numbers of societies. Whereas cross-cultural studies can deal with more than 1,000 cultures simultaneously (the Ethnographic Atlas contains over 1,200 cases, for example), and cross-societal studies often involve 100 or more societies, cross-national studies are generally restricted to no more than five or six countries at maximum, and most involve only two.

Note here that it is possible to compare multiple societies, in some cases, without collecting original data from each one. We may conduct a study in one society to replicate a study previously done in another. It is also possible to compare two or more studies done in multiple societies "after the fact," even if the studies were not originally intended for this purpose, although one must be constantly aware of problems of comparability, which I discuss shortly. But the best cross-national studies are generally those that are explicitly planned and designed to be cross-national, because problems of comparability can be addressed at the design stage of the research project and methods adapted to the explanatory objectives of the project.

Davis and Robinson (1991) studied consciousness of gender inequality in Austria, West Germany, Great Britain, and the United States. Among a variety of findings, they discovered that employed women in the United States were more favorable to efforts to reduce inequality than were nonemployed women; however, this pattern did not appear in the other three countries. Because the studies in each country were designed to be comparable in terms of sampling and measurement, it is likely that the difference in the effect of employment Davis and Robinson observed is a real difference rather than an artifact of noncomparable research methods.

True cross-national studies are rare because of their difficulty and expense. They are, however, valuable, for the reasons discussed earlier. But each type of comparative research has its own value, and each encounters its own versions of problems common to scientific researchers in all fields. In the next section, I briefly discuss a few of the major issues in the conduct of comparative research.

ISSUES IN COMPARATIVE RESEARCH METHODOLOGY

In any scientific investigation into human behavior, there are many issues that must be managed successfully in order to produce useful evidence and to come to defensible conclusions. Many of these issues fall under three headings. First, *sampling* involves the selection of observations to be made from among the universe of all possible observations. Second, *measurement* is the process of assigning values to variables for each case. Third, *explanation* has to do with the interpretation of the evidence and the development of theory. Each of these issues is critical in any type of research, and the principles that guide the researcher to successful solutions to the problems each issue poses are identical regardless of whether research is comparative or noncomparative (Lee, 1982). However, comparative research presents some unique problems, and the ways in which the principles of good research are applied to these problems are somewhat different.

Sampling

The objective of behavioral science is to study the behavior of all human beings, or at least all members of a defined human population. However, no single study can possibly do this, and in most cases it is not necessary. Instead, studies are conducted on "samples" of relevant populations. The sample is the set of observations we actually make, which is a subset of all observations we could possibly make (the population). Provided that our samples possess certain properties, it is possible to "generalize" the results obtained from samples to populations with a high degree of confidence that we are correct.

Good samples possess two properties. The first is size. Although there is no handy rule that covers all cases, larger samples are better than smaller samples. This stands to reason because the possibility that unusual events could occur in a high proportion of cases is greater in a smaller sample. For example, it is not at all inconceivable that we could observe heads on two consecutive tosses of a fair coin. In other words, if you flipped a coin twice and it came up heads both times, you would not be sure that it was a two-headed coin. But if you observe heads on 2,000 consecutive tosses, the hypothesis that the coin is "fair" becomes highly untenable. The larger a sample, the more likely it reflects the characteristics of the population from which it was drawn.

However, this also depends on another property of good samples: representativeness. A sample is representative to the extent that it possesses the same elements as the population in the same proportions. In other words, if a population contains half males and half females, a sample should too.

Because it is impossible to know all the relevant characteristics of a population in advance of a study, or to intentionally choose observations that would collectively reflect these characteristics, behavioral scientists rely on *random* sampling methods to produce representative samples. Random simply means that we select the observations (cases) that comprise our samples by chance: Every member of the population has an equal chance of appearing in the sample, and the actual selection of cases is done by chance. If a random procedure is followed, and if the sample is large enough, the laws of probability ensure that the sample is highly likely to reflect or mirror the characteristics of the population. Then we can have some confidence that what we find to be true of the sample is also true of the population (Babbie, 1990).

This, in brief, is the theory behind sampling. The same principles of sampling apply to all forms of behavioral research. Unfortunately, in the case of comparative research, it is essentially impossible to apply these principles to produce large, representative samples of the world's societies. The reasons for this differ according to the type of comparative research under consideration.

In cross-cultural research, as noted earlier, it is possible to work with fairly large samples of cultures—well over 1,000 in the case of the Ethnographic Atlas (Murdock, 1967), and over 100 even in samples researchers construct independently (see, e.g., Ellis & Petersen, 1992). However, it is not possible to obtain representative samples of the world's cultures because we only have data on some of them and cannot get data on many of the others. Many societies that have existed over the course of human history no longer exist, or exist in a form highly altered from earlier forms as a result of contact with other societies. Those for which we have ethnographic data are surely different from those for which we do not (Lee, 1982, 1984a). Even if we were to use all of the ethnographic data available, we would have a biased (nonrepresentative) sample of the world's cultures, making generalizations from our sample to the population hazardous indeed.

We have a similar problem with cross-societal research even though the societies at issue are contemporary. There is a great deal of variation across societies in the amount and types of data that are collected from their populations and made available to the scholarly community. Trent and South (1989), in their cross-societal study of divorce, were able to come up with data on the divorce rate and other relevant variables for 66 societies around the world. Because there are less than 200 contemporary nations, this is a high sampling fraction. But, as they demonstrated, the societies on which they had the necessary data were different from those on which they did not. The societies in their sample had higher gross national products, higher life expectancies, and lower fertility rates and were different from those not in the sample in several other ways as well. Generally, it is the more technologically advanced societies that are best able to collect population data and most likely to make it publicly available. This means that cross-societal samples also cannot be fully representative of the world's societies; if the necessary data simply do not exist for certain societies, we cannot create them.

The problem in cross-national research is somewhat different. Theoretically, we could choose any societies in the world to study and could therefore employ random methods of selection. But this is not usually possible for political and logistic reasons, and, furthermore, the laws of probability do not apply to small numbers—remember, cross-national studies can only include a few societies. Although samples of individuals within societies may be large and representative, samples of societies themselves are inherently small and nonrepresentative.

The bottom line is that, for varying reasons, the principles of good sampling cannot be applied to the selection of societies for comparative research. Does this mean that good comparative research cannot be done? No. But it does mean that the objectives of this type of research must be adapted to the realm of the possible. Also, generalizing from samples to populations, which is a primary objective of survey research in contemporary societies, simply cannot be done. In other words, there is no type of comparative research that allows us to describe the population of societies in the world.

The objective of comparative research, however, is explanatory, not descriptive. We do this sort of research to test our ideas about *why* things go together as they do. What we need for this are samples of societies that allow our ideas to be tested fairly. We may, for example, have a theory that suggests a variety of reasons why arranged marriages should be more likely to occur in societies with extended family systems than in those with nuclear families (Lee & Stone, 1980). Whereas the ideal would certainly be a representative sample of all societies in the world, we can get by with a sample that includes a number of societies with extended family systems and a number with nuclear family systems. If, after comparing them according to type of mate selection system, we observe the difference we predict, our reasoning (theory) gains credibility. If we do not observe this difference, something about our reasoning is faulty and needs correcting, or perhaps our theory needs to be traded in for a completely different model.

In cross-cultural and cross-societal research, the general strategy is to employ all possible data—that is, if data are available for a society, use them. In cross-national research, it is vitally important to select societies that are appropriate for the comparison we wish to make. If we have a hypothesis we believe to be universally applicable—that is, true in all human societies—we are well advised to test it in societies that differ as dramatically as possible, under the assumption that if it works at the extremes of a continuum it is likely to work in the middle. If, on the other hand, we have a hypothesis that a specific characteristic of a society has a specific effect on behavior, we should select societies that are as similar to one another as possible except on the characteristic in question. In this way, if the predicted differences are observed, we have narrowed the list of possible factors that might explain them because a difference cannot be explained by a similarity. In the study mentioned earlier by Davis and Robinson (1991), on consciousness of gender inequality, education was shown be positively related to consciousness of gender inequality among U.S. women but negatively related to women's support for government efforts to combat inequality; this pattern did not hold in Austria, West Germany, or England. The authors argued that the United States may be different due to a tradition of emphasizing individualism and the primacy of the individual's role in solving problems. They suggested that "well-educated U.S. women adopt more individualistic solutions to women's disadvantaged position because of the U.S. educational system, which may emphasize personal effort and achievement more than systems in Britain and other European countries" (Davis & Robinson, 1991, p. 82). Although there are no available means of verifying this speculation in the authors' data, their suggestion is reasonable because the four societies they studied are similar in so many other respects. (For more on the subject of selecting societies for cross-national research, see Kohn, 1987, 1989; Lee & Haas, 1993; Przeworski & Teune, 1970; and Warwick & Osherson, 1973.)

The point here is that comparative research is much more useful if it begins with a good theory. The theory predicts what will be discovered if certain observations are made. By making those observations and checking their outcomes against the predictions, we can learn something about the validity of the reasoning that produced the predictions. Without theory, we can only describe, and comparative research is limited for descriptive purposes because of the impossibility of obtaining representative samples of the world's societies. If we do not have a theory that should be tested comparatively, and that clearly stipulates what kinds of comparisons should be made to provide a constructive test, the value of the research probably will not justify its difficulty and expense (Kohn, 1987).

Measurement

Measurement is the process of assigning values to variables. Once observations are selected for inclusion in the sample, we must determine what value each observation takes. This may be as simple as ascertaining whether a respondent is male or female, or as complex as determining how "developed" a society is on a multidimensional index. In all research, each observation must be assigned a score for each variable.

In cross-cultural and cross-societal research, the values of variables are provided to the researcher in many cases. For example, in the Ethnographic Atlas the type of family system that characterizes a society is precoded in such a way that family type (nuclear vs. extended) and marital type (monogamy, polygyny, polyandry) may be determined. The values for the variables, of course, refer to the "typical" or normative practice in the society, not to any specific family or set of families. In other cases, variables must be coded from original ethnographic reports or from compilations of the texts of these reports, such as the Human Relations Area Files. Problems may arise in each case.

In precoded data sets, variables are not necessarily provided to the researcher in the form he/she finds most useful. Decisions must be made according to the objectives of the research, and codes for variables must often be recombined and reordered to suit those purposes. For example, Blumberg and Winch (1972) developed a theory of the relationship between "societal complexity" and family structure, which argued that the most complex families (i.e., extended family systems) are most likely to be found in the intermediate ranges of societal complexity. They decided that in addition to consanguineally extended family systems, they would count societies as having complex families if they practiced frequent polygyny—the marriage of one husband to two or more wives. Their test of the theory was highly supportive. However, the theory was about family structure, not marital structure, but marital structure was an important component of their measure. It turns out that if marital and family structure are separated, their theory predicts marital structure quite well but predicts family structure rather poorly (Lee, 1983). This is unfortunate because the entire theory was about family structure.

Problems are also encountered, usually much more obviously, when variables are coded directly from ethnographic reports. Balkwell and Balswick (1981) studied the status of the elderly and tested a theory that said that older persons have higher status in agricultural than hunting-and-gathering societies. To do this test, they had to code "status of the elderly" from ethnographic reports. They decided that any indication that older persons were ritually abandoned or killed would indicate low status for the elderly, regardless of other indicators. This seems eminently reasonable, particularly to contemporary scholars who cannot imagine abandoning or killing people simply because they have become too old. Their test was supportive: Older persons were shown to have higher status in agricultural societies.

However, Balkwell and Balswick (1981) overlooked the fact that older persons are killed or abandoned primarily in nomadic societies; it occurs when they become too weak or sick to keep up with the group in its travels. As many groups must move in pursuit of food, slowing or stopping for older persons threatens the survival of the entire group. They are therefore faced with difficult choices between keeping their elders alive a little while longer or pursuing the food they need to keep the adults and children alive; if they stop, everyone may die.

The problem for Balkwell and Balswick was that these nomadic societies are almost exclusively hunting-and-gathering types. The members of agricultural societies do not move because they must stay with the land on which their food is grown, so abandoning or killing old people who cannot keep up simply is not an issue. Of course, when the researchers coded the status of the elderly the way they did, hunting–gathering societies received much lower scores on this variable than did agricultural societies. When the variable is coded without regard to the practice in question, the direction of the relationship remains the same, but the relationship is much weaker (Lee, 1984b; Lee & Ishii-Kuntz, 1987). Balkwell and Balswick (1981) overestimated the strength of this relationship because they coded one variable in such a way that it was automatically and necessarily correlated with another variable, for a reason that had nothing to do with their theory.

Trent and South (1989), in their cross-societal study of divorce mentioned previously, showed that divorce rates are higher in more modern, complex, "developed" societies such as the United States than in those that are less technologically developed. The divorce rate they used, however, was the "crude" divorce rate, which is simply the number of divorces in a given year per 1,000 total population of the society in that year. With this measure, it is possible for a society to have a low divorce rate either because few marriages end in divorce or because few people are married and thus are not exposed to the risk of divorce. Less developed societies typically have higher birthrates, lower life expectancies, and consequently high proportions of children in their populations; this means high proportions of unmarried persons. Thus, Trent and South's findings may mean, in part at least, that less developed societies have few divorces for the innocuous reason that relatively few people are married. A better indicator for their purposes would have been the "refined" divorce rate, which is the number of divorces per 1,000 married women in the population. Unfortunately, this was not available to them, so they did the best they could with what they had and warned their readers that there are problems with the use of the crude divorce rate.

Measurement in cross-national research can be difficult. Besides all the usual problems of constructing good measures that are faced in noncomparative research (and there are many), the cross-national researcher is faced with the additional problems of comparability across societies and, frequently, across languages. Having comparable measures is essential to comparative research because if measures mean different things in different societies, then observed differences between those societies may be artifacts of the measures rather than true differences. The same measure (i.e., the same set of items or questions) may measure different things in different cultures, even if perfectly translated (Kohn, 1987; Lee, 1982; Lee & Haas, 1993; Przeworski & Teune, 1970; Warwick & Osherson, 1973).

Haas (1986) studied attitudes toward the breadwinning (provider) role among women in Sweden and the United States. To measure her dependent variable, she used two slightly different items in the two countries. In the United States, she asked respondents to agree or disagree with the statement, "The husband should be the main breadwinner in the family." In Sweden, the comparable statement was, "The man should be the primary breadwinner in the family." The difference between the two statements is subtle but important because the rate of cohabitation is much higher in Sweden than in the United States, and many of Haas's Swedish respondents were cohabiting and technically did not have husbands. It is entirely possible to measure the same phenomenon in two or more societies by asking substantially different questions (Miller, Slomczynski, & Schoenberg, 1981; Przeworski & Teune, 1970).

Fortunately, a great deal of work has been done on how to create comparable measures and how to ascertain whether measures are in fact comparable (Kohn, Slomczynski, & Schoenbach, 1986; Kuechler, 1987; Miller, Slomczynski, & Schoenberg, 1981; Przeworski & Teune, 1970). Unfortunately, space prohibits a careful treatment of these efforts here. Comparable measurement is difficult to achieve in cross-national research, and in all likelihood measures are never perfectly comparable, but it is possible to come close. It is, nonetheless, important to be aware that noncomparability of measures may produce artifactual differences between nations in cross-national research. As Kohn (1987, 1989) points out, findings of cross-national similarity are unlikely to be due to noncomparable methods, but findings of differences between nations may be. One must always consider measurement error as a possible explanation for cross-national differences.

Although it takes somewhat different forms, measurement error is also a paramount concern in "qualitative" studies such as ethnographic reports. Here the researcher observes the behaviors and customs of a group of people and interprets these observations in the context of the culture of the people as he/she understands it. A primary danger is the unintentional application of the researcher's own cultural background on the interpretive process—in other words, ethnocentrism. Ethnographers are highly trained in methods designed to minimize the possibility of ethnocentric interpretations (see, e.g., Barnard & Good, 1984). It is important, for example, for the ethnographer to live with the people he/she is studying for some time, to learn the language, and to interview key informants extensively not only about customary behaviors but also about the motivations and meanings underlying the behaviors. Interpreting the behavior of members of one society according to the culture of another society constitutes a serious form of measurement error.

Explanation

In the terminology employed here, "theory" is synonymous with "explanation." Theory is the body of concepts, premises, assumptions, and knowledge that makes our empirical observations understandable; it is the attempt to answer the *why* question. There is no particular type or form of theory that is unique to comparative family scholarship because comparative researchers tailor their explanatory strategies to the objects of their particular research efforts. There are, however, certain common problems that arise in the course of constructing comparative explanations. We can deal with only a few of these problems here.

One generic explanatory problem common to both cross-cultural and cross-societal research is often referred to as the ecological fallacy. This is the assumption that what is true of aggregates is also true of individuals. This assumption is often false. As an example, let us return to the study of divorce rates by Trent and South (1989). They discovered that across most of their sample, divorce rates and rates of female labor force participation are positively related; that is, societies in which higher proportions of women are in the labor force have higher divorce rates than do other societies. This does not mean, however, that employed women are more likely to divorce than are nonemployed women. This may or may not be true (Greenstein, 1990; White, 1990). It is possible that nonemployed women are more likely to divorce in populations in which most women are employed. The discovery that two properties or characteristics of aggregate populations go together does not automatically imply that these same characteristics go together on the individual level; this must be determined separately.

A second major explanatory issue in comparative research is termed "overidentification." Technically, overidentification refers to a situation in which there are more ways to explain a difference among cases than there are cases in the analysis. This problem occurs most frequently and obviously in cross-national research because it is a problem that is inherent in all small-sample research, and cross-national studies can deal with only a few societies. The problem arises when we attempt to explain a cross-national difference, either in the value of some dependent variable or in a pattern of relations among variables. The difference in question must be attributable to some other difference between the societies (because a difference cannot be caused by a similarity), but any two societies have an infinite number of differences between them even if they were selected to be as similar as possible. Which difference accounts for the difference we are trying to explain?

There is no statistical means of answering questions such as this because, for a sample of two societies, any difference between them will rank the societies in the same order (or its mirror opposite, which comes to the same thing). The consequence is that any difference between two societies perfectly explains any other difference between the societies in statistical terms, so we have no way of distinguishing between alternative explanations.

Again, the best defense against overidentification is a good theory (Kohn, 1987; Lee & Haas, 1993). If a particular difference between societies is predicted on some theoretical grounds, and that difference is in fact observed, the theory gains in credibility, although we certainly cannot rule out other possible explanations. If the predicted difference is not observed, the theory loses credibility. This is one more reason why comparative research should not be done without a theory, which provides the rationale for the comparison one is making as well as a credible explanation for the observed differences.

CONCLUSION

Good comparative research does not result from simply following a predesigned set of rules and procedures (Kohn, 1987; Zelditch, 1971). Instead, it involves creativity in assembling appropriate observations and employing these observations in a constructive manner. I have touched only briefly on some of the major issues in the method of comparative social inquiry here, and the reader is certainly not prepared by this abbreviated treatment to go out and do useful comparisons. But at least I have highlighted some of the issues.

Comparative research remains the only means of ascertaining how the characteristics of societies in which people live affect their behavior. It is, in fact, the only means of observing variation in the characteristics of societies, thereby rendering them amenable to scientific analysis by the method of covariation. There are no easy solutions to the methodological problems posed by comparative inquiry, but our methods have become a great deal more sophisticated in recent years, and we are at least aware of the many pitfalls and obstacles to comparability.

Perhaps the best way to conclude this chapter is to echo Kohn's (1987) observation that unless we have a compelling reason for doing comparative research, we are well advised not to do it. Comparative research can be a powerful means of analyzing the effects of society on behavior, which is what sociology is all about, but it is difficult to do well and is hard on resources. There are many specific compelling reasons to do comparative research, but they can all be summarized by one generic term: theory. We compare societies in order to shed light on our thinking, to determine whether our ideas about the way the world works have merit. If we do not have ideas that need to be tested in this manner, there is little point in comparison. But if we do have ideas about how the characteristics of societies affect the behavior of their members, comparative research is the only way to generate empirical tests of these ideas.

NOTE

1. The discussion of types of comparative research is based heavily on several previous publications on comparative methodology. See Lee (1982) for a general treatment of the issues, Lee (1984a) for a detailed discussion of cross-cultural research, and Lee and Haas (1993) for an analysis of cross-societal and cross-national methods. Also compare Lee's division of comparative research into types with Ragin's (1987) distinction between "case-oriented strategies" and "variable-oriented strategies."

REFERENCES

Babbie, E. (1990). *Survey research methods* (2nd ed.). Belmont, CA: Wadsworth.

Balkwell, C., & Balswick, J. (1981). Subsistence economy, family structure, and the status of the elderly. *Journal of Marriage and the Family, 43,* 423–429.

Barnard, A., & Good, A. (1984). *Research practices in the study of kinship.* New York: Academic Press.

Barry, H., & Schlegel, A. (1980). *Cross-cultural samples and codes.* Pittsburgh: University of Pittsburgh Press.

Blumberg, R. L., & Winch, R. F. (1972). Societal complexity and familial complexity: Evidence for the curvilinear hypothesis. *American Journal of Sociology, 77,* 898–920.

Davis, N. J., & Robinson, R. V. (1991). Men's and women's consciousness of gender inequality: Austria, West Germany, Great Britain, and the United States. *American Sociological Review, 56,* 72–84.

Ellis, G. J., & Petersen, L. R. (1992). Socialization values and parental control techniques: A cross-cultural analysis of child-rearing. *Journal of Comparative Family Studies, 23,* 39–54.

Greenstein, T. N. (1990). Marital disruption and the employment of married women. *Journal of Marriage and the Family, 52,* 657–676.

Haas, L. (1986). Wives' orientation toward breadwinning: Sweden and the United States. *Journal of Family Issues, 7,* 358–381.

Ishii-Kuntz, M., & Lee, G. R. (1987). Status of the elderly: An extension of the theory. *Journal of Marriage and the Family, 49,* 413–420.

Jacobs, J. (1974). *Fun city: An ethnographic study of a retirement community.* New York: Holt, Rinehart & Winston.

Kohn, M. L. (1987). Cross-national research as an analytic strategy. *American Sociological Review, 52,* 713–731.

Kohn, M. L. (Ed.). (1989). *Cross-national research in sociology.* Newbury Park, CA: Sage.

Kohn, M. L., Slomczynski, K. M., & Schoenbach, C. (1986). Social stratification and the transmission of values in the family: A cross-national assessment. *Sociological Forum, 1*, 73–102.

Kuechler, M. (1987). The utility of surveys for cross-national research. *Social Science Research, 16*, 229–244.

Lee, G. R. (1982). *Family structure and interaction: A comparative analysis* (2nd ed.). Minneapolis: University of Minnesota Press.

Lee, G. R. (1983, October). *Economic and familial complexity: A further investigation of the issue of curvilinearity.* Paper presented at the annual meeting of the National Council on Family Relations, St. Paul, MN.

Lee, G. R. (1984a). The utility of cross-cultural data: Potentials and limitations for family sociology. *Journal of Family Issues, 5*, 519–541.

Lee, G. R. (1984b). Status of the elderly: Economic and familial antecedents. *Journal of Marriage and the Family, 46*, 267–275.

Lee, G. R., & Haas, L. (1993). Comparative methods in family research. In P. G. Boss, W. J. Doherty, R. LaRossa, W. R. Schumm, & S. K. Steinmetz (Eds.), *Sourcebook of family theories and methods: A contextual approach* (pp. 117–131). New York: Plenum Press.

Lee, G. R., & Ishii-Kuntz, M. (1987). Status of the elderly: An extension of the theory. *Journal of Marriage and the Family, 49*, 413–420.

Lee, G. R., & Stone, L. H. (1980). Mate-selection systems and criteria: Variation according to family structure. *Journal of Marriage and the Family, 42*, 319–326.

Middleton, J. (1965). *The Lugbara of Uganda.* New York: Holt, Rinehart & Winston.

Miller, J., Slomczynski, K. M., & Schoenberg, R. J. (1981). Assessing comparability of measurement in cross-national research: Authoritarian–conservatism in different sociocultural settings. *Social Psychology Quarterly, 44*, 178–191.

Murdock, G. P. (1967). Ethnographic atlas: A summary. *Ethnology, 6*, 189–236.

Murdock, G. P. (1981). *Atlas of world cultures.* Pittsburgh: University of Pittsburgh Press.

Murdock, G. P., & White, D. R. (1969). Standard cross-cultural sample. *Ethnology, 8*, 329–369.

Przeworski, A., & Teune, H. (1970). *The logic of comparative social inquiry.* New York: Wiley–Interscience.

Ragin, C. C. (1987). *The comparative method: Beyond qualitative and quantitative strategies.* Berkeley: University of California Press.

Salamon, S. (1992). *Prairie patrimony: Family, farming, and community in the Midwest.* Chapel Hill: University of North Carolina Press.

Smith, A. H. (1970). *Village life in China.* Boston: Little, Brown.

Trent, K., & South, S. J. (1989). Structural determinants of the divorce rate: A cross-societal analysis. *Journal of Marriage and the Family, 51*, 391–401.

United Nations. (1992). *Demographic yearbook 1990.* New York: United Nations Publishers.

Warwick, D. P., & Osherson, S. (Eds.). (1973). *Comparative research methods.* Englewood Cliffs, NJ: Prentice Hall.

White, L. K. (1990). Determinants of divorce. *Journal of Marriage and the Family*, 52, 904–912.
Wolf, D. L. (1992). *Factory daughters: Gender, household dynamics, and rural industrialization in Java*. Berkeley: University of California Press.
Zelditch, M. (1971). Intelligible comparisons. In I. Vallier (Ed.), *Comparative methods in sociology* (pp. 267–307). Berkeley: University of California Press.

PART TWO

FAMILY VARIATION

Courtesy Suzanna Smith.

Introduction

Part II explores some of the ways in which families throughout the world are similar to, or different from, each other. During the time in which most of the work reviewed here was conducted, researchers were guided by the theory of structural–functionalism. They were interested in the positions (or structure) of the various members of the family group and the functions the family system performed for society as a whole.

Chapter 4, "Family Origin and Universality," focuses on the importance of the family as an institution to human societies worldwide. Bron B. Ingoldsby begins by addressing the question, "When and how did the family, as we understand it, begin?" He then turns to central questions in the debate about the universality of the family. "Are there certain tasks important to any civilization that the family performs better than any other institution? If so, does this mean that family organization is essential for the survival of any society, and that it is therefore universal?" This chapter shares the best thinking on these questions.

In Chapter 5, "Patterns of Kinship and Residence," Max E. Stanton broadens the scope of the investigation. He takes us beyond the immediate family to a consideration of the larger kin group, that is, all others we may consider to be relatives. Some surprising variety emerges. Differing needs and conditions, such as the availability of natural resources, lead to variation in definitions of kin and kinship obligations. We will be introduced to the terminology for describing kinship patterns and the rules by which different societies govern kin relationships, such as whom individuals can marry and where they can live.

In the final chapter in this section, "Marital Structure," Bron B. Ingoldsby addresses the fascinating complexity of the organization of marriage itself. Monogamy, or one husband to one wife, is only one of a number of ways of dealing with the interconnected issues of love, intimacy, sex, reproduction, economics, and power. Having multiple husbands and/or wives is an accepted and even preferred marital structure in many cultures, and Ingoldsby discusses how some of these arrangements function.

CHAPTER FOUR

Family Origin and Universality

BRON B. INGOLDSBY

How did "family" as an organization in human society begin? What features make it attractive to so many of us, and is it universal? That is, what does the family "do," and is it found in all cultures? This chapter grapples with these difficult questions.

Looking at the family from the structural–functional framework, I examine the research dealing with the following questions: How is the family defined? What are its functions in a society? What is its origin? Is it universal? I then conclude with a new look at defining the family.

FAMILY DEFINITIONS

Before we can study the family, we have to know what it is; therefore, it must be defined. However, in order to define it, we must find it in nature first—which is difficult to do without the definition to guide us. The first modern professional to attempt this was George Peter Murdock (1949). In his landmark work, Murdock approached the chicken and egg simultaneously: He had a definition in mind, and he searched the world's cultures to see if it held true.

Anthropologists have been doing field work for centuries, writing accounts of societies they visited and studied from their Western perspective. Murdock surveyed 250 of these ethnographic reports (collected today in most university libraries as the Human Relations Area Files) focusing on "family" descriptions. His work resulted in this definition: "The family is a social group characterized by common residence, economic cooperation, and reproduction. It includes adults of both sexes, at least two of whom maintain a socially approved sexual relationship, and one or more children, own or adopted, of the sexually cohabiting adults" (p. 1).

Murdock went on to use the term "nuclear family" for what he considered to be the most basic societal structure "a married man and woman with their offspring" (p. 1). He considered this to be a minimal structure which was the norm in about one-quarter of the societies he evaluated. In another quarter the dominate mode was polygamous, meaning two or more nuclear families united by the plural marriages of a spouse. The remaining half Murdock characterized as extended, where the nuclear family of a married adult resides with the family of his/her parents.

Murdock concluded that "the nuclear family is a universal human social grouping" (p. 2) that either stands on its own or serves as the basis for the more complex forms. For Murdock, this nuclear family fulfills so many essential functions that he declared it inevitable and therefore universal, at least in his impressive sample. Since that time, his claim has been tested, which is reviewed later in this chapter.

In 1963, William Stephens's classic cross-cultural family text was published. He began with Murdock's definition, which he personally liked, but went on to discuss some problems with it. First, the ethnographic data, on which we must all depend for this kind of work, often have an incomplete description of family customs. Second, some evidence had since surfaced that appeared to contradict Murdock's claims about family structure, function, and universality.

Stephens (1963) developed this definition of marriage: "Marriage is a socially legitimate sexual union, begun with a public announcement and undertaken with some idea of permanence; it is assumed with a more or less explicit marriage contract which spells out reciprocal rights and obligations between spouses, and between the spouses and their future children" (p. 5).

He added to this a definition for family: "a social arrangement based on marriage and the marriage contract, including recognition of the rights and duties of parenthood, common residence for husband, wife, and children, and reciprocal economic obligations between husband and wife" (p. 8).

Stephens then went on to explain each of his keys points, indicating that although they were generally true, there did seem to be exceptions to each point somewhere. In the end, Stephens concluded that all societies have some kind of family kinship system but he was unable to define it precisely.

FAMILY FUNCTIONS

Before examining the issue of what the family *is* and how it is structured, we need to examine what the family *does*. Social institutions exist because they perform certain valuable functions for their members and for the society of which they are a part. The family is such an enduring institution among humans because of the critical societal functions it handles.

Some of these functions which the family used to perform have been taken over by other institutions in the modern world. One of these is formal education. Public and private schools now teach the academic skills at a generally superior level to that which parents used to pass on to their children.

In many ancient cultures, religion was family based. The father served as priest and directed the rituals of the local belief system. Today, most people attend the services of an organized denomination if they desire religious instruction.

A complex medical practice has replaced home health care, and people tend to turn to movie theaters and other enterprises for entertainment rather than the home. No doubt the reader can think of other examples where an institution has taken over a traditional family function because it can meet that need better than the family can. As this occurs, the family adapts and focuses on what it does best.

And what does it do best? Once again we go to Murdock, who has postulated that the family fulfills four essential functions for society. Murdock (1949) claimed that the family must be universal because no other societal institution could take these over.

The first function is *sexual*. Murdock (1949) points out that sexuality must be controlled, and is, in all societies: "As a powerful impulse, often pressing individuals to behavior disruptive of the cooperative relationships upon which human social life rests, sex cannot safely be left without restraints. All known societies, consequently, have sought to bring its expression under control by surrounding it with restrictions of various kinds" (p. 4).

However, if sex is overregulated, personality maladjustments and insufficient population may result. All cultures have resolved this issue of needing to allow sexual expression, but not so much as to be socially destructive, through the institution of marriage. Sexual gratification is always a part of marriage, and that privilege serves to solidify the relationship.

This is not to say that sex only occurs in marriage, of course. Nonmarital sex occurs in all cultures, with varying degrees of acceptance. But it may be safe to say that the majority of adult sexual expression occurs in marriage, and that it is the one context in which sexual behavior is always socially acceptable.

Even within marriage, however, there are times when many societies frown on intercourse, such as during pregnancy or menstruation and in connection with certain religious observances. In fact, Stephens (1963) speculates that for the average primitive society, sexual intercourse between husband and wife is only legitimate about half the time.

The key point here is that marriage (which is part of the nuclear family) is the *primary* sexual relationship in all societies, which leads to the second function, which is *reproduction*. This one follows naturally from the first; if husbands and wives are having intercourse, they will be the ones having children as well. We all know that many children are born out of wedlock, but the majority are born according to society's preference, which is into a legal family. Any society must have children born into it in order to perpetuate itself, and in every case they turn to the nuclear family (which is what a marriage becomes once children are introduced) for that critical element.

The third function of the family is *socialization*: "It is also necessary for a society to do more than simply produce children; they must be cared for in a physical sense and they must be trained to perform the adult roles deemed appropriate for them in their culture. This involves more than the teaching of occupational skills; it revolves around the basic processes of language development and the transmission of culture" (Lee, 1982, p. 58). In other words, society depends on the parents to love and nurture their children; to toilet train them and teach them to speak and otherwise act in what would be considered a civilized manner.

The final basic function of the nuclear family, according to Murdock, is *economic*. By this, he was referring to the division of labor by sex. Due chiefly to the greater physical strength of men and the fact that women are the ones who bear the children, marital pairs have found it logical to divide responsibilities according to their capacities in order to enhance the survival of the group. Murdock (1949) says: "By virtue of their primary sex differences, a man and a woman make an exceptionally efficient cooperating unit. . . . All known human societies have developed specialization and cooperation between the sexes roughly along this biologically determined line" (p. 7).

Whereas in the modern world there is little reason for a complete separation between the provider and domestic roles, few would argue against the notion that a man and a woman can provide for the needs of a family more easily than a single parent generally can. Nevertheless, the implication that women should be limited to expressive roles is a frequent criticism of structural–functionalism.

Murdock (1949) claimed that society would cease to exist without the sexual and reproductive functions, that life would cease without the economic, and that culture would end without socialization. "No society, in short, has succeeded in finding an adequate substitute for the nuclear family, to which it might transfer these functions. It is highly doubtful whether any society ever will succeed in such an attempt, utopian proposals for the abolition of the family to the contrary notwithstanding" (p. 11).

It can be said, of course, that there may be other functions in addition to these four that are central to the family. William Ogburn (1929) was one of a number of sociologists who took the position that urbanization and industrialization had stripped the modern family of many of its traditional functions. With other agencies taking over much of the economic, educational, protective, recreational, and religious functions, providing companionship and emotional support became the primary function of the family. Being relieved of some of the external social roles has allowed the family to better fulfill the remaining functions.

In fact, being the chief source of love and affection may well be what the modern Western family does best. Many would argue that this is what gives the family its strength in our ever-changing and fast-paced world. In looking at the cultures throughout the world, it would be difficult to make a convincing claim that this is presently a universal family function not adequately provided for in other nonfamily ways. However, I believe that psychological intimacy is rapidly becoming the cornerstone of modern family life.

FAMILY ORIGIN

Many cultures have creation myths, and often they focus on what we call family relations. More than an actual recounting of the origin of the family, they can be seen as guidelines for how the family in that culture ought to be organized. Drawing from the book of Genesis in the Old Testament of the Bible, we can draw the following conclusions concerning Judeo–Christian societies:

1. It is expected that men and women will form sexual relationships (4:1).
2. Children are expected to result from this union (1:28).
3. The husband–wife bond (conjugal) is more important than are other relationships, such as the parent–child (consanguineal) (2:24).
4. There is a division of labor by sex, with females responsible for child-rearing and males responsible for providing food (3:16–19).
5. Husbands have legitimate power over their wives (3:16).

The well-known story of Adam and Eve posits a family structure and function similar to the one described in the previous section and makes the claim that the family began when humans did. The implication is that the husband–wife–child unit is a natural group that enhances survival and happiness.

It is presently considered beyond the reach of science to determine how and when the family originated. As a result, writings on the subject are necessarily speculative. A number of 19th-century social scientists, referred to as Social Darwinists, tried to place the family in an evolutionary sequence.

Building on the idea of progressive development from savagery to barbarism to civilization made popular by the work of Charles Darwin, the Social Darwinists proposed a similar process for the family. They did not all agree on the particulars, but basically the idea was that the family has progressed from some form of matriarchal group marriage to patriarchy to present-day monogamy. Not only is such a view ethnocentric and value based, but there is no valid reason to assume that all cultures would follow the same family structure track. Historical research cannot tell us how the family originated, but we do learn from it that there are many different patterns of family life in addition to one's own (Queen, Habenstein, & Quadagno, 1985).

Karl Marx and Friederich Engels adapted this evolutionary thesis to their own ideas about the role of economics in human civilization. They also presumed an original matriarchal group marriage system, which was replaced by the patriarchal oppression of monogamy when men gained control of the means of production (Hutter, 1988). A version of this view is held by some feminist scholars today, who would also like to see a more fluid and equal family life replace an overly rigid and unfair structure.

In contrast, Westermarck (1891/1925) was closer to the religious texts of the West in postulating that monogamy was the original form of marriage. He concluded that the nuclear family is based in biological instinct and referred to the monogamous habits of some lower animals to support his theory.

More recent work on the origin of the family has focused on sex roles. Whatever form the family takes, it always includes adults of both sexes and the pattern of interdependence between the sexes (Lee, 1982). The most illustrative example of this perspective is the work of Gough (1971).

She postulated that during the Miocene period of prehistory, the climate became dryer, resulting in open grasslands replacing many subtropical forests. This caused some of the tree-dwelling primates to adapt to terrestrial life. These ground dwellers had to become active hunters rather than simple foragers. Success was maximized by working in groups, which led to the development of language and eventually resulted in greater brain complexity.

The key to this theory is not only that our new humans were smarter, but that living on the ground caused them to develop an upright stance, which resulted in a smaller pelvis size for the female. This meant that females could no longer carry a fetus for as long as before and still survive the birth process. Thus, human babies began to be delivered sooner in their development.

As a result, these babies were born more helpless and therefore required more complete care than do other animals. This necessitated a mother–child closeness in which the mother must spend much of her time and energy ensuring the child's survival. It then became efficient for the mother to obtain the help of others in carrying out the other life tasks of providing food and shelter, and so on. The obvious solution was to bond with males, who were not encumbered with child care and had the natural strength and fleetness for the other tasks.

As Lee (1982) expressed it:

> According to this logic, then, the family originated among human beings because a certain division of labor between the sexes was found to be convenient or efficient and maximized the probability of survival for individuals and groups. . . . The logic here implies that the origin of sex roles, or the differentiation between the sexes in terms of socially defined behavioral expectations, coincided with the origin of the family. If the argument is correct, then men have been assigned protective and productive tasks, and women have assumed domestic and child-care responsibilities, since the earliest periods of the existence of mankind. (p. 54)

Social and technological changes have significantly reduced this traditional division of labor, but it is not illogical to suppose that economic efficiency, as well as sexual attraction, is what has always brought men and women together. So we find that the scientists like Murdock and Gough came to the same conclusion as the religious texts such as the one referred to earlier. That is, that adult men and women come together in a sexual union and share in the life skills necessary for their own survival and the rearing of their children.

Most modern scholars have abandoned the investigation of the details of the origin of the family. However, based on the sex-role theory, those factors resulting in the origin of the family would be the same for all humans everywhere, as our biology and response to the environment are similar. Thus, many social scientists conclude that the family as I have described it must be universal.

FAMILY UNIVERSALITY

Is the family universal, and what does it mean if it is? I am not asking whether everyone lives in a family. What we want to determine is whether or not the family exists everywhere as a social institution. If so, it can be concluded that the family *may* be necessary, that is, that human society cannot survive without it. However, if just one society can be found that does not have the family as I define it, we would have to conclude that while common, alternatives to the family can be devised.

Murdock (1949) threw down the gauntlet, so to speak, when he declared that his study found the nuclear family to be universal. This conclusion can be tested empirically by sifting through the available data on the world's cultures, much as Murdock himself did. If we find just one society that does not have the family, we can conclude that either (1) the family is not universal or (2) it may be, but not as previously defined.

There are two aspects to Murdock's definition. The first has to do with *structure*, which is that it will consist of at least a married man and woman and their dependent (natural and/or adopted) children. The second part has to do with *function*, or what the family does for society. In this case there are four functions: sex, reproduction, socialization, and economic. Therefore, we can reject Murdock's thesis by finding just one society in which the positions of husband, wife, and offspring do not go together; or even if they do, one or more of the four functions are not fulfilled by the family institution (Lee, 1982).

Over the years, researchers have accumulated data on some cultures that appear to contradict Murdock's conclusions. Some data are fairly weak, but there are data from three cultures that make a strong case. These cultures are (1) lower-class black unions in Jamaica, (2) the Israeli kibbutz, and (3) the Nayar of southern India.

Jamaica

Stephens (1963) described the work of Edith Clarke, who declared that marriage among the Jamaican poor was rare. A proper church wedding, with the accompanying feast and other costs, is too expensive. Those who cannot afford it settle for illegal common-law unions, which Clarke referred to as concubinage. In some, the father stayed with his family, but in other cases the woman might have a succession of lovers, with her children often "fatherless."

Although families without someone in the husband/father position are common throughout the world due to death, divorce, or desertion, the claim that the mother–child dyad is a viable alternative to the nuclear family is better made if a society can be found where that form is in the majority. It has been reported that about two-thirds of all children born to lower-class black Jamaicans are illegitimate. However, this does not mean that these are fatherless families. Rodman (1966) points out that although couples tend not to marry until they are past the childbearing stage (when they can afford it), most do eventually marry.

In addition, children do grow up with their mother and the man she is living with, who tend to have relatively stable and permanent relationships. So we find that legal marriage and the nuclear family are the cultural preference, and that although cohabitation may not be strictly legal, it is culturally acceptable.

The Kibbutz

Both Stephens and Lee discuss the Israeli kibbutz, which provides a stronger case against Murdock's assertions than does Jamaica. Kibbutzim are self-contained communities based on communistic ideals brought to Palestine in the 1920s by European Jews. Throughout history there have been many communal social movements, and many of them have tried to replace the family as we know it. In general, few survive more than a few years. However, the kibbutz may be the most successful of them all.

In 1954, Melford Spiro reported extensively on one particular kibbutz. In the traditional kibbutz, when a couple wishes to be together they simply have the manager move them into a two-person apartment. There is no marriage ceremony, but they are considered a "couple" until they decide to end the relationship. Children do not live with their parents but in a special area of the community where they are reared and educated by the adults assigned to that responsibility. All adults work somewhere in the community and couples do not depend on each other economically. All domestic service is done at the community, rather than household, level, and all members are provided for.

At first glance, then, many aspects of Murdock's definition are not met. Parents and children live separately, violating the nuclear structure. Moreover, although sex and reproduction are family functions, socialization and economy are not. Closer inspection since the time of Spiro's original work, however, indicates that the kibbutz may be more familylike after all.

First, the couple relationships appear to be as stable and permanent as in the greater culture. Couples and their children know each other and spend as much time together as one might find in many modern busy dual-career families. During the evening and weekend visits, much of the traditional socialization occurs, and although they may not live in the same room the family is quite close geographically. The strongest point is the economic one, where interdependence is at the group, rather than couple, level, even though there is evidence that members usually end up with traditional tasks. That is, the men are more likely to be assigned agricultural work while the women find themselves in the kitchen or the nursery.

The Nayar

Possibly the most interesting of the examples is the Nayar. According to Lee (1982), "they have been used as a counterexample to just about every empirical generalization regarding cross-cultural family uniformity ever offered" (p. 101). Murdock recognized them as a society in his original work but rejected the conclusions about them, saying that the little work done on them could not be substantiated.

After extensive work by Gough in the 1950s supported the original contentions, Murdock tried to claim that the Nayar were not really a society after all. Although Gough's (1959) work is accepted as reliable, it is important to note that her ethnographic account is after the fact. That is, the culture I am about to describe no longer exists, due to outside pressures, in this form. Gough has reconstructed it from available documents and the memories of informants.

The Nayar were a warrior Hindu caste living principally in the Kerala province of South Malabar in India. Although part of the larger society, the Nayar were basically self-sustaining and could have continued their practices indefinitely if they had avoided outside interference. As warriors, the men traveled and were away from home a great deal, and their marital practices were an apparent adaptation to that situation.

Girls began adulthood at puberty with a ceremony, lasting about 4 days, in which they were united with a "ritual husband." This was called the *tali-tying* marriage and had no real significance in the girl's life after the ceremony. After this rite of passage, girls could then enter into *sambandham* relationships with other men, who were called visiting husbands.

All adult females could marry as many visiting husbands as they liked. These relationships were formed and ended as the participants desired, resulting in a kind of fluid group marriage. These were basically sexual relationships, as there were very few economic responsibilities. The males gave small gifts on certain occasions but had no obligation to provide for the livelihood of the woman or their children. This was not considered promiscuity, however, but legally sanctioned and culturally approved marriages of the Nayar.

The legitimacy of children was important in the sense that a child should not be fathered by someone from a lower caste. In each case, one of the visiting husbands was asked to be designated as the father, which he accepted by paying for the midwife. At this point, his responsibility for and involvement in the child's life ended.

All spouses continued to live in their family of orientation, which was matrilineal. That is, a woman lived with her children, siblings, and mother and was provided for by her brothers (her children's uncles). Likewise, a man lived with his sisters and provided for their children but often spent the night with one of his wives. As mentioned before, this worked well for men who traveled too much to develop a conjugal family life. The children who mattered to them were those of their sisters rather than those of their wives.

Here we find that most of Murdock's conditions are not met. The family is not nuclear because spouses did not live together. Sex and reproduction were couple functions, but socialization did not involve the father and he had no economic responsibility for his wives and children. If we accept the Nayar as a once viable society, they are clear evidence that the nuclear family is not universal (Lee, 1982).

In 1975, Hendrix carefully analyzed Murdock's work with a review of 213 cases from the Human Relations Area Files. He found four cases in which husband and wife each remained in their mother's home throughout their lives, like the Nayar. Four other cases were like the kibbutz, where parents and children have separate residences, and a few others where the educational and/or economic functions were not performed by the nuclear family.

In summary, then, whereas the nuclear family with its four functions is extremely common, and clearly the most efficient way to generally organize family life, some alternatives are possible. Rather than rejecting the notion that the family is universal, it may be the definition that needs some adjustment.

THE FAMILY REDEFINED

Reiss (1965) proposed an alternative definition for the family to Murdock's. The one function that he found to be universal was the socialization of the young, but just a certain kind which he referred to as "nurturant socialization." Although it may not be the parents who provide for the physical care and education of their children, there are always relatives of some kind who give the love and emotional support necessary for healthy development.

Reiss (1965) concluded that the one common element in all societies is the nurturance of infants by a small primary group of kin: "The family institution is a small kinship structured group with the key function of nurturant socialization of the newborn" (p. 449). Commonly that group is the parents in a conjugal relationship (the nuclear family), but occasionally it is the mother and/or other relatives of the mother.

This accounts for groups like the Nayar and some Native American Indian tribes (see Driver, 1961) where residence is matrilocal and the father has minimal interaction with, or financial responsibility for, his wife and children. However, Reiss's definition, although unchallenged, is less specific and ambitious than is Murdock's. That is, although it is more technically correct, it is less satisfying because it tells us less about family structure and function.

For most practical purposes, Murdock's definition is useful and more informative, with the other cases being exceptions to the general rule. One problem with Reiss's definition is that although it correctly captures the notion of family, it does not address marriage, which has always been a subpart of the definition. However, it may be the tendency to make family flow from marriage that has given much of the trouble to Murdock, Stephens, and others.

Without exception, marriage is a sexual adult relationship (and usually an economic one as well) from which children may result. Family life focuses on the care of those children, but in rare cases the father plays no role in it. In those cases, people remain forever in their *family of orientation* and do not establish a new and separate *family of procreation*. So, although marriage and family generally go together, they do not always.

To help deal with this circumstance, the following definitions of marriage and family are offered. They are detailed enough to be useful and broad enough to qualify as universal.

> *Marriage*: a culturally approved sexual relationship that often also contains economic and psychological expectations.
> *Family*: a kinship group providing the nurturant socialization of their children (natural or adopted).

CONCLUSION

There is a tendency to use the terms "marriage" and "family" somewhat broadly in our society today, where any long-term adult relationship is referred to as a marriage and any group of people who love each other call themselves a family. However, the use of these terms needs to be restricted if they are to have a useful cultural and scientific meaning. Even though there are many kinds of human relationships, the technical use of "marriage" and "family" should include the concepts of reproduction and child care.

Part of the push to extend the definition of family is so that more individuals can benefit from government programs and benefits that depend on the public definition of the term. Although understandable, this view also implies that families are the only legitimate groupings for long-term emotional and social support (Coontz, 1988). Perhaps new terms need to be developed for these other kinds of relationships.

Homosexual marriages, for instance, are not legal in the United States and do not yet have widespread cultural approval. This could change in the future, even though a homosexual marriage cannot naturally develop into a family because the couple cannot create their own children from it, but they could adopt, use artificial insemination, or bring in children from previous heterosexual relationships. The definition of marriage noted previously is general enough to include these unions.

In addition, psychological intimacy may eventually become a universal function of marriage and family. The direction of modern society points to a continuing deemphasis of economic interdependence in marriage and to the increasing importance of the family as the critical source of love and affection in a fast-paced world.

To summarize, marriage and family are universal cultural institutions that perform critical functions for the preservation of human society. As Stephens (1963) has pointed out, even though there are logical alternatives, such as freely cohabitating bands, they have not been adopted. Moreover, whereas there are some mother–child dyad cultures, they are rare, leading to the conclusion, strongly supported by child development research, that social fathers are sufficiently important to maintain the preeminence of the nuclear structure.

However, this does not mean that the debate is over. Whereas many serious scholars (see Popenoe, 1993) still maintain that the intact nuclear family is critical for proper childhood socialization, there are others (Stacey, 1993) who point out that this structure is more functional for men than it is for women. Recent work points to more personal rather than societal definitions of family (Gubrium & Holstein, 1990).

In the end, there are various ways to look at family, depending on what it is that one wants to understand. Until recently, most studies focused on macrosocial issues, asking what it is that the family does for the larger community. Present research is beginning to turn that approach on its head and ask what the family does for its respective members.

REFERENCES

Coontz, S. (1988). *The social origins of private life: A history of American families 1600–1900*. New York: Verso.

Driver, H. (1961). *Indians of North America*. Chicago: University of Chicago Press.

Gough, K. (1959). The Nayars and the definition of marriage. *Journal of the Royal Anthropological Institute* 89(1), 23–34.

Gough, K. (1971). The origin of the family. *Journal of Marriage and the Family* 33(November), 760–771.

Gubrium, J., & Holstein, J. (1990). *What is family?* Mountain View, CA: Mayfield.

Hendrix, L. (1975). Nuclear family universals: Fact and faith in the acceptance of an idea. *Journal of Comparative Family Studies* 6(Fall), 125–138.

The Holy Bible. King James Version.

Hutter, M. (1988). *The changing family: Comparative perspectives* (2nd ed.) New York: Macmillan.

Lee, G. (1982). *Family structure and interaction: A comparative analysis*. Minneapolis: University of Minnesota Press.

Murdock, G. P. (1949). *Social structure*. New York: Free Press.

Ogburn, W. (1929). The changing family. *Publication of the American Sociological Society 23*, 124–133.

Popenoe, D. (1993). American family decline, 1960–1990: A review and appraisal. *Journal of Marriage and the Family, 55*(3), 527–541.

Queen, S., Habenstein, R., & Quadagno, J. (1985). *The family in various cultures.* New York: Harper & Row.

Reiss, I. (1965). The universality of the family: A conceptual analysis. *Journal of Marriage and the Family 27*(November), 443–453.

Rodman, H. (1966). Illegitimacy in the Caribbean social structure: A reconsideration. *American Sociological Review 31*(October), 673–683.

Spiro, M. (1954). Is the family universal? *American Anthropologist 56*(October), 839–846.

Stacey, J. (1993). Good riddance to "the family": A response to David Popenoe. *Journal of Marriage and the Family, 55*(3), 545–547.

Stephens, W. (1963). *The family in cross-cultural perspective.* New York: Holt, Rinehart & Winston.

Westermarck, E. (1925). *The history of human marriage.* London: Macmillan. (Original work published 1891)

CHAPTER FIVE

Patterns of Kinship and Residence

MAX E. STANTON

Virtually all human beings have a deep need to affiliate with others. This affiliation may be in the form of political alliances, friendship bonds, religious congregations, work gangs, and any number of other types of assemblages. Membership in some of these groups creates strong, lifelong bonds and will be, for the most part, quite satisfying and rewarding for the individuals involved. Other types of affiliation may be short-lived but, nonetheless, often quite important—such as a party of workers who have banded together to fight a forest fire which might be threatening their collective homes and property.

Of all types of human affiliation, kinship is, with few rare exceptions, the most permanent and has the greatest long-term impact on the life, behavior, and social identity of an individual. There is no question that some other associations may have deep and significant impact on a person's identity and loyalties (e.g., the traditional military societies of the North American Great Plains peoples, the "clans" of the pre-1745 Scottish Highlands, or the age-sets of East Africa), but even these types of affiliation, and others which command so much social effort on the part of those who belong, do not replace the basic kinship units of their respective societies as the single most important locus of social obligations and identities (Fox, 1967).

Stack and Burton (1993) noted recently that the lives of individuals are strongly affected by kinship network, even in modern Western society. Patterns of family interaction are "scripted" by kin in the areas of work, time, and roles. That is, such important activities as reproduction, care of dependent children or the elderly, and economic survival are often assigned to individuals by the larger family. Pressure to assume certain responsibilities for the good of the family can be both subtle and significant.

Because kinship is so central and "natural" in the life of the average person, most people do not give too much thought to the ways and manners in which various other societies reckon their terminology. If we hear such terms as "family," "mother," or "relatives," we usually tend to think of them and other such terms in the context of our own personal experience, with little regard to the fact that there are a great number of ways throughout the world in which people in various societies do (or have in the recent past) relate to these same terms. The tendency to think that our own type of kinship organization is normal and "correct" is especially strong if we have little or no contact with people from other societies.

The rural to urban migration trends of the latter half of the 20th century have brought millions of people from different cultures together in numbers unprecedented in history. Contemporary travel by air and over hard-surface long-distance highways has also brought people of diverse heritages together. International tourism is rapidly becoming the world's largest industry. It is important, therefore, to be aware of the fact that significant differences exist between people and groups. In this chapter, I focus on kinship as one of these "significant differences." Kinship is one of the basic "building blocks" of any society. It is also one aspect of social interaction that can cause confusion between people of different cultural heritages.

Members of ethnic minorities within a given society are usually acutely aware of the differences between their own patterns of kinship terminology and affiliation and those of the majority group. This reality first came to my attention when, in the mid-1960s, I visited the Hopi Indian Reservation in northeastern Arizona in the company of some fellow anthropology students. We were eager to see whether some of the things we had learned in the classroom would actually prove to be the case in the reality of the field. We had learned enough about Hopi kinship terminology to know that a person would refer to his/her mother's sister as mother and that her children would be referred to as brother or sister. We spoke to a shy but cooperative girl of 8 or 9 years of age and asked her whether her mother had any sisters. She said, "Yes," so we asked the girl what she called her. She replied, "Aunt Martha." We were somewhat disappointed but persisted and asked the girl whether there was a Hopi word she used and she said, "Ya, I call her my mother." We asked the girl whether her Aunt Martha had any children, and the girl replied that she did. We then asked what the girl called them. She replied, "Jimmy," "Annie," and so on. We asked her whether there was any word she used when she did not refer to them by name and she said, "I call them my cousins." One of the students in our group then patiently asked whether she did not refer to them as her brothers and sisters. Her reply was classic and has had a profound impact on my understanding of the world view of ethnic minorities: "Yes, I do call them my brothers and sisters—but I didn't know you white guys knew about that!" She was fully aware that we "white guys" as a general group knew very little about Hopi life and gave us the most appropriate answer for the specific context in which she found herself at the time.

Because there are still many Native American groups that continue to follow their traditional kinship rules and because there are so many people entering the United States from all parts of the world, many from places in which dramatically different types of kinship patterns are still practiced, and because ours is an ever-shrinking world wherein all inhabitants have become part of a "global community," it is essential for us as well-informed people to understand and appreciate the many varieties of kinship systems that persist throughout the world. It is also essential not to think of differences as being inferior to our own system. There are many people to whom these various forms of terminology make good sense and are preferred. In this chapter I discuss the various societal norms that have to do with lineage and family affiliations, rules, and terminologies.

BASIC KINSHIP AFFILIATION

The most intimate group of kin for the majority of us are those in our immediate family. Whether they are our relatives by birth or adoption they form the core of the world of our relatives. Beyond this first tier of relatives, there are other people to whom we are related, either through a genealogical link or through marriage. Those individuals to whom we are related through a direct genealogical link are our *consanguine* kin, meaning *by blood*. (Anthropologists continue to use this term as a popular convention even though it is now well-known that our blood does not directly transmit our hereditary traits.)

There are two types of consanguine kin. Those people who are related to one another in a direct genealogical line are *lineal* kin (such as parent to child). In some cases, there is a distinction made between lineal kin who are descended from the direct line of a male and those who are descended from a direct line of a female. Kin who reckon their descent line through a common male ancestor are *cognatic* kin; those who trace their line through a common female ancestor are *agnatic* (sometimes also referred to as *uterine*) kin. Those relatives who are not in a direct parent-to-child line but who have a common more distant genealogical tie (such as siblings or first cousins) are *collateral* kin.

There are also those relatives to whom one is related by legal, nongenealogical ties. This would include all those individuals who have some sort of kinship affiliation through marriage (such as a spouse, brother-in-law, or what most Americans would refer to as an aunt- or uncle-by-marriage). These people are our *affinal* relatives. In most societies, affinal relatives are considered to be close and important members of the kinship network and are most often treated as important, vital parts of one's immediate kinship group. Another nongenetic tie is the *adoptive* relationship. In this situation, the expectation is that a person who is adopted into a kinship network assumes the social role equal to that of a person born into the same position, having all of the social rights, privileges, duties, and obligations as if he/she had inherited that position through birth (Lowie, n.d./1968).

Research by Rossi and Rossi (1990) provides us with an excellent understanding of the structure of kinship norms in the United States. Responses to vignettes that tapped the sense of obligation to help various relatives in times of crisis and celebration allowed them to uncover basic principles underlying the U.S. kinship system. Briefly, their results were as follows:

1. In accordance with sociobiological theory, our sense of obligation to another person is a function of how closely related we are. That is, we show the highest levels of obligation to our own parents and children, followed by siblings, grandparents and grandchildren, aunts and uncles, and nieces and nephews, and finally cousins.

2. Reflecting the emphasis on conjugal relations in our society, the position a person occupies is important even when the person is not blood related. That is, in-laws and stepparents and children are accorded the same level of obligation as are siblings and grandparents and children.

3. More distant kin (aunts/uncles, nieces/nephews, and cousins) have about the same salience in our lives as do those nonrelatives with whom we frequently interact: our friends and neighbors.

4. Due to especially close bonds between mothers and daughters, there is a maternal tilt in the U.S. kinship system. Generally, women evoke more obligation than do men, especially if they are unmarried. There is also a tendency to be closer to the wife's relatives than to the husband's.

TYPES OF FAMILIES

The most common type of family is the *nuclear family*. It consists of at least one responsible adult male and one female living commonly in a marriage arrangement with their children. The nuclear family may be part of a greater collection of families that are ultimately grouped together into an *extended family* which has as its head a responsible adult (or, in some cases, a group or council of responsible adults). The extended family is a corporate economic and political unit, as well as a kinship-based group. Members of this type of family work for the mutual benefit and welfare of all individuals and (nuclear) families that are recognized to be part of the unit. The extended family is an ongoing body with a geographical base and it transcends the lifetime of its members. The composition of the extended family with its nuclear families and independent single adults changes constantly, but the extended family itself continues on with new leaders and new members as individuals depart or as the generations pass away.

The *joint family* has many of the elements of the extended family in that it is made up of any number of separate nuclear families and is an economic, geographical, and political entity as well as a kinship-based group. It too is ultimately headed by one person or a small coalition of leaders. The distinction between the two types is that the joint family is not an ongoing, long-term unit. It is made up of close relatives, usually brothers, who are affiliated together under the rule of their father. When the father dies or becomes physically or mentally unable to continue on as the leader, the oldest brother assumes the role of head of the family. It now becomes the task of this older brother to work to help his younger brothers within the joint family to set up their own independent family units separate from his own family. As he does this, his own children mature and remain within the joint family until he, the older brother himself, dies or is unable to continue on at its head. In the meantime, the brothers of the original joint family have gone on to establish a separate joint family arrangement with their own children.

Historical research on the family has found a variety of family types in addition to those mentioned above. They often have a complex relationship to the larger society, principally the economic structure, but to other aspects as well (see Farber, Mogey, & Smith, 1986; Fox, 1967).

In many parts of the world, there are social trends such as widespread divorce or bearing (or adopting) children by a single person. Families having the presence of one adult as a permanent member of the household are known as single-parent families. Divorce in particular can complicate multi-generational family relationships, as grandparents struggle to stay in contact with their grandchildren and perhaps their ex-children-in-law as well (Johnson, 1988).

It is also becoming recognized that some families are headed by homosexuals who function as would a husband–wife pair. This type of family is known as a same-sex type of union. Single-parent families are given the same legal status as those headed by a husband and wife. Same-sex families, as a socially acknowledged phenomenon, have yet to receive legal standing in most places in which they are found and, therefore, lack the legitimacy enjoyed by the other forms of family units.

RULES OF DESCENT AND AUTHORITY

Because kinship typically implies special obligations and rights between its members that would not be expected between neighbors or strangers, it is too important to be left just to biology or chance. All cultures, then, have rules for defining who our important relatives are. This does not mean that they are ignorant of the other biological connections but simply that for the purposes of inheritance, marriage, and other aspects of life, certain lines matter and others do not.

In many societies, an individual is affiliated to his/her family group exclusively through either the father's or the mother's family line: *unilineal descent*. If the inheritance passes through the father's side of the family, the arrangement is *patrilineal*. This means that primacy is given to ties from father to son to grandson, and so on through the male relatives. Taking one's surname from the father or husband is a patrilineal concept.

If the kinship affiliation is recognized through the mother's side, it is *matrilineal*. In this case, descent is traced through the mother and all the women in the line. Here we would find that societal expectations about mutual aid or inheritance would focus on the mother's side of the family and would not apply to the father's. The Jewish people are an example of matrilineal religious descent. In order to be a Jew, your mother must be one, and the religion or ethnic identity of the father does not matter. Therefore, if a child's father is Jewish but the mother is not, that child is not a Jew.

There are also some societies that practice *double descent*. In these groups, a person (who is the referent, or center of discussion, whom I shall call ego) has distinctive rights and privileges that relate to both the line of inheritance from the father and other, distinct, rights that stem from the mother. The rules of double descent differ widely from group to group, but basically, one may inherit political or social rights from the father's group and land and other property from the mother—or another set of rights and privileges, depending on the specific rules of the particular group in question. The significant fact to remember in double descent is that whatever is inherited from the mother is not also inherited from the father.

Finally, there is the *bilateral* type of inheritance, in which ego has full and equal rights of inheritance to all property, social status, and privileges from both the father and the mother. This is the type of system common in the United States and most other modern Western societies. Like double descent, it is a nonunilineal descent system. Simply by following the rules of biology, bilateral descent cultures are indicating that kinship obligations are relatively minor and therefore can be shared with many people.

In 1949, the anthropologist George Peter Murdock made an in-depth survey cross-sampling of 250 societies through out the world (a somewhat small, but carefully selected representative sample of the more than 5,000 known social groups) and came up with the following statistics for the prevalence of the four types of descent rules: patrilineal, 42%; matrilineal, 20%; bilateral, 30%; double descent, 7% (Murdock, 1949). The remaining 1% refers to a small number of societies that determine kinship in ways even more complicated than those listed above. In one, odd-numbered children are affiliated with the father's family and even-numbered offspring go with the mother's. In a few other societies, kin group varies by the sex of the child.

In societies that recognize a known human ancestor as the common progenitor of either the patrilineal or the matrilineal group, the term "lineage" is used to designate a group of relatives. In those societies in which closely related people trace their common ancestry to a mythical being or natural force (often an animal, plant, natural object, or fictitious character) the term "clan" is used to designate the patrilineal or matrilineal group. It must be noted that there will not be both matrilineages and patrilineages in the same society. They are mutually exclusive groups. Also, there will not be a mixture of lineages and clans within a given society.

The terms "patrilineal" and "matrilineal" must not be confused with "patriarchal" and "matriarchal." They are kinship designations and do not imply rule by men or by women. An analysis of Stephens's (1963) data indicates that about two-thirds of all known societies are patriarchal. This means that the husband/father is given (by societal agreement and not by force) power over the members of his family and access to the best resources and privileges.

Matriarchies—societies in which women rule men within the home—are extremely rare. Stephens found maybe 5 in a sample of 96 cultures. However, in most of these, the idea of Amazon women is more legend than real. Typically, women appear to have higher status than do men because transmission of property is matrilineal, but actual authority resides in male members of the female line. The people of the Five Nations of the Iroquois in Ontario and upper New York State are frequently cited as being matriarchal. For example, the senior women of a clan selected a person (or persons) who would assume the position of *sachem* (chief) in one of the 50 leadership seats in the Iroquois council. However, the *sachem* was always a senior male of the clan to which the women who made the selection belonged (Fenton, 1978; Tooker, 1978).

There is a trend toward the *egalitarian* type of authority structure within the context of the independent nuclear families of the urbanized areas of the world. This is a recent trend and is most likely related to the fact that many of the traditional kinship supports for the family no longer function effectively within the reality of the mass culture of the urban setting and that, by necessity, the husband and wife must see each other as equals in an isolated team. Also, women are now able to honorably support themselves and their children in the absence of a husband/father in the household, which has surely made them far more independent than in previous generations.

In the Stephens sample, 12% of the cultures had a general egalitarian pattern, where the husband and wife made decisions jointly, and 15% divided authority into separate spheres. In the latter case, they were roughly equal in overall decision making, but each controlled their own domains. In a typical blue-collar marriage in the United States, for instance, the wife may be in charge of household decisions and childrearing while the husband makes the "outside" decisions about lawn, cars, and occupations.

TYPES OF POSTMARITAL RESIDENCE

In most urban, industrialized nations a newly married couple will choose a residence wherever social and economic conditions dictate. They may live in the near proximity of the relatives of either the bride or the groom, or they may move to a new location hundreds of miles away from any close relatives. This type of a residence pattern is known as *neolocal* residence.

In the majority of societies, the conventional practice is for the husband to remain in close association with his close male relatives (father, paternal uncles, brothers, etc.). This pattern, *patrilocal* residence, is quite common in groups that have patrilineal lineages or clans. Patrilocal residence increases the authority of the groom's family because he remains in his childhood home but the bride is removed from hers.

In societies that have matrilineal lineages or clans, it is quite common for the wife to reside with her husband and children in the close proximity of her female relatives. This type of residence pattern is *matrilocal* (or *uxorilocal*). In some cases, the newly married couple resides with the family of the bride for a given period after the onset of the marriage (usually until the birth of the first child or shortly thereafter) and then moves to the vicinity of the groom's family to dwell for the remainder of their marriage. This pattern is *matri-patrilocal*.

In some cases, the family has the choice of dwelling either in close proximity to the relatives of the husband or in near proximity to the relatives of the wife. This type of residence pattern, *bilocal*, is quite common where extended families are found. Young married college students in neolocal societies occasionally resort to this pattern temporarily as part of their effort to become financially independent.

Finally, there are a few societies in which a young man, on reaching adolescence, leaves his parental household and goes to live with his maternal uncle (mother's brother). This pattern, *avunculocal*, is only found in societies that have matrilineal clans. The young man inherits his clan affiliation through his mother (she and her brother having commonly inherited their clan membership from their mother) and will, therefore, assume his social rights and responsibilities through his mother's clan. The mother's brother will pass on his social statuses and positions to his sister's son and not to his own son (who is a member of his wife's clan). A woman in a clan-type society will have a wide range of male relatives (her own siblings as well as her male parallel cousins) whom she will count as her brothers. There will, therefore, always be someone to whom the young man may go to spend his adolescence and young adult years (Goodenough, 1955/1968).

In the 1949 survey conducted by George Murdock, the following percentages for residence patterns were found: patrilocal, 58%; matrilocal, 15%; matri-patrilocal, 9%; bilocal, 8%; neolocal, 7%; avunculocal, 3%. Murdock also determined from the survey that there was some correlation between residence patterns and kinship types. Of the groups represented, it was found that 92% of those that practiced the patrilineal kinship arrangement were also patrilocal (or eventually became patrilocal by practicing the matri-patrilineal system). Of the matrilineal groups, 63% also practiced either matrilocal or avunculocal residence patterns.

Lee (1982) provides us with an excellent summary of the explanations for this pattern. Briefly stated, economic subsistence patterns determine the rules of residence, which in turn affect the rules of descent. The most primitive societies are based on hunting, which is almost exclusively a male activity. Because knowledge of the territory can be crucial for success, it is important that men stay in the same area as adults in which they learned to hunt as children. This mandates patrilocal residence and then patrilineal descent, so that males will control the land.

Agricultural societies tend to be matrilocal and matrilineal when the major activities are crop and animal tending and harvesting. Women typically are assigned to these activities, so the land is passed on through their lines. If the sexual division of labor is such that working the land is mostly done by men (plow-based or pastoralist economies), then the males control the land. This results first in patrilocal residence, so that the male workers can stay together, and then in patrilineal descent in order to pass on this same condition to their sons.

Industrialized nations have economies based on wages rather than land, and it is not in the best interests of individuals to cooperate with large kinship groups. As a result, nuclear families predominate, residence is neolocal and descent is bilateral.

Returning to the issue of postmarital residence by itself, surprisingly only 7% of the societies in Murdock's sample were neolocal in their residence patterns. Keep in mind, however, that the groups chosen by Murdock were not all the same size. The large, urban industrialized societies of Europe, East Asia, and North America were given no more significance and weight than were the smaller, often more isolated groups of the Pacific, the Amazon basin, or sub-Sahara Africa. Nor were many of the groups as involved in the same degree of technological complexity and urbanization as they might be today. Also, in 1949, when Murdock published his findings, many of the trends toward urban migration and rapid technological change were not yet under way in many of the groups found in the sample, or these trends had just begun and had not yet appreciably affected the nature and structure of the societies represented.

Ethnographic data are only as current as the publication of the field data of the most recent researcher to emerge from the field, and Murdock's data were, in many cases, representative of the social reality that was reported in groups that had not been studied by anthropologists or other trained social scientists since before the worldwide economic depression of the 1930s and World War II. The great mass movement of people from isolated, rural, tradition-oriented societies to the rapidly expanding urban areas of the world did not get under way until the 1950s. Also, with the changes in traditional habitats brought on by such phenomena as deforestation, mineral exploitation, urban expansion, political strife, rapid population growth, and desertification, many groups have had to restructure their social organizations in such a way as to meet the demands of a cash economy, mass education, national politics, resource depletion, and other factors incompatible with the maintenance of a traditional way of life. It is highly probable that if the same 250 societies Murdock surveyed in 1949 were to be reentered into the statistics using the current social and economic realities, far more than 7% would be recognized as practicing de facto neolocal residence patterns because of the dramatically changed circumstances of recent years. We need only to look at ever-increasing rates of international migration and the rapid growth of the urban areas of Africa, Asia, Latin America, and elsewhere in the Pacific basin to know that significant social changes must be taking place that will have profound effects on the nature and expression of kinship relationships.

To illustrate this dramatic change, consider Polynesia over the past four decades. In 1950, only a few Polynesians had left their home villages and districts. The capital cities of the Polynesian islands were, for the most part, small colonial outposts. Virtually all Polynesians of central Polynesia still spoke their traditional languages and most practiced their traditional extended family form of kinship. The cash economy made an impact only in the realm of plantation labor, which, for the most part, was manned by young adult males who would leave their families for a few years to earn enough to return to their homes to finance the construction of a home and to provide themselves with some incidental goods and supplies (Oliver, 1961; Doumenge, 1966).

Today, just a generation later, more than half of the Cook Islanders now live in New Zealand, especially in the urban areas of Auckland and Wellington. Of the 350,000 Samoans in the world, more than 60,000 live in New Zealand, also principally in the urban areas. Approximately the same number of Samoans are found in the following metropolitan areas of the United States: Honolulu, Los Angeles, Seattle, and Salt Lake City.

Approximately one-third of all Tongans in the world now live in the urban areas of Auckland, Sydney, Honolulu, Los Angeles, San Francisco, and Salt Lake City. Sizable concentrations of Polynesians are also found in and near San Diego, Phoenix, Washington, D.C., Kansas City, Melbourne, and Vancouver.

French is now the language of preference for the adolescents of Tahiti. Over half of the 200,000 people in French Polynesia live in or near the capital of Pape'ete, now the bustling urban center of eastern Polynesia. The capitals of the Polynesian island groups serve as magnets, drawing large numbers of the rural villagers into rapidly growing urban centers. It is difficult to find any remaining families in the outlying areas that have not been severely disrupted by this flow to the cities (Stanton, 1993).

A typical example is a Samoan classmate of mine who was reared in Samoa with his four brothers and sisters. They all lived in a small village on the island of Savai'i in Western Samoa. He left his home and family in 1963 to study in the United States. He stayed in the United States to fulfill a career in the Navy, living in the San Diego area until his 20-year retirement. One sister, married to an officer in the U.S. Army, has lived in Germany for the past 7 years. Another sister lives in Hawaii. His third sister lives in Auckland, New Zealand, and his brother lives in Virginia. My friend and his four siblings are married to Samoans, but not one of them reared their children in the context of the traditional Samoan extended family of their youth. By the necessity of their circumstances, each of the brothers and sisters had their children in a neolocal family arrangement and in the midst of an urbanized, non-Samoan society. The experience of this friend and his siblings is not unusual; it is repeated many times throughout Polynesia.

COUSIN RELATIONSHIPS

Anthropologists have developed a means of kinship reckoning whereby kinship ties are calculated in terms of one's cousins. This may seem to be a somewhat unusual way to look at kinship, but it helps us to get a much better look at the nature and function of kinship alliances within a society than if we were to only consider close consanguine or affinal relatives. In many societies, there is no differentiation between one's cousins (e.g., the Anglo-American system). In this context, the term "cousin" does not convey any sense of relationship as to whether one's cousin is related through the mother's side of the family or that of the father. It does not indicate the gender of the cousin or imply whether the person is the offspring of one's mother's sister or brother or one's father's sister or brother. A cousin is a cousin, and that is all that is important.

Many Anglo-Americans have close and affectionate ties with their cousins which are often lifelong in nature and, in some cases, as intense and valuable as the relationship with one's own siblings. However, the society that has a broad, general classification for one's cousins rarely imposes any important duties and responsibilities that bind such cousins into strong legal and political ties with each other.

In North American society, there is considerable confusion regarding the terminology used to classify cousins. This is especially true with regard to second cousins and first cousins once removed. Most North Americans know that their first cousin is the child of a sibling of their mother or father. For example, if your mother or father has a brother or sister, the child of this person is your first cousin. The child of your first cousin is your first cousin once removed, and you are the first cousin once removed to that same child. Your child and the child of your first cousin are second cousins to each other, but he/she will not be a first or second cousin to you. That person is your first cousin once removed. This is where the confusion lies.

In popular discussion, most North Americans merge the term for their first cousins once removed and their second cousins into the same terminological classification of second cousin. We rarely use the terms "third cousin," or "second cousin once removed," "second cousin twice removed," and so forth. It is just best to remember the generational distance you are from a given set of grandparents. If you are both two generations removed from your grandparents (your parents being the first generation away), you are first cousins. If you are both three generations removed, you are second cousins. If you are two generations removed from the specific set of grandparents and another cousin is three generations removed, you are one generation apart from one another making you first cousins once removed.

In cases in which the only distinction between cousins is gender, this relationship is generally no more significant than that discussed above. This is especially the case in those societies that have gendered nouns and would have a term for a male or female cousin that is determined by a definite article (such as *el primo* or *la prima* in Spanish). There are, however, many cases in which a cousin might transfer his/her family loyalties and affiliations at marriage that would effectively terminate the kinship ties that existed before marriage. In such cases, the use of gender to differentiate male and female cousins would imply that those cousins who are referred to by one specific term are guaranteed to be one's lifelong relations and those who are given another term will no longer count as close relatives after they are married.

There are many cases in which the gender of the siblings of one's parents determines the type of terminology one would use in reference to cousins. We shall see later that societies that have strong clans, or in which either the male lineage or the female lineage is the exclusive means by which one inherits his/her social identity, usually make a clear distinction between specific groupings of cousins. In such cases, it is vital to distinguish between those cousins who are members of one's clan or lineage and those who are not. This is accomplished by having a set of terms for "in-family" and "out-of-family" cousins. In such systems, the cousins who are the children of an aunt or uncle who are of the same sex as the parent in question (mother's sister or father's brother) would be "parallel cousins." Those cousins who are the offspring of an aunt or uncle who are the opposite sex of the parent in question would be "cross-cousins."

Those societies that make a distinction between parallel cousins and cross-cousins regard parallel cousins as close consanguine relatives and expect their members to behave toward these parallel cousins as they would toward their own siblings. It is common for a person of the opposite sex to treat such cousins with close respect. Persons of the opposite sex would show their respect for parallel cousins by practicing "avoidance relationships" during and after puberty. Such avoidance relationships also exist between brothers and sisters in these societies and would include such things as refusing to be alone in the same room with a sibling or parallel cousin of the opposite sex, refusing to dance with such a person, averting direct eyesight in public, refraining from profanity or coarse jokes, and so on. In these same societies, cross-cousins are not regarded as close relatives. In fact, there often exists a strong "joking relationship" between cross-cousins, especially between persons of the opposite sex. Such relationships might include extensive teasing, telling ribald jokes, flirting, and even sexual experimentation. Often, the relationship between cross-cousins of the opposite sex is so important to the people in these types of societies that they become *preferred* marriage partners and are encouraged to marry one another.

The practice of cross-cousin marriage is commonly found in societies that have clan systems. We might ask whether this type of close genetic inbreeding causes physical or mental problems in the groups in which the practice is found. The answer is, "Apparently not." It stands to reason that if there were noticeable genetic defects resulting from first-cousin marriages of cross-cousins, the practice would prove to be dysfunctional and would not be continued as frequently as it is. As there are so many individuals who would qualify socially as cross-cousins, there is probably no noticeable increase in genetic defects because although the marriage partner is closely related genetically, the pool of potential partners is so large that there is little chance of repeating the genetic pattern generation after generation. In cases in which close inbreeding has been known to cause problems, we find that not only was the genetic relationship close but the group had a rather limited number of members to begin with and that they were located in a geographically or socially isolated situation.

An interesting exception to the parallel-cousin avoidance practice of marriage exists in traditional Islamic societies. In Muslim Arab societies (and non-Arab Muslim societies that have adopted the Arab social model), the children of two brothers (parallel cousins through male siblings) are considered to be preferred marriage partners to the extent that a woman must receive the express permission of the son of her father's brother if she desires to marry another person. However, the children of two sisters (parallel cousins through female siblings) are considered to be as close in their relationship to one another as would be siblings and any intimate relationship between them would be looked on as a type of incest.

The marriage of the children of brothers in Islamic societies has roots in the Old Testament and the Koran and follows a pattern that was once widespread throughout the region of Southwest Asia and North Africa. The avoidance of marriage between the children of sisters has less obvious roots. In Arab tradition, it is assumed that sisters maintain close relationships into adulthood (frequently becoming the wives of the same man in cases in which the husband chooses to follow the allowed practice of plural marriage). Because of this close affiliation between sisters, it is assumed that there will be times when both sisters are nursing their respective infants and will, occasionally, offer to nurse the child of the other sister if, for example, the mother is ill, tired, or busy with some other task and does not want to be interrupted. According to Arab tradition, children who have nursed from the same woman are considered to be siblings. Because of the potential for two women to marry the same man, the children of two sisters could well be the offspring of a common father and it would make good sense to disallow any marital unions of this type.

KINSHIP TERMINOLOGY: THE SIX BASIC TYPES

As should already be apparent, there are many ways for the thousands of societies throughout the world to reckon their kinship affiliation. Fortunately, it is not necessary to learn the intricacies of each system in order to be conversant on the subject of kinship. As discussed earlier, most anthropologists have recognized the importance of the classification of cousins in unraveling the web of kinship. Approximately 90% of all of the world's societies can be grouped into one of six basic kinship types, which can be identified by the names used to refer to cousins and siblings. (Not all societies fall within one of these six kinship categories. Notable exceptions are the Navajo–Apache people of the American Southwest, the Ainu of Japan, the Fijians, and virtually all the aboriginal people of Australia.) These kinship types are named after a society that uses (or recently used) the terminology characteristic of the classification. Because two groups happen to use the same type of kinship terminology does not imply in any way that there are any historical or cultural affiliations between them (Hocart, 1937/1968).

Some kinship types tend to merge a large number of people into a single term such as "brother" or "mother." This tendency to "lump" a large number of relatives into one category is known as a classificatory system (Kroeber, 1909/1968). In other kinship types, a different set of terms is used for people who are the same genealogical distance from the referent (the person from whom the relationships are being described, known as ego in a kinship chart). This may mean that the mother's brother is referred to by a different term from the father's brother, or that parallel cousins are given different designations from cross-cousins. Such a "splitting" of relationships is said to be a *descriptive* system. Of course, it is not possible to be totally classificatory (e.g., siblings—brother and sister—and parents—father and mother—are distinguished in all societies by their sex). Also, a strictly descriptive system does not include all the possible kinship combinations possible to describe (e.g., it would be somewhat cumbersome to have a specific term for the third-born son of your mother's oldest sister). The differences between classificatory and descriptive systems are a measure of degree of the number of separate kinship terms used. The six common kinship systems are described here in order of complexity of terminology from the most classificatory (the "lumpers") to the most descriptive (the "splitters").

The *Hawaiian* system employs the least number of specific kinship terms. All the adults in ego's parental generation are grouped together under the term "mother" or "father." A person is fully aware of his/her specific biological parents, but all adults in the kin group are referred to as one's parents and each person within this level of the kinship grouping will be treated as a parent by ego; in return, each person to whom ego refers as his/her parent will treat that person as his/her own biological child. All the members of the family in ego's own generation would be referred to as brother and sister and all the members of the generation of ego's children would be called son or daughter. This type of kinship terminology is most commonly found in the context of extended families (although not all groups that employ the Hawaiian kinship terminology have extended families as their basic kinship unit and not all groups that have extended families employ the Hawaiian system in their terminology).

In the *Eskimo* (or *Inuit*) kinship system, the relatives in ego's direct genealogical lineage are referred to as either mother or father in the parental generation, brother or sister in one's own generation, or son or daughter in the generation of one's children. The siblings of ego's parents are grouped together according to their sex as either uncle or aunt, and their children are collectively referred to as cousins. Although in some Eskimo-type systems there is a distinction made as to whether the cousins are males or females, no distinction is made as to whether a kinship linkage is from either the mother's side of the family or the father's side. The Eskimo system is most often used where neolocal residence is practiced and when the independence of the nuclear family as a socioeconomic unit is necessary. As most of us will recognize, the Eskimo type is the one that is predominantly used in Anglo-American and western European societies.

The next three kinship types are found in societies that depend on clans as their basic family organization. When most North Americans hear the term "clan," they tend to think of the so-called Scottish clans. Actually, the clans of Scotland were based on obligations and loyalties as much (or more) to the geographical landlord as to someone who was a close kin. In the anthropological sense, therefore, the Scottish clans did not operate as clans in the precise technical definition but much more as feudal fiefdoms (Fox, 1976).

Before proceeding, it will be helpful to discuss four basic characteristics of clan affiliation. These four characteristics should aid in gaining a better understanding of how clan systems operate. The four characteristics are:

1. Clan membership is for life (one never changes clans, even in marriage).
2. All siblings belong to the same clan.
3. Clans are strictly exogamous units.
4. The ultimate leadership of a clan will always rest on a senior male (or coalition of males) who is a member of the clan.

In the *Iroquois* clan type of arrangement, ego merges the term for his/her parents with the parents' sibling of the same sex (thus, the father's brother will also be referred to as father and the mother's sister becomes mother). A separate term will be used for the mother's brother and the father's sister. In some cases, societies that have masculine and feminine markers for a person's gender will employ the feminine marker to the term used in reference for father to the father's sister (which in English would roughly be equivalent to "father-ette"), or the masculine marker would be added to the term for mother in reference to the mother's brother (roughly equivalent to "male mother"). In the Iroquois system, parallel cousins would belong to one's own clan (or to a closely affiliated clan) and would be referred to by the term "brother" or "sister." It would not be possible for cross-cousins to be closely related through clan membership, and a term roughly equivalent to "cousin" would be employed. In many Iroquois-type systems cross-cousins become preferred marriage partners.

The Iroquois system is found in both patrilineal and matrilineal type societies. It works out that regardless of which type is used, parallel cousins will always belong to ego's own clan (or to a very closely affiliated clan) and cross-cousins will never belong to a closely related clan.

The next two clan-type kinship systems are quite similar to the Iroquois system in many ways. The major difference is that in the *Omaha* system, which is only patrilineal, parallel cousins are treated in the same manner as in the Iroquois system, but cross-cousins are all lumped together with the term of either father or father's sister (on the father's side of the family) regardless of the generation of the person. In this system, therefore, not only is ego's mother's brother (maternal uncle) given a designation roughly equivalent to "uncle," but so is his son called uncle, and so would all the male descendants of that line be called by this same term (Taylor, 1969). Because the Omaha system is patrilineal, using the same term to refer to the mother's brother and all his male descendants is equivalent to saying, "He who is a male in my mother's clan." The females in ego's matriline would all be referred to as mother regardless of the generation. Thus, "mother" becomes a term used for any female who belongs to the mother's clan, including (of course) ego's mother herself. This practice of "lumping" all relatives of the mother's clan into a general category based on their sex is "cross-generational equivalence" (Keesing, 1975).

The matrilineal *Crow* kinship can be referred to as a sort of "mirror image" of the Omaha type. It follows the Iroquois system for the naming of ego's parallel cousins and all other relatives in the mother's clan (the clan to which ego also belongs). It employs cross-generational equivalence for the members of the father's clan. Ego uses the same term for cross-cousins on the father's side as he/she would use for the father or the father's sister (Taylor, 1969). The Crow system does get more complex when dealing with the members of ego's children's generation, but it is not necessary to discuss the intricacies of this system here.

The important key to understanding any of the clan-related kinship systems (the Iroquois, Omaha, or Crow type) is that each one allows the speaker (ego) to clearly differentiate between those relatives who are members of his/her clan and those who belong to the clan of the parent who is not of ego's own clan. Often, a person who is not a fellow clansperson but who is related through a genealogical tie will recognize a special social bond to ego and thus be of some help in times of need or grief.

In the three clan-based systems described here, clans are usually grouped together into alliances of closely affiliated clans. The most common such arrangement is one in which the whole society is divided into two basically equal units. Each of these two units would be referred to as a moiety (meaning *half*). There are other societies in which the clans are divided into three or more allied groups. Each of these alliances of closely related clans would be referred to as a phratry. Technically, a moiety is a phratry, but it is such a common phenomenon in clanlike societies, that such alliances are specifically referred to as moieties to set them apart from other types of phratries. People who belong to the same moiety or phratry treat one another in much the same manner as they would members of their own clan.

The final, most descriptive of the six kinship types is the *Sudanese* type (named after a region in eastern Africa and not a specific group). Ego employs a special term for each set of relatives in the parental generation. There is a specific and separate term for father, father's brother, and father's sister and for mother, mother's sister, and mother's brother. Also, each set of cousins has a separate term. Therefore, in ego's generation there would be a term for one's siblings and one each for the children of the father's sister, father's brother, mother's sister, and mother's brother. The Sudanese system is found most commonly in societies that have segmentary lineages. Ego would be able to trace his/her ancestry back to a known ancestor along with a large number of relatives. As long as the common relationship is not too distant in the past, all the members of ego's lineage would consider themselves to be close relatives. However, as the generations produce new children and these children grow to adulthood, the lineage becomes too large to be an effective kinship unit so it is eventually necessary to divide the group into two or more new segments. When this division takes place, it becomes necessary for ego to be able to quickly identify those individuals who will remain in his/her lineage from those who are now part of another lineage. By having specific terms for a large number of relatives, ego will know who is a kinsperson and who is no longer a kinsperson by the terms that have been used all of his/her life (Evans-Pritchard, 1950).

CONCLUSION

Systems of kinship, marriage, and residence make sense to those who use them. Moreover, they are the first exposure a person has to his/her society. What we learn as young children tends to remain normal and comfortable throughout our life. As many who work in cross-cultural settings know, insights into the family system of a group of people lead to a fuller understanding of their whole way of life.

An experience related by one of my professors illustrates this understanding. This professor began his anthropological field research among the Iroquois of the Six Nations Reserve near Brantford, Ontario. Each Sunday he attended a church service with his family in the non-Indian city of Brantford. One Sunday, a member of the congregation who was a successful businessman approached the young anthropologist and asked him whether he had been "out on the reserve" long enough to get to know something about what went on "out there". When my professor acknowledged that he had some basic idea of was happening, the businessman then asked whether he could get an idea of the Iroquois concept of honesty. The businessman explained that he had a very hard-working employee who was an Iroquois. The Iroquois was one of his best workers, but, it seemed, he had a serious character flaw.

When the Iroquois man had come to work for him 8 or 10 years before, he had not been employed for more than a few months when he asked whether he could have a week off to go to the reserve to participate in his mother's funeral in the traditional Indian manner. He offered to make up the lost time by deducting it from his vacation, but the owner of the business saw no need for that and excused him with his blessings and condolences. A few months later the owner was again approached by this same employee, now wanting to attend to his father's funeral. This time, the owner decided that maybe it would be necessary to make up for the extra week by deducting it from the

Iroquois's vacation time. Not too much later, the Iroquois worker asked for time off to attend his sister's funeral and not much later on it was a brother and then another sister. Finally, the businessman felt that he had had enough when he was approached so that the man could attend his mother's funeral. A man might have quite a large number of brothers and sisters, but it stood to reason to the owner that once a person's mother had died, it would not happen again.

The business owner told the Iroquois that he now was convinced that the man was using funerals as an excuse to skip work and that if he wanted to spend so much time back home with his people he should just stay there. That had just happened a few days ago and the businessmen was now asking the anthropologist whether he, as a Christian, had done the right and decent thing by terminating the employment of the Iroquois worker. At that point, my professor told the businessman that it might be beneficial for him to understand that every Iroquois probably refers to as many as 15 or 20 people as mother and an equal number as father, and perhaps as many as 100 persons would be considered their brothers or sisters. After learning about their kinship system, the businessman had a better appreciation of Iroquois customs. He apologized to the man he had fired, rehired him, and made arrangements for all of his Native American workers to use their vacation time to leave work for important traditional events such as funerals.

Because kinship is so central to the lives of us all, and because we all live in a complex world occupied by so many people from so many different cultures and groups, it would be wise to become more aware of and sensitive to the point of view of those around us.

REFERENCES

Bohannan, P., & Middleton, J. (Eds.). (1968a). *Kinship and social organization* (*American museum sourcebooks in anthropology*, Vol. Q10). Garden City, NY: Natural History Press.

Bohannan, P., & Middleton, J. (Eds.). (1968b). *Marriage, family, and residence* (*American museum sourcebooks in anthropology*, Vol. Q9). Garden City, NY: Natural History Press.

Bowen, E. S. (1964). *Return to laughter*. Garden City, NY: Anchor Books.

Doumenge, F. (1966). *L'Homme dans le Pacifique sud* (Publications de la Société des Océanistes No. 19). Paris: Musée de l'Homme.

Evans-Pritchard, E. E. (1950). Kinship and the local community among the Nuer. In A. R. Radcliffe-Brown & D. Forde (Eds.), *African systems of kinship and marriage* (pp. 360–391). London: Oxford University Press.

Farber, B., Mogey, J., & Smith, K. (1986). Kinship and development. *Journal of Comparative Family Studies, 17*(2). [Special issue]

Fenton, W. N. (1978). Northern Iroquoian culture patterns. In W. C. Sturtevant

(Ed.), *Handbook of North American Indians: Vol. 15. Northeast* (pp. 296–321). Washington, DC: Smithsonian Institution.

Fox, R. (1967). *Kinship and marriage: An anthropological perspective.* London: Penguin Books.

Fox, R. G. (1976). Lineage cells and regional definition in complex societies: The case of Highland Scotland. In C. A. Smith (Ed.), *Regional analysis: Vol. II. Social systems (Studies in Anthropology)* New York: Academic Press.

Goodenough, W. (1955). Residence rules. *Southwestern Journal of Anthropology, 12,* 22–37. (Republished in Bohannan & Middleton, 1968b, pp. 297–316.)

Hocart, A. M. (1937). Kinship systems. *Anthropos, 32,* 345–351. (Republished in Bohannan & Middleton, 1968a, pp. 29–38.)

Johnson, C. L. (1988). *Ex familia.* New Brunswick, NJ: Rutgers University Press.

Keesing, R. M. (1975). *Kin groups and social structure.* New York: Holt, Rinehart & Winston.

Kroeber, A. L. (1909). Classificatory systems of relationship. *Journal of the Anthropological Institute, 39,* 77–84. (Republished in Bohannan & Middleton, 1968a, pp. 19–27.)

Lee, G. R. (1982). *Family structure and interaction: A comparative analysis* (2nd ed.). Minneapolis: University of Minnesota Press.

Lowie, R. H. (n.d.). Relationship terms. In *Encyclopedia britannica* (14th ed.). (Republished in Bohannan & Middleton, 1968a, pp. 39–59.)

Murdock, G. P. (1949). *Social structure.* New York: Macmillan.

Oliver, D. (1961). *The Pacific islands* (rev. ed.) (*Natural History Library*). New York: Anchor Books.

Rossi, A. S., & Rossi, P. H. (1990). *Of human bonding: Parent–child relations across the life course.* New York: Aldine de Gruyter.

Stack, C. B., & Burton, L. M. (1993) Kinscripts. *Journal of Comparative Family Studies, 24*(2), 157–170.

Stanton, M. (1993). A gathering of saints: The role of the Church of Jesus Christ of Latter-Day Saints in Pacific Islander migration. In G. McCall & J. Connell (Eds.), *A world perspective on Pacifis Islander migration: Australia, New Zealand and the USA* (Center for South Pacific Studies, Pacific Studies Monograph No. 6, pp. 23–37). Sydney: University of New South Wales.

Stephens, W. N. (1963). *The family in cross-cultural perspective.* New York: Holt, Rinehart & Winston.

Taylor, R. B. (1969). *Cultural ways: A compact introduction to cultural anthropology.* Boston: Allyn & Bacon.

Tooker, E. (1978). The league of the Iroquois: Its history, politics, and ritual. In W. C. Sturtevant (Ed.), *Handbook of North American Indians: Vol. 15. Northeast* (pp. 418–441). Washington, DC: Smithsonian Institution.

CHAPTER SIX

Marital Structure

BRON B. INGOLDSBY

This chapter looks at marriage rather than the more complex issue of family. Family structure is determined by the number of *social positions* that make up a family. With marriage, however, there are only two positions: husband and wife. Cohabitating couples are considered as if they were legally married for this type of analysis. Therefore, marital structure refers simply to the number of *individuals* who occupy each of those two positions or roles within a given marriage.

Homosexual unions cannot be considered here for two reasons. First, we have no global data on same-sex domestic relationships. In the United States, for instance, census statistics only tell us about opposite-sex cohabitation. Second, if we take away one of the two positions, this type of analysis makes no sense. As a result, an investigation of same-sex marital structure is beyond the scope of this chapter.

There are, then, four possible types of marriage structure, depending on the number of persons of each sex who occupy each position within a given marriage (Lee, 1982; see Table 6.1). The type most familiar to those from modern Western societies is *monogamy* or one husband and one wife. As it is often the only legal option, it is so common that many people make the mistake of considering monogamy the only natural or legitimate marital form.

The other three possibilities are all forms of plural marriage, or *polygamy*. In each case, the structure is determined by the number of husbands or wives simultaneously married to their opposite-sex counterparts. Drawing on medical terms for the sexes, "polygyny" means many females, whereas "polyandry" refers to many males. "Cenogamy" is the term for group marriage. More recently, the term "polygynandry" (Sangree & Levine, 1980) has also been applied to the situation of a marriage consisting of plural husbands and wives.

117

TABLE 6.1.   Types of Marital Structure

Marital type	Husbands	Wives
Monogamy	One	One
Polygyny	One	Two or more
Polyandry	Two or more	One
Cenogamy	Two or more	Two or more

It has been tempting for some to consider the plural marriage forms to be at least exotic, if not unnatural. Book titles such as *Strange Customs of Courtship and Marriage* (Fielding, 1942) reveal the Eurocentric bias of some writers who have helped shape public opinion.

Monogamy is certainly the most common of the marital types; the generally equal sex ratio throughout the world sees to that. It works well with our modern economic structure and probably provides for greater interpersonal intimacy, but this does not make it more "natural." As we shall see, polygyny in particular has been a common adaptation to the complexities of the human condition.

In the most extensive examination of the Ethnographic Atlas, Murdock (1967) analyzes marital structure in 1,157 societies. As with all studies in which societies rather than individual marriages are counted, polygyny emerges as the preferred marital structure in the world. Monogamy was the only permitted form of marriage in 14.5% of the cultures, polyandry was the norm in only seven cultures or 0.6%, cenogamy does not show up as the preferred marital style in any of the cases surveyed, and polygyny is practiced in 84.8% of the world's cultures. In 42% of the polygynous societies, it was practiced only occasionally, which means in fewer than 20% of all marriages.

It must be remembered that modern industrialized societies are not included in the data banks of the Ethnographic Atlas, but the results are nonetheless impressive. It should also be kept in mind that even in polygynous societies, the majority of marriages may be monogamous due to sex-ratio constraints. However, polygyny is the ideal for which the citizens strive.

Modern societies, heavily influenced by European colonialism, are overwhelmingly monogamous, but many citizens end up practicing "serial monogamy." They marry, divorce, and remarry; sometimes more than once. In this way, one has more than one spouse but only one at a time. Those who enter into cohabitation relationships increase their total number of partners even more.

POLYGYNY

The Baganda are one of the larger Bantu tribes living in present-day Uganda in East–Central Africa. They are an agricultural people who enjoy a mild climate. Before English domination brought Western social changes, polygyny was the dominate marital form. The king may have had literally hundreds of wives, chiefs dozens, and commoners two or three. Queen, Habenstein, and Quadagno (1985) provide an excellent summary of this well-known example of polygyny.

Girls usually married at about age 14, and boys shortly thereafter, as soon as they could acquire property. A wife could be inherited or captured in war but was usually purchased from her parents. The brideprice, what the groom pays the bride's family in order to marry her (see Ingoldsby, Chapter 7, in this volume, for a complete explanation), typically involving goats, cattle, and cowrie shells, could often take up to a year to accumulate. Once agreed on, the wedding would take place as soon as the brideprice was paid. The bride would be fed well to make her plump, and she would be veiled in bark cloth.

Wives were valued for two things. The first was their economic productivity. A wife's primary responsibility was to cultivate a family garden plot, and whenever she wore out her hoe, her husband would reward her with a goat (and probably a new hoe) for her diligence.

Wives were also valued for producing children. The Bagandans had a number of beliefs concerning children, especially legitimacy. A woman would give birth in her garden, hanging on to a plantain tree and supported by a female assistant. The medicine man was only called in difficult cases, but he was generally not wanted because of his primitive obstetrics and because needing him indicated to the Bagandans that the child had been conceived in adultery.

If the firstborn to a chief were male, he would be killed as it was considered to be bad luck for the father. Babies born breech were also killed (it was believed that they would grow up to be murderers), but twins were cause for rejoicing. A child's umbilical cord was saved and brought to a special clan ceremony. It would be dropped into a container of beer, water, and milk, and if the cord sank, the child was considered to be the product of adultery and disowned.

The day after the clan ceremony the child was named. The paternal grandfather would recite the names of clan ancestors and when the child laughed it was believed that the soul of that ancestor had entered the child's body and that was the name given. Children generally lived with a brother of the father after weaning. Grandparents could also, at any time, ask for a child to live with them.

Explanations for Polygyny

Western scholars first supposed that the sex drive was at the root of the practice of having plural wives. Men were presumed to have a greater desire for sexual variety than do women, and because they typically control the authority structure, they then simply imposed their will on the women to gratify themselves. But as Lee (1982) demonstrates, this explanation has a number of flaws to it. First, there is no evidence that the sex drive for males is innately stronger than it is for females. Second, women also favor the polygynous system. There are a number of economic advantages to living in a polygynous household (e.g., greater wealth for all), and it is often a senior wife who encourages her husband to marry again.

Third, the fact of the roughly equal sex ratio makes it so that only some men can enter plural marriage. As a valuable resource, each wife usually commands an expensive brideprice, so it is only the older men, who have had the time to gain wealth, who can afford additional wives. It is the younger men who are believed to have the more intense sexual urges, but they may not yet have even a first wife.

Finally, even though there may be some theoretical evidence that males value sexual variety (see Ingoldsby, Chapter 15, this volume), it does not necessarily follow that they would try to acquire multiple wives. Instead, they would seek multiple sexual partners, which is not the same thing. Men in most societies are able to obtain sex without marriage, even though marriage always includes sexual privilege. Because sex is available elsewhere, marriage would be a high price to pay for that aspect alone.

Other arguments have been offered as well. Whiting (1964) claims that polygyny is more likely to be acceptable in cultures that have postpartum sex taboos until the infant is weaned. This taboo enables the couple to space children so that the mother can properly feed each one. Polygyny therefore provides a regular sexual outlet for the husband. Ember (1974) reports that polygyny fills the need for all women to marry in societies in which there are fewer men due to high warfare mortality rates.

Marriage and Economy

The explanation that has shown the most promise, and received the most attention among scholars (see Lee, 1982), has been the link between marital type and economic subsistence patterns. It has been widely reported that in polygynous societies, the wealthiest families are most likely to be polygynous. The implication is that the more women and their children can contribute to the production of wealth, the more likely polygyny is to be practiced. We find this in light agriculture and animal husbandry economies, where the more wives a man has, the more fields can be tended and the more animals cared for. The wealth generated exceeds any additional consumer as virtually everyone can be a worker.

As a result, women are attracted to the economic advantages of being a multiple wife. Sociobiologists (Devore, 1979) have reported similar strategies in the animal kingdom as well. Male blackbirds that control the richest wetland will have many females attach to them, while the less fortunate males on the rocky edges may be lucky to entice even a single mate.

A good example of this argument that having plural wives is for economic reasons, rather than to have an exotic harem, is the Siwai:

> It is by no mere accident that polygynous households average more pigs than monogamous ones. Informants stated explicitly that some men married second and third wives in order to enlarge their herds. They laughed at the writer's suggestion that a man might become polygynous in order to increase his sexual enjoyment. ("Why pay bride price when for a handful of tobacco you can copulate with other women as often as you like!"). (Oliver, 1955, p. 352)

With the family as the unit of production, it follows that the economy might influence family size. In primitive hunting–gathering societies, children will consume much more than they produce, and the same is true for modern industrialized societies. These societies tend to be monogamous, while the agricultural ones, which have a high female contribution to subsistence, tend to be polygynous.

However, this explanation does not fit the facts as perfectly as originally thought. Goody (1973) points out that although polygyny is practically universal among native African societies, it is more frequent in West Africa, even though women contribute more to production in East Africa. Also, about 90% of preagricultural societies practice polygyny even though women make relatively low contributions to subsistence in those hunting, fishing, and herding cultures.

In these cases it may be women's reproductive value that leads to the taking of plural wives. That is, more wives means more sons being born, who will be the workers in a male-oriented economy. Recent research (Lee & Whitbeck, 1990; Verdon, 1983) has indicated that the reasons for polygyny are many and complex: economy, social status, tradition, biosocial, political connections and lineage advantages, and others, even possibly including the previously discredited idea of sexual access. In light of the fact that most societies permit the practice of at least occasional polygyny, it may be that scholars have pursued the explanation from the wrong vantage point. Goody (1976) argues that it is monogamy that requires an explanation, and that we should be looking for the constraints that push a society away from polygyny and toward monogamy.

Mormon Polygyny

One reason for polygyny that has received little attention is religion. Modern Christianity has been strongly promonogamy and has ignored the institutionalization of polygyny among the Old Testament Hebrews. One exception has been the Church of Jesus Christ of Latter-Day Saints (LDS), commonly known as the Mormons. The LDS church is one of the largest and fastest-growing denominations in the United States today, and its members practiced polygyny on a fairly large scale during its early history. It has received little attention from family sociologists, however, and much of what has been reported is biased.

Mormon prophet Joseph Smith founded the LDS church in New York State in 1830. He later stated that he had received a revelation from God indicating that as part of the restoration of ancient Christian practices, the Saints (as church members call themselves) should return to the practice of plural marriage. Wyatt (1989) makes it clear that this practice did not begin for the traditional sexual or economic reasons. First, early Mormons came from puritan New England and found polygyny personally distasteful; second, they correctly predicted the persecution that would come to them because of it; finally, it was older men who had the plural wives, just as in other cultures, and not the younger ones at their sexual peak.

In addition, there is no evidence that there was an excess of Mormon females who needed husbands, or that there were any economic benefits to plural marriage. Most plural wives had to support themselves and lived at a subsistence level. In short, Mormons practiced polygyny for the ideological reason that they believed God required it of them.

Joseph Smith carefully introduced the practice to trusted associates in the early 1840s, after the church had moved its headquarters to Nauvoo, Illinois. There was much secrecy involved as polygamy was illegal and attracted much persecution from nonmembers. Moreover, many of the church members themselves had difficulty accepting the doctrine.

After Smith's murder by an anti-Mormon mob in 1844, the church was led to the Salt Lake valley in present-day Utah by their new prophet, Brigham Young. In 1852, the church publicly admitted to the practice and in the following decades suffered ever greater federal prosecution and persecution. Finally, in order to avoid imprisonment, disenfranchisement, and the seizure of property and other financial assets, Church President Wilford Woodruff declared an end to the practice of plural marriage in 1890 (Ingoldsby, 1989).

Although Wyatt (1989) claims that it was the lack of an economic basis that doomed Mormon polygyny in the long run, he offers no evidence for this. In actuality, the practice of "the principle," as the Mormons called it, was given up because the church prophet declared that it was now God's will for them to submit to secular authority.

In the American case, polygyny was purely ideological. It was embedded in an antipolygamy culture and lacked an economic rationale. In spite of this, polygyny persisted for more than 50 years, and there are still some small splinter groups from the LDS church that practice plural marriage in the American West.

Early Mormons believed that having many wives and children were signs of God's favor and a requirement for his blessings. Having large families is still an expectation for devout Mormons, and it is clear that the key philosophical reason for Mormon polygyny was to bring children into the true religion. Although the husband was, of course, older with each plural wife he married, the average age for each wife was always 19, and a man tended to remarry when his present wife passed the childbearing years. First wives averaged eight children, whereas subsequent wives averaged six (Ingoldsby, 1989).

Life "in the principle" (as Mormons referred to plural marriage) was difficult. Husbands were often absent, on church missions or avoiding federal marshals, and the wives worked at home or on their farm with their children. The divorce rate was higher for polygynous marriages than it was for the monogamous ones, and after a generation or so from the formal ending of polygyny, church members were content to be in the cultural mainstream of U.S. society with monogamous marriages.

Drawbacks to Polygyny

In polygynous societies, wives are scarce, and therefore valuable, resources. As a result, they are expensive to obtain, and we find that the custom of paying the girl's family a brideprice is more common in polygynous cultures. This custom helps to deal with the problem of the sex ratio, as men need time to generate the wealth necessary to afford additional wives. Women often marry shortly after puberty and are therefore much younger than their husbands. This means that there are always more women in the marriage pool than there are men, making polygyny possible.

Stephens (1963) recounts problems with jealousy in some polygynous households, and indeed many Western women today consider it to be only natural that a woman would resent sharing her husband with others. However, the idea of sexual exclusivity is learned rather than innate, and therefore jealousy would be less common in cultures that do not espouse that value (Lee, 1982).

In short, there may be nothing intrinsically anxiety producing about plural marriages. In Ware's (1979) study of polygyny in Nigeria, she found that the majority of women were pleased to have their husband take an additional wife, mainly because it gave them help in their domestic tasks. It must be remembered that even though it is expensive to establish a polygynous arrangement, in the long run it usually creates more wealth for all members than it costs.

Stephens (1963) mentions that in the political system of the Trobriand Islands, a husband receives an annual large food gift from the kinsmen of each wife. This makes it economically profitable to have as many wives as possible. In other cases, plural wives are a status symbol for prominent families. In general, polygyny has not been associated with low status for women, so they tend not to oppose it.

However, Stephens (1963) also quotes the following Indian Hindu proverb: "A thousand moustaches can live together, but not four breasts" (p. 56). So how is the possibility of jealousy dealt with? Essentially there are two approaches: (1) If the co-wives are sisters or other close relatives, they tend to share the same residence; and (2) if they are not related, they are usually given separate households. This first approach, "sororal polygyny," is very common in polygynous societies. It is apparently assumed that sisters can handle sexual jealousy and close quarters better than others would (Lee, 1982).

In nonrelative plural marriage, or "hut polygyny" each wife has her own home, or "hut," and the common husband visits each in rotation. This practice reduces interaction between the wives and their children and also results in periods of father absence.

In summary, polygyny has flourished everywhere except in Christian Europe and North America, and it brings advantages to the wives as well as to the husband. This is particularly true for the senior wife, who often has authority over the others. It remains popular in places even when not economically advantageous and has mechanisms for dealing with family conflict.

POLYANDRY AND POLYGYNANDRY

Murdock (1957) originally identified four societies as being characterized by polyandry: the Toda, the Tibetans, the Nayar, and the Marquesans. In 1967, he found three more, and since that time a few others have been identified. While certainly rare compared to monogamy and polygyny, entire cultures have found it suitable for their particular circumstances, and it would be inaccurate to call polyandry unnatural, as early ethnographers sometimes did.

In addition to permitting women to marry multiple husbands, many of the polyandrous societies allow the husbands to marry additional wives under various circumstances, resulting in group marriage. As the two often go together, I will discuss them together.

For the sake of clarity, we need to distinguish between two types of group marriage. Typically, people think of group marriage as a situation in which a group of men are all married to the same group of women and vice versa.

They all know each other and may share the same residence. I restrict the term "cenogamy" for this type of group marriage. Another type, "polygynandry," is also likely to occur in polyandrous cultures. In this case, both men and women may have plural spouses but the spouses are not the same people. The woman visits her various husbands and the man visits his wives, but each may not know the spouses of their partner.

Because there are not many recognized polyandrous societies, I will describe some of them and then attempt to explain the predisposing conditions for this particular marital structure.

The Todas

The Todas are a pastoral tribe living in small villages in southern India. Western anthropologists began studying them in the late 1800s. They have a complex kinship system and care for herds of sacred buffalo. Polyandry has existed for centuries as the dominate marital type.

When a Toda woman marries a man, she is automatically married to all his brothers, even those who may not be born yet. This is called fraternal polyandry, and like its counterpart, sororal polygyny, practitioners show little evidence of jealousy. There is no concern about who the biological father is, but a social or legal father is chosen for each child. One brother, usually beginning with the eldest, will make a ceremonial bow and arrow and "give the bow" to his pregnant wife to achieve that status.

Female infanticide is practiced, as is true for many nonliterate societies. In the Toda case, of course, it reduces the number of potential wives so that polyandry can (or must) occur. Unlike the Baganda, twins are considered bad luck and one is killed even if they are both boys. Todas prefer to marry cross-cousins. In fact, if a Toda dies unmarried, he/she is ritually married to a cross-cousin so that there will be no singles in the Toda afterlife.

Todas maximize heterosexual outlets for males in various ways. Because Todas are often married as children, there are typically few mature women available for marriage. An older man, perhaps widowed, who does not have the time for a child bride to grow up, can negotiate for an already married woman from her husbands. This wife transfer is effected by giving some buffalo, which increases the wealth of the original husbands. This in turn enhances their competitiveness for a new and younger wife.

Another marital type is a system we might call consort–mistress. The Todas are divided into two endogamous groups, or moieties. One marries within his/her own moiety but may enter into a legitimate sexual relationship with someone from the other group. Typically, a man obtains permission, through payment, from the desired woman's husbands. A ceremony is held and visits are scheduled.

Although betrothals were often arranged during the infancy of those involved, a girl did not move into her husband's home until after puberty. Shortly before puberty, it is reported that the girl would be deflowered by a young man from any clan except the girl's. Not to do so was considered disgraceful.

The Toda household revolves around care of the buffalo and dairying activities. Women have relatively little to do as they may not engage in anything having to do with the sacred buffalo, including preparing food that includes milk products. Wives could be divorced for being incompetent or lazy, but adultery was considered normal and not grounds for censure. If a wife was barren, the husbands would try to take on an additional wife.

Inheritance is patrilineal, with only males inheriting. Women own very little, only personal possessions and their dowry. Although males are dominant in many ways, few societies give as much freedom and leisure to women as the Toda do (Queen et al., 1985).

Tibetans

Before the Chinese conquest of Tibet, anthropologists (Prince Peter, 1965) reported its inhabitants to be practicing a classical polyandry. The economy was agricultural, but land was scarce due to the high altitude. In addition, all the land was owned by the church, the government, or the landed aristocracy. The peasants had to rent the land at a cost that often exceeded half their income. There was little incentive to try to increase one's holdings as surplus production usually went to rent and taxes.

Like the Todas, the Tibetans practiced fraternal polyandry and female infanticide. Still, there was often an excess of females as many men joined monastic groups. Unmarried females had the option of also joining religious orders, becoming prostitutes, or living in their brother's household. The Todas differ from the Tibetans in that the predisposing condition seems to be a lack of productive activities for women, where each man does not need a spouse of his own. For the Tibetans, it is more a strategy to keep the birthrate down in a poor environment. The land cannot support many people, and if each generation of sons were to subdivide their inheritance, the plots would become too small (Lee, 1982).

Other South Asian Groups

Other polyandrous groups for which we have data include the Nyinba of Nepal (Levine, 1980). As with their neighbors, polyandry is fraternal, though all other marital structure possibilities are present among the Nyinba. Polyandry once again seems to be a successful adaptation to a harsh environment and scare resources and a way to avoid subdividing land holdings. In case of infertility, men prefer to marry an additional wife who is a sister of the first.

Another Himalayan culture is the Pahari. The Pahari justify polyandry with a Hindu tradition of five deified brothers who shared a common wife. Once again, there is a narrow survival margin for population versus land. Monogamy and polygyny are also acceptable, depending on each family's financial condition (Berreman, 1980).

Sri Lanka is home to the ancient Kandyan culture (Kemper, 1980). Their Buddist traditions deemphasize the ritual importance of marriage, so there is very little ceremony. This is especially true for cross-cousins, who are considered married from birth. Monogamy is the norm, and the only legal option since 1859; however, cases of polyandry have been found even later than the 1950s. As with most of the cultures permitting polyandry, sexuality is rarely restricted and not considered to be a defining characteristic of marriage.

When a man allows other husbands into his marriage, it is generally for economic reasons and is positively associated with sacrifice and solidarity. Polygyny, on the other hand, is far less respectable. Kandyans say that polyandry is to unify the family, meaning to concentrate male earning power. Women define their polyandrous marriages not in terms of shared sexuality but in terms of shared food. A husband is someone for whom a wife cooks rice, and although a man's extramarital affairs are tolerated, society would not accept his eating in public with a mistress. So it is economy rather than sexuality that defines marriage.

Finally, there are the Nayar (see Ingoldsby, Chapter 4, this volume, for a description). Even though Murdock (1957) saw them as an example of polyandry, they are clearly a case of polygynandrous group marriage and do not meet the general characteristics found in most polyandrous societies.

Rationale

What are those characteristics? First, polyandry as we have discussed it so far is generally fraternal. That is, brothers stay together on the family farm and one wife moves in with them. Second, polyandry is a response to economic poverty, which demands that land not be divided and that the birthrate remain low. Third, female infanticide is often practiced. Fourth, the economy tends to be male oriented, with few productive tasks assigned to women, making them less necessary. Fifth, sexuality has few restraints and does not generate the jealousy found in romantic cultures. Finally, in every case except possibly for Tibet, additional wives are also permitted, resulting in cenogamy. However, group marriage is merely an acceptable by-product to certain conditions such as infertility or unexpected wealth, not the goal.

Polyandrous groups in other parts of the world support many of these predisposing conditions to various degrees. The Marquesans (southern Polynesia) practiced fraternal polyandry and female infanticide, and well-to-do households might marry additional wives and become cenogamous. Jealousy was considered inappropriate, and family heads might arrange for additional husbands for an already married daughter because each male worker would add to the family wealth (Stephens, 1963).

The Kaingang were wandering hunters in the jungles of Brazil among whom about 14% of all marriages were polyandrous (Lee, 1982). Women were encouraged to attract additional lovers and husbands, as each man could help hunt and protect the group.

The Yanomama Shirishana have been extensively studied by Peters (1982). In the 1950s polyandry was the dominant marital type for this small Amazonian tribe. Fraternal polyandry was common, but "associated polyandry," where the husbands are not brothers (as with the Kandyans), also occurred. Female infanticide was practiced but did not appear to be related to food shortages.

Marriages begin monogamously, with a young adult male paying a brideprice for an infant girl and consummating after puberty. After they had had a few children, another male would join the group, usually because he could find no mate of his own. He would be welcomed as another meat provider for the group.

Later, if the younger husband could obtain a wife of his own through capture in a raid, he would leave the polyandrous arrangement. It was also common for a man to leave his wife when she reached menopause and move in with a younger bride. The first wife would then be cared for by her sons or sons-in-law. In the case of the Yanomama, economic considerations do not seem to play a part. Instead, polyandry was a short-term adjustment to a sex-ratio imbalance.

Nigerian Polygynandry

Recent articles (see Cassidy & Lee, 1989) indicate that polyandry is adequately understood. Essentially, it is a response to (1) extreme societal poverty, mandating a low birth rate, and (2) limited productive economic roles for women. However, more recently investigated cases in the Jos Plateau of northern Nigeria point to greater complexity. In South Asian cases, the wife has a fixed residence which she shares with her husbands, who tend to be close relatives. The polyandrous Nigerian tribes, however, have a system in which each husband (who tend not to be related) has his own separate residence, and the wife shifts from one to another (Sangree & Levine, 1980).

The Abisi

The Abisi number around 3,300 (Chalifoux, 1980) and are divided into six clans. A woman cannot have more than one husband per clan. Typically, a young woman is married to three men on the same day, but she will live with them separately in a certain order. She begins with the "first marriage," which is arranged by her parents. After this betrothal, the girl is free to select her second husband, for the "love marriage," whom she chooses from her various suitors. This marriage is popular with the young people but does not have the same social status as the first marriage.

The third groom is selected by the parents, usually from the remaining suitors, for the "home marriage," referring to the girl's home whose family arranged it. (Parents also select the first marriage, but on a more formalized basis of clan exchanges.) Most men also enter into each of these three types of marriages, so marriage is polygynous for them while it is polyandrous for the women, resulting in polygynandry for the culture.

A woman usually stays with her first husband for a year (to leave earlier means a smaller dowry for her), at which time she must move in with her love marriage husband. At the end of the next year, the third husband may claim his wife, but more than half of Abisi women refuse to go to their home husband. All these men, even the rejected suitors, have paid a brideprice, often in the form of work prestations, to the girl's family. This free labor is the economic incentive for parents to promote polyandry for their daughters.

Women may move back and forth between husbands as they desire, and they may also enter into a fourth marriage, the "grass marriage." Typically, the woman is enticed while gathering wood in the bush by an older man who is better established financially than are her younger husbands and can therefore offer more economic security. Parents are informed of the liaison later and the union is validated by payment of a goat and two hoes.

The Abisi system is one of polygynandrous group marriages in that the plural marriages of each sex are separate. The focus is on polyandry for the women, with polygyny as a natural by-product. While there are economic considerations, first marriages have important lineage and political significance. The system also seems to be designed for dealing with the legitimization of sexual attraction to more than one person and could be seen as more healthy than the monogamy-with-adultery pattern common in modern Western society. It also avoids the psychological tension one might expect to find at a higher level in cenogamous households, where all the marital participants share the same residence.

The Irigwe

Another Nigerian society is the Irigwe (Sangree, 1980), for whom divorce did not even exist until 1968. First marriages are arranged by parents while the individuals are still small children. Substantial farm labor is performed by the prospective groom's family for several years before the marriage is consummated. Parents will do this in spite of the fact that most "primary marriages" rarely stay together for more than a few weeks. The main incentive for the boy's family is that the work shows the community that this family's sons and daughters are good candidates for "secondary marriages."

Secondary marriages are initiated by the couple themselves and involve a much smaller brideprice. Daughters are encouraged by their parents to enter into several secondary marriages during the teen years. The woman is only obligated to spend a few nights with each husband, and the parents benefit from the flow of bride gifts.

A woman remains married to all her husbands throughout her life, but there is a culturally determined system for residence. Once she becomes pregnant for the first time, she will stay with that husband, who is designated the legal father. Subsequent shifts from one husband to another are determined by health crises with the children. A diviner often ascertains that the particular illness is rooted in the child's poor "soul state," which can only be improved by a change of residence.

Competition for secondary wives fosters hostility between tribal sections but also controls it. That is, Irigwe men are suspicious of men from other sections who might want to take their wives in secondary marriage, which can lead to fights among the competing males. However, once a man's wife has cohabited with another man he must be treated with caution and respect because of the Irigwe belief that a co-husband can cause the first husband's death, if he is ill or injured, merely by the new husband's presence. As a result, men sharing the same wife tend to be polite to each other and to avoid one another when possible.

The Irigwe, then, have a system different in approach but similar in result to the Abisi's. Both societies are polygynandrous, with men paying for wives who will control the living arrangements. The traditional exchange of economic security for sex and children seems evident, with variety substituted for stability.

The Birom

The Birom (Smedley, 1980) practice "cicisbeism," which is not quite polyandry, because the multiple unions do not result in legal status. This term refers to a situation in which a married woman is permitted socially approved sexual relations with men not defined as a legal husband. She retains her full status with her "real" husband throughout their lives. Prior to colonialism, this custom was widespread, overt, and considered a necessary part of the social system.

The key aspects of this system are as follows. The right of sexual access to another man's wife is obtained by the payment of a fee, usually a goat, to the woman's husband. A woman chooses her own *cicisbeo*, or lover, and is expected to have some. The woman does not leave her husband but receives her lovers in her own home. Any children she may have from these men belong to her husband, the one person to have paid a brideprice for her.

The advantages for Birom women include expanded economic support and sexual variety, but what benefits do the men derive? For one thing, of course, they are the *cicisbeos* to other men's wives, thereby maximizing sexual variety for everyone in a legitimate context and minimizing (by sharing with others) economic and other marital obligations. More important, however, is that the practice provides an alliance system for men called *njem*. To become a leader in the community, a man needs a group of followers, and these are the lovers of a man's wives and the husbands of his own mistresses. Men gain wealth and power through *cicisbeism*, but it is the women who determine who the leaders will actually be since they are the ones who choose the *njem* partners.

Also the women receive material support for themselves and their children every year from their *cicisbeos* which they do not have to share with their husband. This annual support provides them with economic security. The men gain politically but have been more willing in recent years to do away with the *njem* than have the women.

Summary

The previously mentioned polyandrous African societies and others exhibit complicated systems of spouse circulation (Muller, 1980) that are very different from "classic" South Asian polyandry. For multiple-husband cultures in Asia, the explanation is chiefly economic: a poverty and land scarcity which forces brothers to share a wife. Classic polyandry intensifies affinal relationships.

The Nigerian version, in contrast, increases the extent and variety of affinal ties (Levine & Sangree, 1980). Husbands are not brothers and coresidence does not occur. The land is not as poor, so economics is an issue of lesser importance. Polygyny always occurs along with the polyandry, and the status of women seems to be higher. As with the Asians, sex is "looser" than in monogamous societies, but it is more central to the meaning of marriage.

Prince Peter (1980) disagrees that polyandry, or any marital structure, can be purely the result of economic, kinship, social necessity, or other rational cultural factors:

> But do human creatures act rationally in response to so deep an emotion as the passionate, sexual instinct of reproduction? Are they sufficiently aware of their unconscious urges and drives, not to speak of complexes carried over from childhood and securely entrenched by infantile amnesia, to be able to do so? Is there not a predominant psychodynamic correlate of polyandry which is being neglected here, as an intermediary between ecological and sociological reasons for the custom and its actual institution? Personally, I think so, and feel that this factor is sadly left out by those investigating polyandry. (p. 374)

Prince Peter goes on to suggest homosexual tendencies and the Oedipus complex as the psychodynamic correlate, in spite of researchers' inability to empirically connect these Freudian concepts with family structure. However, his general point is well taken in that there probably is more to marriage than just culture and economy. The relevance of sexual and psychological intimacy and other microsocial and clinical concepts in the understanding of marital structure seems warranted.

CENOGAMY

The fourth and final type of marital structure is cenogamy. This is group marriage where the husbands and wives share the same spouses. Although we find the practice of group marriage in polyandrous societies, Murdock found no cases of a society that had group marriage as its dominant or preferred structure.

Stephens (1963) mentions two groups that he considered marginal. The Siriono of Bolivia are technically monogamous but permit and frequently engage in sexual intercourse with the wife's sisters or the husband's brothers, real and classificatory. Unlike the Birom, however, there appears to be no economic or political component to this system.

The other case that looks like cenogamy, but which most writers have concluded is another example of sexual hospitality, are the Reindeer Chukchee. Stephens (1963) quotes the ethnographer Bogoras, who wrote about them in 1909:

> The Chukchee group marriage includes sometimes up to ten married couples. The men belonging to such a marriage-union are called companions in wives. . . . Each companion has a right to all the wives of his com-

panion, but takes advantage of his right comparatively seldom, namely, when he visits for some reason the camp of one of the companions. Then the host cedes him his place in the sleeping-room. . . . The union, in group marriages, is mostly formed between persons who are well acquainted . . . especially between neighbors and relatives. Second and third cousins are almost invariably united by ties of group-marriage; brothers, however, do not enter into such unions. The inmates of one and the same camp are seldom willing to enter into a group-marriage, the reason obviously being that the reciprocal use of wives, which in group-marriage is practiced very seldom, is liable to degenerate into complete promiscuity if the members of the group live too close together. . . . Not to be connected with such a union, means to have no friends and good-wishers, and no protectors in case of need. (pp. 48–49)

It may be that the purpose of Chukchee cenogamy is the same as it is for Nigerian polygynandry. That is, men trade their wives' sexuality for a male network, which exists for their political or economic benefit. There is, however, one clear case of true cenogamy as the dominant marital structure in a society. It is a U.S. example and, as with Mormon polygyny, it was religiously based.

The Oneidans

John Humphrey Noyes was an apprentice lawyer turned minister by a religious revival that occurred in Vermont in the early 1830s. He developed a "Perfectionist" doctrine, which stated that Christ had already returned to earth for the second time, and that redemption from sin was already an accomplished fact. The group's discussions focused on spiritual, economic, and sexual equality. His radical ideas outraged the community, so in 1848 Noyes moved his flock from Putney, Vermont, to former Indian lands along Oneida creek in central New York State.

What became known as the Oneida Community grew, and in many ways flourished, over the next few decades. In 1862, the Oneidans built the Mansion House, a spacious brick building which still stands, in which many of the members lived. The Oneidans practiced economic communism in which there was no private ownership of property. Holding "all things in common" was designed to help the members overcome selfishness.

To avoid problems of discrimination, community jobs were rotated every year. It functioned much like an Israeli kibbutz and was quite successful. Their economic base was originally the sale of excellent steel traps developed by a member, but in 1877 the Oneidans began manufacturing silverware—an enterprise that continued after the demise of the religious group.

Noyes considered monogamy to be selfish love, and developed the idea of "complex marriage," which the Oneidans all apparently practiced. He felt that it was natural for all men to love all women and vice versa, and therefore each adult in the community was considered married to all the adults of the opposite sex.

The community was managed by committees, and the feelings of women were considered in the practice of complex marriage. If a man desired sexual relations with a particular woman, he would submit a request to the Central Committee. A female go-between would deliver the message so that women could turn down proposals that did not appeal to them without embarrassment. Noyes did not believe that sex was the duty of women for the pleasure of men; in fact, women had considerably more responsibility, freedom, and respect than were found in the larger culture at this time.

Noyes had two programs related to children that were important to the Perfectionist doctrine. First, he felt that scientific principles used in breeding superior animals could also be successful with humans. Second, for the first 20 years of the community, he had the Oneidans refrain from bearing children so that they could become economically stabilized.

For birth control, Noyes advocated coitus reservatus, which is sexual intercourse without male ejaculation. Common medical opinion of the time indicated that frequent ejaculation was not good for men, but developing such control is difficult. Older women in the community benefited as Noyes mandated that until a male could learn this coital control, sexual relations had to be limited to women past menopause.

In 1869, the group began a eugenics (called "stirpiculture" by Noyes) program. Couples wanting to become parents had to make a formal application to the appropriate committee, which decided if the couple had the superior physical and mental traits desired. The program was in effect for the last decade of the group's existence and 58 children were born during that time. Reports indicate that as a group these children were very healthy and well adjusted.

Outside pressure against this radical reformulation of family life and structure led to public campaigns against what was labeled "free love" and "animal breeding." Probably to escape charges of statutory rape (Noyes had fathered about a dozen children, some apparently with women who were legal minors), Noyes fled to Canada in 1879, and the community disbanded shortly thereafter (Kephart & Jedlicka, 1991).

As is true with most modern communal groups, the Oneidans did not survive the loss of their charismatic leader. Nevertheless, a truly cenogamous culture did thrive for an entire generation. This indicates that group marriage is possible, barring outside opposition. Moreover, once again, the causes have nothing to do with economics or other traditional explanations and everything to do with religious belief.

CONCLUSION

Stephens (1963) suggests that monogamy as a cultural preference gained preeminence in modern societies because the early Catholic fathers outlawed polygyny. Their general repugnance for sexual pleasure resulted in an ideologically based marital structure now considered normal. Monogamy's foundation is stronger than that, of course. One spouse at a time best fits the even sex ratio and the economic structure of the non-family-based, consumer- oriented society in which most of us presently live. It also provides for the deeper psychological intimacy now widely valued in marriage and implies greater equality between the sexes than do some of the plural marriage forms.

Polygamy, in its various forms however, has been a successful strategy in many societies for dealing with the complexities of human civilization and intimacy. Each culture must find a balance in handling the issues of economy, status, sexual exclusivity and variety, chastity, parental power, paternity, kin networks, politics, jealousy, religion, and related concerns. Depending on the relative importance of these considerations, men and women have been very creative in dealing with marital structure. The Abisi, for instance, settled on four different marriages for each person, so as to meet the needs of kin organization (first marriage), romance (love marriage), parental authority (home marriage), and economic security (grass marriage). In contrast, modern Western culture generally ignores the first and third considerations and tries to combine the fourth (economics) with the highly valued second (romance).

In marital structure, then, we find a fascinating variety. The various approaches reflect our attempts to deal with the complexities of human intimacy, with all its beauty and pain, joy, and confusion.

REFERENCES

Berreman, G. (1980). Polyandry: Exotic custom vs. analytical concept. *Journal of Comparative Family Studies, 11*(3), 377–384.

Cassidy, M., & Lee, G. (1989). The study of polyandry: A critique and synthesis. *Journal of Comparative Family Studies, 20*(1), 1–12.

Chalifoux, J. (1980). Secondary marriage and levels of seniority among the Abisi (Piti), Nigeria. *Journal of Comparative Family Studies, 11*(3), 325–344.

Devore, I. (1979). *Sociobiology.* Paper presented at the National Council on Family Relations, Boston.

Ember, M. (1974). Warfare, sex ratio, and polygyny. *Ethnology 13*(April), 197–206.

Fielding, W. (1942). *Strange customs of courtship and marriage.* New York: Garden City.

Goody, J. (1973). Polygyny, economy and the role of women. In J. Goody (Ed.),

The character of kinship (pp. 175–190). London: Cambridge University Press.

Goody, J. (1976). *Production and reproduction: A comparative study of the domestic domain.* London: Cambridge University Press.

Ingoldsby, B. (1989). Mormon marriage: A review of family life and social change. *Family Science Review, 2*(4), 389–396.

Kemper, S. (1980). Polygamy and monogamy in Kandyan Sri Lanka. *Journal of Comparative Family Studies, 11*(3), 299–324.

Kephart, W., & Jedlicka, D. (1991). *The family, society, and the individual.* New York: HarperCollins.

Lee, G. (1982). *Family structure and interaction: A comparative analysis.* Minneapolis: University of Minneapolis Press.

Lee, G., & Whitbeck, L. (1990). Economic systems and rates of polygyny. *Journal of Comparative Family Studies, 21*(1), 13–24.

Levine, N. (1980). Nyinba polyandry and the allocation of paternity. *Journal of Comparative Family Studies, 11*(3), 283–298.

Levine, N., & Sangree, W. (1980). Conclusion: Asian and African systems of polyandry. *Journal of Comparative Family Studies, 11*(3), 385–410.

Muller, J. (1980). On the relevance of having two husbands: Contribution to the study of polygynous/polyandrous marital forms of the Jos Plateau. *Journal of Comparative Family Studies, 11*(3), 359–370.

Murdock, G. P. (1957). World ethnographic sample. *American Anthropologist 59*(August), 664–687.

Murdock, G. P. (1967). Ethnographic atlas: A summary. *Ethology 6*(April), 109–236.

Oliver, D. (1955). *A Solomon Island society.* Cambridge, MA: Harvard University Press.

Peter, Prince of Greece and Denmark. (1965). The Tibetan family system. In M. Nimkoff (Ed.), *Comparative family systems* (pp. 192–208). Boston: Houghton Mifflin.

Peter, Prince of Greece and Denmark. (1980). Comments on the social and cultural implications of variant systems of polyandrous alliances. *Journal of Comparative Family Studies, 11*(3), 371–376.

Peters, J. (1982). Polyandry among the Yanomama Shirishana revisited. *Journal of Comparative Family Studies, 13*(1), 89–96.

Queen, S., Habenstein, R., & Quadagno, J. (1985). *The family in various cultures* New York: Harper & Row.

Sangree, W. (1980). The persistence of polyandry in Irigwe, Nigeria. *Journal of Comparative Family Studies, 11*(3), 335–344.

Sangree, W., & Levine, N. (1980). Introduction. *Journal of Comparative Family Studies, 11*(3), i–iv.

Smedley, A. (1980). The implications of Birom cicisbeism. *Journal of Comparative Family Studies, 11*(3), 345–358.

Stephens, W. (1963). *The family in cross-cultural perspective.* New York: Holt, Rinehart & Winston.

Verdon, M. (1983). Polygyny, descent, and local fission: A comparative hypothesis. *Journal of Comparative Family Studies, 14*(1), 1–22.

Ware, H. (1979). Polygyny: Women's views in a transitional society, Nigeria 1975. *Journal of Marriage and the Family, 41*(February), 185–95.

Whiting, J. (1964). Effects of climate on certain cultural practices. In W. Goodenough (Ed.), *Psychological anthropology* (pp. 511–544). Homewood, IL: Dorsey Press.

Wyatt, G. (1989). Mormon polygyny in the nineteenth century: A theoretical analysis. *Journal of Comparative Family Studies, 20*(1), 13–20.

PART THREE

FAMILY DEVELOPMENT

Courtesy Bron B. Ingoldsby.

Introduction

Part III takes a developmental approach to major stages in family life—mate selection and marriage, childhood, divorce, and later life. Just as an individual changes as he/she passes through time, so does a family. How these family changes are experienced depends in large part on the culture in which one lives, as these chapters illustrate.

In Chapter 7, "Mate Selection and Marriage," Bron B. Ingoldsby looks at the beginning stages of the family life cycle. Historical and cross-cultural evidence points to a variety of practices concerning the processes and rules of mate selection and the wedding itself. Aspects of adjustment to marriage also vary in importance by culture. The original meanings behind some of the marriage customs in Western societies are also explained in this chapter.

In Chapter 8, "Parents' Socialization of Children," D. Terri Heath searches for the commonalities and differences among contemporary cultures in approaches to childrearing. She finds striking similarities across cultures: High parental involvement leads to positive child outcomes in many important areas.

In Chapter 9, "Divorce: A Comparative Perspective," Patrick C. McKenry and Sharon J. Price provide a sweeping look at what has become the most common source of marital disruption. They examine societal forces in and responses to divorce in historical and cultural contexts.

Part III concludes with Chapter 10, "Chinese Families in Later Life," in which William H. Meredith and Douglas A. Abbott discuss the last and often longest stage in the family life cycle. Rather than comparing various cultures, as the other chapters have done, the authors focus on China. This gives the reader a more in-depth look at how one particular society, long known for its veneration of the elderly, deals with its aging population.

CHAPTER SEVEN

Mate Selection and Marriage

BRON B. INGOLDSBY

The institution of marriage is very popular throughout the world. For instance, in the United States today about 95% of all citizens marry at least once by the time they reach the age of 40. The median age for first marriage is 23.8 for women and 26.2 for men (Wells, 1991). There are many others who choose not to formalize their stable sexual relationship and cohabit instead (2.6 million in the United States in 1988).

Marriage, as normative as it is, is approached in many different ways. Even though it is common for most North Americans to marry in their 20s, they do so much earlier in some other cultures. It has been common for girls especially to marry at puberty, and infant betrothals have not been unknown. How mates are chosen also varies considerably from one culture to another. As we see in this chapter, the free mate choice based on love which is common to the modern West has not been the way people in most other societies have selected their mates. The rituals connected with the wedding ceremony have been many and varied as well. What one expects from a spouse and how they get along are also areas that are heavily influenced by culture.

I examine three general topics: (1) mate selection procedures, (2) wedding customs, and (3) marital adjustment. Few, if any, areas of human activity have been invested with as much specified activity and meaning as has marriage.

MATE SELECTION PROCEDURES

Historically, there have been three general approaches to choosing one's mate: marriage by capture, marriage by arrangement, and free-choice mate selection. I examine each of them in turn.

Marriage by Capture

Although it has probably never been the usual method of obtaining a wife, men have taken women by force in many times and places. This typically occurred in patriarchal societies in which women were often considered property. Often women were seized as part of the spoils of war, and other times a specific woman was forced into marriage because the man wanted her and could not afford the brideprice or obtain the permission of her parents. The capture and marriage of a woman was legal in England until the reign of Henry VII, who made it a crime to abduct an heiress (Fielding, 1942).

The ancient Hebrews would seize wives under certain circumstances. A dramatic example is recounted in the Old Testament (Judges, chapter 21), where it was arranged for young women to be kidnaped from two different areas to serve as wives so that the tribe of Benjamin would not die out after a war that they had lost.

There was also a formal procedure for dealing with wives captured in warfare:

> When thou goest forth to war against thine enemies, and the Lord thy God hath delivered them into thine hands, and thou hast taken them captive, And seest among the captives a beautiful woman, and hast a desire unto her, that thou wouldest have her to thy wife; Then thou shalt bring her home to thine house; and she shall shave her head, and pare her nails; And she shall put the raiment of her captivity from off her, and shall remain in thine house, and bewail her father and her mother a full month: and after that thou shalt go in unto her, and be her husband, and she shall be thy wife. And it shall be, if thou have no delight in her, then thou shalt let her go whither she will; but thou shalt not sell her at all for money, thou shalt not make merchandise of her, because thou hast humbled her. (Deuteronomy 21:10–14)

At least she was given time to get used to the idea and never sold into slavery! Fielding (1942) cites a number of different cultures, including the Australian aborigines, who frequently resorted to marriage by capture in the recent past. The Yanomama of Venezuela (an Amazonian tribe) are reported (Peters, 1987) to use capture as one of their mate selection options. One village is often raided by another for the specific purpose of finding wives. If a man captures a young, attractive female, he must be careful as other men from his own village will try to steal her from him.

In the popular musical *Seven Brides for Seven Brothers,* the concept of marriage by capture is acted out, and one of the songs is based on the historical incident of the rape of the Sabine women. There are many cultures that still have remnants of the old practice of marriage by capture in their wedding ceremonies. In each of them, the match is prearranged, but the husband pretends to take his bride by force, and she feigns resistance.

One example are the Roro of New Guinea. On the wedding day, the groom's party surrounds the bride's home and acts out an assault on it. The bride attempts to run away but is caught. Then a sham battle ensues, with the bride's mother leading the way and crying at the loss of her daughter when she is taken off to the groom (Fielding, 1942).

Marriage by Arrangement

It appears that the most common method of mate selection has been by arrangement. Typically, the parents, often with the aid of certain relatives or professional matchmakers, have chosen the spouse for their child. This form of mate choice is more common when extended kin groups are strong and important. Essentially, marriage is seen as of group, rather than individual, importance, and economics is often the driving force rather than love between the principals.

Arranged marriages have been considered especially important for the rulers of kingdoms and other nobility. Care had to be taken to preserve bloodlines, enhance wealth, and resolve political issues. It is believed, for instance, that the majority of King Solomon's 700 wives and 300 concubines were acquired for the purpose of political alliances.

Stephens (1963) identifies four major considerations that determine mate choice in societies in which marriages are arranged. The first is *price*. The groom's family may need to pay for the bride, with either money or labor. In some cultures, the situation is reversed, with the bride's family paying a dowry to the husband. In other cases, there is a direct exchange, where both families make payments to each other or simply trade women for each other's sons.

The second consideration is *social status*. That is, the reputation of the family from which the spouse for one's child will come is very important. A third determinant is any *continuous marriage arrangement*. This refers to a set pattern for mate selection, which is carried on from generation to generation. For instance, cousin marriages are preferred in many societies.

The final criteria for mate choice are *sororate and levirate* arrangements, which refer to second marriages and tend to be based on brideprice obligations. These terms are more fully explained later in the chapter. Stephens also notes 19 societies (including, for example, some large ones such as China and Renaissance Europe) that have practiced child betrothals or child marriages. This means that the marriage is arranged before puberty and can even be worked out before the child is born.

In addition to marriage by capture, the Yanomama also practice variety within arranged marriages. The ideal match is between cross-cousins, and the majority of unions fall into this category. Most betrothals are made before the girl is 3 years of age. Men initiate these arrangements at about the time they become hunters, which is shortly after they turn 15. Another acceptable form of mate selection is sister exchange. Two unrelated single males wish to acquire wives and have sisters who are not promised to anyone, so they simply trade sisters (Peters, 1987).

Some societies have provided an "out" for couples who have strong personal preferences that go against the arrangement of their families. This is to permit elopement. Stephens (1963) gives this account of the Iban of Borneo:

> When a young woman is in love with a man who is not acceptable to her parents, there is an old custom called *nunghop bui*, which permits him to carry her off to his own village. She will meet him by arrangement at the waterside, and step into his boat with a paddle in her hand, and both will pull away as fast as they can. If pursued he will stop every now and then to deposit some article of value on the bank, such as a gun, a jar, or a favor for the acceptance of her family, and when he has exhausted his resources he will leave his own sword. When the pursuers observe this they cease to follow, knowing he is cleared out. As soon as he reaches his own village he tidies up the house and spreads the mats, and when his pursuers arrive he gives them food to eat and toddy to drink, and sends them home satisfied. In the meanwhile he is left in possession of his wife. (p. 200)

Following is a detailed look at some of the specific mechanisms of arranged marriages.

Brideprice

Throughout much of human history, marriage has been seen as chiefly an economic transaction. As an old German saying goes, "It is not man that marries maid, but field marries field, vineyard marries vineyard, cattle marry cattle" (Tober, 1984, p. 12). The purpose of a brideprice is to compensate the family of the bride for the loss of her services. It is extremely common and is indicative of the value of women in those societies. Stephens (1963) reports that Murdock's World Ethnographic Sample yields the following breakdown on marriage payments:

Brideprice—260 societies
Bride service—75 societies
Dowry—24 societies
Gift or woman exchange—31 societies
No marriage payment—152 societies

This means that in 62% of the world's societies, a man must pay in order to marry a woman. The price is usually paid in animals, shell money, or other valuable commodities and often exceeds one's annual income. Some cultures prefer payment in service, often many years of labor to the bride's parents, or at least permit it for suitors who cannot afford to pay in goods. One famous example from the Old Testament is that of Jacob, who labored 7 years for each of Laban's two daughters, Leah and Rachel.

Dowry

The dowry appears to be an inducement for a man to marry a particular woman and therefore relieve her family of the financial burden of caring for her. Although relatively rare, it is a sign of a culture that places a low value on women. Actually, the key purpose of a dowry is probably to stabilize a marriage, because it is not given to the husband but is something that the bride brings with her into the marriage. For example, in Cyprus before the time of English influence, the expected dowry was often a house. If the husband divorced his wife or mistreated her and she left him, the dowry went with her. Like modern-day wedding gifts, or the bride's trousseau, it was an investment in the marriage and intended to reduce the chances of a breakup (Balswick, 1975).

The dowry has been around for a long time. The Babylonian code of Hammurabi (1955 B.C.) clearly stated that the wife's property stayed with her if her husband divorced her and passed on to her children when she died. Ancient Greece and Rome also considered the dowry to be essential in any honorable marriage (Fielding, 1942).

Recent research in the southern Indian state of Kerala (Billig, 1992) differentiates between the traditional dowry and an actual "groomprice." Groomprice is money paid by the bride's family directly to the husband to use as he sees fit. In the 1950s and 1960s, rapid population growth resulted in more younger women looking for husbands a few (average of 7) years older than themselves. This surplus of potential brides increased the value of husbands. Popular revulsion for the groomprice has resulted in a decrease in the age difference (now 5 years), women lowering their social status expectations for their husband or increasing their own education, and a government outlawing of the practice.

Sororate and Levirate

These terms refer to marriage practices designed to control remarriages after the death of the first spouse. In cultures that practice the sororate, a sister replaces a deceased wife. Assume that a man has paid a good brideprice for his wife but some time later she becomes ill and dies. He has lost his wife and the brideprice. Therefore, to make good on the original bargain, the parents who received the brideprice provide the man with a new wife. This new wife is an unmarried sister or other close relative of the first wife. Here we see how marriage is often more of an economic transaction than it is a personal relationship.

Much more widely practiced has been the levirate. Under this system, it is the husband who dies, and his wife must be married to a brother of the deceased man. There are various reasons for this practice. One is that the wife belonged to her husband as part of his property and as such would be inherited along with the other possessions by a near relative. Another is that it is presumed that women need someone to take care of them, and brothers-in-law (which is the meaning of the Latin word *levir*) should assume that responsibility. It has been reported that the levirate has been practiced by the New Caledonians, the Mongols, the Afghans, the Abyssinians, the Hebrews, and the Hindus, as well as certain Native American and African tribes (Fielding, 1942).

The chief reason that the Hindus and Hebrews practiced the levirate was religious and had to do with the importance of having a son in the family. Hindu men needed a son to perform certain sacrifices, so if a man died before having one, a boy born to his former wife and brother would carry out those ceremonies in his name (Fielding, 1942).

For the Hebrews, it was also important that every man have a son, so that his name would not die out. There was a ritualized penalty for men who refused to marry their brother's widow and rear a son in his name:

> And if the man like not to take his brother's wife, then let his brother's wife go up to the gate unto the elders, and say, My husband's brother refuseth to raise up unto his brother a name in Israel, he will not perform the duty of my husband's brother. Then the elders of his city shall call him, and speak unto him: and if he stand to it, and say, I like not to take her; Then shall his brother's wife come in to him in the presence of the elders, and loose his shoe from off his foot, and spit in his face, and shall answer and say, So shall it be done unto that man that will not build up his brother's house. (Deuteronomy 25:7–9)

The punishment for refusing to practice the levirate used to be more severe than the above-quoted ritual. In Genesis, chapter 38, we read of Judah's son Onan and how he was killed by the Lord for refusing to impregnate his dead older brother's wife. The book of Ruth in the Old Testament is also an excellent example of how the levirate worked. It is an account of how Naomi has no more sons for her daughter-in-law Ruth to marry, so she arranges for another male relative, Boaz, to take on the responsibility.

Matchmaking

There are various ways in which two young people can be brought together. Typically, the parents of both boys and girls will work out the details among themselves and then announce it to their children. The initial go-between in Turkey has been the boy's mother, who would inspect possibilities at the public baths and then give reports to her son (Tober, 1984). The popular musical *Fiddler on the Roof* is about father-arranged marriages. Often, hired go-betweens, or matchmakers, assist in making the arrangement. They might act as intermediaries between the families or suggest potential spouses. Checking for astrological or other religious signs and requirements could also be part of their job.

In the 1800s, bachelor pioneers in the American West would sometimes find a wife by ordering one from a mail-order catalog. Even today, many Asian families publish matrimonial want ads in search of a respectable spouse for their child (Tober, 1984). I recently found the following in the classified section of a Philippine newspaper:

> FOREIGNERS: video match a decent friendship marriage consultant office introducing a beautiful single educated Filipina view friendship to marriage.

> LADIES: Australian European businessmen newly arrive in town sincerely willing to meet decent Filipina view friendship to marriage. Ambassador Hotel suite 216.

Computer dating services in the United States, Japan, and elsewhere manifest the continued utility of professional matchmaking, even in societies in which the individuals involved make the final decisions themselves. There are also magazines designed for singles that include matrimonial or relationship want ads.

There are immigrants to Western societies who are not comfortable with love-based unions and prefer to have their marriages arranged by their parents or through a mediator. It is estimated, for instance, that up to 90% of the marriages in the East Indian community in Edmonton, Alberta, are to some degree arranged (Jimenez, 1992). Some ethnic Indians return to the Indian subcontinent to find a spouse, whereas others allow their parents to find a match locally for them. Some place ads in newspapers such as *India Today* or *India Abroad*, which focus on desired background characteristics such as education, religion, and age. In deference to Western customs, the young people can veto any match that does not appeal to them, and a dowry is rarely accepted.

Free-Choice Mate Selection

As noted in Chapter 2, love gradually became the principal criterion for marriage in the Western world after the Renaissance. The shift from kinship and economic motives to personal ones in mate selection led to the conclusion that the individuals themselves, rather than their parents or others, were best qualified to make the decision. In societies in which the basic family unit is nuclear, both romantic love and free mate choice are more common. This is because extended kin groups are not important enough to see marriage as needing to be group controlled.

Even though free choice is the mate selection method of the modern United States, one should not conclude that it is the most common approach in the world. In a survey of 40 societies, Stephens (1963) found only 5 in which completely free mate choice is permitted. An additional 6 allowed the young people to choose their spouse, but subject to parental approval. Twelve other cultures had a mix of arranged marriages and free-choice (usually subject to approval) unions, and the final 16 allowed only arranged marriages.

Moreover, even free choice does not mean that one can marry anyone. All societies have marital regulations. The rule of *exogamy* declares that a person must marry outside his/her group. Typically, this means that certain relatives are unavailable as marriage partners. Exogamous rules are generally the same as the incest taboos of the society, which prohibit sexual intercourse between close blood relatives. Others go beyond that, however. In classical China, two people with the same surname could not marry even if there was no kinship relation (Hutter, 1981).

The rule of *endogamy* declares that a person must marry within his/her group. This rule applies social pressure to marry someone who is similar to oneself in important ways, including religion, race, or ethnic group; social class; and age. These factors have been found to be related to marital compatibility and are precisely the kinds of things considered by parents in arranged marriages. One reason why the divorce rate seems to be higher in free-choice societies may be that many couples ignore endogamy issues and allow romantic love to be practically the sole consideration in mate selection. There is a tendency for marriages to be fairly homogamous, however, even in free-mate-choice societies.

A final factor is *propinquity* (geographical nearness). It is, of course, impossible to marry someone who lives so far away from you that you never meet. At another level, however, this principle refers to a human tendency to be friends with people with whom it is convenient to interact. Let us say that you leave your hometown to attend college elsewhere. You left a boyfriend or girlfriend back at home and you also meet someone new at college. All other things being equal, which one will you marry? Generally, it will be the one at school simply because it is easier.

Some Examples

Free mate choice is on the rise in China today. However, it is very different from the courtship pattern in North America. Young people gather information about each other first and check for mutual suitability before going public with their relationship. In fact, dating follows, rather than precedes, the decision to marry. Typically, the couple knows each other for well over 2 years before marrying. This cautious approach is paying off, as the quality of these marriages seems to be higher than that of arranged unions (Liao & Heaton, 1992).

The Igbo are a people living in present-day Nigeria (Okonjo, 1992). About 55% of the Igbo have their marriages arranged, while the remaining 45% are in free-choice unions. Most of the latter are younger, indicating a move from arranged to free choice, which we see occurring throughout much of the world today. Regardless of type, premarital chastity is very highly valued among the Igbo.

As the Igbo move to free mate choice based on love, their various arranged practices are falling into disfavor. Customs that are quickly disappearing include *woman-to-woman* marriage. In this situation, an older childless woman pays the brideprice to marry a younger female, usually a cousin. A male mate is chosen for the "wife" to have children with, but they belong to the older female spouse, who has the legal role of "husband."

Another way of securing an heir is *father-to-daughter* marriage. If a man has no sons, he may prohibit a daughter from marrying. She has children from a male mate (not the father) but her sons are considered her father's. Women whose husbands turn out to be impotent are allowed to have a lover from whom to have children, who are considered to be the legal husband's. Other arranged practices seldom practiced anymore are the levirate and child marriages.

Courtship and Sex

One final issue in the area of mate selection is premarital sexuality in courtship. There is considerable variation across cultures concerning the acceptability of premarital sexual relations. Most are fairly permissive, however. Of 863 societies in Murdock's Ethnographic Atlas, 67% impose little restriction on premarital sex. The largest proportion of permissive societies are found in Pacific regions, and the most restrictive are the Arab and Muslim nations (Wen-Shing & Jing, 1991).

In the Marshalls of Micronesia, sexual activity begins around puberty. It is common to have many different partners, to cohabit with a few, and eventually to marry a more permanent mate. There is no stigma to being an illegitimate child or an unwed mother, and having children does not seem to reduce a woman's chances of finding a future mate (Wen-Shing & Jing, 1991). In this culture, sexuality is just seen as part of life, with no special taboos or significance attached to it.

The Hopi also included sexuality as part of their courtship procedure. A girl was allowed to receive suitors in her late adolescence. The boys would sneak into her house at night and sleep with her, and the parents would pretend not to notice if he was considered a good marriage prospect. Eventually, she would become pregnant and then select her favorite lover as her husband. The families involved would then arrange the marriage. As a result, a Hopi boy would never have intercourse with a girl whom he was not willing to marry (Queen, Habenstein, & Quadagno, 1985).

In the United States today, one estimate is that about 80% of college men and 63% of women in college have had premarital intercourse (Kephart & Jedlicka, 1991). The "sexual revolution" of the 1960s and 1970s had a major impact on premarital behavior: In the 1930s, only 15% of U.S. women had experienced premarital coitus. In spite of fairly high rates of sexual experience, there is still widespread disapproval of premarital coitus in U.S. society. In comparison, other Western countries appear to be more relaxed about it. Much of today's caution has to do with the dangers associated with sexually transmitted diseases and unwanted pregnancies.

WEDDING CUSTOMS

There are many rituals and practices that occur in connection with the act of getting married. Contemporary couples typically participate in many of these without giving much thought to what they might mean and why they are being done. My purpose here is to provide some insight into the depth and richness of marriage by recounting some of the principal Western wedding customs along with their history and meaning. Unless otherwise noted, the following information comes from Chesser (1980) or Tober (1984).

The Ring

This may be the oldest and most universal symbol of marriage. Some ancient peoples used to break a coin in half, with each partner taking one piece. The idea of this love match is still found in today's necklace jewelry. This practice may have evolved into wearing rings, which we know were used by ancient Egyptians, Greeks, and Romans.

The right hand is considered to be dominant over the left, and originally men wore the engagement ring as a symbol of their control of the relationship. When women began wearing engagement and wedding rings they were moved to the left hand as a sign of submission. Another possible theory is that the ring should be worn on the fourth finger of the left hand because there is a vein in that finger that runs straight to the heart. The *vena amoris* does not exist but is still a logical place for jewelry as it is probably the finger least used in daily activity (Fielding, 1942).

The ring's shape is indicative of never-ending love, and in the 17th century, social pressure led to the preference of gold as the material because it does not tarnish. The ring gains even greater symbolism with the inclusion of a precious stone. The clarity and durability of the diamond make it the most popular, as does the idea that it represents innocence. Other stones have been assigned special meaning as well. For instance, the emerald promises domestic bliss, and the ruby is a sign of love. Its red color is also supposed to have the power to ward of evil spirits.

Setting the Date

One important decision that a couple must make is when to marry. Today, convenience seems to be the determining factor. However, many cultures and religions have had beliefs about good and bad luck times of the year for marrying, and much effort was often expended to set the date at a time when the gods, or stars, would smile on the new couple. For example, January is a good-luck month because the Greeks dedicated it to Hera, a goddess of fertility. February and March are bad for Catholic and Orthodox adherents because one should give up good things during Lent. The folklore says, "Marry in Lent, live to repent."

April is considered to be a good month since springtime is illustrative of the reproduction wished on the new couple. May is not so good since Catholics dedicate the month to the Virgin Mary, the patron saint of chastity.

July and August are inconvenient times for farmers, who need to be getting the harvest in. The Irish believed that "they that wive between sickle and scythe shall never thrive."

The autumn months are considered to be good times to marry because of the connection between harvest and fertility and because of good astrological signs. December, finally, is a bad-luck month due to the British belief that "you always repent of marriage before the year is out."

Candles

Another symbol of love are candles. Apparently an evolution from the Roman torches used to light the way of the wedding procession, one popular ritual today is to have a large candle representing God's love used to light two other candles, which stand for the couple getting married.

The Bridal Veil

Many cultures believe in the "evil eye," where one can be made ill by the covetous stares of powerful individuals. The veil, then, is designed to protect the bride from the evil spirits that might attend all the looking at she is certain to get. The Romans preferred that the veil be red, as that is the most effective color for warding off evil.

The Wedding Gown

Most people are aware that a white gown is intended to represent the bride's virginity, a guarantee that groom's expected from her family. This rhyme tells us of some attitudes toward bridal gown colors:

> Married in red, wish yourself dead;
> Married in black, wish yourself back;
> Married in blue, you'll always be true;
> Married in green, ashamed to be seen;
> Married in grey, go far away;
> Married in brown, live out of town;
> Married in white, chosen all right.

Children

The purpose of including children in the wedding party (today's flower girl and ring bearer) is to serve as a visible encouragement for the age-old purpose of marriage: fertility.

The Kiss

Although not a legal requirement, the kiss historically sealed the wedding vow. Whereas wedding participants prefer to do their own kissing today, the priest used to give the groom the "kiss of peace" and then he would kiss his bride. The priest assistants would then kiss all the wedding guests.

The Wedding Cake

There are many superstitions surrounding this important centerpiece of most receptions. Often multitiered and decorated with hearts, lovebirds, and flowers, small figures of the bride and groom often adorn the top. It is considered bad luck for a bride to bake her own cake, or to taste it before it is formally cut. If a section is saved, however, it will perpetuate the couple's love.

The cake is actually another symbol of fertility and used to be broken over the bride's head. It was believed that cutting the cake would magically facilitate the breaking of the bride's hymen, or maidenhead, and thereby aid in the birth of the first child. We have since developed the less messy custom of throwing rice (also representative of fruitfulness) or other materials on the couple.

Attendants

The bridesmaids and groom's attendants appear to be remnants of the marriage by capture sometimes practiced. The bride had women trying to protect her from capture, while the groom had his friends to assist him in the assault (Fielding, 1942).

Flowers

In the Middle Ages, the wealthy adorned themselves with their finest jewelry. Peasant brides could not afford such things, so they imitated the practice by using flowers. Flowers have since assumed a place of prominence in wedding plans with a bouquet for the bride, corsages for others, and floral arrangements throughout the room. Modern selections are based on personal preference but originally some had special significance. One favorite, the orange blossom, meant fruitfulness.

Talismans

There are various good-luck articles that superstition dictates a bride should work into her wedding clothes. A penny in your shoe is supposed to guarantee a lifetime of good fortune. A family heirloom, "something old," gives a sense of continuity from one generation to the next. "Something new," as most of the bride's clothes will be, puts things on an optimistic note. "Something borrowed," usually from a happily married friend, is based on the idea that happiness rubs off. "Something blue" is a symbol of fidelity.

Throwing the Garter and Bouquet

The person who catches these objects is to be the next to marry. Custom dictates that when throwing her bouquet, the bride not face her girlfriends, so that the bouquet cannot be directed into the hands of a favorite. Throwing the garter comes from an old English custom, "flinging the stocking." Guests would invade the bridal chamber and the women would take the groom's stockings while the men grabbed the bride's. They would take turns throwing them, and whoever tossed the one that landed on the bride or groom's nose was the next to marry. By the 1500s, the bride's garter was so highly prized that guests would rush her at the altar trying to get it. In self-preservation, she began to take it off and her husband would throw it out to the unmarried males.

Evil Spirits

It has been a common religious belief that malicious spirits are attracted to weddings due to their sacred nature. As a result, many diversions are used to throw them off of the bride's trail. Car decorating, noise making, and following the couple as they leave for their honeymoon are all to frighten the devil away from the newlywed couple. Carrying the bride over the threshold is to shake off demons who have been following along the soles of her feet. Finally, sprinkling holy water on the marriage bed is intended to drive off spirits who are attracted to the sexual act.

The Honeymoon

Honey refers to mead, an alcoholic drink made from fermented honey, and moon refers to the lunar month. Essentially, it indicates a time in which the new couple should be free from the cares of the world and allowed to get to know each other. Its central purpose has been the consummation of the marriage.

In many European and Mediterranean cultures it has been very important that the bride be found to be a virgin. Proof of this would be that she would bleed from first intercourse, and the stained bedsheet might be hung from a window the following morning as evidence to all of her purity and the proper consummation of the new union.

MARITAL ADJUSTMENT

The last topic for investigation in this chapter is the quality of the marriage relationship itself. I shift from a structural–functional focus to a developmental one for this section. This shift will allow us to see how marital concerns can change and be influenced by the stages in the life cycle through which the couple progresses. This information on cross-cultural variation comes from Wen-Shing and Jing (1991).

Intimacy

How one would assess the quality of one's marriage depends on what is expected in a marriage relationship. In the United States and Canada today, the emphasis is on psychological intimacy and emotional sharing, in addition to task performance. That is, one's satisfaction is influenced by whether or not the spouse acts in hoped for ways in the areas of child care, housekeeping, economic support, and sexual activity. Certain negative behaviors, such as gambling, abuse, drug use, and infidelity, can present major threats to marital stability and happiness.

However, what many Westerners want the most, especially women, is a deep and close friendship. The more couples express their feelings to each other, the better the marriage tends to be (Ingoldsby, 1984). The traditional marriage of times past in which each spouse performed the expected tasks would be considered hollow by today's standards. The happiest marriages appear to be those couples who know each other well and enjoy doing things together.

Expected closeness varies by culture, however. For instance, the Japanese family tends to have a very clear sexual division of labor. The husband has his work and associates with his colleagues there. He does not participate in child care or housework and is fairly unaware of how his wife and children spend their time. They also know little about his life. It is not considered wise to overload a single relationship with too many concerns, so adults have various friends and relatives in whom they confide.

In the United States and Germany, research indicates that husbands and wives are significantly more involved in each other's lives. Husbands are home more often and interact more in each other's social lives. Confiding in others about their marital relationship is likely to be considered a betrayal rather than a wise action.

The tolerance of extramarital affairs varies greatly among different societies. Conservative cultures consider it unforgivable and a principal rationale for divorce. In others there is a double standard. In the Philippines, for instance, extramarital sex is not tolerated in the wife but it is acceptable *macho* (see Ingoldsby, Chapter 15, this volume) behavior for husbands to have many lovers. The Toda, discussed in Chapter 6 (Ingoldsby, this volume), consider affairs for either sex to be natural and not a cause for concern. In Micronesia, there is a long postpartum sex taboo, and extramarital behavior on the husband's part is considered to be frequent.

Stress

There are many events that are stressful to family functioning. Some are unexpected, such as certain disasters, illnesses, or work-related conflicts. Others are more normative, which include the life-cycle stresses expected from parenthood, children leaving home, retirement, and widowhood.

Certain types of stresses are more important in some cultures than they are in others, however. For example, Nigerian families consider procreation to be very important in marriage. Fertility is a blessing and barrenness is a curse. Infertility can be a major source of conflict and unhappiness for many Nigerian couples as a result.

In Korea, it is still considered important that married women be housewives and not work outside the home. Many young women are well educated but fewer than 15% have jobs. Modernization has made housework easier and more monotonous, and as a result many Korean housewives are developing neurotic symptoms in response to their unfullfilling life-style. It is common enough that psychiatrists have labeled this phenomenon the "housewife syndrome."

Finally, household structure can have an impact on how stress is experienced. In extended families, there are other family members to provide a buffer when there is conflict in a couple relationship. These other members can give psychological as well as economic support. However, extended families have interpersonal conflicts that are less likely to occur when the households are nuclear. Problems are most likely to erupt between the wives of brothers and between mothers-in-law and daughters-in-law over issues of household duties and power structure. Most young couples would prefer to establish their own nuclear family if they could.

Life-Cycle Issues

Each phase of the marital life cycle has its own unique challenges, which may be viewed differently from one society to the next. In the "marriage establishment phase," the couple must replace fantasy with reality and make the adjustments necessary for living with another person. Each spouse has his/her own ideas about how family life should be, and these adjustments are even more complicated when we enter a large or extended family system. Many cultures are patrilocal, requiring the bride to move in with and be subject to her in-laws. There are many stories of the hardships endured by these young wives when they lose the support of her own family of origin.

There are various interactive patterns a couple might develop. The dominant–submissive pattern is common. One spouse controlling the other is considered dysfunctional in many societies, but a dominant husband and submissive wife would be seen as not only normal but even ideal in a patriarchal culture. Another pattern is the "obsessional husband and the hysterical wife." In this one, the husband is intellectual and emotionally distant and the wife complains about his being cold and uninvolved. Whereas Western clinicians would consider this to be a mismatch, a couple in Japan would not be likely to be labeled dysfunctional.

In the "childbearing and childrearing phases," couples deal with fertility and child socialization. In some cultures, having large families or having children of a certain sex is more important than it is in others. Asian cultures are most likely to value having sons over having daughters. Not meeting those societal expectations can result in anxiety and conflict for the couple.

It is not uncommon for husbands and wives to disagree on how children should be reared and disciplined. Cultures also differ on whether the focus of childhood should be enjoyment or learning through hardship. These differences will be even more difficult if the husband and wife come from different cultures and bring with them the conflicting approaches of their society. For instance, a husband of Hawaiian heritage may feel that children should be quiet at mealtime, and that physical punishment is the best approach for discipline. A wife from the mainland United States is likely to feel that dinner time should include discussions between parents and children, and that striking children is abusive.

In the "empty-nest phase," the couple must get used to having their children leave home and being alone again. The impact of this would be much less in extended families, where there are always others around, and to which many married children return. In nuclear families, as children leave and workers retire, the couple may need to reestablish their relationship. This could be especially difficult for those couples that had separate life activities. In Japanese families, for instance, the retired husband has lost his social network and has no involvement in his wife's activities. Some couples consider divorce once the children are gone and they see that they have little to keep them together.

"Widowhood" is the final phase. Generally women are most likely to outlive their husbands, and how they deal with that loss depends to some degree on culture. Traditional Hindu society is very hard on widows. No matter how young she may be, a widow is expected never to remarry and to live a life of seclusion, interacting only with close family members.

The matrilineal Trobriand Islanders have highly structured mourning rituals followed by a seclusion for the widow for a time between 6 months and 2 years. After that, she puts on a gaily decorated outfit and after some ceremonial dancing is allowed to remarry. Evidence indicates that societies that see death as natural and provide grieving ceremonies and family support—such as the Samoans—find widowhood less painful than do those that are uncomfortable with it and ignore the subject as much as possible (e.g., in the United States).

CONCLUSION

This chapter has examined mate selection practices that have been common throughout the world. Although largely an economic or political transaction beyond the control of the couple themselves, it is becoming in modern times a free-choice situation based on affection.

The wedding day is often considered to be the most important day in a person's life. There are many customs and rituals associated with getting married, many with deep meaning unknown to today's couples. I have tried to analyze some of the principal ones. Finally, I have discussed some of the major influences on marital adjustment and how these influence can differ by culture.

REFERENCES

Balswick, J. (1975). The function of the dowry system in a rapidly modernizing society: The case of Cyprus. *International Journal of Sociology and the Family, 5*(2), 158–167.

Billig, M. (1992). The marriage squeeze and the rise of groomprice in India's Kerala state. *Journal of Comparative Family Studies, 23*(2), 197–216.

Chesser, B. (1980). Analysis of wedding rituals: An attempt to make weddings more meaningful. *Family Relations, 29*(2), 204–209.

Fielding, W. (1942). *Strange customs of courtship and marriage.* New York: New Home Library.

The Holy Bible. King James Version.

Hutter, M. (1981). *The changing family: Comparative perspectives.* New York: Wiley.

Ingoldsby, B. (1984). Emotional expressiveness and marital satisfaction: A cross-cultural analysis. *Journal of Comparative Family Studies, 11*(4), 501–515.

Jimenez, M. (1992, July 26). Many Indo-Canadians follow age-old custom. *The Edmonton Journal,* p. B3.

Kephart, W., & Jedlicka, D. (1991). *The family, society, and the individual.* New York: HarperCollins.

Liao, C., & Heaton, T. (1992). Divorce trends and differentials in China. *Journal of Comparative Family Studies, 23*(3), 413–429.

Okonjo, K. (1992). Aspects of continuity and change in mate-selection among the Igbo west of the river Niger. *Journal of Comparative Family Studies, 23*(3), 339–360.

Peters, J. (1987). Yanomama mate selection and marriage. *Journal of Comparative Family Studies, 18*(1), 79–98.

Queen, S., Habenstein, R., & Quadagno, J. (1985). *The family in various cultures.* New York: Harper & Row.

Stephens, W. (1963). *The family in cross-cultural perspective.* New York: Holt, Rinehart & Winston.

Tober, B. (1984). *The bride: A celebration.* New York: Harry N. Abrams.

Wells, J. (1991). *Choices in marriage and family.* San Diego: Collegiate Press.

Wen-Shing, T., & Jing, H. (1991). *Culture and family: Problems and therapy.* New York: Haworth Press.

CHAPTER EIGHT

Parents' Socialization
of Children

D. TERRI HEATH

Students interested in cross-cultural research learn quickly that there are more similarities than differences in the experience of parenthood for people of different countries. Worldwide, parents have for centuries been responsible for the socialization of their children. Although it is true that parents receive assistance from others (e.g., extended family, neighbors, and professional caregivers) in fulfilling these obligations, societies throughout the world charge parents with the primary protection, socialization, and nurturance of the children they bear or adopt. Communities mandate these obligations out of a belief that parents are the most suitable adults to rear the children they bear. Parents are assigned legal responsibility to raise their children to be productive, responsible adults in accordance with the expectations of each particular community.

This chapter presents research and discussion of three influences of parents on children predominantly from a "social mold" perspective. This perspective was chosen because the cross-cultural research that exists in the area of parent–child relationships is largely driven by this theoretical framework. However, this lack of variety in approaches is a weakness in the literature that should be remedied by future comparative researchers, researchers whose new approaches and fresh insights will, it is hoped, include tests of additional theoretical perspectives.

The three parental influences presented in this chapter—(1) styles of parenting, (2) parental class status, and (3) closeness with parents—were chosen for inclusion here because each has demonstrated a significant impact on the academic achievement, psychological well-being, substance use and juvenile delinquency, and general behavior of children worldwide. By selecting literature from those cross-cultural studies that have been published since

161

1988, this chapter presents the most current research on cross-cultural parenting influences. In each of the three sections, the cross-cultural research is preceded by presentations of theoretical foundations which serve to describe how parents influence their children. The cross-cultural research that follows illustrates these influences.

As we will see, one limitation of this chapter is that only a few examples from developing countries are presented here. This is not because they were deemed unimportant but, rather, because they were unavailable. Research requires significant financial support, support that is rarely available in developing countries and more often used by researchers in developed countries to study their own cultures. As developing countries acquire economic resources for sponsorship of research in their own communities, and as researchers of European, North American, and other developed countries elect to invest more of their financial resources in cross-cultural research, future presentations of cross-cultural family research are likely to be more balanced.

COMPONENTS OF PARENTING STYLES: CONTROL, SUPPORT, AND POWER

Few areas of research on parent–child relationships have received more attention than parents' childrearing styles. Researchers seem fascinated by both the variety of childrearing behaviors among parents and the effects of these behaviors on children. Social mold theorists have long argued that parents influence their children's behavior through three main categories: control, support, and power. Parental control includes (1) the rules set by parents for appropriate child behavior, (2) specific actions used by parents to influence child behavior, and (3) the final results of the parents' attempts at control (i.e., whether the parental behavior achieved the desired results) (Peterson & Rollins, 1987) and is a combination of three subdimensions: coercion (the exertion of considerable psychological or physical force to secure a child's compliance in behavior), love withdrawal (indicating disapproval by ignoring or rejecting the child until the behavior is changed), and induction (avoiding a contest of wills by explaining the consequences of a child's behavior to secure voluntary compliance by the child) (Rollins & Thomas, 1979).

Parental support is the verbal and nonverbal encouragement parents give children to reinforce valued and appropriate behavior. The purpose of parental support is to validate particular behaviors, which strengthens the parent–child bond and enhances the child's self-image. A variety of terms have been used to describe the unitary dimension of parental support, including warmth, affection, nurturance, and acceptance (Peterson & Leigh, 1990; Peterson & Rollins, 1987). However, more recent studies have identified subdimensions of parental support: general support (dependability, trust, shared interests), companionship (shared activities and time, conversations together), sustained contact (holding child for safety or fun), and physical affection (kissing and hugging) (Barber & Thomas, 1986).

Parental power is the *potential* power parents have to influence the behavior of their child in another direction from the child's own desires (Hoffman, 1960). The greater the parent's power, the more likely the child will comply with the wishes of the parent. However, potential is an important concept here because although the parent may not choose to actually exercise this power, its very existence is the source of the parent's ability to influence the child's behavior. A parent's power originates in four areas. Reward power and coercive power refer to a parent's ability to use either rewards or punishments to encourage modifications in a child's behavior to more closely align with the parent's desires. Expert power and legitimate power refer to a parent's special knowledge and mandated authority, respectively. Parents use expert power when they teach their child a particular skill such as riding a bike or harvesting a local crop. They use legitimate power when they arrange a marriage or demand that their child attends school. Each of these four sources of power is a resource enabling parents to evoke behavior from their children that the parents deem desirable (French & Raven, 1959, cited in Rollins & Thomas, 1979).

Influence of Components on Child Characteristics

It has become increasingly apparent that different combinations and varying degrees of parental control, support, and power are predictive of specific child outcomes. This section, based on the comprehensive literature review by Rollins and Thomas (1979) and a variety of related studies since 1979, describes the relationships between these three components (parental control, support, and power) and the child outcomes of cognitive development, academic achievement, creativity, moral behavior, internal locus of control, self-esteem, drug and alcohol abuse, and general social competence. Most of the study designs discussed here have not included specific subdimensions of parental support. Consequently, parental support is most often reported here as a general dimension. More researchers have examined specific subdimensions of control (most often coercion and induction). Therefore, this chapter presents a more detailed examination of the subdimensions of control than those of support. Although there are a minority of documented exceptions to what is described here, this section presents the most commonly found relationships between these three parenting style components and the selected child outcomes in the current research literature.

In general, it appears that high levels of parental support enhance cognitive development in both sons and daughters. When parents use high levels of control, and specifically coercive methods of control, children demonstrate lower levels of cognitive development (Rollins & Thomas, 1979). But these influences on cognitive development do not parallel the influences on academic achievement according to a review of studies by Rollins and Thomas. Most studies have found that daughters demonstrate greater academic achievement when parents are less supportive and more controlling. This may be because these daughters feel more challenged and less dependent, and are therefore more persistent and competitive in their studies. However, a more recent study of urban ghetto black youth in the United States has challenged this notion for girls. In this study, low-income girls actually excelled in academic pursuits when parents exhibited high levels of both support and control. The researchers speculated that the ghetto environment itself fostered the toughness and assertiveness required for girls to be competitive in school (Clark, 1983). Academic achievement for sons, whether low or middle income, seems to be highest when parents use high levels of both control and support (Clark, 1983; Rollins & Thomas, 1979).

Creativity is fostered by low to moderate parental support but appears to decrease when parental support is moderate to high. General parental control does not appear to influence creativity in either direction. However, when specific subdimensions of control are examined, the pattern is more clear. Coercive methods of control are associated with less creativity in a child, and inductive methods are associated with more creativity. This may be the result of the mediating variable of stress which appears to play a significant role. A low to moderate level of stress, fostered by inductive methods of control, is associated with greater creativity, possibly because it acts as a motivator. But coercive methods are more often associated with greater levels of stress that appear to inhibit creativity (Rollins & Thomas, 1979).

Of great concern to many parents is the moral behavior of their children. Moral behavior is associated with greater levels of support, general control, and specifically, inductive methods of control. High levels of parental coercion are associated with lower levels of moral behavior in children. In a related area, helping children develop an internal locus of control (feelings of internal power and the ability to control one's life rather than be controlled by fate) is associated with high levels of parental support and inductive methods of control. High levels of coercion are associated with low levels of internal locus of control (Rollins & Thomas, 1979), most likely because coercive methods of control rely on the use of external pressure. Induction relies on internal pressure, which is more closely associated with the internal power of an internal locus of control.

Self-esteem follows a similar pattern to that of an internal locus of control. High levels of parental support and general control, specifically inductive methods of control, are all associated with greater self-esteem in children. High levels of coercion are associated with lower self-esteem (Rollins & Thomas, 1979). In examining the subdimensions of support, self-esteem in daughters appears to be associated with high levels of mother's general support and father's physical affection (Barber & Thomas, 1986) and the general support and participation (time spent in activities) of both mothers and fathers (Gecas & Schwalbe, 1986). The self-esteem of sons is associated with mother's companionship and father's sustained contact (Barber & Thomas, 1986) and parental, especially paternal, control (Gecas & Schwalbe, 1986).

Drug and alcohol abuse among adolescents also appears to be associated with particular levels of parental control and support. High levels of support from both mothers and fathers are associated with less alcohol abuse in adolescents. Low and moderate levels of control act in a similar fashion— less abuse—especially when combined with high levels of parental support. Adolescents who are heavy users of alcohol often have parents who use low levels of support and high levels of control in their childrearing (Barnes, Farrell, & Cairns, 1986).

Social competence in children and adolescents has been the focus of much research attention in the last two decades. The ability to foster social competence in children is a critically important skill for parents as they socialize their children for success in school, work, and the social world. Parents who exhibit high levels of support and inductive methods of control have children and adolescents who are socially competent. Socially incompetent children and adolescents most often have parents who exhibit high levels of coercive control and low levels of support (Rollins & Thomas, 1979). Parental power also influences several subdimensions of social competence: conformity to parents, identification with parents, and autonomy in reference to parents (Henry, Wilson, & Peterson, 1989; McDonald, 1977, 1979, 1980; Peterson, Rollins, & Thomas, 1985; Smith, 1970, 1983, 1986). Specifically, adolescents are more responsive and conforming to parents, who they perceive to have power: power to deliver advice and information (expert power), power to give positive reinforcements (reward power) or negative ones (coercive power), and power to exercise community sanctioned authority (legitimate power) (Peterson & Leigh, 1990).

In summation, high levels of support, specifically physical affection, have demonstrated positive outcomes in every area described here except academic achievement for middle-class girls. Second, inductive methods of control are more often linked to positive outcomes in children and adolescents than are coercive methods. Third, perceptions by youth of parental power are associated with high levels of conformity and identification with parents.

One cautionary note is important here, however. Even though much of the research in this area is based on how parents "cause" or influence behaviors in their children by their own actions, this may simply be the result of our overreliance on the social mold perspective. The social mold perspective in the research literature is plagued with cross-sectional and correlational designs that fail to reveal the direction of influence in families. For example, children and adolescents who demonstrate prosocial behavior that pleases a parent may elicit a supportive behavior from the parent. In this situation, it is a child-initiated interaction rather than one directed by the parent that is responsible for the association between parental support and social competence in children. Adults may be the reactors here, not the directors, as social mold theorists have contended (Peterson & Leigh, 1990).

A Typology of Parenting Styles

The particular balance of these three components (control, power, and support) reflects the childrearing style of the parent. This area of research was energized by Baumrind's (1966) categorization of childrearing into authoritative, permissive, and authoritarian parenting styles and their associated influences on children. *Authoritative* parents are firm in their limits but warm and nurturing in their approach. They explain their reasons for their actions, encourage parent–child discussions about problems, and are responsive to their children's needs. They recognize their own power as parents and use this power to gain compliance in their children if reasoning is ineffective. The children of authoritative parents are usually self-reliant, self-controlled, cheerful, cooperative with adults, achievement oriented, and friendly with peers.

Permissive parents avoid supervision and control of their children either by not establishing standards of acceptable behavior for their children or by setting standards that are lower than their children's capabilities. They are accepting of their children and consult with them on family matters. They encourage autonomy, use reasoning, and are rarely punitive. Permissive parents may either indulge or ignore their children's needs. The children of permissive parents are usually aggressive, aimless, domineering, lacking in self-control and self-reliance, and noncompliant with adults.

Authoritarian parents demand obedience from their children, impose and enforce many rules and restrictions, and favor punitive methods to gain compliance. They value and encourage order and tradition, do not permit parent–child negotiations, and are uncompromising in their standards and rules. The children of authoritarian parents are usually fearful, moody, aimless, unhappy, easily annoyed, and less able to cope effectively with stressful circumstances (Jaffe, 1991).

Baumrind concludes that it is authoritative parenting that fosters those qualities associated with Western notions of social competence in youths:

social responsibility, vitality, independence, achievement, friendliness, and cooperativeness (Baumrind, 1975, 1978). Few researchers have tested Baumrind's typology and theories on parenting practices in either developing countries or Eastern developed countries (e.g., Japan). This type of cross-cultural research is critically important in furthering our understanding of cultural differences of Baumrind's typology and resultant child outcomes.

CROSS-CULTURAL RESEARCH EXAMPLES: PARENTING STYLES

Because space limitations here preclude a comprehensive presentation of this literature, four selected studies illustrate the variety of cross-cultural work in this area. The examples come from China, Japan, the United States, and Israel. The first illustrative example, from China, was included here because it describes the influence of parental control, support, and power even when parents are only able to interact with their children a few hours each week. The second example, from Japan, illustrates the influence parents have on personality development by their use, or lack thereof, of parental support in childrearing. Third, is an illustrative example from the Mexican American subculture in the United States. Researchers here examined one of the subdimensions of control, coercion via corporal punishment, in a comparative study between native-born and foreign-born mothers. The last illustrative example is indirectly related to parental support. Mothers in two different cultures, Japanese and Israeli, support identical behaviors in their children but label these behaviors as either obedient (Japan) or autonomous (Israel), depending on which is more valued in their respective culture.

China

A team of six researchers recently completed "the first large-scale psychological study of socialization in China" (Zhengyuan, Wen, Mussen, Jian-Xian, Chang-Min, & Zi-Fang, 1991, p. 241). Using research on U.S. samples as models, this team documented the complex relationship between childrearing and child behaviors that exists in contemporary Chinese culture.

China has a long, rich history of collectivism and places a priority on community over individual needs. Although there have been recent internal challenges to this established ideology, China remains a model for parenting practices within a collective society. For example, even when their children are very young, many Chinese parents bring them to child centers before breakfast and retrieve them after supper, for an average of 10 to 11 hours in care each day, 6 days a week. With children in group care for such a significant portion of their childhood days, can parents influence the development of their children during the few hours each week available to them? A team of researchers surveyed 2,254 Chinese children, ages 3 to 6, and their parents to assess the influence of various subdimensions of parental support and control on children's personality development (Zhengyuan et al., 1991). The results suggest that parents have a significant influence on the development of their child's personality even though the amount of parent–child interaction time is limited in many Chinese families. Chinese parents who exert strong control over children foster the development of good character, positive attitudes toward others, self-confidence, self-control, a high frustration tolerance, and positive attitudes toward work. Chinese parents who use inductive discipline (e.g., reasoning and persuasion methods even if the child does something to make them very angry) contribute to the development of self-control, self-confidence, independence, and positive attitudes toward work in their children. When parents encourage independence in their children, they help children develop positive attitudes toward others, self-confidence, independence, self-control, high tolerance for frustration, and positive attitudes toward work. Parents who demonstrate a respect for individuality have children who are curious, show positive attitudes toward others and work, are self-confident, independent, demonstrate high levels of self-control, and show good character. Finally, intellectual stimulation by parents is associated with children who are independent and self-confident and show a high frustration tolerance and good character. In sum, Chinese parents appear to be powerful socialization agents for their children even though their children spend few hours each week in the presence of parents. Differences in parenting styles contribute to significant differences in child behavior and personality development for Chinese families.

Japan

Many studies have been done on individuals who exhibit Type A behavior (an emphasis on time urgency, competitive achievement–striving, and aggression–hostility) because of its high correlation with coronary heart disease in adults. Recently, child development scholars have begun to examine this same relationship for children to determine how and when Type A behaviors begin. The relationship between parental childrearing behaviors (negative rejection, positive rejection, strictness, expectation, interference, anxiety, dotage, blind obedience, inconsistency, and disagreement between parents' attitudes) and the Type A and Type B behavior in Japanese preschoolers, ages 3 to 6, reveals an interesting pattern. Responding parents were first divided into four groups by gender of parent and child (i.e., mothers of boys, mothers of girls, fathers of boys, and fathers of girls) and then divided into two subcategories within each of the four groups by behavior of the child (mothers of Type A boys, mothers of Type B boys, etc.), and this pattern became apparent. Both mothers and fathers of Type A boys showed lower anxiety about their sons than did parents of Type B boys. For girls, only mothers showed a similar relationship. That is, mothers of Type A girls, but not fathers, reported lower anxiety about their daughters than did mothers of Type B daughters (Yamasaki, 1990). Yamasaki speculates that children of less anxious parents may develop Type A behaviors in order to elicit more expressions of concern or affection from parents. If this is true within the Japanese culture, higher levels of parental support may protect children from developing Type A behaviors, with its subsequent risk for adult-onset coronary disease.

Foreign-Born and Native-Born Mexican American Subculture in the United States

There has been much speculation about the influence of culture on parental control and its subdimensions, especially among subcultures in the United States. High rates of reported child maltreatment have been linked to the perceived tendency among minority populations in the United States to use corporal punishment as a disciplinary strategy. But in a recent study of foreign-born and native-born Mexican American mothers in the United States, mothers in both groups chose corporal punishment as their last choice of control method when their children misbehaved. Therefore, no cultural differences were apparent. For both groups, mothers were most likely to use "no television/no play with a friend" and least likely to use "spanking" as their most common method of control. "Scolding" and "verbal reasoning" ranked second and third, respectively. However, there were subtle yet significant differences in how these mothers carried out this control. Foreign-born mothers were more likely to use "physical discipline" and "verbal reasoning" than were native-born mothers because they often used a combination of these two methods. They would first spank their child and then explain the reasons for the spanking. Native-born mothers more often used scolding than the combination of spanking and verbal reasoning (Buriel, Mercado, Rodriguez, & Chavez, 1991). The researchers concluded that Mexican American mothers did not choose corporal punishment as their preferred style of control. Although there were subtle differences between foreign-born and native-born Mexican American mothers on how control was administered, the preferred method for both groups was withdrawal of privileges rather than physical punishment. This challenges the notion that the high rates of reported child maltreatment among minority populations are a result of a culturally based reliance on methods of corporal punishment for parental control.

Japan and Israel

The last illustrative study in this section compares an Asian culture and a Middle Eastern one on the value of autonomy (independence) and obedience. The results suggest that parents use supportive techniques to encourage identical behaviors in each culture but label these behaviors as either autonomous or obedient according to whichever trait is more valued in their respective cultures.

Israeli and Japanese cultures are based on family cohesiveness, educational achievement, and collectivism. However, unlike Japanese culture, Israel also values a Western-based emphasis on individualism. This individualism promotes a parental emphasis upon developing independence and self-sufficiency in children. Japanese parents expect obedience to parents who teach early mastery of skills that demonstrate emotional maturity, self-control, self-reliance, and compliance with adult authority (Osterweil & Nagano, 1991). When Japanese mothers of preschoolers are compared with Israeli mothers of preschoolers on their views of independence and obedience in their children, the cultural differences become apparent. Although obedience is defined by both groups as compliance with parental demands, Japanese mothers are more likely to describe their child as obedient when they perform personal care functions (e.g., brushing teeth and dressing self) than do Israeli mothers who report similar functions as examples of autonomy. In other words, on these indicators of instrumental independence (e.g., child gets dressed, washes, and goes to school by him/herself) Israeli mothers more often express these as examples of independence, whereas Japanese mothers more often use these same examples to reflect obedience. In examining emotional independence, some interesting differences emerge between these two cultures. Israeli mothers emphasize a child's ability to be alone as an example of emotional independence; they appreciate it because they tend to value initiative in self-expression and the capacity for self-occupation. However, Japanese mothers value the development of the capacity for establishing social relationships and view it as the measure of emotional independence. Osterweil and Nagano (1991) conclude that "instrumental independence is viewed as a manifestation of separateness in Israel, but in Japan it indicates a close relationship with mother and compliance with her wishes" (p. 373). Therefore, it appears that both Israeli and Japanese mothers value independence but for different reasons. Israeli mothers value it as an indication of separation between mother and child, whereas Japanese mothers value independence as an indication of a child's closeness, as manifested in obedience to teachings about social competence.

Summary

From the cross-cultural research presented in this section, it is apparent that there are more similarities than differences in parents' socialization of children across cultures. This discussion of parental socialization techniques describes and illustrates how the balance and interaction of parental control, power, and support result in particular child behaviors.

Although Chinese parents spend little time each week with their young children, they serve as powerful socialization agents in the development of their children's personalities. In Japan, parental support can be influential in fostering Type B personality traits to prevent the development of adult coronary heart disease for Japanese preschoolers. Although much speculation exists about why minority populations are overrepresented in reports of child maltreatment in the United States, it is apparently not because corporal punishment is a preferred method of parental control for either native-born or foreign-born Mexican Americans. Finally, parental support of particular child behaviors encourages the development of what Israeli mothers describe as autonomy and Japanese mothers describe as obedience.

PARENTAL CLASS INFLUENCES

In nearly every culture, parental differences in class result in different expectations of and outcomes for children. In industrialized societies, class is most commonly measured by socioeconomic status, education, accumulated wealth, and occupation. However, these measures have sometimes failed to discriminate class statuses in developing countries so contemporary researchers have begun to identify measures such as housing conditions, proficiency in the dominant language, and the demands placed on the children's labor as more relevant measures of class in some cultures (Lockheed, Fuller, & Nyirongo, 1989). In general, higher class, however measured, is associated with (1) parents who encourage their children, invest more time helping them in academic activities, and hold greater academic aspirations for them; and (2) children who exhibit higher reading scores, greater academic motivation, and greater self-esteem (Amato & Ochiltree, 1986; Gecas, 1979; Kohn, 1977; Maccoby, 1980; Lockheed et al., 1989). These qualities often result in higher academic performance.

Family background variables appear to influence status attainment in children via three interconnected clusters of influences, commonly referred to as the Wisconsin Model (Falk & Cosby, 1975; Hanson, 1983; Otto & Haller, 1979). Family-of-origin variables (e.g., mother's and father's educational attainments) specify the family's socioeconomic status and social circumstances. The family-of-origin variables join with personal characteristic variables (e.g., child's IQ) to influence sons and daughters to achieve levels of academic achievement compatible with their family's social position, expectations, and personal ability. These influences are further modified by social psychological variables (e.g., academic performance, significant others, and aspirations). Thus, family-of-origin variables create a class position for the family, which limits the number and range of significant others in the child's environment who communicate role expectations and support specific aptitudes in the child (Otto, 1986; Sewell, Haller, & Ohlendorf, 1970). This milieu is further shaped by the personal characteristics of the child that influence their occupational aspirations. Furthermore, the occupational experiences of parents are often linked to their socialization practices in childrearing, which give children the tools to succeed in specific occupations (Farmer, 1985; Peterson, Rollins, Thomas, & Heaps, 1982). Consequently, educational attainment is closely associated with occupational status because occupations require specific academic prerequisites (Wilson, Peterson, & Wilson, 1993).

In examining successful children, family processes are also important. Those children who are academic achievers have parents who set standards that are both challenging and attainable, and these parents encourage and support their children in their attempts to meet these challenges. Such parents are knowledgeable about what their child is capable of achieving. Children who are encouraged to meet a challenge that is too difficult are vulnerable to failure. Children who consistently fail are unwilling to try new experiences. On the other hand, parents who fail to challenge their children often raise children who are bored and lack high self-esteem. Balancing challenge with opportunities to succeed results in children who take appropriate risks and demonstrate high self-esteem.

Differences in home environments have an additional, significant impact on which children will excel academically. In industrialized countries, children who live in homes in which reading material for children and adults is present, television is deemphasized, and children are encouraged to explore and solve problems are more likely to succeed in their academic careers. Although fewer researchers have investigated parallel contributions to success for children living in developing countries, it is intuitive to expect that when demands for children's labor are less and housing and sanitary conditions are better, children probably achieve greater literacy and academic success. Five components of family life are associated with school achievement: (1) high levels of verbal interaction between parent and child (e.g., asking children questions and permitting children to participate in meal conversations), (2) high expectations by parents for the child's achievement, (3) a warm and nurturing parent–child relationship, (4) an authoritative style of parental discipline (Baumrind, 1968) (e.g., demands for maturity, inductive control techniques, and high levels of parental support), and (5) parental belief that the child is capable of success (Hess & Holloway, 1984).

Occupations of parents also play a significant role in the childrearing and therefore success outcomes of children. Parents' attitudes toward childrearing have been found to correlate with their occupations, partially explaining the differences between parents who foster academically successful children and those who do not. Working-class parents participate in the labor force in positions that demand reliability, respect, and adherence to rules. In turn, they value and teach such qualities as conformity, orderliness, and obedience to their children. Because middle-class parents work in jobs that demand creativity, ambition, independence, and self-control, these parents emphasize autonomy and internalized control. Like working-class parents, those qualities that enable middle-class parents to succeed at work become the foundation for what they teach their children (Kohn, 1977; Peterson & Rollins, 1987). Both sets of values can aid children in their academic success, but especially so if parents value education and support academic achievement in their children.

However, social forces outside the family may have a competing influence. For example, Peters (1981) reports that black U.S. families place a greater emphasis on qualities that conflict with the behavior encouraged for U.S. school children in the classroom. Because educational institutions are operated predominantly by white, educated, middle-class teachers and administrators, the school environment may be more supportive of children who exhibit parallel middle-class behaviors (e.g., self-assertion and independence) than of children who exhibit behaviors learned in black, working-class families (respect for elders and authority figures).

Let us turn now to research from around the globe on the role of parents, their socioeconomic status, and education levels in the fostering of academically successful children. Some studies found parents' class status to be the primary influence in academic achievement and others found that parents' educational attainment exerted the strongest influence. Both factors appear to be important to children's academic success. Five examples from vastly different cultures illustrate this nearly worldwide relationship.

The Mizos of India

Mizoram is a state in northeastern India inhabited almost entirely by a tribal people known as Mizos. Agriculture is the primary occupation of the Mizos people, with all able-bodied adults participating in the work. Men clear the jungle for new fields, and women sow the seeds, weed, and harvest the crops.

Arranged marriages, once the standard, are now gradually diminishing within the Mizos culture, and free selection of marital partners is more common today. However, a brideprice is still paid to the bride's relatives by the groom. When the couple bears children, responsibility for childrearing rests with them. All Mizos parents, irrespective of their status and wealth, consider the education of their children a privilege, yet it is the higher-status families that report greater parent–child interaction, which, in turn, leads to significantly greater academic achievement for boys (Sudhir & Sailo, 1989). Boys who experienced greater parent–child interaction demonstrated significantly higher achievement scores in general science and social science. However, girls who experienced greater parent–child interaction showed no significant differences in academic achievement from girls who experienced lower parent–child interaction. One cultural explanation for this gender difference is that given the male-dominated patrilineal culture of the Mizos, boys are more encouraged to compete and achieve than are girls (who may even be discouraged from academic achievement) even though both girls and boys have legal access to formal educational opportunities (Sudhir & Sailo, 1989). In this situation, greater parent–child interaction has no effect on girls' achievement because the cultural behavior of the society neutralizes any academic achievement differences between daughters of higher-socioeconomic-status parents and those of lesser-status parents.

Thailand and Malawi

In the developing countries of Asia's Thailand and Africa's Malawi, family background appears to influence the school performance of youth in a variety of ways. In Thailand, the influence of family background on the mathematics scores of eighth-grade students paralleled findings in many industrialized countries; higher mathematics scores were associated with higher paternal occupational status, higher maternal education, higher per capita income for the district, and use of the language of instruction in the home (Lockheed et al., 1989). In Malawi, however, these conventional measures of family background were not associated with differences in mathematics scores of similar-age children in fourth and seventh grades. When measures of class more relevant for a developing country were used, students who did well in mathematics were associated with (1) a greater number of modern attributes of their home (e.g., modern house without a thatched roof, ownership of a radio, and electricity), (2) congruence between the language of home and instruction, and (3) less demand for child labor by the parents. Consequently, family background and class status demonstrate a fairly consistent association with academic success when they are measured in a culturally relevant manner.

Urban Blacks and Whites in Great Britain

An example from Great Britain further illustrates that time spent with children is associated with improved academic achievement, and that time invested is often a function of parental education (Hamner & Turner, 1985). When two cultural subgroups of inner-city London 6-year-olds were compared, researchers found that race and educational attainment of the mother both influenced the amount of time mothers spent with their children reading, doing mathematics, and writing. Black (Afro Caribbean) mothers read aloud to their children more often than did white mothers. Children of more highly educated mothers spent more time on all learning activities than did children of mothers with less education (Plewis, Mooney, & Creeser, 1990).

The Xhosa of South Africa

The black Xhosa-speaking people of Transkei, South Africa, offer yet another example of the relationship between parent education and children's academic achievement. The socioeconomic status (SES) of Xhosa-speaking students, ages 13 to 17, and of average ability (as measured on a standardized aptitude test) was categorized as either low, middle, or high SES. When these three groups of students were compared on academic ability, the academic performance of each youth was associated with his/her parents' SES. Students in the higher SES category scored better on academic achievement tests than did students in either the middle or low SES categories. Furthermore, taken separately, maternal and paternal aspirations for academic achievement increased the child's academic performance. In other words, the aspirations of each parent appeared to have separate, yet powerful, influences on the academic performance of both daughters and sons in this South African subculture (Cherian, 1991).

Thailand and the United States

In addition to the important influence of parents' education and SES on academic achievement in children, parental encouragement also appears to exert a clear influence on children's academic success as described earlier. When comparing the perceptions of their parents' encouragement of the mathematics skills of Thai and U.S. adolescents (age 13), some clear trends emerge. Strong parental encouragement of success in mathematics is associated with adolescents who are less anxious when doing mathematics, and who do not view mathematics as more appropriate for males than females. Both Thai and U.S. adolescents hold more positive views of the usefulness and importance of mathematics to society, as well as more positive views of themselves as learners of mathematics, when they believe their parents encourage them to succeed in mathematics. Furthermore, there are no differences between Thai and U.S. students in these relationships, which lends support for the universality of this relationship between parental encouragement for success and children's academic achievement (Tocci & Engelhard, 1991).

Summary

Socioeconomic status, amount of parent child interaction, parental education, and parental encouragement of success in a specific academic subject all demonstrate positive significant effects on children's academic performance. Using examples from vastly different cultures, economies, and political states, it appears that parental time invested in children, with its resultant payoff in greater academic achievement, is more common among higher SES families. This may be partly the result of possessing greater resources, enabling these parents to spend more time in such pursuits with their children.

However, we must use caution in interpreting these seemingly consistent results. Another plausible explanation for these findings is that the measures researchers used to test academic achievement in these studies may measure the skills taught to middle- and higher-class children more than the skills taught to lower-class children by less educated parents. For example, a child who lives in a remote, agricultural village in a developing country may be exceptionally gifted in the tasks required of the local industry but may not be able to demonstrate these on a standardized academic instrument. More studies are needed from developing countries to understand cross-cultural similarities and differences in academic achievement. A separate but related problem in this area is the lack of attention to the issue of literacy. By necessity, this section has been limited to discussion on the more narrow topic of academic achievement because of the dearth of cross-cultural studies of parental influences on literacy. When sociologists and psychologists invest more research resources into the examination of cultures in developing countries, future literature in this area may focus on the broader concept of literacy, a more elementary skill but of great global value.

THE BENEFITS OF CLOSE PARENT–YOUTH RELATIONSHIPS IN ADOLESCENCE

Having established how parents influence their children via their control, power, and supportive socialization techniques, and via their socioeconomic and class statuses, this last section describes how a positive relationship between parents and children later enhances the life satisfaction and psychological well-being of older youths and protects them from juvenile delinquency and substance abuse. As the cross-cultural examples illustrate, youth who perceive a close relationship with their parents exhibit more positive outcomes in each of these four areas. Life satisfaction and psychological well-being are described first, followed by illustrative cross-cultural examples. Next is a description of the impact of close parent–child relationships and their protective value on the substance abuse and juvenile delinquency of adolescents. Relevant, illustrative cross-cultural examples conclude this section.

Life satisfaction is a subjective measure of an individual's perception of his/her quality of life. Rather than objective measures of income, education, accumulation of wealth, and home ownership, life satisfaction is the level of individual satisfaction each person perceives in his/her own life: that which is privately known and privately evaluated. A multitude of factors influence life satisfaction, and because it is a personal evaluation, these factors differ for individuals. A study of life satisfaction among Hong Kong adolescents illustrates the profound effects peers and parents can exert on an adolescent's life satisfaction.

Psychological well-being is a measure of multiple subdimensions: self-esteem, locus of control, anxiety, loneliness, and sociability. Persons who exhibit high self-esteem, an internal locus of control, low anxiety and loneliness, and high sociability are considered to have strong psychological well-being. Just as with life satisfaction, many factors can influence psychological well-being, but this section focuses specifically on the association between strong relationships with parents and positive outcomes for youth and young adults.

Hong Kong

Adolescence is a transitional period in the life cycle. Associations with family and peers are changing, and adolescents often feel increased pressure to succeed in social relationships outside their families. Their level of attachment, identification, and frequency of consultation with parents relative to that with peers influences the life satisfaction of adolescents in general and, specifically, their satisfaction with school, family, and others. Hong Kong, on the south coast of China, is heavily influenced by current political and economic changes in China. Chinese culture, with its emphasis on family and community over individual independence, continues to play a significant role in the culture of Hong Kong. Because the orientation of adolescents toward their peers and parents has important implications for their satisfaction with life, Hong Kong offers a unique look at this relationship in a rapidly developing society. In a study of 1,906 students, ages 13 to 16, adolescents who were more oriented toward their parents, as well as those who were more oriented toward their peers, were equally satisfied with school, their acceptance by others, the government, and the media. However, those adolescents who are most oriented toward their parents were additionally satisfied with life in general, their families, and the environment (Man, 1991). Man (1991) concludes that "in a predominantly Chinese society like Hong Kong, the family remains a highly important determinant of the adolescents' life satisfaction" (p. 363).

Iran

Parents continue to influence the lives of their children as young adults through parental interactions, guidance, and shared history. When young adults are dissatisfied with their parents, their adult psychological well-being appears to be negatively influenced. When Iranian students, ages 17 to 39, studying at universities in Iran and the United States were asked about their childhood dissatisfactions with their parents, an interesting pattern emerged. Those adults who perceived the most childhood dissatisfaction with parents were most likely to experience current loneliness, anxiety, external locus of control, misanthropy, neurosis, and psychosis when compared to adults who scored low on the dissatisfaction scale. They were also more likely to experience lower self-esteem and lower sociability, as well as decreased satisfaction with peer relationships, than were adults who had perceptions of childhood satisfaction with parents (Hojat, Borenstein, & Shapurian, 1990). There were no differences between the Iranian students studying at U.S. universities and those studying at Iranian institutions. The authors conclude that when a child's needs for closeness, attachment, and intimacy are not fulfilled to the child's satisfaction in early childhood, the result can be adult dissatisfactions with peer relationships and decreased psychological well-being in adulthood.

Puerto Rico

Can a child's need for closeness and intimacy be adequately fulfilled when the parents of the child are either alcohol dependent or mentally ill? By comparing three groups of children—those with an alcoholic parent, with a mentally ill parent, and with other parents without obvious diagnoses— researchers in Puerto Rico believe that children and adolescents, ages 4 to 16, with alcoholic or mentally ill parents are more likely than other children to be exposed to adverse family environments, such as stressful life events, marital discord, and family dysfunction. In addition, the children in these families were more maladjusted than were children in families without a diagnosed parent, according to reports by psychiatrists, parents, and the children themselves (Rubio-Stipec, Bird, Canino, Bravo, & Alegria, 1991). (However, the teachers of these three groups of children were unable to detect differences in child behavior, probably because 43% of them rated their familiarity with the child as "not good.") It appears from this research that children of alcoholic or mentally ill parents suffer negative consequences during childhood, and these consequences are readily apparent to psychiatrists, their parents, and even the children themselves.

In many cultures, adolescence is a period of rapid psychological growth and a shift in orientation from parents to peers. Adolescents move through this period from childhood at the beginning to adulthood at the end. Most choose educational and career paths during this period. Many choose marriage partners. They move from residing with their parents to residing with peers, with spouses, or by themselves. Because this is a time of such change, some adolescents cope with the transitions by engaging in problematic behaviors (e.g., drug and alcohol abuse and juvenile delinquency). This section presents some of the factors that contribute to problematic behaviors for youth in Canada and three subcultures in the United States: Native American, white, and Hispanic.

Canada

Social control theorists contend that adolescent alcohol consumption is influenced by the degree to which youth are influenced by peers more than parents. A study of alcohol consumption by Canadian 11th and 12th graders demonstrates this relationship (Mitic, 1990). Students were divided into three groups: (1) those who drank only with their parents, (2) those who drank only with their peers, and (3) those who drank both with and without their parents. The consumption rates of this last group were further divided into the amount of drinking with and without parents. As might be expected, students who drank only with parents consumed the least amount of alcohol. Those who drank with both parents and peers consumed the most alcohol and drank more heavily when they were with peers. It appears that what parents model for their children regarding alcohol consumption has only a small influence in the youths' consumption behaviors when the parents are not present.

Hispanics and Whites in the United States

Researchers found that Hispanic and white youth (ages 9 to 17) in the United States are also significantly influenced in their drug and alcohol consumption by their relationships with friends and parents. For white and Hispanic adolescents who used either licit substances (e.g., cigarettes and alcohol), marijuana, or other illicit substances (e.g., cocaine, heroin, and prescription drugs used for recreational purposes), the single most important influence was the percentage of friends who used marijuana. Those youths who had higher percentages of friends who used marijuana were more likely to use each category of drug (licit, marijuana, and other illicit) than were youths who had fewer friends who used marijuana; this is equally true for both Hispanic and white youth. Although both users and abstainers were more affiliated with their parents than their peers, users were more strongly influenced by their peers; more likely to disregard parental objections to their friends; more likely to believe that their friends, rather than their parents, understand them best; and more likely to respect the ideas of their friends in difficult situations. The only cultural difference was that, in general, Hispanic youths respected their parents' views more than did white youths, regardless of whether they used or abstained from drugs and alcohol (Coombs, Paulson, & Richardson, 1991). Coombs et al. conclude that "youths having viable relationships with parents are less involved with drugs and drug-oriented peers" (p. 87).

Ojibway Native Americans

Delinquent behavior represents a dysfunctional response to stressors and strains in adolescence. On Native American reservations in the United States, an orientation toward parents and tribal elders appears to protect some youth from these negative behaviors. High percentages of Native American Ojibway adolescents, ages 12 to 18, reported inappropriate or illegal activities, such as using alcohol (85%), stealing something (70%), skipping school (64%), smoking marijuana (53%), and intentional damage to property (45%). However, those who spent more time with their family in chores, recreation, family discussions, and meals were less involved in negative behaviors. As expected, those youth who spent more time in activities away from their families— such as listening alone to the radio, and partying with drugs and alcohol— were at greatest risk for delinquent behaviors and court adjudications (Zitzow, 1990). Ojibway youth who spent more time in activities with parents and tribal elders were less likely to engage in delinquent behaviors resulting in court adjudications.

Summary

This last section focused on how close parent–youth relationships are associated with the life satisfaction, psychological well-being, lack of substance use, and absence of delinquent behavior in adolescents. Without exception, adolescents in all six studies benefit from increased involvement with healthy parents. Parental involvement enhanced life satisfaction among adolescents in Hong Kong and contributed to psychological well-being among Iranian college students and Puerto Rican youths. The presence of parents was associated with less alcohol consumption among Canadian adolescents, a strong bond with parents was associated with less drug consumption by Hispanic and white youth in the United States, and spending time with parents and tribal elders was associated with less involvement in delinquent behaviors for Native American adolescents in the United States.

CONCLUSION

In reviewing the literature on cross-cultural research on parent–child relations for this chapter, a clear trend became increasingly apparent. When parents are more involved and/or have greater expectations of their children's behavior, children demonstrate better outcomes. As is apparent from the illustrative examples, greater parental involvement is an active involvement, not a passive one. It is acquired not simply by the amount of time parents and children spend together but rather by how that time is spent. An involved parent is not one who spends the majority of the day near his/her child but rarely interacting with the child. It is, instead, the parent who uses opportunities to share activities such as teaching the child a local trade, reading together, or fostering a close, supportive relationship through companionship. This active, involved parent appears much more likely to rear a successful child. Illustrative cross-cultural examples presented here of high-quality interaction between parents and children, such as spending time reading together in Great Britain, establishing firm limits and offering support in China, and engaging adolescents in activities with parents and tribal elders in the United States has been associated with better child outcomes. These patterns emerged even when examining parent–son versus parent–daughter relations, relationships among family members in developing versus developed countries, or parent–child relationships in families that resided in Western cultures versus Eastern ones.

Table 8.1 lists alphabetically by country each of the 15 cross-cultural research articles presented in this chapter. Across the top of the table, the first three columns represent the three sections presented in this literature review: components of parenting styles, parental class influences, and benefits of close parent–youth relationships. The fourth column lists those studies that concluded that greater parental involvement and/or greater expectations are associated with better child outcomes (80% of those presented in this chapter). In none of the studies presented here did the researchers conclude

TABLE 8.1.   Selected Studies in Cross-Cultural Research, by Country

Country/ study	Parenting styles	Parental class	Close parent–youth relationships	Parental involvement = positive outcomes
Canada Mitic (1990)			×	×
China Zhengyuan et al. (1991)	×			×
Great Britian Plewis et al. (1990)		×		×
Hong Kong Man (1991)			×	×
India Sudhir & Sailo (1989)		×		×
Iran Hojat et al. (1990)			×	×
Japan Yamasaki (1990)	×			×
Japan/Israel Osterweil & Nagano (1991)	×			
Puerto Rico Rubio-Stipec et al. (1991)			×	×
South Africa Cherian (1991)		×		×
Thailand/Malawi Lockheed et al. (1989)		×		
Thailand/ United States Tocci & Engelhard (1991)		×		×
United States Buriel et al. (1991)	×			
Coombs et al. (1991)			×	×
Zitzow (1990)			×	×

that greater parental involvement or greater expectations were associated with poorer child outcomes, although a minority did not include this relationship in their research design. The implications of this trend are important because this literature search represents the most current work in parental influences on children throughout the world. Greater parental involvement and/or higher parental expectations are associated with better child behaviors in China and Japan; higher academic achievement among children in Great Britain, India, South Africa, Thailand, and the United States; greater psychological well-being and life satisfaction in children and young adults in Hong Kong, Iran, and Puerto Rico; and less juvenile delinquency and substance abuse among adolescents in Canada and in the United States. Using currently available cross-cultural literature, there appears to be little cross-cultural difference in this association, further supporting the argument that there are more similarities than differences in parental influences on children across cultures. However, this conclusion is based on currently available literature. Parental involvement and parental expectations are broad, general concepts. It is likely that when future cross-cultural research designs include subdimensions of these two broad concepts, results may offer descriptions of cultural differences in parental involvement and expectations for children around the world.

REFERENCES

Amato, P. R., & Ochiltree, G. (1986). Family resources and the development of child competence. *Journal of Marriage and the Family, 48,* 47–56.

Barber, B. K., & Thomas, D. L. (1986). Dimensions of fathers' and mothers' supportive behavior: The case for physical affection. *Journal of Marriage and the Family, 48,* 783–794.

Barnes, G. M., Farrell, M. P., & Cairns, A. (1986). Parental socialization factors and adolescent drinking behaviors. *Journal of Marriage and the Family, 48,* 27–36.

Baumrind, D. (1966). Effects of authoritative parental control on child behavior. *Child Development, 37,* 887–906.

Baumrind, D. (1968). Authoritarian vs. authoritative parental control. *Adolescence, 3,* 255–272.

Baumrind, D. (1975). Early socialization and adolescent competence. In S. E. Dragastin & G. Elder, Jr. (Eds.), *Adolescence in the life cycle* (pp. 117–143). Washington, DC: Hemisphere.

Baumrind, D. (1978). Parental disciplinary patterns and social competence in children. *Youth and Society, 9*(3), 239–276.

Buriel, R., Mercado, R., Rodriguez, J., & Chavez, J. M. (1991). Mexican-American disciplinary practices and attitudes toward child maltreatment: A comparison of foreign- and native-born mothers. *Hispanic Journal of Behavioral Sciences, 13*(1), 78–94.

Cherian, V. I. (1991). Parental aspiration and academic achievement of Xhosa children. *Psychological Reports, 68*(2), 547–553.

Clark, R. (1983). *Family life and school achievement.* Chicago: University of Chicago Press.

Coombs, R. H., Paulson, M. J., & Richardson, M. A. (1991). Peer vs. parental influence in substance use among Hispanic and Anglo children and adolescents. *Journal of Youth and Adolescence, 20*(1), 73–88.

Falk, W. W., & Cosby, A. G. (1975). Women and the status attainment process. *Social Science Quarterly, 56,* 307–314.

Farmer, H. S. (1985). Model of career and achievement motivation for women and men. *Journal of Counseling Psychology, 32,* 363–390.

Gecas, V. (1979). The influence of social class on socialization. In W. R. Burr, R. Hill, F. I. Nye, & I. L. Reiss (Eds.), *Contemporary theories about the family* (Vol. 1, pp. 365–404). New York: Free Press.

Gecas. V., & Schwalbe, M. L. (1986). Parental behavior and adolescent self-esteem. *Journal of Marriage and the Family, 48,* 37–46.

Hamner, T. J., & Turner, P. H. (1985). *Parenting in contemporary society.* Englewood Cliffs, NJ: Prentice Hall.

Hanson, S. L. (1983). A family life-cycle approach to socioeconomic attainment of working women. *Journal of Marriage and the Family, 45,* 323–338.

Henry, C. L., Wilson, L. M., & Peterson, G. W. (1989). Parental power bases and processes as predictors of adolescent conformity. *Journal of Adolescent Research, 4,* 15–32.

Hess, R. D., & Holloway, S. D. (1984). Family and school as educational institutions. In R. D. Parke (Ed.), *Review of child development research* (Vol. 7, pp. 179–222). Chicago: University of Chicago Press.

Hoffman, M. L. (1960). Power assertion by the parent and its impact on the child. *Child Development, 31,* 129–143.

Hojat, M., Borenstein, B. D., & Shapurian, R. (1990). Perception of childhood dissatisfaction with parents and selected personality traits in adulthood. *Journal of General Psychology, 117*(3), 241–253.

Jaffe, M. L. (1991). *Understanding parenting.* Dubuque, IA: Brown.

Kohn, M. L. (1977). *Class and conformity: A study in values* (2nd ed.). Chicago: University of Chicago Press.

Lockheed, M. E., Fuller, B., & Nyirongo, R. (1989). Family effects on students' achievement in Thailand and Malawi. *Sociology of Education, 62,* 239–256.

Maccoby, E. E. (1980). *Social development: Psychological growth and the parent–child relationship.* New York: Harcourt Brace Jovanovich.

Man, P. (1991). The influence of peers and parents on youth life satisfaction in Hong Kong. *Social Indicators Research, 24*(4), 347–365.

McDonald, G. W. (1977). Parental identification by the adolescent: A social power approach. *Journal of Marriage and the Family, 39,* 705–718.

McDonald, G. W. (1979). Determinants of adolescent perceptions of maternal and paternal power in the family. *Journal of Marriage and the Family, 41,* 757–770.

McDonald, G. W. (1980). Parental power and adolescents' parental identification: A reexamination. *Journal of Marriage and the Family, 42,* 289–296.

Mitic, W. (1990). Parental versus peer influence on adolescents' alcohol consumption. *Psychological Reports, 67,* 1273–1274.

Osterweil, Z., & Nagano, K. N. (1991). Maternal views on autonomy: Japan and Israel. *Journal of Cross-Cultural Psychology, 22*(3), 362–375.

Otto, L. B. (1986). Family influences on youth's occupational aspirations and achievements. In G. K. Leigh & G. W. Peterson (Eds.), *Adolescents in families* (pp. 226–255). Cincinnati: South-Western.

Otto, L. B., & Haller, A. O. (1979). Evidence for a social–psychological view of the status attainment process: Four studies compared. *Social Forces, 57,* 887–914.

Peters, M. F. (1981). "Making it" black family style: Building on the strengths of black families. In N. Stinnett (Ed.), *Family strengths: Roots of well-being.* Lincoln: University of Nebraska Press.

Peterson, G. W., & Leigh, G. K. (1990). The family and social competence in adolescence. In T. P. Gullotta, G. R. Adams, & R. Montemayor (Eds.), *Developing social competency in adolescence* (pp. 97–138). Newbury Park, CA: Sage.

Peterson, G. W., & Rollins, B. C. (1987). Parent–child socialization. In M. B. Sussman & S. K. Steinmetz (Eds.), *Handbook of marriage and the family* (pp. 471–507). New York: Plenum Press.

Peterson, G. W., Rollins, B. C., & Thomas, D. L. (1985). Parental influence and adolescent conformity: Compliance and internalization. *Youth and Society, 16,* 397–420.

Peterson, G. W., Rollins, B. C., Thomas, D. L., & Heaps, L. K. (1982). Social placement of adolescents: Sex-role influences on family decisions regarding the careers of youth. *Journal of Marriage and the Family, 44,* 647–661.

Plewis, I., Mooney, A., & Creeser, R. (1990). Time on educational activities at home and educational progress in infant school. *British Journal of Educational Psychology, 60*(3), 330–337.

Rollins, B. C., & Thomas, D. L. (1979). Parental support, power, and control techniques in the socialization of children. In W. R. Burr, R. Hill, F. I. Nye, & I. L. Reiss (Eds.), *Contemporary theories about the family* (Vol. 1, pp. 317–364). New York: Free Press.

Rubio-Stipec, M., Bird, H., Canino, G., Bravo, M., & Alegria, M. (1991). Children of alcoholic parents in the community. *Journal of Studies on Alcohol, 52*(1), 78–88.

Sewell, W. H., Haller, A. O., & Ohlendorf, G. W. (1970). The educational and early occupational status attainment process: Replication and revision. *American Sociological Review, 35,* 1014–1027.

Smith, T. E. (1970). Foundations of parental influence upon adolescents: An application of social power theory. *American Sociological Review, 35,* 860–873.

Smith, T. E. (1983). Parental influence: A review of the evidence of influence and a theoretical model of the parental influence process. In A. C. Kerckhoff (Ed.), *Research in sociology of education and socialization* (Vol. 4, pp. 13–45). Greenwich, CT: JAI Press.

Smith, T. E. (1986). Influence in parent–adolescent relationships. In G. K. Leigh & G. W. Peterson (Eds.), *Adolescents in families* (pp. 130–154). Cincinnati: South-Western.

Sudhir, M. A., & Sailo, L. (1989). Parent–child interaction and academic achievement among secondary school students in Aizawi. *Indian Journal of Psychometry and Education, 20*(1), 19–28.

Tocci, C. M., & Engelhard, G. (1991). Achievement, parental support, and gender differences in attitudes toward mathematics. *Journal of Educational Research, 84*(5), 280–286.

Wilson, S. M., Peterson, G. W., & Wilson, P. (1993). The process of educational and occupational attainment of adolescent females from low-income, rural families. *Journal of Marriage and the Family, 55,* 158–175.

Yamasaki, K. (1990). Parental child-rearing attitudes associated with Type A behaviors in children. *Psychological Reports, 67*(1), 235–239.

Zhengyuan, X., Wen, W. C., Mussen, P., Jian-Xian, S., Chang-Min, L., & Zi-Fang, C. (1991). Family socialization and children's behavior and personality development in China. *Journal of Genetic Psychology, 152*(2), 239–253.

Zitzow, D. (1990). Ojibway adolescent time spent with parents/elders as related to delinquency and court adjudication experiences. *American Indian and Alaska Native Mental Health Research, 4*(1), 53–63.

CHAPTER NINE

Divorce: A Comparative Perspective

PATRICK C. McKENRY
SHARON J. PRICE

The preoccupation of U.S. society with current divorce rates often obscures the fact that some form of marital dissolution exists in all societies. In fact, provisions for divorce itself are almost universal.

Historically, provisions for divorce are of ancient origin. The first written regulation was incorporated into the Babylonian legal code of Hammurabi, around 2000 B.C. This regulation provided that a husband could divorce his wife at will, with no stated reason required. Throughout much of Western history, divorce was more a prerogative for husbands than for wives. However, at present, most industrialized societies accord equal rights of divorce to both spouses (Kephart & Jedlicka, 1988).

Viewed in cross-cultural and historical perspective, modern U.S. divorce rates are viewed as relatively modest (Lee, 1982). For example, Murdock (1950), in a study of 40 preliterate societies, estimated that rates of divorce in about 60% of these societies exceeded contemporary U.S. rates. And Hutter (1988) notes that other industrialized nations have had higher rates of divorce in the recent past than the United States.

The universal existence of marital dissolution across societies is viewed by social scientists as functional rather than reflecting personal failure or the failure of the family institution itself. Divorce is typically viewed as an important element in family systems—an escape valve for the tension that inevitably rises from a dysfunctional relationship (Goode, 1963). However, almost no society places a positive value on divorce. Most societies, in fact, penalize parties to a divorce. Preliterate groups have imposed fines, prohibited remarriage, levied alimony, or insisted that the brideprice be returned. Industrialized societies have applied religious, economic, and legal pressures to encourage the continuation of marriage. All societies have used equally

187

effective informal controls such as censure, gossip, disparagement, and condescension (Kephart & Jedlicka, 1988).

Legal grounds for divorce vary to some extent across societies. In societies in which divorce is difficult to obtain, the grounds for divorce may not represent the real reason for the divorce; in such cases there is a tendency toward dishonest annulment, fabrication of legally accepted offenses, migratory divorce, and separations (Price & McKenry, 1988). There are, however, some common grounds across cultures: adultery, sterility, economic incapacity, thievery, impotence or frigidity, desertion, and cruelty (Kephart & Jedlicka, 1988).

Much scholarly attention has focused on the societal reasons behind the increasing option to divorce, especially in Western society. It is commonly believed that industrialization and the conjugal family system that accompanies it operate together in such a way as to drastically increase the frequency of divorce over that prevalent in nonindustrial societies. Lee (1982) notes that in industrialized societies, families are no longer obligated to remain together as self-sufficient economic and productive units but instead are voluntarily held together for emotional gratification. As voluntary unions without strong kin support, the mutual dependence of the husband and wife creates high expectations for companionship, intimacy, and emotional support. With the kin group less available, there is also less pressure on the married couple to remain together when there are marital problems. Also, it appears that women's economic independence is highly associated with higher divorce rates in industrialized nations; opportunities for labor force involvement provide women with an option for independent living if traditional marriage proves unsatisfactory (Glick, 1973; Goode, 1963; Lee, 1982). Goode (1963) notes that one of the most striking reasons for higher divorce rates among industrialized nations today is the declining stigma attached to divorce; there is little loss of respectability or individual rights after a divorce in most industrialized societies today.

Divorce, in fact, has increasingly come to be seen as a civil rights issue in developed Western cultures. Its availability is seen as an important advancement in the social status and position of women because separations are formalized and provision is made for alimony, child maintenance, and housing (Prendiville, 1988).

As divorce has become more common, there has developed a large pool of other divorcees with whom divorced individuals may remarry. Thus, in most nations the rate of remarriage has paralleled increases in divorce rates. In fact, in most adult age groups in the United States, the chances of eventual marriage are higher for divorcees than for single people of the same age.

This chapter explores patterns of divorce in various cultures. The focus is on the historical and cultural context of divorce, societal factors affecting divorce rates, and societal responses to individuals and families after divorce.

Comparative research on divorce is limited and often dated. Also, researchers have been preoccupied with etiology to the neglect of postdivorce adjustment, including remarriage. There is still a common assumption that divorce is morally "wrong," or at least dysfunctional, and thus should be studied in terms of prevention.

NORTH AMERICA

U.S. Subcultures

The United States is often thought of as a "melting pot" wherein various subcultures are well integrated and indistinguishable. In reality, however, significant cultural differences remain in the family patterns and life-styles of Americans. These are clearly reflected in the patterns of divorce and remarriage among the three largest minorities: African Americans, Hispanics, and Asian Americans.

African Americans

During a period of relative stability in overall divorce rates, the divorce rate for African Americans increased by 17% in the 1980s (Martin & Bumpass, 1989). Staples (1985) notes that while the white divorce–marriage ratio is approximately 50%, the corresponding ratio among African Americans is about 67%. Racial differences in divorce rates persist independently of such compositional variables as education, religiosity, region of residence, and parental marital stability (Teachman, 1986). Perhaps because divorce is so common among African Americans, their adjustment to divorce as variably measured appears to be better than that of white Americans (e.g., Gove & Shin, 1989; Kitson, with Holmes, 1992; Menaghan & Lieberman, 1986). The better adjustment of African Americans to divorce also has been explained by (1) strong extended family resources, (2) greater acceptance of alternative childrearing structures, and (3) fewer perceived barriers to divorce (Fine, McKenry, & Chung, 1991).

African Americans, particularly women, are also less likely to remarry following divorce (Sweet & Bumpass, 1988). Possible explanations for this racial difference are that (1) single-parent status may be more normative among African Americans than it is among whites (Kitson, with Holmes, 1992), (2) marriage may be less central to the well-being of African Americans than it is for Whites (Ball & Robbins, 1986), and (3) African American women, as compared to white women, are less constrained by marriage because of their relative economic independence from men (Hampton, 1980).

Hispanics

The rate of divorce among Hispanics varies considerably by Hispanic sub-group. After controlling for age, age at marriage, and education, Mexican Americans and Cubans have odds of stability greater than those of whites; however, Puerto Rican marriages have quite low odds of stability, similar to those of African Americans (Frisbie, 1986). A cultural interpretation suggests that the traditional, familistic orientation of certain Hispanic groups is responsible for the greater stability of the families (Frisbie, Bean, & Eberstein, 1978). The difference in marital stability between Puerto Ricans within the United States and the other Hispanic groups is thought to be related to the perpetuation of poverty within and greater discrimination toward this ethnic group as a whole (Sanchez-Ayendez, 1988).

Divorce in Puerto Rico has been a puzzling phenomenon for social scientists. Despite being mainly Catholic and Hispanic, with well-defined patriarchal roles, Puerto Rico has one of the highest divorce rates in the world, surpassed only by the United States and Guam. Various reasons have been offered to explain this phenomenon. Puerto Rico has experienced rapid social change since 1950, moving from an agricultural to an industrialized state. This has affected marital stability by changing the traditional role of women in terms of (1) a need for increased income due to a decrease in household production and a change in consumption patterns, (2) an increase in employment opportunities for women outside the home, and (3) an increase in the educational level of the population, which has also contributed to an increase in women's employment. Sociopsychological changes needed for adaptation to such change have been lacking in Puerto Rico, resulting in conflict between expected gender roles of a traditional patriarchal society and the presence of women in a breadwinner role. Other related factors include the mass exodus of the population from rural to urban areas and the extensive and successful campaign by private groups and the government in promoting the use of contraceptives and sterilization (Canabal, 1990).

Asian Americans

Asian Americans constitute a hard-working, conforming, and cohesive family group that is a carrier of a traditional culture similar to that of middle-class, white America (Sue & Kitano, 1973). They exceed white Americans in terms of marital stability as well as educational achievement and median family income. The Asian American culture traditionally has stressed the importance of the family unit over the individual. Divorce still carries with it much stigma. Because of the diversity of this group in terms of historical origin and the extent of time in the United States, there is little empirical data on the extent of divorce among Asian Americans. The divorce rate among Asian Americans is estimated to be less than half the overall rate of the United States, yet divorce rates appear to be rising among younger and/or more assimilated Asian Americans (Min, 1988; Staples & Mirande, 1980).

Canada

Canada has long held the distinction of having one of the lowest rates of divorce among industrialized nations. Despite social and economic development in the mid-20th century, Canada moved rather slowly in changing its restrictive divorce laws. Prior to 1968, divorce was granted primarily on grounds of adultery. In 1968, divorce laws were changed to include various other grounds (Peters, 1983). However, in Canada today, a marriage still cannot be terminated because the relationship has stagnated or because one or both partners wish a change unless there is a 1-year separation with the idea that the marriage is over (*Canadian Almanac and Inventory*, 1992). Current divorce legislation represents a compromise between the wholly restrictive law of the 19th century and the move to unilateral divorce (Eichler, 1988). Canadian society, particularly the conservative influences of religion, government, and family, has sought to maintain the status quo despite attempts for change in access to divorce similar to that of other Western industrialized nations. More specifically, the federal government has not wanted to offend the Roman Catholic Church or the Roman Catholic majority in Quebec. However, the Roman Catholic hierarchy has finally recognized that its specific beliefs should not necessarily restrict wider society (Peters, 1983).

Divorce rates increased significantly after the liberalization of divorce legislation, increasing fivefold from 1968 to 1981. The 1989 divorce rate was 2.8 per 1,000 individuals, almost half the U.S. rate (4.8 per 1,000 individuals) (United Nations, 1992). Similarly, about 10% of Canadian families with children are single parents compared to 25% in the United States (U.S. Bureau of the Census, 1991). As in the United States, there is an east–west difference in divorce rates with the western provinces generally having higher divorce rates due to younger populations, greater individualism, and lesser influence of the Catholic church (Peters, 1983). Also, it should be noted that Canada is distinguished by its high immigrant and ethnic population, with much variation in marriage and family patterns. Historically, divorce rates of Canada have paralleled those of the United States, even though the magnitude of the rates has been different (Robinson & McVey, 1985). Reasons cited for increasing divorce rates in Canada include better opportunities for women that allow them to be independent, decreasing stigma, and higher expectations. Simpler divorce laws and family reform laws that give separated women a larger share of the family assets have also been cited as major factors (Eichler, 1988; Peters, 1983)

Remarriage has become a significant element in the total marriage scene in Canada. The majority of divorced individuals remarry, often within 3 years of the divorce. Remarriages account for over 25% of all marriages. However, the marriage and remarriage rates in general are declining in Canada because of economic uncertainties, changing values toward marriage, and changing roles of women (Robinson & McVey, 1985).

EUROPE

Divorce and remarriage rates in Europe have paralleled those in the United States in many respects. As in the United States, by the turn of the 20th century, industrialization and urbanization introduced radical reforms in divorce and the view of family (French Embassy, 1981). Also, similar to the United States, European divorce rates have risen markedly since the mid-1960s, reaching a plateau in the 1980s. Remarriage rates have generally declined in the past decade due to a decline in economic incentives and lesser cultural pressure to marry.

In general, the pattern of post-World War II family change has been similar in North America, Western Europe, and even parts of Eastern Europe, suggesting that more global rather than particular national explanations need to be sought. Nearly all these countries experienced (1) a postwar baby boom followed by baby bust; (2) an increase in nonmarital cohabitation, marital dissolution, and single-parent families; (3) a fall in average household size; and (4) a steady rise in the proportion of married women who work outside the home (Cherlin & Furstenberg, 1988).

In addition to the forces of industrialization and urbanization, there has been a parallel trend in ideology similar to the trend in the United States stressing independence and self-fulfillment. Thus, increasingly the positive and liberating effects of divorce on adults and children are being sought as individual rights (Mitterauer & Sieder, 1982). Also, European governments have been cited as facilitating divorce by providing greater economic support to single parents. However, the extent of such support is increasingly being questioned as divorce becomes more normalized and Europe deals with problems of a slow growth economy.

Yet these general social forces are modified by historical experience, common values, and political structure (Cherlin & Furstenberg, 1988). A wide variation in divorce rates exists among European nations, ranging from the former Soviet Union (3.39 per 1,000 individuals) to Italy (0.44 per 1,000 individuals) (United Nations, 1992), and societal response to divorce also varies somewhat. In general, the rates of divorce are higher in more highly industrialized and urbanized Northern Europe than in Southern Europe (see Table 9.1). Nations representative of different regions of Europe and/or unique cultural variations are discussed below. Little was ever known about divorce in Eastern European nations, and what was known has probably dramatically changed with the democratic revolutions of 1990–1991. Divorce in Communist Eastern Europe was always common and continued to increase in spite of fairly strict divorce legislation (Haderka, 1987). What was once known as the Soviet Union is discussed as representative of Eastern Europe because of greater availability of data.

United Kingdom

The United States most resembles Britain in its pattern of divorce and remarriage largely because of the influence of the common English-speaking culture. Britain has the highest divorce rate in Western Europe (2.86 per 1,000 individuals) (United Nations, 1992). The divorce rate doubled from 1970 to 1980 (Family Policy Studies Center, 1984). The more lenient legislation incorporated within the Divorce Law Reform Act of 1969 facilitated the increase and is related to increases in the levels of divorce at all durations of marriage (Kiernan, 1988). Recent research also indicates the strong role of socioeconomic characteristics in predicting divorce in Britain today (Haskey, 1984).

Divorce has been the major contributor to the growth in single-parent families in Britain. In 1984, 13% of all British families with dependent children were single-parent families, and in approximately 90% of these fami-

TABLE 9.1. Crude Divorce Rates (per 1,000 Individuals) in Selected Nations in North America and Europe

North America	
United States	4.83
Canada	2.80
Mexico	0.57
Puerto Rico	3.89
Europe	
United Kingdom	2.86
Sweden	2.20
France	1.90
Italy	0.44
Former Soviet Union	3.39

Note. Data from United Nations *1990 Demographic Yearbook* (1992). The years of these data range from 1987 to 1989.

lies, the mother was the custodial parent (*General Household Survey Report*, 1984).

Similar to the United States, a frequent consequence of single parenthood is poverty. Over one-half of all single-parent families were living below the national poverty line in 1980. Fifty-two percent of single parents today rely on state benefits as their major source of income. The high reliance on government benefits can be explained by adverse economic conditions, gender inequities in income, and limited availability of child care. The tendency of British social policy has been to assume that single mothers are parents first and workers second. Thus, single mothers are guaranteed economic support for as long as their children are dependent (usually to age 16) with no pressure to seek employment (Kiernan, 1988). Unlike the United States, British policy also permits a man to pay a residual amount to his first family while concentrating his resources on his current family (Maclean, 1987)—thereby giving priority to his present family. At present, the British government appears to be moving away from the welfare state notion of extensive support after divorce. There is greater emphasis on enforcing laws that require fathers to pay support to children of the first marriage and women to become self-sufficient (Kiernan, 1988).

The remarriage rates in Britain are considered relatively high by British tradition (approximately 50%). A major motivating factor in remarriage has been enhanced economic well-being for single mothers (Miller, 1984).

Sweden

The Swedish rate of divorce was one of the highest in Europe following World War II and has accelerated faster than that of most other European nations since then. However, during the 1980s, the divorce rates stabilized as they have in other Western nations. Currently, the rate of divorce in Sweden (2.20 per 1,000 individuals) is second to that of Britain (Popenoe, 1988).

The divorce rate is thought not to be a highly valid indicator of relationship or family stability in Sweden because of very high rates of cohabitation and declining marriage rates. Although cohabitation is considered part of the courtship process that leads to marriage, the majority of Swedes cohabit for relatively long periods of time prior to marriage, half of all children are born in cohabiting unions, and an increasing number of young Swedes are expected not to marry. Cohabiting couples have much higher rates of dissolution than do married couples because individuals who marry in Sweden have lower risk factors (e.g., older, more children, and higher socioeconomic status) (Hoem & Hoem, 1988). Thus, actual rates of "relationship" dissolution would be much higher if cohabiting unions were included with actual marriages.

The high Swedish divorce rate is somewhat surprising because so many factors associated with divorce in the United States are mitigated in Sweden, including poverty, teen pregnancies, early marriage, interethnic and interfaith unions, and high residential mobility. Also, high divorce rates are contrary to Sweden's long history of social welfare in support of families. Reiss (1988) contends that marriage and family behaviors in Sweden may be less conventional as compared to other Western nations because Christianity historically has been a less dominant influence. However, divorce per se has seldom been addressed by the Swedish government. Popenoe (1988) suggests that much more research is needed to understand the reasons for the high rates of divorce and general relationship instability in Swedish society.

Similar to the United States, Sweden also has a high proportion of single-parent families. Eighteen percent of Swedish families were single-parent families in 1980 compared to almost 25% in the United States (U.S. Bureau of the Census, 1991). Yet there are two noticeable differences between the two nations regarding single parents: (1) in Sweden, almost all children are born to parents who live together, and (2) the economic situation of single-parent families in Sweden is not characterized by the high level of relative deprivation as in the United States (Hoem & Hoem, 1988; Popenoe, 1988).

France

France, like Sweden, has experienced very high rates of cohabitation, out-of-wedlock births, and divorce in recent years. Such rates in France are surprising because they are inconsistent with other European nations outside Scandinavia, and France is a predominantly Catholic nation (Roussel & Thery, 1988). The divorce rate in 1988 was 1.90 per 1,000 individuals (United Nations, 1992).

Two of the reasons given for the relatively high rates of divorce in France include the massive movement of women into the labor market and reforms in the divorce laws. Such changes are thought to reflect a wider cultural change related to (1) a new image of women and changes they have brought to families and (2) value differences of the "baby boom" cohort (Roussel & Thery, 1988). Also, it should be noted that more lenient attitudes toward divorce have existed in France for many generations; for example, the French Revolution (1789–1799) secularized marriage and introduced very liberal divorce legislation which was repealed about 25 years later (French Embassy, 1981).

Historically, the French government has been concerned with changes from traditional family patterns, especially declining birthrates; thus there has been strong state intervention on behalf of families. Divorced or otherwise single mothers traditionally have been viewed as victims by the state and have received special assistance. However, as in the United States and other European nations, much debate has ensued over the continuation of current welfare policies because (1) it is felt that these policies undermine family solidarity and (2) increasingly, divorced mothers are not viewed as victims but as initiators of their own fate (Roussel & Thery, 1988).

Italy

Historically, Italy has had a strong antidivorce tradition with Italian families characterized by the stability of both their nuclear and their extended family relationships. Italy, in fact, had no legal provision for divorce until 1970, whereas most other European nations permitted divorce under some conditions since the mid-1800s. Also, unlike other nations in Europe, the stability of the family institution lessened only moderately as a result of the introduction of divorce legislation. It should be noted that divorce rates vary greatly by region of the country, with the more urban and industrialized north having divorce rates twice as high as the south (Sgritta, 1988).

There are still strong legal deterrents to divorce in Italy. There must be a legal separation of at least 3 years prior to a divorce petition's being considered. Also, judicial procedures are slow and relatively expensive. Thus, social scientists believe that a number of separations do not end in divorce (Sgritta, 1988).

Another major deterrent to divorce in Italy is the influence of the Catholic church. Other factors frequently related to divorce in Italy include the delay of women moving into the labor force, a chronic housing shortage, economic problems of the nation, and the efficient social control exerted by kin and community, especially in the less urbanized areas. Sgritta (1988) concludes that the legal costs of separation and divorce, along with the hardships and economic costs associated with searching for and renting an independent dwelling, are onerous for most Italians, especially if the wife is not gainfully employed.

Consistent with the tradition of family stability, Italy has a much smaller proportion of single parents due either to divorce or out-of-wedlock births than do other European nations. Yet the increase in this family form in recent years is thought to represent a significant change in the traditional notion of family (Sgritta, 1988). In general, recent research indicates that increasingly marriage is not indissoluble, and thus higher divorce rates are projected for the future (Sabbadini, 1985).

Former Soviet Union

The former Soviet Union experienced an extraordinary increase in divorce prior to its demise as a republic in 1991; the divorce rate tripled between

1960 to 1980. Statistical data in the 1980s placed the divorce rate in the former Soviet Union at a level second only to the United States among major industrial nations (Moskoff, 1983; see Table 9.1). Like other European nations, the Soviet Union liberalized its divorce laws in the mid-1960s. Prior to that time, the Soviet government attempted to suppress divorce by cumbersome and lengthy court procedures that could be very expensive (Moskoff, 1983). Divorce was seen by the Soviet government as a "youth problem" because one-third of all separations occurred in the first year of marriage, and two-thirds by 5 years of marriage (Perevedentsev, 1978). The former Soviet Union included many largely rural republics, and these areas evidenced much lower rates than did the more urban western republics.

The reasons for the significant increase in divorce were not thoroughly studied. Scholars primarily focused on complaints given by petitioners for divorce (Perevedentsev, 1978). The vast majority of divorces (two-thirds) were initiated by women, and the most frequent reasons given for divorce were psychological in nature. Incompatibility of character was most frequently mentioned and was a catch-all term that included such complaints as value conflicts, distrust, cruelty, disrespect, and jealousy. Also, alcoholism was frequently mentioned by these women. Perevedentsev (1978) reports that almost one-half of all women filed for divorce because of their husbands' alcoholism. Yet it is not clear whether alcohol was a cause of the divorce or was a result of marital discord (Moskoff, 1983). Adultery was also commonly mentioned, especially in marriages of longer duration. One study indicated that two-thirds of the men's suits and three-fourths of the women's suits mentioned this complaint (Chuiko, 1975).

From a sociological perspective, much has been written about the impact of industrialization, for example, the decline in the economic functions of the family, the dramatic reduction of wives' economic dependence on husbands, and stress associated with urbanization, including a severe and chronic housing shortage, daily shopping to find scarce items, and traveling in crowded mass transit systems (Moskoff, 1983). In addition, the higher education level and the greater level of intellectual and emotional development of the people have increased individualism and raised expectations for happiness (Perevedentsev, 1978). It would be expected that this ideological trend has accelerated since the democratic revolution. Changing gender roles have also been identified as a contributing factor to divorce. The Soviet family changed from a patriarchal unit in which the husband was the distinct and unquestioned head to an egalitarian family with the wife often contributing as much, if not more, of the income to the family than the husband (Perevedentsev, 1978).

Soviet scholars expressed much concern about the negative consequences of divorce. As in the United States, fathers often did not remain involved with their children after divorce. Fatherless households were associated with poor academic performance, teen crime, and problems in psychosexual development; however, socioeconomic status was not controlled for in these studies (Aristova, 1985; Moskoff, 1983).

Women with children faced severe financial constraints after divorce. A father was obligated to pay child support equal only to one-fourth of his income regardless of the number of children, and many fathers defaulted on their child support (Moskoff, 1983).

Loneliness was identified as a major problem for divorced individuals. Fewer than half of all divorced individuals remarry, compared to about 80% in the United States, with men being more likely to remarry than women. Low remarriage rates were related to the absence of housing and the changing role of women (Moskoff, 1983). The Soviet government was very concerned about this low rate of remarriage because of its impact on fertility and thus the labor supply (Moskoff, 1983).

LATIN AMERICA

Two major influences on the divorce laws and practices in Latin American have been identified: (1) the Catholic church's view that marriages should not be broken and (2) the beliefs of the 16th-century Spanish and Portuguese conquerors that men should provide for their wives and children, maintain proper links with kin, maintain their honor against attack, and seize honor from others (i.e., *machismo*). Divorce laws, however, have gradually changed, frequently in the midst of protest. Uruguay enacted divorce legislation in the early 20th century and "it was as socially revolutionary as when Italy did so" (Quale, 1988, p. 273). The revolutionary nature of these changes was also evident in Mexico when governors were thrown out of office for attempting to pass divorce legislation in 1915 and 1923. Similarly, Perón was thrown out of office in 1965 when Argentina liberalized divorce laws, passed legislation enabling women to vote, and mandated equal pay for equal work. Columbia legalized divorce for civil marriages in 1973, Brazil in 1977, and Argentina in 1987 (Quale, 1988). In Mexico, when the state broke with the church during the revolution (1911–1917), divorce was made possible and in some places very easy (Cubitt, 1988).

In 1987, the only remaining Latin American countries that did not recognize divorce were Chile and Paraguay (Quale, 1988). In addition, in these countries, annulments were available only under the rules of the Catholic church.

In spite of divorce not being legal, Latin American countries appear always to have had provisions for ending unhappy marriages. For example, prior to 1977 in Brazil, if a man unknowingly married a women who was not a virgin, he could have the marriage "voided" (Presel, 1980). Furthermore, if a man found his wife had been unfaithful, he was "supposed to go into a raging fit" (Presel, 1980, p. 119), could legally kill or severely beat her lover, and would almost inevitably insist on a legal separation. In these cases, husbands were allowed to take concubines with no damage to their reputations. Thus, "informal consensual unions" were common (Quale, 1988). There is a serious lack of reliable marriage and divorce data in Latin America countries, which has been attributed to the prevalence of consensual unions, which are systematically not registered. Wives often view social and legal divorce as a threat to their position; therefore, they strive to avoid divorce even when legally available (Quale, 1988).

Several factors, however, have been reported to be related to divorce rates in Latin America. Specifically, Goldman (1981) studied divorce in Colombia, Panama, and Peru. She reported that unlike several other countries, there was virtually no relationship between level of education and the probability of divorce. In contrast, she found that separation and divorce rates were higher if women married before age 15, and that consensual unions were much more likely to end in separation than were legal marriages (Colombia, 7:1; Peru, 7:1; Panama, 3:1). The higher dissolution rates of consensual unions, however, could not be accounted for by age, area of residence, or level of education. These findings were viewed as being generalizable to other Latin American countries.

ASIA

Divorce laws and practices, similar to many other parts of the world, have changed significantly in Asian nations. These changes are attributed to religious laws, political revolutions, urbanization, industrialization, and, in some cases, Western influences.

Japan

Japan has experienced significant changes in divorce laws and trends. In 1883, it was believed that Japan had the highest divorce rate (3.4 per 1,000 population) in the world. However, the Civil Law Act in 1892 reduced the divorce rate by half (Yuzawa, 1990), and this low rate continued until after World War II when, because of impoverishment, men and women stayed together in order to survive (Katsutoshi, 1986). Japan still has a low divorce rate, even though it has increased since 1964 (Hutter, 1988). This increase has been attributed to several factors, including (1) the growth in the Japanese economy accompanied by an increase in employment opportunities for women, thereby reducing anxieties about how they can make a living after divorce; (2) the first wave of baby boomers reaching divorceable age; (3) more favorable attitudes toward divorce; (4) decrease in the influence of the extended family; and (5) women's desire to live more rewarding lives (Katsutoshi, 1986; Yuzawa, 1990). Furthermore, it is expected that the divorce rate in Japan will continue to increase as the roles of women continue to change.

Japan's relatively low level of divorce (1.5 per 1,000) has been attributed to the high value on family life, suppression of individual freedom of choice, and the education of women to be good wives and wise mothers (Yuzawa, 1990). In addition, divorce in Japan creates scandals, and children of divorced parents find their marriage prospects diminished (Hutter, 1988).

In the 1800s, only men were allowed to initiate divorce in Japan. In contrast, in 1988, 74% of all petitions for divorce were initiated by women. Data indicate, however, that in 90% of the divorces in Japan, the husband and wife mutually agree and merely notify the registration office (the simplest form of divorce in the world) (Yuzawa, 1990).

Approximately 70% of all divorces in Japan involve children, a complete reversal of 30 years ago. Prior to 1947, only fathers received custody of children; since that time custody can be awarded to either parent. In 1984, mothers received custody in 72% of the cases (Katsutoshi, 1986). This change is the result of (1) a decline in the notion that children belong to the household and thus to the father as head of the household and (2) the increase in nuclear families wherein grandparents are no longer available to take care of the children.

Only a little more than 20% of all children in their mother's custody have ever received monetary support from their fathers (Yuzawa, 1990). Because the income of custodial mothers is only about 40% of ordinary households, many claim the "child allowance" granted by the state. This lack of support may be due to no provision for visiting rights between the noncustodial parents and their children, with the result being that rarely do an absent parents and child meet after divorce. There are several indications, however, that currently these issues are being addressed. Proposed changes may make it easier for couples to seek a divorce by providing formal agreements regarding custody and financial support, with the government claiming payment from the person responsible for child support.

India

Because the social sciences focus on areas considered "important," there has been a lack of research in areas such as marriage and divorce in India (Pothen, 1986, 1989). Thus, statistical information on divorce and remarriage is limited. It is assumed, however, that prior to 1970, there were few divorces, with a gradual increase occurring between 1970 and 1976 as a result of the 1976 amendment to the 1955 Hindu Marriage and Divorce Law; since then, the number of divorces has steadily increased each year (Hussain, 1983).

Because Hindus constitute more than 80% of the population in India, it is assumed that Hindu laws impact the larger society, and these laws have changed over the last few decades. Hindu marriage was historically viewed as important for men but essential to women; wives were expected to be completely devoted to their husbands and were bound to them even after the husband's death (Pothen, 1989).

The 1955 Hindu Marriage and Divorce Act offered equal opportunity to the wife and husband to separate from each other and legally terminate their marriage (Hussain, 1983; Pothen, 1986, 1989). According to this act, divorce could be granted on several grounds, including adultery, cruelty, venereal disease, and being missing for 7 years. In 1976, this act was amended to include mutual consent.

For the Muslim population, law and religion are blended to form personal laws. Furthermore, while Islamic public law in India has grown more and more receptive to foreign concepts, family law has tended to be less flexible and more conservative (Hussain, 1983).

Under Islamic law, historically the husband held the arbitrary measure of *talaq* (the three-word formula, "I divorce thee"), which was a constant threat to a wife; the Muslim husband held absolute and unlimited power (Hussain, 1983). Mohammad, however, instituted reforms that limited the power of divorce possessed by husbands, gave women the right to obtain a separation on reasonable grounds, and practically forbid the practice of *talaq* without the intervention of arbiters or judges. In 1939, the Dissolution of Muslim Marriages Act recognized the right of the wife to dissolve a marriage on selected grounds. In 1986, however, Islamic law in India was changed and a divorced husband is now obligated only to return the *mehr* (marriage settlement) and to pay his wife maintenance only during the *iddat* (3 months following the divorce) (Pathak & Rajan, 1989; Mody, 1987). Therefore, if a woman is not able to maintain herself after divorce, it would be the responsibility of her children, parents, or other relatives. This latter law is viewed as having negative consequences for Muslim women and has resulted in the government's drafting a uniform civil code (Pathak & Rajan, 1989; Hussain, 1983).

Many authors have concluded that it is a combination of factors, similar to Western cultures, that leads to marriages terminating in India. The most prevalent reasons cited by women are cruelty, interference from in-laws, and illicit sex. The most common reasons cited by men are women's poor management of income, insufficient income, interference from in-laws, and infidelity. According to Mehta (1975), however, the primary reason the divorce rate in India is increasing is that women are no longer willing to occupy a subordinate position in the family while men still hold a traditional outlook and consequently treat women as inferior beings.

Similar to other cultures, divorce often creates an economic crisis for women and, unlike married women, divorced women often seek employment. Seeking employment may be more likely because children are viewed as the responsibility of the mother and her family. Pothen (1986, 1989) has reported that some children were upset as a result of their parents' divorce, whereas others were reconciled to the situation and were viewed as happy and well adjusted. Indian culture, however, has the advantage of the support of a large number of relatives in addition to parents.

China

Divorce has been possible in China for more than 200 years. For example, in ancient law, three types of divorce were recognized: (1) mutual consent, (2) repudiation (seven grounds for men, three grounds for women), and (3) "intolerable acts" against principles of conjugality. The 1931 Chinese Soviet Republic Laws, however, were antifamily legislation based on the 1926 Soviet Family Code and permitted unrestrained divorce (for the first time women could initiate divorce) (Naltao, 1987).

Divorce practices in China vary by different regions of the country, and divorce statistics are not considered reliable. Indications are, however, that divorce was on the increase prior to 1949 (United Nations, 1985, 1986) and exploded with the passage of the marriage law of the People's Republic of China. Specifically, although China's divorce rates were lower than those of Sweden, England, the United States, and some Asian countries, it was the only country that almost doubled its divorce rate between 1979 and 1984 (United Nations, 1985, 1986).

The most recent (1981) law in China is based on the premise that marriage is found on "love, understanding, and mutual respect . . . which will result in loyalty and dedication to the nation" (Robinson, 1989, p. 651). No precise grounds for divorce were included in this law, but divorce is granted "in the event of complete and permanent breakdown of a marital relationship" (Platte, 1988, p. 436).

Divorce in China is not an easy or quick process. Rather, a process of education and mediation at several levels generally precedes the granting of divorce. The emphasis is on reconciliation (unless wife abuse or forced marriage is an issue); the court is only the last stage in the process and cases may be returned to work units in the neighborhood (Platte, 1988; Naltao, 1987; Robinson, 1989).

Reasons for divorce in China are similar to those in other countries. They vary between rural and urban areas and include wife battering, infidelity (Naltao, 1987), disagreement over the division of household duties, and maltreatment of women after the birth of a daughter (Platte, 1988). Similar to other countries, there is an inverse relationship between age at marriage and divorce, with most divorces taking place early in the marriage. Also, remarriages have a high rate of divorce (Platte, 1988).

Child custody favors the mother and property owned individually before marriage is retained after marriage. Property acquired during marriage is divided unless received as a gift or inheritance. In rural China, however, many women forfeit claims of property, and in all cases court judges are given wide discretion in the distribution of marital property.

It is generally assumed the divorce rate in China will remain low when compared to that of other countries, especially in the rural areas where 80% of the population lives. However, countervailing forces, including modernization, urbanization, and the "baby boomers," who are of divorceable age, may challenge this assumption.

Iran

Historically, in Iran men could simply say "I divorce thee" in front of two witnesses to effect a divorce (*talaq*). However, in 1967, the Shah passed the Family Protection Act, which prohibited men from exercising this right and marrying a second woman without the permission of the former wife (Aghajanian, 1986). This new law, strongly opposed by religious leaders, required legal procedures and evidence that spouses could not reconcile and is credited with changing the expectations of Iranian husbands.

As a result of the 1979 Islamic Revolution, and a return to more traditional Islamic religious practices, the Special Civil Court replaced the Family Protection Court with judges who were Islamic scholars. In addition, new laws were based on the Koran and the Islamic strong desire to protect the family from instability and divorce. Under Islamic law, the judge is advised to do his best to convince the husband and wife to reconcile (Aghajanian, 1986). However, couples who mutually consent to divorce may simply register their divorce with a notary public before two witnesses. (Women's consent, however, in such a strongly patriarchal society is questionable.)

The rate of divorce has increased in Iran since 1981 because of (1) the ease of getting a divorce, (2) many young people rushing into marriage during the revolution, (3) threats to family stability created by the war with Iraq, and (4) the difficulty urban middle-class families have had in adjusting to the Islamic value system.

Variables related to divorce in Iran are similar to those in several countries; for example, younger women, couples with no children, and couples where women are in the labor force are more likely to divorce. In addition, women who marry at later ages are more likely to divorce, possibly because they are better educated, better able to earn a living, and less willing to tolerate a bad marital situation.

Similar to other countries, divorce is viewed as more difficult for women than for men in Iran. Men remarry at considerably higher rates and have more nonfamilial activities to relieve their loneliness. Unless men have to repay a large dowry, they are not adversely affected financially by divorce.

In contrast, women seldom remarry and cannot extend social relationships outside the family. Women are entitled to alimony for only 3 months after divorce, and they usually have to use their dowries for living expenses. In addition, in order to escape a bad marriage, women often forfeit their dowries or receive only a portion of it. In addition, women cannot live by themselves, especially if they are young and do not have a child. Therefore, they usually must move back home with their brothers and/or father.

According to Islamic law, fathers are responsible for their children and have the right of custody of boys from age 2 and girls from age 7. In practice, however, mothers take care of the children, and in almost 75% of divorces, children live with their mother. Fathers, however, are required to provide for their children, which helps the mother financially (Aghajanian, 1986).

AFRICA

By the 1950s, almost all countries within Africa had introduced monogamous civil statutory marriages (as an option). Independent Liberia did so in the 19th century, whereas Ethiopia did not do so until the 1970s. However, statutory civil marriages took place alongside customary and usually polygynous forms of marriage. In spite of these changes, marriage and divorce laws and practices vary widely within Africa (see Hutchinson, 1990; Lee & Pol, 1988; Saunders, 1980; Ellovich, 1980; Dorjahn, 1990; Reyna, 1977).

Libya

In Libya, men are more free to divorce than are women; however, wives are not entirely helpless in this area (Khalidi, 1989). In general, there is no stigma attached to divorce in Libya and divorces tend to occur early in marriage.

The different perception of marriage for Libyan men and women may be a major contributor to divorce (Khalidi, 1989). For example, men more often feel marriage is essential for stability and preservation of the family institution, whereas women more often reported that necessity and family pressure influenced their decision to marry. In several countries, the formation of the nuclear family has been viewed as contributing to an increase in the divorce rate. However, in Libya the opposite is true. For example, the tendency for nuclear families to create their own households is seen as a possible way to reduce the rate of divorce. This trend is seen as reducing the amount of control families have on couples.

By law, if divorce occurs, men do not have to pay alimony (women are entitled to a salary from the state), except when there is an infant child who is too young to leave the mother. If there are other children, they become wards of the father at the time of divorce. However, because most divorces take place within 3 years of marriage, the number of children who are affected by divorce is small. Because men retain custody, there is an incentive for them to remarry, and because they do not pay alimony, they can afford to do so. Because the costs of remarrying a virgin are often prohibitive, remarriages are more often between two divorced persons.

Egypt

The divorce rate in Egypt is considered high (2 per 1,000 population compared to a marriage rate of 10 per 1,000) (Rugh, 1984). Data regarding divorces, however, are often combined with data on widows; therefore, there are questions about their reliability.

Divorce may take several forms in Egypt. A Muslim man may dissolve a marriage contract without court intervention by repudiating his wife three times (*talaq*). Women were not legislatively allowed to initiate divorce until after 1981, and they must go to court to seek a dissolution of marriage by judicial decree (Quale, 1988). Although husbands are not limited by conditions to secure a divorce, a woman may only petition on grounds that her husband (1) has failed to support her, (2) has a serious defect or ailment, (3) has a deleterious moral or social effect on her, (4) is absent for a long period, or (5) has been imprisoned (Rugh, 1984). Two additional means of effecting a divorce include mutual consent (where a woman pays a designated amount to her husband for compensation of his expenses) and annulment of a marriage that has been contracted in violation of prohibitions.

Men initiate approximately two-thirds of all divorces in Egypt, and divorce rates are higher in urban areas than in rural areas. In addition, divorce more often takes place when family size is small (fewer than three children) and spouses are younger than 25 years old; 95% of all divorces occur among persons who are illiterate (Rugh, 1984). Causes of divorce in rank order for females are polygamy, conflict with the husband's family, and finances. Men most often report incompatibility or lack of harmony and conflict with in-laws.

By law, girls remain with their mother until age 12, and boys until age

10, or longer if a judge views it in the child's best interest. Fathers, however, are fully responsible for financial maintenance of children, and women are entitled to alimony for 1 year, which covers the period during which a woman is forbidden to remarry (*idda*, or 3 months) in order to determine whether she is pregnant by her former husband. Women can protect themselves from the negative economic consequences of divorce by amassing a quantity of gifts (usually gold jewelry) during marriage and/or including in the marriage negotiations a set amount of money to be transferred upon divorce. These, however, are considered cynical strategies and evidence of mistrust.

Ghana

In general, divorce is viewed as undesirable in Ghana, especially when a bridewealth has been paid. There has been, however, an increase in divorce, and there is currently a high rate of divorce in this country. Overall, after 20 years of marriage, approximately 32% of the women have dissolved their marriages through separation and divorce (Amoateng & Heaton, 1989). There are several factors reported to be related to varying divorce rates: women who have a primary education (compared to no education or advanced education) have the highest divorce rates, women from matrilineal subcultures are more likely to divorce than those from patrilineal subcultures, and Christians dissolve their marriages at a higher rate than do traditional believers and Moslems. In addition, people who live in urban regions, influenced by modernization and mass media, have higher divorce rates. Young women, women who work after marriage, and women who have children after marriage (as compared to before marriage) are more likely to divorce (Amoateng & Heaton, 1989). In addition, Hagan (1976) viewed fluctuations in the divorce rate to coincide with the seasonal fluctuations in fishing activities and the developmental cycle of the family. These cycles alter the spousal relationship; when a man is unable to fish (because of season or age), he becomes an economic liability and the divorce rate increases.

A woman who divorces after a statutory civil marriage usually receives little help from her kin because, in their eyes, she has effectively refused her own side of the reciprocal obligations of kin. However, few women are in modern statutory marriages, and even when they divorce, rules still tend to make it easier for men to obtain a divorce than for women (Quale, 1988).

Nigeria

Divorce in Nigeria is considered to be a "bad thing" because social relationships are highly valued. At the same time, there are no barriers to divorce if couples do not wish to remain married. In fact, some data indicated that as high as 75–90% of all completed marriages end in divorce (Cohen, 1971). In general, a man may pronounce the divorce in front of three witnesses (*talaq*), and women can initiate divorce if they are willing to pay for it and tolerate the complicated court system.

Cohen (1971) contends that Nigerian society supported marital instability through household organization; that is, divorce breaks up contiguous and continuous contacts among family members but does not break up households, which are the basic corporate units of the society. Children continue to be cared for, and the husband's household survives divorce, with women either returning home or becoming independent. Specifically, older women are taken care of by younger relatives (usually sons or brothers) and young women become *zowers* and return to their families until they remarry. With subsequent divorces, women's freedom increases and they may rent rooms in a city and have several paramours who support them. (*Zowers* are not considered prostitutes but simply women between husbands.)

Most children "lose" a mother, however, as a result of divorce, although the mother may continue to visit and bring gifts. Boys seem more affected than girls, and co-wives often do not function as proper mothers to these children; therefore, paternal aunts may take over some of these functions.

There are several variables related to lower rates of divorce in Nigeria, including marriages (1) that have live children, (2) in which the woman contributes to the economic well-being of the man (especially in rural areas where she helps on the farm and goes to the well to get water), (3) in the lower social strata, with lower bridewealth payments, (4) in which the husband and wife exchange secrets (greater intimacy), (5) in rural areas where the wife does not have to move away from her family when she marries, and (6) in which the wife is obedient. In contrast, divorce rates are higher among marriages (1) in which the wife runs home to her family, (2) that are polygynous (3) in which *purdah* (female seclusion) is practiced, and (4) in which the spouses exhibit greater involvement with their own kin.

It is predicted that as urbanization increases, the divorce rate in Nigeria will also increase. However, it is also expected that divorce rates in rural areas will rise as a result of increasing mechanization and less dependence on women in farming. This increase may also be the result of different expectations between men and women. For example, both young men and young women indicate that they want to include some modern changes in their own marriages. In general, however, boys appear to be influenced by traditional Islamic values while girls are influenced by Christian Western values. Specifically, boys tend to see their marriages as part of and related to the wider kin networks, which stress more traditional values (male dominance, wifely obedience, and polygyny), whereas girls seems themselves as more independent and not deferring to others (Cohen, 1971).

CONCLUSION

This comparative analysis of divorce has been limited by a dearth of scholarship. Research is limited to macrostructural factors, demographic determinants, the process of obtaining a divorce, and historical trends. Research on postdivorce adjustment, including remarriage, is negligible.

However, it can be concluded that no culture has found a formula for marital success even though all societies traditionally have erected barriers to facilitate marital stability. Thus, divorce, or some other form of marital dissolution, exists as an escape from a marriage that one or both spouses view as intolerable. Yet, such allowances may not be equitable for all spouses.

Based on this review, it appears that social and economic development as well as patterns of reproduction affect the decision to leave a marriage. Major influences include urbanization, industrialization, Western thought, and changes in the roles of women. It is anticipated that as these demographic and social changes continue, the rate of marital dissolution will continue to increase throughout the world.

Societies have responded to the problems of divorced individuals and families with a wide range of responses, from punitive measures to supportive social welfare programs. However, the increasing numbers of divorced individuals has necessitated cultures to move toward more ameliorative approaches, either at the family or the societal level. Divorce has become a human rights and equity issue in recent years, with demands for the right of divorce and fair settlements increasingly being made.

REFERENCES

Aghajanian, A. (1986). Some notes on divorce in Iran. *Journal of Marriage and the Family, 48,* 749–755.

Amoateng, A. Y., & Heaton, T. B. (1989). The sociodemographic correlates of the timing of divorce in Ghana. *Journal of Comparative Family Studies, 20,* 79–96.

Aristova, N. G. (1985). Chto dumaiut o razvodakh budushchie nevesty? *Sotsiologicheskie Issledovaniia, 2,* 111–114.

Ball, R. E., & Robbins, L. (1986). Marital status and life satisfaction among Black Americans. *Journal of Marriage and the Family, 48,* 389–394.

Canabal, M. E. (1990). An economic approach to marital dissolution in Puerto Rico. *Journal of Marriage and the Family, 52,* 515–530.

Canadian alamanac and inventory. (1992). Toronto: Author.

Cherlin, A., & Furstenberg, F. F. (1988). The changing European family. *Journal of Family Issues, 9,* 291–297.

Chuiko, L. V. (1975). *Braki i Razvody.* Moscow.

Cohen, R. (1971). Dominance and defiance: A study of marital instability in an Islamic African society. *Anthropological Studies, 6,* 1–30.

Cubitt, T. (1988). *Latin American society.* New York: Wiley.

Dorjahn, V. R. (1990). The marital game: Divorce and divorce frequency among the Temne of Sierra Leone. *Anthropological Quarterly, 63,* 169–182.

Eichler, M. (1988). *Families in Canada today: Recent changes and their policy consequences.* Toronto: Gage.

Ellovich, R. S. (1980). Dioula women in town: A view of introethnic variation (Ivory Coast). In E. Bourguignon (Ed.), *A world of women: Anthropological studies of women in the societies of the world* (pp. 87–103). New York: Praeger.

Family Policy Studies Center. (1984). *One-parent families.* Fact sheet.

Fine, M. A., McKenry, P. C., & Chung, H. (1991). Post-divorce adjustment of Black and White single parents. *Journal of Divorce and Remarriage, 17,* 121–134.

French Embassy. (1981). Women and divorce in France. *International Journal of Family Therapy, 3,* 62–82.

Frisbie, W. P. (1986). Variation in patterns of marital instability among Hispanics. *Journal of Marriage and the Family, 48,* 99–106.

Frisbie, W. P., Bean, F. D., & Eberstein, I. W. (1978). Patterns of marital instability among Mexican Americans, Blacks, and Anglos. In F. D. Bean & W. P. Frisbie (Eds.), *The demography of racial and ethnic groups* (pp. 143–163). New York: Academic Press.

General household survey report. (1984). London: HMSO, Office of Population Censuses and Surveys.

Glick, P. C. (1973). Perspectives on the recent upturn in divorce and remarriage. *Demography, 10,* 301–314.

Goldman, N. (1981). Dissolution of first unions in Colombia, Panama, and Peru. *Demography, 18,* 659–679.

Goode, W. (1963). *World revolution and family patterns.* London: Collier & Macmillan.

Gove, W. R., & Shin, H. (1989). The psychological well-being of divorced and widowed men and women: An empirical analysis. *Journal of Family Issues, 10,* 122–144.

Haderka, J. (1987). Problems of the divorce rate in European socialist countries in the light of the sociology of the law. *Sociologicky-Casopis, 23,* 55–65.

Hagan, G. P. (1976). Divorce, polygyny, and family welfare. *Ghana Journal of Sociology, 10,* 67–84.

Hampton, R. (1980). Institutional decimation, marital exchange, and disruption in black families. *Western Journal of Black Studies, 4,* 132–135.

Haskey, J. (1984). Social class and socio-economic differentials in divorce in England and Wales. *Population Studies, 38,* 419–438.

Hoem, B. & Hoem, J. M. (1988). The Swedish family: Aspects of contemporary developments. *Journal of Family Issues, 9,* 397–424.

Hussain, S. J. (1983). *Marriage breakdown and divorce law reform in contemporary society: A comparative study of U.S.A., U.K., and India.* New Delhi: Concept.

Hutchinson, S. (1990). Rising divorce among the Nuer, 1936–1983. *Man, 25,* 393–411.

Hutter, M. (1988). *The changing family: Comparative perspectives.* New York: Macmillan.

Katsutoshi, Y. (1986). Divorce, Japanese style. *Japan Quarterly, 33,* 416–420.

Kephart, W. M., & Jedlicka, D. (1988). *The family, society, and the individual.* New York: Harper & Row.

Khalidi, M. S. (1989). Divorce in Libya: A critical commentary. *Journal of Comparative Family Studies, 20,* 118–126.

Kiernan, K. E. (1988). The British family: Contemporary trends and issues. *Journal of Family Issues, 9,* 298–316.

Kitson, G. C., with Holmes, W. M. (1992). *Portrait of divorce: Adjustment to marital dissolution.* New York: Guilford Press.

Lee, B. S., & Pol, L. G. (1988). Effect of marital dissolution on fertility in Cameroon. *Social Biology, 35,* 293–306.

Lee, G. R. (1982). *Family structure and interaction: A comparative analysis.* Minneapolis: University of Minnesota Press.

Maclean, M. (1987). Households after divorce: The availability of resources and their impact on children. In J. Brannen & G. Wilson (Eds.), *Give and take in families* (pp. 42–55). Boston: Allen & Unwin.

Martin T. C., & Bumpass, L. L. (1989). Recent trends in marital disruption. *Demography, 26,* 37–51.

Mehta, R. (1975). *Divorced Hindu women.* Delhi: Vikas.

Menaghan, E. G., & Lieberman, M. A. (1986). Changes in depression following divorce: A panel study. *Journal of Marriage and the Family, 48,* 319–328.

Miller, J. (1984). *Living standards of low-income, one-parent families: Movements out of poverty.* Discussion Paper 209, University of York, Social Policy Research Unit.

Min, P. G. (1988). The Korean American family. In C. H. Mindel, R. W. Habenstein, & R. Wright (Eds.), *Ethnic families in America* (pp. 199–229). New York: Elsevier.

Mitterauer, M., & Sieder, R. (1982). Marriage, reproduction and sexuality. In M. Mitterauer (Ed.), *The European family: Patriarchy to partnership from the middle ages to the present* (pp. 136–137). Chicago: University of Chicago Press.

Mody, N. B. (1987). The Shah Bano judgment and its aftermath. *Asian Survey, 27,* 935–953.

Moskoff, W. (1983). Divorce in USSR. *Journal of Marriage and the Family, 45,* 419–425.

Murdock, G. P. (1950). Family stability in non-European cultures. *Annals, 272,* 195–201.

Naltao, W. (1987). Divorce: Traditional ideas receding. *Beijing Review, 11,* 23–25.

Pathak, Z., & Rajan, R. S. (1989). Shahbano. *Journal of Women in Culture and Society, 14,* 558–582.

Perevedentsev, V. I. (1978). The Soviet family today. *Sociology and Social Research, 67,* 245–259.

Peters, J. F. (1983). Divorce: The disengaging, disengaged, and re-engaging process. In K. Iswaran (Ed.), *The Canadian family* (pp. 225–248). Toronto: Gage.

Platte, E. (1988). Divorce trends and patterns in China: Past and present. *Pacific Affairs, 61,* 428–445.

Popenoe, D. (1988). What is happening to the family in Sweden? In N. D. Glenn & M. T. Coleman (Eds.), *Family relations* (pp. 92–99). Chicago: Dorsey.

Pothen, S. (1986). *Divorce: Its causes and consequences in Hindu society.* New Delhi: Shakti.

Pothen, S. (1989). Divorce in Hindu society. *Journal of Comparative Family Studies, 20,* 377–392.

Prendiville, P. (1988). Divorce in Ireland: An analysis of the referendum to amend the constitution, June 1986. *Women's Studies International Forum, 4,* 355–363.

Presel, E. (1980). Spirit magic in the social relationships between men and women. In E. Bourguignon (Ed.), *A world of women: Anthropological studies of women in the societies of the world* (pp. 107–127). New York: Praeger.

Price, S. J., & McKenry, P. C. (1988). *Divorce.* Newbury Park, CA: Sage.

Quale, G. R. (1988). *A history of marriage systems.* New York: Greenwood.

Reiss, I. L. (1988). *Family systems in America.* New York: Holt, Rinehart & Winston.

Reyna, S. P. (1977). The nationality of divorce: Marital instability among the Barma of Chad. *Journal of Comparative Family Studies, 8,* 269–288.

Robinson, B. W., & McVey, W. W. (1985). The relative contributions of death and divorce to marital dissolution in Canada and the United States. *Journal of Comparative Family Studies, 16,* 93–109.

Robinson, J. (1989). Family policies, women, and the collective interest in contemporary China. *Policy Studies Review, 8,* 648–662.

Roussel, L. & Thery, I. (1988). France: Demographic change and family policy since World War II. *Journal of Family Issues, 9,* 336–353.

Rugh, A. B. (1984). *Family in contemporary Egypt.* Syracuse, NY: Syracuse University Press.

Sabbadini, L. L. (1985). *Matrimonie e convivenza nell'opione publica in Italia.* Rome: IRP, WP 02.

Sanchez-Ayendez, M. (1988). The Puerto Rican American family. In C. H. Mindel, R. W. Habenstein, & R. Wright (Eds.), *Ethnic families in America: Patterns and variations* (3rd ed., pp. 173–193). New York: Elsevier.

Saunders, M. O. (1980). Women's role in a Muslim town (Mirria, Republic of Niger). In E. Bourguignon (Ed.), *A world of women: Anthropological studies of women in the societies of the world* (pp. 56–87). New York: Praeger.

Sgritta, G. B. (1988). The Italian family: Tradition and change. *Journal of Family Issues, 9,* 372–396.

Staples, R. (1985). Changes in black family structure: The conflict between family ideology and structural conditions. *Journal of Marriage and the Family, 47,* 1005–1113.

Staples, R., & Mirande, A. (1980). Racial and cultural variations among American families: A decennial review of the literature on minority families. *Journal of Marriage and the Family, 42,* 157–173.

Sue, S., & Kitano, H. (1973). Asian American stereotypes. *Journal of Social Issues, 29,* 83–98.

Sweet, J. A., & Bumpass, L. L. (1988). *American families and households.* New York: Russell Sage.

Teachman, J. D. (1986). First and second marital dissolution: A decomposition exercise for whites and blacks. *Sociological Quarterly, 27,* 571–590.

United Nations. (1985). *Demographic yearbook.* New York: Author.

United Nations. (1986). *Demographic yearbook*. New York: Author.
United Nations. (1992). *1990 Demographic yearbook*. New York: Author.
U.S. Bureau of the Census. (1991). *Statistical abstract of the United States: 1991*. Washington, DC: Author.
Yuzawa, Y. (1990). Recent trends of divorce and custody in Japan. *Journal of Divorce, 13,* 129–141.

CHAPTER TEN

Chinese Families in Later Life

WILLIAM H. MEREDITH
DOUGLAS A. ABBOTT

China is quickly becoming an aging nation. The number of its citizens over 60 years old has reached 100 million. These senior citizens account for one-fifth of the elderly people in the world. The number of elderly in China grows every year at a rate faster than the world average. By the year 2000, China's elderly population will reach 130 million, making up one-tenth of the country's population, a milestone that will mark the beginning of an aging society in China ("China to Enter," 1992; "Senior Citizens," 1992; Zhu & Xu, 1992). The aged population is expected to increase by 3% annually over the next 50 years, far greater than the 1% growth rate for the total population. By the year 2040, senior citizens will total 380 million, accounting for an estimated 25% of the population (Zhuang, 1992). This dramatic shift in population demographics is known in China as the "white-haired shock" (Wang, 1992).

After more than 2,000 years of stability in terms of family roles, obligations, and expectations, Chinese families and the elderly who live in them are changing. In order to understand the role of the elderly in the modern Chinese family, it is first important to understand the traditional family in China. Past traditions are an important starting point for this analysis.

THE TRADITIONAL CHINESE FAMILY

The beliefs that form the basis of the Chinese family can be traced directly to Confucius (551–479 B.C.), whose ideas became the basis of Chinese social and political life for more than 2,000 years. Confucius's ideas penetrated to the core of the lives of ordinary Chinese people, effectively defining for them what it meant to be human and acting as the guiding principles of Chinese social life (Smith, 1991; King & Bond, 1985).

There were many distinctive characteristics of the traditional family in China. First, and foremost, the Chinese family was patriarchal. Roles were clearly defined, with males, particularly the father and eldest son, having the most dominant positions (Hsu, 1971a). Authority passed from the father to the eldest son, whose authority and decisions were absolute. Females, relegated to a subordinate position in the traditional Chinese family, were expected to please and obey their fathers, and if married, were subordinate to their husbands and their husbands' parents. The norm for women was compliance (Kitanao, 1985; Smith, 1991).

A second characteristic of the traditional Chinese family was that it was patrilocal; that is, the married couple lived with the husband's parents. According to this custom, the grandparents, their unmarried children, and their married sons together with their wives and children all lived in one household. Because of patrilocal residence, daughters were considered less valuable than sons because parents felt that daughters were being reared at their expense for the benefit of another family or clan (Sung, 1967). In some cases, particularly if the family was extremely poor, infanticide of the female child was practiced.

Because of its patrilocal residence pattern, the traditional family in China was also an extended family within which many generations and their offspring lived under one roof. Ideally, the more generations living under the same roof, the more status the family had. Besides the prestige factor, the extended family structure of the Chinese family provided another important function. In an agriculturally based economy, there was an urgent need for many workers to cultivate and till the land and harvest the crops. An isolated nuclear family would be at a disadvantage in this economy. The extended family system was a much more suitable arrangement, providing the family with additional laborers as well as providing the members of the extended family with some degree of economic security.

According to the Chinese system of patrilineal descent, the household property and land were to be divided equally among the sons, either at the father's death or at the marriage of the youngest son. However, in exchange for the property and land, the sons were expected to reciprocate by sharing equally in the responsibility for the care and support of their parents in their old age (Hsu, 1971b; Wong, 1988).

Ancestor worship was greatly emphasized in the traditional family in China. It was believed that a Chinese male could achieve some sense of immortality only if his family line was continued through the birth of sons. One of the greatest sins that a man could commit was to die without having any sons to carry on the family line and perform the ancestor worship rituals; therefore, an intense desire to have sons existed among the Chinese.

Filial piety was a highly cherished value in the traditional Chinese family. Filial piety is a set of moral principles, taught at a very young age and reinforced throughout one's life, that emphasizes reverence toward the nation's leaders and one's elders. Duty, obligation, importance of family name, service, and self-sacrifice to the elders, all essential elements of filial piety, characterized Chinese family relations. The meaning of filial piety is threefold: to have gratitude for the care given by one's parents, to respect and love one's parents, and to be attentive to one's parents' desires (Hsu, 1971a; Li, 1985). Complete devotion to parents was expected. Such devotion was taught in childhood through emphasis on obedience, proper conduct, moral training, and the acceptance of social obligations (Ho, 1986). A familiar proverb states: "Of all the teachings of the classics, filial piety comes first" (Kong, 1989, p. 22).

Chinese families were obsessed with social order and the need to "do the right thing." In families, this required children, no matter how old, to remain fanatically loyal to their parents and to value them. An old Chinese saying goes, "The elderly are a family's greatest treasure" (Yu, 1987, p. 211).

Filial piety required children to give priority to the parent's need for material comfort not only while they were alive but after death as well. After a parent's death, filial children spared no expense to provide an elaborate funeral ceremony. Professional musicians were hired to escort the coffin through the streets to the grave. Before and after the burial, survivors gathered for family banquets, and after the funeral, lineal descendants observed 49 days of mourning. Many people, particularly those who were older, kept memorial tablets on a family altar and offered appropriate sacrifices on the anniversary of a parent's death and on the 1st and 15th of each month (Davis-Friedmann, 1991). It was felt that the funeral would shape the destiny of the deceased and their descendants. Within Confucian tradition, the funeral of an elderly parent became a public testimony to the worth of the deceased and the intensity of the child's mourning. This aspect of filial piety has been severely criticized by the Communist government.

Marriage was a family concern, not a private matter between a couple in love. The major purpose of marriage was to carry on the family line (Wu, 1987). Love was not a prerequisite for marriage and was discouraged. Because the bride lived with the husband's parents, the parents felt that they should have an important voice in the decision about who would live with them. The arranged marriage, another characteristic of the traditional Chinese family, kept parents from leaving things to chance.

Of course, as one looks at the Chinese family in the historical perspective, it is important to keep in mind that the preceeding discussion represents the ideal; reality was not always so generous. Much depended on one's class and economic resources. The Confucian ideal of the extended family, with its carefully ordered relationships based on age and sex, was possible only for wealthier families in which older men of the upper class were the absolute rulers of their extended families and their wives commanded the obedience and respect of younger women in the household. The families of the many Chinese who were poor often broke down under the stress of intermittent or chronic famine and poverty. Sometimes children had to be sold and old people left to fend for themselves. Much peasant folklore centers around the often tragic and futile efforts of the poor to live up to Confucian standards of filial piety and obedience toward elders.

THE COMMUNIST REVOLUTION AND THE FAMILY

The Confucian concern for social order and for obeying those in a higher position resulted in few changes occurring in the family system of China for more than 2,000 years. However in 1949, the Communist revolution shook the very foundations of the family system as it had been known. The Marriage Law of 1950 abolished arranged marriages, restricted payments for brides as well as much of the ritual and ceremony associated with marriages, and provided greater access to divorce. In effect, the law not only put an end to the feudal marriage code but also encouraged marriages based on mutual affection. A new Marriage Law of 1981 retained the basic spirit of the earlier law while extending some of its provisions. Later marriages were to be officially encouraged, men and women were supposed to enjoy equal status in the home, both partners were to share the responsibility of caring for their parents and their children, and divorce was to be granted in cases of "complete alienation" even if only one party felt it was necessary (Smith, 1991).

While the law "officially" changed many aspects of traditional marriage and family, the age-old concept of filial piety as it relates to the care of elderly parents was legitimized. The General Principles of the Marriage Law state that "the lawful rights and interests of the aged are protected" and that "within the family, maltreatment and desertion is prohibited." Article 15 of the Marriage Law further states that "children have the duty to support and assist their parents. When children fail to perform the duty of supporting their parents, parents who have lost the ability to work or have difficulty providing for themselves have the right to demand that their children pay for their support." Article 22 stipulates: "Grandchildren or maternal grandchildren who have the capacity to bear the relevant costs have the duty to support and assist their grandparents whose children are deceased." Chapter Seven of the Criminal Law states: "Whoever vilely mistreats an aged member of his family shall be sentenced to imprisonment for not more than two years, or to detention, or to public surveillance. Whoever, having responsibility for supporting an aged person, flagrantly refuses to support that person, shall be sentenced to imprisonment for not more than five years, to detention, or to public surveillance" (Tsai, 1987). It should also be noted, too, that children, in turn, may depend on the support, both economic and emotional, of their parents (Li, 1985).

The Chinese government sees filial care as the best solution for the future to the problems of aging in China. The parent–child reciprocal relationship is the backbone of Chinese culture (Tsai, 1987). Respect, love, and care for the elderly have always been traditional Chinese virtues. The proverb "We should respect our elders" dates back at least 2,000 years (Lin, 1984). Caring for the aged is regarded as an obligation in each household and grown-up children have a duty to care for their parents according to the law.

In addition, as a result of China's large population of 1.1 billion people and a lack of resources to adequately care for continued population growth, in 1980 the People's Republic of China instituted a major population program that shocked the world: the one-child policy. Based on projections, the government determined that unless new families were limited to one child per family, the rate of economic development in China would be substantially reduced. Furthermore, allowing new families to have more than one child would worsen the already severe environmental degradation and famine could be a real possibility. To avoid these problems and accelerate economic development, the government initiated a family planning policy, often known as the one-child-per-family policy, which stated that each new family formed should include only one child. Exceptions are now made for rural families whose first child is a daughter.

At first glance, this policy may not appear to be related to the elderly. It will, in fact, have major long-term effects on Chinese senior citizens. In time, as only children marry each other over several generations, there will be no cousins and no aunts or uncles. This will occur most dramatically in the cities and less so in rural areas. This will change the social fabric of a society previously reliant on extended, large families to care for the elderly. The proportion of elderly will increase rapidly as people live longer and as new births are controlled. The future care of the elderly becomes a major issue as a result of this one-child policy, because there will be fewer children to care for a greater number of elderly. This will place a heavy burden on only children when the time comes for them to care for their parents; and even their grandparents. In fact, it is refered to as the 4–2–1 problem: four grandparents, two parents, one child. In view of this situation, Chinese leaders have stressed that the elderly are not just the responsibility of their children but of the entire country.

As the size of Chinese families becomes smaller and the dependence among family members wanes, social welfare institutions are slowly replacing many individual family functions in terms of caring for elderly family members ("Senior Citizens," 1992). The Chinese government is working to increase its support in five areas: medical service, educational programs, recreation, social activities, and housing (Wang, 1992). Much of the government work is accomplished through the establishment of senior centers and retirement homes. Of course, such provision of services will further impact on the future of the elderly in the family and the Confucian values on which it is based. Whereas in the past the Chinese generally saw themselves in relation to the family, now they are encouraged to see themselves in terms of something much larger: their community and China itself.

It would appear that the obligations to the elderly are as protected under the legal codes of the Communist government as they were in the traditional past; nevertheless, the status of the elderly has declined. The elimination of ownership of private land that occured with the Communist revolution weakened the hold that elderly parents had on their children. If their parents could not pass on land to their children, they might have fewer feelings of obligation. The official curb on ancestor worship further reduced the past prerogatives of the elderly because without state sanction for these beliefs and rituals, parents cannot as effectively invoke the threat of supernatural punishment against those children who desert them or fail to support them (Davis-Friedmann, 1991).

THE ELDERLY IN THE CHINESE FAMILY TODAY

Retirement

Whereas age 65 most often marks the onset of old age in the West, in China withdrawal from the full-time work force usually comes well before age 65. In urban China, women workers may retire at age 50, women cadre (government- and state-sponsored employees) retire at 55, and men retire at age 60. Recent articles in the Chinese press have suggested that the retirement age should be extended because China's early retirement has spurred pension increases that turn into a heavy financial burden on government and enterprise budgets. Extending the retirement age would lower the cost of supporting the elderly and would generate more wealth for the country. This, in turn, may improve the elderly's income. The country also could benefit from continued use of their talent ("State Should," 1992).

Urban workers generally work for government owned enterprises and, as a result, receive 70–80% of their last wage as retirement benefits (Davis-Friedmann, 1991). Urban retirees, therefore, enjoy a high degree of flexibility in their leisure activities. Many retirees spend their years in various ways such as gardening, taking care of their grandchildren, reading, doing arts and crafts, or visiting with friends. The elderly are often seen in parks visiting or doing morning exercises such a *tai-chi* or *qi-gong* (Li, 1985). Elderly men are often seen carrying pet birds in cages, a common hobby of older persons, or playing cards and chess ("Old Folks," 1992). Urban elderly represent an elite group, relative to retirement, compared to their rural counterparts.

However, in recent years the elderly have been taking different roles. The trend is for older persons, particularly men, to take new positions after retirement. Going back to work after retirement is displacing the traditional "baby-sitting with the grandchildren at home" as a life-style for older people in China ("Back-to-Workers," 1991). Older persons may be self-employed, starting up part-time businesses, acting as advisers to their original work units, or counseling middle-school students and helping them organize activities in their spare time. China's retirees are returning to work for reasons that include financial problems due to inflation, invitations from their original work units, or a strong commitment to their work. Because of the one-child-per-family policy, Chinese extended families have become smaller. There are no longer many grandchildren for the urban elderly to care for, which gives them considerably more time to utilize. Approximately one-third of the urban elderly are now working (Hu, 1991). Numerous articles are appearing in the Chinese press encouraging the urban elderly to return to work because their talent is of benefit to the country (Hu, 1991; "Retiree Talent," 1991; "Old Folks," 1992).

One activity that has increased among the urban elderly in recent years is going to school. Continuing education centers specifically for the elderly are becoming more popular. The first one was established in 1983 and the number has grown to more than 2,300 (Ou, 1991). Continuing education for the elderly is a growing trend and considered a positive way to overcome their sense of loneliness and frustration. The curriculum is designed according to elderly individuals' interest and needs. Vocational training classes and special-interest courses such as painting, gardening, music, poetry, exercise, and history are popular. Correspondence classes have also been organized for the elderly. Although increasing in popularity in the past 10 years, still only a small portion of the elderly avail themselves of these opportunities.

In rural areas, where 80% of the population lives, retirement age for men is determined by their health status. They retire when they can no longer do the physical labor on the farm. Women retire when they achieve the status of a grandmother. Age, itself, is of less importance. Men gradually take on less strenuous jobs as their physical strength declines or until family fortunes permit them to pass on primary financial responsibilities to their sons. Because of lack of machine modernization in agricultural production, more than half of men over age 60 in the countryside continue to engage in manual labor (Tian, 1988). After retirement, women focus their energies on child care and household tasks (Davis-Friedmann, 1991).

Men drastically reduce their overall workload when they do stop working and have time to socialize and relax with friends away from home. Women continue working in the home to assist family members as long as their health allows. Rural elderly remain very much a part of their families and are very dependent on them.

Living Arrangements

In rural families, the model is for an elderly parent to live with a married son. In the cities, other alternatives are available. The elderly may live with unmarried children or with a married son, and some live with a married daughter. Retirement homes have recently provided another option for urban elderly. Although the Communist Party has sought to limit the patriarchal power often associated with three-generation households and actively supports more egalitarian relations between husband and wife and between parents and children, the Party has made no large-scale effort to change the expectation that elderly parents should live with adult children (Davis-Friedmann, 1991).

The majority of elderly in China live with one child. Those elderly who live in separate households generally have above-average wealth. Despite the similar incidence of multigenerational households among urban and rural elderly, there is a distinction in terms of preferences. For the rural elderly, living with an adult child (married son) represents a culmination of years of planning and represents the natural order of things. If the elderly parent did not live with a married son, it would be seen as a sign of failure on the part of the parent. To make room for their son's future family, the elderly often build on to existing houses.

For the urban elderly, living with adult children is more a response to economic necessity. In the urban family, the ideal is for married children and their parents to live separately until the time that the parents are too old to manage on their own. At that time of need, a married child will rejoin the parents or an elderly parent will move to the home of a married child. In practice, however, few apartments are available to newly married couples. As a result, many urban families are forced to form three-generation homes earlier than they might prefer. Although urban residents are more dissatisfied with the necessity to live with elderly parents than are rural residents, and actively search for alternatives, urban elderly maintain multigenerational homes as often as rural elderly do. Housing shortages, government restrictions on change of residence, and the economic advantages of joint living consistently limit housing choices (Davis-Friedmann, 1991).

Whereas the previously cited reasons encourage joint living, the economic benefits of large households make multigenerational living desirable. In both urban and rural areas, one household is usually a more efficient unit of consumption than are two smaller ones. Food costs are lower, as well as the cost of furniture and most other items. The need for child care is also an important consideration. In both urban and rural China, mothers work outside the home. In rural areas there is little day care and even in urban areas where day care is more common there are still times that it is unavailable and the parents cannot be present. In addition, with infants, the Chinese believe that it is best for the child to be cared for at home. In both rural and urban areas, the typical solution is for the grandmother to stay at home with the grandchildren (generally only one grandchild in the cities), do the housework, and take care of other important tasks such as food shopping and cooking, tasks that take much longer in China than in the United States because of the lack of modern conveniences and limited use of refrigeration. Washing clothes is another task that falls to the elderly in the multigenerational household. Even when young people live separately from their parents, which occurs more frequently than it did in the past even in the rural areas, they all try to live close by in order to render mutual help (Jia, 1988).

Younger family members regard the role of the elderly in household work and child care as being important for the maintenance of the family's lifestyle. When the elderly parents can no longer care for themselves because of poor health, which places heavy burdens on their children, they will be viewed as having provided several decades of support to their children and grandchildren (Davis-Friedmann, 1991).

Although most families still live together, in the large cities an increasing number of elderly are living in retirement homes ("More Facilities," 1988). Originally such homes were shelters for childless widows and widowers unable to earn a living by themselves. Now, however, care centers for the elderly are available for paying residents who have children and a regular income. In the past, living in such residential centers would have been considered unthinkable for elderly persons who had living children.

The reasons for the increase in the popularity of retirement homes generally falls into three categories: elderly who are seeking company, those elderly needing care by specialists while their grown-up children are working, and those who are sidestepping the conflicts and tension that may occur when elderly parents live with their married children in crowded conditions. Working couples find it difficult to care for the old while working. Hiring somebody to do the nursing care is generally beyond the financial capability of ordinary wage earners. This problem will only increase in the future as the present only-child generation grows up to take care of potentially four elderly parents ("Welfare Homes," 1992; Zhuang, 1992). Although not all elderly live with their children as they would have wanted to do in the past, children generally remain in close contact with their parents ("Respect for," 1992). Approximately 14% of the elderly now live in retirement homes (Zhu & Xu, 1992).

Financial Arrangements

The majority of China's urban elderly derive their income from pensions or part-time employment, although about 22% are supported by their children. In the rural areas, the situation is quite different: Two-thirds of elderly parents are supported by their children whereas 31% support themselves through working. The remainder are supported by other relatives or by government collectives (Tian, 1988; Ming, 1989). It is apparent that China's urban elderly are more reliant on the state, while those who live in the rural areas are bound more closely to their families. However, change is evident in the rural areas as well.

Although urban retirees receive 75% of their last wages as a pension, the pension is in fixed dollars and does not rise with inflation. In addition, retirees do not receive the bonuses and subsidies that they got before retirement, which often exceed salary. China now allocates more than 37 billion yuan (about $7 billion) to retirement pensions. This represents about one-seventh of its budget. The government believes that increasing pensions is not possible because of the nation's limited economic resources and the rapid increase in the number of older people (Hu, 1991). A recent survey by the China Elderly People's Affairs Commission and the Chinese Academy of Social Sciences of 7,000 elderly discovered that their average monthly income was 96 yuan ($18). Monthly expenses of the elderly averaged 75 yuan ($14). Pensions and salaries accounted for 68% of their total income. The remainder came from financial support from children and spouses ("New Light Cast," 1991).

Although filial piety and the parent–child reciprocal relationship are the backbone of Chinese culture, there are also practical reasons in urban areas why children provide care for their elderly parents. The elderly person's pension may be larger than the child's salary as pay is based on years worked. In a country of limited means, such economic support may be very welcome in a household, particularly when one considers the household and child-care work assistance that the elderly are expected to provide in the household (Tsai, 1987). Therefore, the elderly provide both tangible and intangible returns for the family.

Because of the changing dynamics of the Chinese family, many couples who expected their children to care for them are fearful that their children may not be willing or able to support them in retirement. These parents, who are now nearing retirement, are saving as much as possible. In rural areas, and especially developed rural areas, this saving for retirement has also become a trend ("Insuring a Way," 1991). Because the elderly in the rural areas do not receive pensions, the government is encouraging rural one-child families to purchase retirement insurance. Parents of only children who buy the insurance will be paid monthly by the insurance company after reaching retirement.

This represents a fundamental change in the approach to the care for the elderly. The traditional intergenerational approach is gradually being replaced by an investment approach. People in the less developed areas still rely on their sons for old-age support. This, of course, is the reason why they want more sons and try very hard to accumulate money and housing for their sons. However, increasingly, in the more developed rural areas, the people are saving for old age or are relying on pensions or insurance. Rural peasants, particularly the more affluent ones, are moving from investing in their children for old age to relying on government social security programs (Jia, 1988).

Another change in China is the movement of people from rural areas to urban areas. They may then settle down in the cities when they find jobs. Although they may send money back to their parents, nevertheless the function of caring for the elderly by the family is being weakened (Zhu & Xu, 1992).

Relationships between Elderly Husbands and Wives

As we discussed previously, in traditional China women had few rights and limited power. Regardless of their class, women were property owned first by their fathers and later by their husbands. A famous Chinese proverb illustrates this attitude: "A woman married is like a pony bought to be ridden or whipped at the master's pleasure." Of course, the best example of this abuse (as our present-day culture views it) was foot binding. Young female children had their feet bound at age 4 or 5 to prevent their growth. Tiny feet were viewed as an object of beauty. The result, however, was women who were crippled for life.

The Communist revolution represented a major change toward increased egalitarianism in the lives of women in China. Most older women in China today were married under the old conditions, but now under Chinese law they can demand a divorce and share the family property equally with their husbands.

Of course, laws may change but relationships do not change as rapidly. Older husbands and wives were both raised under a different set of rules. Nevertheless, there does appear to be a growing egalitarianism in later life between men and women, and social pressure is put on older men as well as men of all ages to share household chores. One often sees old men and old women performing the same household functions such as shopping for food, preparing food, doing the laundry, or cleaning the house. Both care for their grandchildren as well. Change in the urban areas in terms of elderly husband and wife relationships toward egalitarianism is much faster than the rural areas.

Relationships between Elderly Parents and Children

Few elderly, particularly in the countryside, find it possible to even imagine a life isolated from their children's everyday lives. However, within the multigenerational family setting, the relationships between the generations often vary because of the child's gender. Mothers generally develop strong emotional ties with their children as opposed to fathers, and in old age, mothers receive the benefits of their early attention in terms of especially close ties with adult sons and daughters. Many parents, however, still place more emphasis on their sons than on their daughters, and ties with adult sons are especially strong. Because parents continue to be more likely to live with their sons, it is difficult for married daughters to sustain the same level of daily interactions as their brothers do (Davis-Friedmann, 1991).

Particularly in the urban areas, patterns of behavior are changing. Elderly parents are increasingly likely to divide their attention between sons and daughters. In fact, parents are often as intensely involved with their daughters as with their sons. In general, urban elderly are more likely to observe bilateral kinship as opposed to the patrilateral loyalties of the rural elderly (Davis-Friedmann, 1991). This is in part due to the government's conscious attempt to raise the status of women in society.

The preferred parent–child relationship remains one of mutual interdependence. When they live together, parents and children are in almost constant contact, share their meals, and pool their money in a common household budget. Contact with children who do not live together with their parents is more variable. They are more likely to visit their parents on their days off if they live in the same city or on holidays if they live farther away. During the Lunar New Year holiday period, all children make a major effort to return to the parents' home. Failure to visit one's parents at this time would be a major affront to the prevailing social customs (Davis-Friedmann, 1991).

In rural areas, children not living in the same village rarely visit their parents except on major holidays. Because rural women generally marry into other families and often in other neighboring villages, the relationships between the elderly and their daughters are often much less close than those with their sons. In fact, they may not visit except for once every 2 to 3 years (Davis- Friedmann, 1991). Those rural women who remain in the same village as their parents do remain close to their parents, particularly their mothers.

As mentioned, interdependence is important in the Chinese family. In fact, from early childhood people are socialized for lifelong interdependence with others by developing skills and values that promote harmony (Bond, 1991). Rural and urban elderly view interdependence differently. Rural elderly view joint living as essential to economic survival and a means of maintaining patrilineal loyalties. In contrast, the urban elderly view joint living as a coping strategy, and attachments to their adult children are more emotional than economic (Davis-Friedmann, 1991).

Because of the extreme concern about security in old age and the belief in continuance of the male lineage that exists among rural Chinese, parents of only daughters and those unable to have children face significant problems. Daughters often leave to become a part of another family and may live far from their parents. The traditional solution for the absence of male children, still used today, is to adopt a young boy or to adopt a son-in-law at the time of a daughter's marriage. In the latter case, the parents may require the son-in-law to take the surname of the father-in-law. The son-in-law might choose to do this in order to honor the father-in-law or for economic reasons such as inheritance. Generally, a young man would not take the surname of his father-in-law unless he had a brother to carry on his own father's name.

In the cities, in contrast to the rural areas, parents rarely form favored relationships with just one child if they have more than one child. Rather, they are more likely to move from child to child depending on family size and room available at any given household. Urban elderly maintain strong ties with all their children throughout old age. It is common for siblings to split the financial obligations for elderly parents (Davis-Friedmann, 1991).

In both urban and rural areas, children provide for elderly parents and parents turn for help to adult children without guilt because both believe that the past care of the children requires the children to reciprocate in their parents' old age. However, most Chinese do agree that there is one limitation on this responsibility. All generations believe that the needs of the elderly are less important than the immediate needs of the grandchildren. Both grandparents and parents give priority to the grandchildren because they represent the future of the family (Davis-Friedmann, 1991).

Although harmony in relationships is highly valued between older parents and their children, conflict still occurs. One situation that may bring serious conflict is the remarriage of an elderly widow. This action may provoke irresolvable tensions between her and her adult children ("Remarriage of," 1987). Although urban children may deeply resent the replacement of their dead mother or father with a stepparent, they do not act in as negative a fashion as do their rural counterparts because of greater acceptance of remarriage in the cities. Legally, since the Marriage Reform Law of 1950, family could no longer interfere with the remarriage of widows (Davis-Friedmann, 1991). However, in spite of the law, children may deny their usual filial responsibilities, and the general community may tolerate a higher level of deprivation by the children.

Even for the elderly and their children who live together, conflict certainly occurs. Everyday life in China is strenuous. Homes are overcrowded and families struggle to live within tight budgets. Naturally, patience wears thin at times; therefore, parents and their children argue over finances, the care of the grandchildren, ordinary household decisions, misdeeds outside the home, and so on. Often the main protagonists are the women of the household, as they take responsibility for home management. Even in families in which problems exist, over the long run, both generations generally accept their lot and keep their conflicts out of public view.

In the past, the mother-in-law–daughter-in-law dyad frequently was characterized by exploitation and conflict. Today in China, tension continues in this dyad; however, the daughter-in-law is no longer a servant in the family as in the past. In the past, in disputes, the son was expected to support his parents rather than his wife. In modern China, the son's role in such conflicts tends to be more or less impartial, although in many cases, the son tends to be on the side of his wife rather than his mother (Yang & Chandler, 1992). In other words, this represents another example of the shift of power from the older generation to the younger generation.

Death and the Family

Death of an elderly parent is an important event in China. Traditional practices around death and funerals continue to play a particularly important role in the rural areas. A traditional funeral ceremony in rural China is usually an extravagant event where family members of the deceased often provide a free banquet for all the villagers. Sacrifices for the dead include money and various expensive material objects. Groups of seven or more Buddhist or Taoist monks perform rites that last up to a week in order to save the souls of the dead. Children still may have lengthy funeral processions for their parents, complete with marching bands. To shun accusations of not demonstrating filial piety by their villagers, many farmers go into debt for several years to pay the costs of their parent's funeral ceremony (Cai, 1991; "Old-Style Burials," 1991). In many areas, funerals continue to be seen as an important sign of a person's social responsibility. Many children will spend lavishly as much from fear of public censure as from fear of the supernatural. In rural areas, such social pressures are very strong, and adult children who do not hold a proper funeral are viewed as mean and selfish. To follow the government recommendation of a simple funeral would be seen as a direct affront to the parent's memory (Davis-Friedmann, 1991). Filial piety and social pressure both exert a great deal of influence on the individual.

Since 1956, the Chinese government has strongly encouraged cremation over earthen burial in order to save valuable land for agricultural production and for living space. Cremation is also favored as a means of saving economic resources that are spent on funeral ceremonies. As in many aspects of life, change has been much more evident in the cities, where the government has more influence. The cremation rate in cities has reached 70%, whereas the cremation rate in the rural areas is far less. The cremation rate for the entire country is only 30%. As a result, the government states that more than 100,000 acres of land is used up each year for new burials (Cai, 1991). However, when possible in order to save land, rural residents try to bury their dead on steep hills rather than on cultivable land.

Residents in urban areas generally put the cremated remains in a small casket that is then placed in storage halls. The casket boxes are emerging as a new art form, often made of fine perfumed wood and jade and shaped as miniatures of temples and palaces. Today, however, many choose river and sea burials along with cremation. The family scatters the ashes to the accompaniment of solemn music. This is generally preceded and followed by family dinners.

A number of the older elderly in the cities still try to keep many of the old funeral traditions and are fearful of cremation. Some request that they be given a traditional burial in the earth. Young and middle-age urban residents do not appear to share their parents' beliefs and fears, but rarely would they express open contempt for a relative who wishes to continue with old rituals. Rarely would they ever deny their parents' requests. Even when burial is impossible, as is often the case in the cities, children will spend lavishly, not from fear of angry ghosts or censure from their peers but from a fundamental desire to be the filial son or daughter as traditional Chinese culture requires (Davis-Friedmann, 1991).

Rural residents resist the government's urgings for cremation. They believe that burial is seen as a return to the womb of Mother Earth. Mankind was formed out of the earth and should be buried in it. An old Chinese saying goes: "One's spirit can only be at ease in the earth" (Cai, 1991, p. 3). Cremation is almost seen as barbarous. Rural families believe that filial piety requires children to care for their parents while they are alive, bury them after they have died, and then continue to provide sacrifices for them to consume in heaven. Belief in the efficacy of the Buddhist and Taoist rituals that surround ancestor worship and dictate many of the traditional burial rituals has encouraged resistance to the government's wishes on funerals and ancestor worship. Old rituals have continued, and many people still equate elaborate funerals with proof of family loyalty and moral virtue. Death remains a mystery, and religious belief and familiar traditions give comfort and a sense of control (Davis-Friedmann, 1991). It is unlikely that cremation will become popular in the rural areas unless those in the countryside adopt a different approach to death. In both the cities and the rural areas, funerals remain important family rituals that reaffirm the continuity between the generations regardless of the elaborateness of the service.

The official Communist media outlets often discuss the importance of filial piety in relation to giving care and support to the elderly relative when he/she is alive and not after the person is deceased. Nevertheless, the government does not directly coerce people into changing their views on this topic. The government position is that old traditions will die with the passing of the oldest generation.

The Future for the Elderly in the Family

Traditionally, the elderly in China were highly respected within the family and within society in general. The Confucian concepts of filial piety, devotion to the elderly, and ordered family and societal relationships have been around for 2,000 years. The Communist government broke down many of the inequalities of the traditional social structure; nevertheless, the government has continued to advocate filial care of the elderly, a concept with a strong cultural base in China. The Chinese model of elderly welfare in the cities has been characterized by a combination of filial care and state assistance programs. This system has worked relatively well in the cities, providing the elderly with financial security and continuous contact with family members. However, the future for the elderly in China depends on the continued willingness and ability of the family to provide care for the elderly, the availability of housing space allocated to urban workers, a much improved national economy, and continued observance of the traditional respect for the elderly both in the family and in the larger society.

Undoubtedly, there will be increasing pressure on the government to support the elderly because of the vacuum that will be created by the one-child policy. As each family is permitted to have only one child, the burden of support of parents will be heavy on young couples, who will have to support parents of both husband and wife. Moreover, the relationships between grandparents and grandchildren will be changed as fewer children are being born. The opportunities to live with their children will be more limited as a result of what is referred to as the 4–2–1 problem—four grandparents, two parents, and one child. As a result of more elderly living separately from their children in the future, greater economic difficulties could exist for each living unit as families will not be able to pool resources.

The government seems to recognize the necessity of helping the elderly in the future, but how the government is able to respond to the rapidly increasing elderly population will be critical. At present, the ratio of employees to retirees is 7 to 1. By the year 2000 it is expected to fall to 4 to 1. Difficulty in paying urban retirees is anticipated. In addition, the government will need to continue building more retirement homes as more and more urban elderly will be unable or unwilling to live with their children.

The younger generation of Chinese is seen as being more pragmatic. Some reject the conservatism and traditionalism of the past (Chu, 1985).

There is concern by some that young urbanites in particular may reject the traditional Chinese virtue of caring for one's elderly parents. The Communist Party has begun to publicize caring for elderly parents as a virtue without suggesting the total obedience to parents that occurred in the traditional past. Nevertheless, although weakened, norms of filial piety are still important. A new Chinese culture seems to be emerging. What impact it may have on the elderly in the family remains to be seen.

REFERENCES

Back-to-workers get away from the chores. (1991, June 14). *China Daily*, p. 4.

Bond, M. H. (1991). *Beyond the Chinese face.* Hong Kong: Oxford University Press.

Cai, H. (1991, June 26). Ashes to ashes: The route to a better life after death. *China Daily*, p. 3.

China to enter ageing society by year 2000. (1992, October 2). *China Daily*, p. 3.

Chu, C. C. (1985). The emergence of the new Chinese culture. In W. S. Tseng & D. Wu (Eds.), *Chinese culture and mental health* (pp. 15–24). Hong Kong: Academic Press.

Davis-Friedmann, D. (1991). *Long lives*. Stanford, CA: Stanford University Press.

Ho, D. V. F. (1986). Chinese patterns of socialization: A critical review. In M. H. Bond (Ed.), *The psychology of the Chinese people* (pp. 1–37). Hong Kong: Oxford University Press.

Hsu, F. L. K. (1971a). *The challenge of the American dream: The Chinese in the United States*. Belmont, CA: Wadsworth.

Hsu, F. L. K. (1971b). *Under the ancestor's shadow: Chinese culture and personality*. Stanford, CA: Stanford University Press.

Hu, X. (1991, October 16). There is life after retirement, *China Daily*, p. 3.

Insuring a way to help the aged. (1991, May 28). *China Daily*, p. 3.

Jia, A. (1988). New experiments with the elderly care in rural China. *Journal of Cross-Cultural Gerontology*, 3, 139–148.

King, A. Y. C., & Bond, M. H. (1985). The Confucian paradigm of man: A sociological view. In W. S. Tseng & D. Wu (Eds.), *Chinese culture and mental health* (pp. 29–45). Hong Kong: Academic Press.

Kitano, H. H. L. (1985). *Race relations*. Englewood Cliffs, NJ: Prentice-Hall.

Kong, S. L. (1989). *Chinese culture and lore*. Toronto: Kensington Educational.

Li, X. (1985). The effect of family on the mental health of the Chinese family. In W. S. Tseng & D. Wu (Eds.), *Chinese culture and mental health* (pp. 85–93). Hong Kong: Academic Press.

Lin, X. (1984, September 3). Nationwide concern for elderly. *China Daily*, p. 4.

Ming, T. (1989). Changes in Chinese urban family structure, *Journal of Marriage and Family*, 23(3), 431–453.

More facilities for the elderly. (1988, October 3). *Beijing Review*, pp. 39–40.

New light cast on life as a senior citizen. (1991, December 18). *China Daily*, p. 4.

Old folks find much more to do in society. (1992, February 10). *China Daily*, p. 2.

Old-style burials are thrown on the pyre. (1991, May 28). *China Daily*, p. 4.

Ou, L. (1991, July 10). Universities for elderly are growing. *China Daily*, p. 2.

Remarriage of the elderly. (1987, February 9). *Beijing Review*, p. 37.

Respect for the elderly. (1992, March 9). *China Daily*, p. 38.

Retiree talent helps economy. (1991, June 26). *China Daily*, p. 2.

Senior citizens take up to 8%. (1992, June 25). *China Daily*, p. 3.

Smith, C. J. (1991). *China: People and places in the land of one billion.* Boulder, CO: Westview Press.

State should increase retirement age. (1992, September 24). *China Daily*, p. 4.

Sung, B. L. (1967). *Mountains of gold.* New York: Macmillan.

Tian, X. (1988, November 14). China's elderly surveyed. *Beijing Review*, pp. 26–28.

Tsai, W. (1987). Life after retirement: Elderly welfare in China. *Asian Survey*, 27(5), pp. 567–576.

Wang, R. (1992, September 20). New pro-elderly package upcoming. *China Daily*, p. 4.

Welfare homes change heartless image. (1992, March 7). *China Daily*, p. 2.

Wong, M. (1988). The Chinese American family. In G. H. Mindel, R. W. Hubenstein, & R. Wright (Eds.), *Ethnic families in America* (pp. 230–258). New York: Elsevier.

Wu, B. (1987). The urban family in flux. In Women of China (Eds.), *New trends in Chinese marriage and the family*. Beijing: Women of China.

Yang, H., & Chandler, D. (1992). Intergenerational relations: Grievance of the elder in rural China. *Journal of Comparative Family Studies*, 23(3), 431–453.

Yu, G. (1987). Spending the remaining years at ease. In Women of China (Eds.), *New trends in Chinese marriage and the family*. Beijing: Women of China.

Zhu, C., & Xu, Q. (1992). Family care of the elderly in China: Change and problems. In J. I. Kosberg (Ed.), *Family care of the elderly: Social and cultural changes* (pp. 67–138). New York: Sage.

Zhuang, H. (1992, April 14). A happy home for the elderly. *China Daily*, p. 6.

PART FOUR

GENDER AND FAMILY RELATIONS

Courtesy Suzanna Smith.

Introduction

Each of the three chapters in Part IV addresses gender and family relationships from a different perspective. Taken together, these chapters argue that gender is a complicated and powerful social phenomenon that structures families and societies worldwide.

In Chapter 11, "Women and Households in the Third World," Suzanna Smith focuses on women in the major Third World regions of Africa, Asia, Latin America, and the Caribbean. This chapter includes an overview of indicators of women's welfare, including their health, education, income, and work force participation, and offers some explanations for women's inequality worldwide. Ideological and historical factors are pinpointed, specifically gender stratification, the legacy of colonialism, and a history of providing resources and markets for capitalist expansion. The chapter also analyzes the ways in which women's lives in various regions are influenced by different cultural beliefs and societal norms about proper gender and family roles.

In Chapter 12, "Household Division of Labor in Industrial Societies," Linda L. Haas turns our attention to gender and family relationships in industrialized nations. She examines how families divide responsibility for household work and how this division of labor is related to the status of women and men in society. Haas traces the historical development of the gender-based division of labor that separates men's and women's activities and offers explanations for why this occurred. She then compares various industrial societies on the degree to which they adhere to the "doctrine of the separate spheres," by providing detailed cross-cultural examples of traditional, transitional, and egalitarian societies.

In Chapter 13, "Gender Relations and Marital Power," Jack O. Balswick and Judith K. Balswick examine marital power in a cultural and historical context. They emphasize the impact of social forces on the creation of unequal gender roles that allocate to men greater resources and control in marital relationships. They present examples of how marital power is implemented in various societies, including the harmful effects of inequitable power relations on children and women. Balswick and Balswick analyze traditional theoretical approaches to marital power and conclude by urging us to move beyond accepted models to adopt an "empowerment" perspective that would allow women and men equal access to all valued resources and would result in equitable and mutually respectful relationships.

CHAPTER ELEVEN

Women and Households in the Third World

SUZANNA SMITH

In both industrialized and developing countries, women perform the bulk of the world's paid and unpaid work—two-thirds of it according to the United Nations (1991b). Worldwide, unpaid work such as housework and care of dependents falls almost exclusively on women's shoulders (United Nations, 1991a). They rear younger generations and care for the elderly. They carry out essential household activities such as cooking, cleaning, and managing finances. Women are the majority of the world's food producers. They make up 60–80% of agricultural workers in Asia and Africa and more than 40% in Latin America (Jacquette, 1985).

Women throughout the world also work in paid jobs outside their homes more than ever before. Women's earnings contribute increasingly larger shares to their total household income. In many cases, the income from women's employment ensures family survival (United Nations, 1991a). Yet women control a small share of world resources. They receive only 10% of all earned income and own less than 1% of property (Acosta-Belén & Bose, 1990; United Nations, 1991b).

Three-fourths of the world's population, and the world's women, live in the Third World (Brydon & Chant, 1989). An understanding of women worldwide must be based on knowledge of Third World women's experiences. In this chapter I give special attention to women living in those regions that make up the Third World—Latin America, the Caribbean, Asia, and Africa. This chapter shows that women's experiences vary because of regional differences in environmental, cultural, and social systems.

We will also see that women in all parts of the world have many experiences in common simply because they are women (Mermel & Simons,

1991). In most countries, women struggle to bear and rear children and to provide financially for their families. They do this with fewer resources than men because women seldom have comparable access to land, food, credit, education, jobs, information, or training (Jacobson, 1993). This is largely because their contributions are undervalued and their potential is thwarted by some traditional social and economic systems that limit economic and social autonomy (Friedman, 1992).

Although there is evidence of progress toward equality between men and women in some arenas, such as primary schooling, generally the world is far from achieving gender parity. Women from industrial countries may feel that they are "better off" than their Third World sisters, but the same dynamics keep all women from achieving equality with men, or from reaching their personal goals and full potential as human beings. Some scholars have suggested that First World women tend to underestimate these similarities to avoid confronting inequality in their own home and workplace (Enloe, 1989).

The devaluation of women begins at an early age. For example, a Lebanese school principal noted, "When a boy is born . . . there is joy. When a girl is born, there is silence" (Freidman, 1992, p. 13). Infanticide of girls is common. Hundreds die from starvation, neglect or abuse simply because they are born girls. Girls are primarily viewed as potential mothers and housekeepers who will offer little economic support to their families. Parents assume that sons will provide for them in old age, and usually give sons preferential treatment by financially and emotionally supporting their education and business activities (UNICEF, 1992). Girls are consistently deprived of schooling, immunizations and nutritious foods, and encouragement to improve their skills (Friedman, 1992; UNICEF, 1992).

The first section of this chapter, "The Apartheid of Gender," addresses these disparities between men and women by providing evidence of Third World women's almost universal subordination. We see how women's second-class citizenship is manifested in lower education, marginal employment, and poorer physical health relative to men.

But why are women seldom in positions of economic and political power and men rarely in nurturing roles? Why is a woman's "place" so consistently at home and a man's at work, regardless of women's (or men's) talents, interests, and aspirations? Why are women's significant contributions consistently devalued? Why do we see this same pattern in so many nonindustrialized countries, from Bangladesh to Burkina Faso? In the second section, "Roots of the Apartheid of Gender," I examine the historical and social roots of this phenomenon. I focus on social stratification by gender and race, ethnicity, and class and on the impact of colonialism and capitalist expansion. In the third section, I expand the discussion of "Contemporary Capitalism and Third World Women and Families," looking more closely at inequities between women and men in agricultural and industrial production.

The fourth section begins to look more closely at *diversity* in "The World of Women." I examine women's lives in the various Third World regions, describing how their experiences vary with cultural beliefs and practices and social and economic systems. In the final section, "Empowering Women," I return to the roots of gender stratification and discuss some ways women are taking action to improve their lives.

It is important to understand that although the central focus of this chapter is women, "family" is not out of the picture. Indeed, family is the core of Third World women's lives. Family is the first site of women's socialization into their adult roles as wives, mothers, and workers. Families transmit social values that limit (or expand) women's opportunities in life. Family is where men and women pool and divide their money and labor to ensure survival. Family is the site of power struggles between genders and generations. Family is a force for preserving tradition and intergenerational continuity, but for many women, it is also a catalyst for change. Because family is women's central concern, poor social and economic conditions affecting children and husbands prompt women to take action to improve their families' lives. My approach is to illuminate women's experiences in the *context* of their family lives, their communities, and the larger society.

THE APARTHEID OF GENDER

A look at international statistics illustrates what is termed the "apartheid of gender" (Grant, 1992). Throughout the world, improvements in education, employment, and health achieved by men in the last 40 years were not equaled by women. Even in industrialized countries, this gender gap holds. Only in Sweden, Finland, and France did women approach, but not equal, men's access (Jacobson, 1993). The following sections provide an overview of the disparities between Third World women and men, focusing on three critical "human resource" variables: education, employment, and health.

Education

Worldwide, literacy has improved considerably in the past two decades, from 46% in 1970, to 60% in 1985. However, literacy rose faster among men than women, so the existing gender gap actually widened. Between 1970 and 1984, the number of illiterate women increased by 54 million, and illiterate men by only 4 million (Jacobson, 1993). Two-thirds of the 1 billion illiterate adults are women, with the vast majority of them living in South Asia, sub-Saharan Africa, and the Middle East (Friedman, 1992). The illiteracy rate for women in all Third World countries is 45% (United Nations, 1991b).

Universal primary education for girls has been accepted as a fundamental goal by all countries but has not been reached in South Asia and sub-Saharan Africa. Girls have caught up to boys in primary and secondary school enrollment in Latin America and the Caribbean (United Nations, 1991a). However, of the 130 million children who do not have access to primary schools, two-thirds are girls (Friedman, 1992). Poverty contributes to girls' lower school enrollment because poor women work longer hours to make ends meet and lean on their daughters to help with the additional work (Jacobson, 1993).

In higher education, women and men have achieved nearly equal enrollment in most countries except those in sub-Saharan Africa and South Asia, where fewer than 30 women per 100 men enroll in colleges and universities. Women have also made rapid gains in advanced training for law, business, and science and engineering, except in Africa (United Nations, 1991b). However, some argue that these are wealthy women whose advanced training is irrelevant to improving the lives of poor women (Townsend & Momsen, 1987).

Older women who never had the opportunity to enroll in school have high rates of illiteracy. In sub-Saharan Africa and South and West Asia, illiteracy rates are more than 70% for women 25 and older. The illiteracy rate for women 25 and older is 40% in Southeast Asia and 20% in Latin America and the Caribbean (United Nations, 1991a). Illiteracy is higher in rural areas. Many rural women are two or three times more likely to be illiterate than are their counterparts in urban areas (United Nations, 1991a). Rural women tend to have more children and to be poorer. In their struggle to survive, they have little time or energy to spare for literacy training (United Nations, 1991b).

A girl's education is not just a matter of school *attendance* but of social *acceptance* of her right to an education and the importance of schooling for her and, eventually, her family. This acceptance begins in the family at the moment of birth, not in the classroom at age 5 or 6. In many cultures, preference is given to boys in the belief that they have a better chance of locating employment than do girls. Girls are brought up to believe that they do not need an education since they will marry and rear children rather than work in paid employment where educational qualifications are required. This gender gap in education is heightened when, due to economic crises, governments and families have less money to spend on education (United Nations, 1991b).

Women's lack of education or training prevents them from obtaining steady, well-paid work and taking advantage of technological progress that could improve their lives. They are caught in a downward spiral of poverty that leads to ill health, repeated childbearing and associated physical and financial demands and powerlessness to change the situation. In contrast, women who are educated are more likely to locate employment at higher earnings, to control their fertility, to be in overall good health, and to have children who are more educated and in better health (United Nations, 1991b).

Employment

Women's participation in economic production has increased in the past two decades, in part out of economic necessity. In many Third World countries, women work 60 to 90 hours per week just to maintain the same meager standard of living of a decade ago (United Nations, 1991a, p. 82). Table 11.1 presents women's economic activity rates (i.e., the percentage of women who are economically active[1]). These are highest in sub-Saharan Africa and Southeast Asia. Table 11.1 also shows women's share of the paid labor force in 1970 and 1990. The percentage of women to men in the labor force has been rising in almost all regions except Southeast Asia, where it has remained fairly steady, and sub-Saharan Africa, where it declined, probably because severe economic conditions have reduced or limited job growth (United Nations, 1991a; 1991b).

In at least one-fourth of all households, women's earnings account for more than half of the total family income.[2] In addition, women are the *primary* breadwinners in one-third to one-fourth of the world's households (Jacobson, 1993). Even when a man is present, wives contribute a larger share of their earnings to such household necessities as food, medical care, and

TABLE 11.1.   Women's Employment, 1970–1990

	Women's economic activity rates	Women's share of labor force
Sub-Saharan Africa		
1970	48%	39%
1990	51%	37%
Southeast Asia		
1970	48%	35%
1990	49%	35%
South Asia		
1970	25%	19%
1990	24%	20%
Latin America and Caribbean		
1970	28%	24%
1990	32%	29%
North Africa		
1970	10%	12%
1990	16%	17%

transportation than do husbands, whereas husbands often use their pay for personal consumer items such as tobacco and alcohol (Blumberg, 1988; Jacobson, 1993). It is not unusual for African children's nutrition to deteriorate while wristwatches, radios, and bicycles are purchased by adult male family members (Jacobson, 1993).

Worldwide, the workplace is segregated by sex. The *service sector* (including wholesale and retail trade, restaurants, hotels, transportation, communication, banking, insurance, real estate, business services, and government) is probably the only occupational category where women "corner the market" (United Nations, 1991b). Women fill over half the service-sector jobs in Latin America and the Caribbean, and more than a third of those jobs in Africa and Asia (United Nations, 1991a). In the Third World, women tend to be most heavily involved in the *commerce* branch of the service sector in wholesale and retail trade, restaurants, and hotels. In contrast to the industrialized regions, women make up less than half of Third World *clerical* workers, with the exception of Southeast Asia (Townsend & Momsen, 1987). In many countries, these often prestigious and higher-paying jobs are assigned to men. Unlike the United States, where women dominate clerical work, men represent the majority of the clerical labor force in Latin America, Southeast Asia, and India (Brydon & Chant, 1989).

Third World women are seldom employed in professional jobs, and when they are, they tend to be in the lower-paid and technical occupations. Teaching is the largest employer of women in the professional category. The teaching profession has always been one of the first professions open to women because it is consistent with women's accepted role as nurturers of young children. In the last two decades, the proportion of women primary school teachers increased throughout the world. However, the higher the level of education the fewer the women employed as teachers. This is true of every region except Latin America and the Caribbean, where women's employment in upper educational levels equals men's (United Nations, 1991a).

Women's share of *industrial employment* is usually low (these jobs include mining and quarrying, manufacturing, utilities, and construction). Women tend to be concentrated in the so-called light manufacturing industries such as food processing and the manufacturing of textiles, clothing, and shoes. Women's share of manufacturing employment is higher in the Free Trade Zones of Southeast Asia and Latin America, where these industries are common.

Regardless of the employment sector, women workers are consistently paid less than men and receive fewer benefits (United Nations, 1991a). They are also more likely to work part time, to have lower seniority, and to have fewer opportunities of advancement, due to employers' reluctance to hire and train female workers or to assign them more prestigious jobs (United Nations, 1991a).

Frequently, the only wedge of opportunity women have against occupational segregation, unemployment, and underemployment is the *informal sector* (Brydon & Chant, 1989; United Nations, 1991a). This is the "edge of survival," to which more and more poor women are pushed out of economic necessity (United Nations, 1991b). Informal-sector jobs include small commercial businesses and manufacturing, self-employed trading, or personal services such as domestic services, laundry, or sewing. Some informal income-generating activities—such as beer brewing, streetside vending, and prostitution—are also called the shadow economy because they take place outside the legalized employment system. Informal-sector work is far less secure than are jobs in the formal sector and often pays less than the minimum wage (United Nations, 1991a).

In Africa and Asia, most women work in *agriculture*—nearly half of women in Asia, except West Asia, and 80% of women in sub-Saharan Africa (United Nations, 1991a). Only a small minority of women in Latin America and the Caribbean (around 11%) work in the agricultural sector (United Nations, 1991a). Women's contribution to agricultural production is essential. In Africa, women grow 80% of the food consumed in the household. In India, women produce 70–80% of food crops and in Latin America and the Caribbean, 50% (Jacobson, 1993).

We know that women are almost always responsible for *housework and child care*. Although these activities are unwaged, they certainly can be considered productive work. Domestic activities contribute to family welfare by saving money (e.g., raising a kitchen garden), meeting family members' nutritional needs (e.g., preserving and preparing food), providing services (e.g., health care and house cleaning), instilling certain values and beliefs in children, and upholding the social and economic status quo (Brydon & Chant, 1989).

Housework and child care are often not captured in government surveys, and only a few Third World countries have estimated time spent in household production (United Nations, 1991a). However, when housework and other economic activities are counted, estimates of women's economic contributions increase. For example, when household production and domestic work were included in a survey conducted in India, estimates indicated that 75% of women over age 5 were working, compared with 64% of men. In a study of Nepalese families, estimates of women's contributions to household income rose from 20% to 53% when the value of subsistence production (i.e., production for home use) was factored in (Jacobson, 1993; United Nations, 1991a).

Health

Reproduction is a central part of Third World women's lives. In most parts of the Third World, the total fertility rate (TFR), which refers to the average total number of births per woman at the end of childbearing age, is between three and six children. However, in sub-Saharan Africa, North Africa, and West Asia, the average TFR is more than six children. In many Third World countries, 30% of women are pregnant or lactating at any given time, in large part because women's status in many societies depends on their ability to bear children. In addition, children in many Third World countries are expected to provide for their parents in old age, which is particularly important where there is no public source of support for the elderly (United Nations, 1991a).

For pregnant Third World women, there are a number of risks associated with reproduction. Malnutrition is endemic, putting mother and child at risk. Births are not attended by trained personnel and there are few backup services for high risk-pregnancies. The result is that pregnant Third World women are 80 to 600 times more likely to experience death due to complications of pregnancy or childbearing than are pregnant women in the industrialized countries. Pregnancy adds a particularly heavy burden to an adolescent's developing body. The risk for maternal and infant mortality among teenagers is twice that of women 20 to 24 (United Nations, 1991a). Nearly two-thirds of pregnant women and half of nonpregnant women in the Third World are thought to be anemic, possibly due to a lack of protein and iron-rich foods (Townsend & Momsen, 1987). These nutritional deficiencies compromise women's health, physical development, and ability to bear children (United Nations, 1991b). Their children are also at greater risk for infant and child mortality. In an attempt to make up for these real or anticipated child losses, women often continue childbearing for as long as possible. This increases the stress on their bodies and traps women and children in a cycle of poor health and nutrition (United Nations, 1991b).

Most poor women work long and hard, often with insufficient protein and caloric intakes. In many cases, cultural beliefs and practices result in a tendency for women and girls to consume smaller amounts and less nutritious food. In some countries, food taboos discourage pregnant women from eating fruit, vegetables, milk, rice, and other high-calorie foods. This increases women's susceptibility to illness, pregnancy complications, and death during childbirth (United Nations, 1991a).

Men in many Third World countries have higher status and as a result receive better food, as well as better health care (Agarwal, 1985; Jacobson, 1993; United Nations, 1991a). In many societies, men are fed first and women and children eat whatever is left over. This results in higher mortality rates for girls than for boys (Jacobson, 1993; United Nations, 1991a).

Another concern regarding women's health is *female circumcision*, which involves cutting or removing portions of a woman's external genitalia, presumably to reduce her sexual desires. There are three types of female circumcision. The least invasive (and least common) is the Sunna type, which involves cutting the woman's clitoral hood. This may invoke psychological trauma but does not necessarily impair the woman physically. The excision type involves removal of the clitoral glans or entire clitoris. In the radical infibulation, the clitoris, labia minora, and labia majora are removed and the two parts of the vulva sewn together, leaving only a tiny opening for the passage of urine and menstrual blood (Brydon & Chant, 1989).

Female circumcision is often a rite of passage for female adulthood (Lightfoot-Klein 1992). Excision and infibulation are performed on young girls between 5 and 8 years old. The results are a number of immediate and long-term problems, including shock, hemorrhaging, retention of urine, persistent infections, damage to the reproductive system, continual gynecological and genitourinary complications including infertility, difficulties in childbirth, and death (Brydon & Chant, 1989; Lightfoot-Klein, 1992). Although this practice is illegal in some countries, it is still practiced throughout sub-Saharan Africa. However, it is less common in the Middle East and other parts of North Africa (Brydon & Chant, 1989; Townsend & Momsen, 1987).

Summary

This section discussed indicators of fundamental differences between men and women that appear to be characteristic of gender relations in the Third World. The descriptors of women's social, economic, and physical well-being indicate that women are consistently disadvantaged relative to men in education, employment, and health. Women make substantial contributions to their families' economic and physical well-being (Dixon-Meuller, 1985; Jacobson, 1993). What accounts for these differences between men and women? Answers to this question are considered in the next section.

ROOTS OF THE APARTHEID OF GENDER

This section covers three major reasons for the unequal distribution of resources and power between men and women. First, relying on feminist theory, particularly socialist and materialist feminism (see Smith, Chapter 1, this volume), gender stratification is a fundamental mechanism that subordinates women in the home and in larger social institutions. Second, gender stratification is compounded by other aspects of society that structure unequal relationships—race, ethnicity, and class. Third, historical developments have influenced the articulation of gender relations in Third World societies—colonialism and capitalist expansion.

Gender Stratification

Early theories attributed gender differences in power and privilege to biological differences between the sexes. Men were generally stronger and bigger, but the most important categorical difference was that only women could bear children (Huber, 1988). Gender roles, particularly for women, were considered logical extensions of "natural" proclivity toward nurturing behaviors.

According to feminist theoretical approaches developed in the 1960s and 1970s, the roots of differences between men and women are found not in biological sex but in cultural interpretations of how women should behave and what they should do (Enloe, 1989; Townsend & Momsen, 1987). Feminists attributed women's subordinate position in society to *gender stratification*, also called *patriarchy* (Huber, 1988). This refers to "the extent to which societal members are unequal in their access to the scarce resources of their society on the basis of their membership in a gender category" (Chafetz, 1988, p. 111). Patriarchy is used by those in power to justify the "rights" of a certain privileged group to define, govern, and control others. As a result of gender stratification, women are excluded from experiences and activities that "enhance their growth and development, their access to resources, and their access to positions of power" (Baber & Allen, 1992, p. 7).

The Interplay of Gender, Race, Ethnicity, and Class

In most societies, gender stratification is compounded by discrimination based on race, ethnicity, and class (Jacobson, 1993). Thus, poor women and women of color face a "double" or "triple" jeopardy. The combination of gender, class, and ethnicity or race places them at an even greater disadvantage in society than both men and wealthier, nonminority women (Acosta-Belén & Bose, 1990; Jacobson, 1993). This concept is an important analytic tool for understanding the structure of any given society and the relations among its members.

In many of the examples in this chapter, women's experiences vary depending on their position in the social hierarchy. The following example illustrates how gender roles *interact* with class differences in a particular cultural context.

In the Zapotec region of Mexico, women produce wool textiles that they sell as rugs, wall hangings, purses, and seat covers in local tourist trade and for export. The women of the area share a common ethnic identity and cultural history. But inequality marks their community. One study of 150 households found that women in about 80% of the households weave for others. About 10% of the households contract with weavers to produce goods, often on a piecework basis. These merchant households earn about seven times more than do weaver households.

Weaver households ($n = 100$) have a pool of money that family members share. Men and women (62%) manage this money together in most weaver households. In 35% of the weaver households, women manage the money. Men do so in only 3% of these households. In contrast, men alone manage the finances in over two-thirds of merchant households ($n = 50$). Men and women manage the business together in 29% of merchant households. Women manage the finances in only 4% of these households.

Compared to weaver households, few merchant women make business decisions. Angela Suarez explains: "My husband tells me how much yarn to dye, how many weavers we will hire, and what to cook them for lunch. I also have to buy what he asks me for the house. He gives me a certain amount of money every day for food. He keeps the key to the money and doesn't let me handle it. He says that he knows how to take care of the money." (Based on Stephen, 1992, pp. 25–27.)

Examples of differences and conflicts based on class and racial identity have been reported between majority and minority women and wealthy and poor women, such as black domestic workers and their white women employers (Cock, 1988), urban middle-class women and rural agriculturalists (Burja, 1986), and housewives and tomato producers (Villareal, 1992). However, the *intersection* of race or ethnicity, class, *and* gender is particularly important. Research consistently shows that being poor, minority, *and a woman* is to be at the bottom of the social hierarchy—vulnerable to malnutrition, illness, job exploitation, dangerous living conditions, discrimination, and violence. This is not to say that poor minority men do not suffer. They do. However, by virtue of their gender, poor women of color are consistently at a greater disadvantage than men of their same class and culture (Agarwal, 1985).

Historical Developments: Colonialism and Capitalist Expansion

Beginning in the 15th century, territories in the New World and later in Africa and Asia served as the source of raw materials and labor that fueled the industrial revolution. The natural wealth of newly "discovered" lands and the forced labor of indigenous people and African slaves were used by colonial powers to support the lavish tastes of the European aristocracy and the consuming needs of the rising bourgeoisie. The wealth and natural resources of the colonies were transformed in European factories into market products that eventually found a way back to the colonies (Acosta-Belén & Bose, 1990).

Although there were differences among European powers in their approach to colonization, generalizations can be made about the effects on indigenous societies (Brydon & Chant, 1989). First, nation states were created that carved out geopolitical areas for various colonial powers. Boundaries were imposed on common ethnic groups that were dispersed over a wide territory, resulting in the division of kin groups into states ruled by different administrative authorities. Second, Christian missionaries established outposts that transformed indigenous cultures, not only by conversion but by educating people for posts as low-level functionaries in government, commerce, and industry.

Third, under capitalism, previous subsistence agricultural economies became increasingly tied to the larger marketplace and dependent on outside investors to purchase agricultural products. Commodities used for domestic consumption and production, such as land and animals, acquired monetary value and could be sold. Human labor could be purchased by wealthy producers from landless farmers who needed cash to purchase food and other consumer goods. In effect, previously self-sufficient agrarian cultures became peasant societies dependent on a cash-based economic system and the sale of their wage labor (Brydon & Chant, 1989). Families could no longer survive on the fruits of their own labors—their crops, animals, and vegetable gardens—and the small-scale sale or trade of produce for cloth, decorative items, and needed goods (Acosta-Belén & Bose, 1990).

Colonialism was carried out primarily by European men with a certain ideology regarding women's proper place in society. Women who accompanied male colonizers as wives, missionaries, or teachers also reinforced stereotypes about proper "feminine" behavior (Enloe, 1989). Consistent with the prevailing Western gender ideology, colonialists imposed or offered new sources of cash to men but not to women, including cash crops or wage labor on plantations and in mines (Acosta-Belén & Bose, 1990; Rogers, 1980).

Gender stratification existed to different degrees in various nonindustrial cultures (Coltrane, 1992) but became more firmly established during colonial rule of Third World nations from the 1880s to about 1960. European missionaries and authorities had very little regard for the traditional community and family relationships that characterized indigenous peoples of conquered lands. Women's rights and productive activities were undercut by the imposition of patriarchal European relationships on traditional cultures. Colonialists presumed that men had supreme authority in the family clan and community. They deprived indigenous women of any property, personal autonomy, and public authority they might have had prior to colonialization (Acosta-Belén & Bose, 1990; Etienne & Leacock, 1980).

By the 19th century, the United States had joined the fight for territorial expansion and sought to become the major economic and geopolitical power in the hemisphere. Even after independence in the 20th century, former colonies continued to be integrated into a global economic system of production through their dependence on the industrial powers, particularly the United States, for imports, export markets and foreign aid (Acosta-Belén & Bose, 1990).

Through international investments, foreign aid, and development projects in Third World nations, capitalist countries have promoted large-scale cash-crop production and private ownership of land. This process has also altered the gender-based division of labor, creating or exaggerating inequities between men and women (Johnson-Odim, 1991). The penetration of contemporary capitalism in rural as well as urban areas has had a profound impact on Third World women and their families, and for this reason I discuss these transformations in more detail below.

CONTEMPORARY CAPITALISM AND THIRD WORLD WOMEN AND FAMILIES

This section looks more closely at the integration of Third World women and their families into contemporary capitalism through their involvement in the agricultural and industrial development and urbanization that has been associated with capitalist expansion. I examine men's and women's daily activities in small farm production, agroindustry production, industry, and domestic labor, paying particular attention to how family relationships are affected.

Small Farm Production

Traditionally, many agricultural societies have been organized around small farm production. Men and women have separate as well as joint activities designed to enhance production for home consumption and market sales.

In many societies, women are traditionally responsible for meeting their children's needs for medicine, clothing, and food, as well as for school fees. They do this by producing food from their own fields for family consumption and generating enough surplus to earn needed cash, for example, by marketing produce or "processed" foods such as fried cakes. If women do not maintain their own food crops, they risk losing their capacity to grow or purchase food and other essentials for their children and increase their financial dependence on their husbands (Blumberg, 1989).

International economic development projects and Western commercial agriculture have often failed to recognize women's contributions to farming (Overholt, Anderson, Cloud, & Austin, 1985). Development professionals tend to have Western stereotypes about traditional men's and women's roles, often assuming that the man is the major breadwinner, farmer, or businessperson and women are homemakers who assist their spouses, not farmers and traders in their own right (Jacobson, 1993). As a result, development projects direct their assistance to men's cash crops, and women farmers are often unable to obtain many of the inputs they need to improve their production, such as fertilizers, pesticides, irrigation, and improved seeds (Cloud, 1985; Saito & Weidemann, 1990). The result is that men tend to control household decisions related to agricultural production and the purchase and use of inputs such as a plow, seeds, or fertilizers.

Out of customary obligations to their husbands, women are often forced to shift their time and energy from their food crops and other income-generating activities to their husband's cash crops, without being assured that they will directly reap the financial benefits (Blumberg, 1989). Under certain conditions, women may gain financially from their involvement in cash-crop production by demanding to be paid a fair wage (Jones, 1986). Generally, however, cash-crop production *combined with* other responsibilities places a heavy burden on women's time, energy, and physical health. Women work many more hours per day than do men in agricultural production and paid and unpaid work—an average of 12 to 18 hours a day for women compared with 8 to 12 hours a day for men (Jacobson, 1993; United Nations, 1991a). Consequently, women find it increasingly difficult to grow the food their families need. In Papua, New Guinea, for, example, men have planted coffee crops on the best slopes, making it difficult for women to find suitable land for food crops and lengthening their day because they have to walk longer distances to their fields. Because women have less time for food crops, families are not able to produce enough food and much of the cash goes to buying rice (Finch, 1992).

Women's ability to survive these pressures has been further eroded by environmental degradation due to deforestation and desertification. Woodlands may only be found at remote distances from the home, forcing women and children to travel long distances to locate enough fuelwood for cooking. This makes rural women's work even more arduous and time-consuming (Brydon & Chant, 1989; Dankelman & Davidson, 1988). The costs of fuelwood have increased, making it more difficult for cash-poor rural women to buy fuelwood in markets. As a result, only one meal a day instead of two may be prepared, or less nutritious but faster-cooking foods may be used, with a negative impact on family health (Brydon & Chant, 1989). Due to economic crises and international policies, government spending on social, educational, and health services that could help women and children has been cut in many countries, thereby depriving rural women of important resources to ease their burdens (Vickers, 1991).

Agroindustry Production

Many farmers are becoming part-time wage workers, combining their own small-scale farming with seasonal part-time work on large-scale, market-oriented farms (Flora, 1988). International banana, pineapple, sugar, tea, coffee, and palm oil companies employ large work forces recruited from poor rural households. Agroindustries are generally owned by multinational firms. There is, however, some evidence from Costa Rica, Honduras, and areas of North Africa that wealthy nationals are establishing smaller "plantations" for specialized food crops (e.g., miniature vegetables) and cut flowers. These can be grown on less land than other crops (M. E. Swisher, personal communication, April 7, 1993).

Agroindustries use a strict division of labor by sex (Arzipe & Aranda, 1986; Flora, 1988). Crops that need a lot of weeding and picking, such as coffee and tea, have a large female work force. Men represent a larger segment of workers on banana, sugar, and palm oil plantations, which require the use of machetes to clear land and harvest fruit (Enloe, 1989). In addition, women's jobs in rural-based agroindustries tend to be in food processing (cleaning, packing, and handling) rather than in clearing land, planting, and harvesting (Arzipe & Aranda, 1986; Flora, 1988). Regardless of the product, women agroindustry employees are assigned to the most tedious, least skilled, and most seasonal jobs. As a result, they make less money, have little opportunity for promotion, and are more likely to be unemployed (Enloe, 1989). (See the following example.)

Tess is a Filipino woman who works for a subsidiary of United Brands. Like thousands of other men and women, she migrated to the plantation from her home to another island in search of work when the sugar industry collapsed. Tess works in the packing plant, preparing bananas to be shipped to Japan. She is paid about $1 per day. With her living allowance, she gets about $45 a month. She sends a third of it home to her family.

Tess uses a chemical solution to wash the bananas. There is a large red spot on her leg where some of the wash spilled accidentally. Tess stands for hours at a time. At the end of the day she goes home to the dormitory she shares with 100 other women, 24 in a room.

Like many other plantation workers, Tess is young and single. She is subjected to harassment in the packing plant and can be fired if she is found to be pregnant. Tess has a secondary education but she cannot find other work, except in the entertainment industry around a military base or subsistence farming. She finds her job dull and isolated. She explains, "We have no choice than to stay here. We are far from the highway and if we went out and spent our money there would be nothing left for our food." (Based on Enloe, 1989, p. 138. Berkeley: University of California Press. Copyright 1989 by Cynthia Enloe. Adapted by permission.)

Employment in agroindustry places additional pressures on rural women in relation to their families (Flora, 1988). When mothers migrate seasonally, they must arrange for child care in their absence, live apart from their families for extended periods, make the transition back to their villages at the end of the production cycle, and live on a meager income from their own production or savings until they return to the plantation and begin the cycle again. When family members live together on or near the plantation (e.g., banana production), women put in long days in packing sheds and return home to carry out their traditional responsibilities of cooking, cleaning, and caring for their children and husbands.

Where plantations employ only migrant male labor, there are scores of women at home performing unpaid domestic work and farm labor. Without a partner, the workload for farm women increases. Yet decision-making authority usually remains in the hands of the woman's husband or his male relatives. Thus, even in men's absence, women often have little control over the farm. Customs block them from making production decisions and men appropriate the benefits of the sales of cash crops (Gailey, 1992; Rudolf, 1992). Often, agricultural production declines and the food supply for family decreases. Family members, particularly small children and lactating women, are at risk for malnutrition and disease (Gisbert, Painter, & Quiton, 1992).

The following sections illustrate how urban economic systems structure women's employment opportunities and family relationships. Looking more closely at employment in both the formal sector and the informal sector and using examples from manufacturing and domestic work, we see that women's employment opportunities are limited.

Industrial Soldiers

Although rural and urban women are separated by geographic distance and differ in economic activities and life-styles, they are bound together by the forces of development. As on family farms and plantations, employment in urban areas is segregated by sex, with women being concentrated in traditional, labor-intensive production such as food processing, electronics assembly, and textile and apparel manufacturing, rather than modern "high-tech" industries. Within these occupations, women hold jobs with less authority, lower income, and fewer benefits than men (Enloe, 1989; Fuentes & Ehrenreich, 1983).

One reason for this gendered division of labor is employers' stereotypes about female workers. Managers define some skills, such as sewing, as something that women do "naturally" or "traditionally" and therefore not worthy of being financially rewarded. In addition, women's labor can be kept cheap if the "skilled" jobs (e.g., cutting and pressing) are reserved for men.

Employers view women first as wives and mothers, not as employees.

Married women are considered secondary wage earners whose earnings are not as important to family well-being as men's, who presumably are the breadwinners. Single women are seen as temporary workers who are expected to leave the labor force when they find a husband and can be supported by him (presumably young women are supported by fathers during this "phase" of employment) (Enloe, 1989).

Parents and communities also socialize young women to think of themselves first in their family roles. Poor families depend on young women's incomes for survival but also support the establishment of traditional families in which the husband provides financially for his wife while she cares for him and the children. For example, many workers in the Export Processing Zones of Korea and Malaysia do not see themselves as workers but as daughters and prospective wives, a view that is reinforced by their families and Confucian religious teachings regarding women's subordination to men (Enloe, 1989; Kim, 1992). (See the following example.)

My daughter, Kim, is working in the Masan Free Export Zone. We can't provide the financial support she needs for a dowry and living expenses. And we need Kim's support to meet our own obligations. But the work is hard, hours are long. Kim is not proud of being a factory worker—others look down on this work. She would rather be an office worker, even though the pay is lower.

Kim doesn't expect to be in Masan long so she thinks she can stand the work. She is 22 and she expects to marry soon—by 25 will be ideal. Some of the girls pressure women over 26 to quit, even if they are not married. Sometimes they do quit—but have to look for other work later. Kim is saving for her dowry. Some of her friends told me they save money by skipping breakfast and dinner and only eating the lunch the company provides. I do not approve, of course, but she leads her own life there.

After marriage, Kim's husband will support her. A husband should be able to provide for the family. One of my friend's daughters had to go back to work because her husband could not support his family. This was harder on his wife than before she married because she had to take care of the children, the house, and her husband, as well as go to work. After awhile she started "putting out" from home. The pay wasn't as good and there weren't any benefits. But she could stay at home and be there for the children, so it wasn't like real work anyway. This also caused less arguments with her husband. (Based on Kim, 1992, pp. 54–56.)

Domestic Workers

Women working in cities tend to be employed in jobs considered "appropriate" based on their traditional roles as wives and mothers. It is not surprising that women tend to be concentrated in service occupations, particularly domestic work. For example, due to rapid rates of urbanization in Latin America, domestic work represents the largest single job category for women (Enloe, 1989). Domestic work is becoming an increasingly common job for women in Asia and other world regions (Brydon & Chant, 1989).

Unlike "nannies" and "au pair" girls, domestic workers are usually women of color from less privileged communities. They do ordinary household chores as well as care for children. They are seldom organized into professional organizations or unions, although they may spend a lifetime serving middle-class families. These workers experience common problems such as isolation, loneliness, and possibly sexual assault (Enloe, 1989). When they work abroad, they also face a formidable immigration bureaucracy and possible deportation. (See the following example.)

"Padmini" is a Sri Lankan maid working in Saudi Arabia on a short-term contract. She makes much more money working here than she would at home. She provides her employer with round-the-clock service, 7 days a week, 18 hours per day. "But," she says, "I have no access to leisure or recreation. I am in a strange cultural environment, without my family, under very trying working conditions. Medical facilities are unavailable. Some women are abused. Their employer becomes impatient because they do not know how to use electrical appliances or they resist sexual advances. I have friends who return to Sri Lanka catatonic or in wheel chairs because they have been assaulted by their employers. Will I come back? Yes, my family is very poor." (Based on Enloe, 1989, p. 192. Berkeley: University of California Press. Copyright 1989 by Cynthia Enloe. Adapted by permission.)

Domestic workers employed in their own countries may experience paternalistic attitudes, conflicts with the employer, and (again) possible sexual harassment. Yet for many Third World women, domestic work offers relatively steady and possibly lucrative employment, as well as flexibility. Women are not bound to an employer and may pursue jobs on a temporary basis.

Summary

In this section, I argued that the economic development and urbanization associated with colonialism and capitalist expansion has generally had detrimental effects on women. Often, integration into the global economic system has increased women's total workload, eroded economic resources and autonomy, and marginalized women's power in family decision making (Agarwal, 1985). It has become increasingly difficult for women to meet their families' needs. Ironically, the urbanization and economic development of

Third World societies was expected by some family scholars to result in the emergence of the nuclear family as the predominant family form. Instead, woman-headed families have proliferated as poor women and men migrate to plantations or cities in an attempt to provide for their families. In cities, women have formed extended kin networks so they can pool resources and share domestic labor and child care (Brydon & Chant, 1989; Deere et al., 1990; Mermel & Simons, 1991).

Thus far, I have emphasized the similarities among women based on the gender stratification systems that structure human societies. Women's experiences are also filtered through the cultural, economic, and environmental systems characteristic of the world region in which they live. The following section explores this diversity of experiences while still observing the common thread that binds women together, gender stratification in societal systems and the family.

THE WORLD OF WOMEN

Women's experiences vary by the geographical area they inhabit. I address these differences primarily by continent or subcontinent, focusing on Latin America, the Caribbean, sub-Saharan Africa, North Africa and the Middle East, South Asia, and Southeast Asia. Although this broad approach may simplify or obscure differences within regions, it does provide a general understanding of the prominent conditions of each area (Brydon & Chant, 1989).

Each world region has been subjected to different political and cultural histories. Within each region, gender roles and relations have been affected by predominant religious belief systems, kinship structures, and the ways countries were colonized by foreign powers. In addition, each region is characterized by certain climatic conditions and natural resources that influence agricultural production. The environment provides the raw materials and conditions for household production and consequently affects the products available and the types of activities needed to transform these products for human use.

Latin America

Three centuries of direct Spanish rule have resulted in cultural, religious, and linguistic similarities across Latin America. Colonists vigorously implanted Hispanic institutions in the New World, diluting and in some cases decimating indigenous populations and their cultures. Although formal ties were broken in the 19th century, informal relations continued with Spain, as well as with other European powers. In the 20th century, particularly after World

War II, the United States exerted a powerful economic and cultural influence on Latin America (Brydon & Chant, 1989).

Latin America as a whole is one of the most urbanized areas of the Third World, with 42% of the population residing in settlements of 100,000 or more inhabitants. Between 25% and 30% of the population are employed in industry-related occupations. Compared to other regions, Latin America has one of the highest rates of women employed in wage work and trading (Brydon & Chant, 1989). Fertility declines and increased educational levels have resulted in a shift toward more egalitarian relationships at home (Safa, 1990).

Nevertheless, women are pressured to conform to traditional ideals of motherhood and domesticity and a cultural and religious system based on male superiority. Even in socialist countries such as Nicaragua and Cuba, where egalitarian marriages are legally sanctioned and financial support is provided regardless of marital status, traditional gender roles persist. Most women are taught that their role in life is to become mothers. Unmarried or childless women are considered deviant and often are pressured to foster relatives' children to validate their femininity and ensure their respectability (Brydon & Chant, 1989). Most women are married or have children by their mid-20s, and a large proportion of women are married in their teenage years (10–25% of 15- to 19-year-olds have been married, compared to 10% for the developed world). In most countries, women bear between four and six children. Although in the past two decades the number of female-headed households in Latin America has increased dramatically, the male-headed nuclear family remains the norm.

The ideology of *machismo* pervades relationships between men and women and perpetuates male privilege in public and private spheres, regardless of social class. Derived from the Spanish word *macho*, it is often associated with male ideological and physical control of women. *Machismo* is manifested in male domination of family decision making and control of women's social, sexual, and economic freedom (Brydon & Chant, 1989).

As an institution, the Roman Catholic church, to which the majority of Latin Americans belong, has encouraged women to be "good" mothers and wives. That is, they are to deny their own needs and resign themselves to their fate in life, even if this means enduring unhappy marriages and financial privation. Women are expected to guard the moral order and to accept the difficulty of life on earth in preparation for a better life in heaven (Brydon & Chant, 1989, p. 18).

In short, men continue to be the principal wage earners, hold the prestigious public posts, and leave women to carry out most of the child care and domestic work (Brydon & Chant, 1989; Huber, 1988). Throughout Latin America and the Caribbean, women may be negotiating some changes within the home, but in the workplace or the state their needs are still not legitimized (Safa, 1990).

The Caribbean

The Caribbean basin was a locus of international slave trade during the 17th and 18th centuries. A major legacy of the Spanish and British colonial period has been economic dependency on plantation agricultural export production as the foundation of national economic systems (less than one-fourth of the regional labor force is employed in industry). Periodic job shortages in agriculture occur as a result of declines in the world market for agricultural products and seasonal changes in production, and men frequently leave their home island for employment elsewhere on a short-term or permanent basis (Brydon & Chant, 1989).

About one-third of women head their households, providing the primary financial support for their families. Regionwide, most women are employed. Caribbean women's economic and social autonomy can in part be explained by men's migration but can also be attributed to historical and cultural factors (Brydon & Chant 1989).

Two eras appear to have been particularly important in shaping women's economic independence, slavery under British rule and the later involvement of the United States in the region. During and after slavery, women were separated from their husbands and thus shouldered the primary responsibility for their children's economic and social welfare and development. In the 1960s and 1970s, U.S. manufacturing companies established offshore manufacturing plants that employed women, thereby enabling them to earn the means to provide for their families (Brydon & Chant, 1989).

Three major family types are common in the Caribbean, the nuclear two-parent family, the African-descended matrifocal household, and the East Indian extended family group (Ellis, 1986). Although legal marriage is the ideal, common-law marriages are widespread and are recognized as formal unions. In addition, there are a large number of "visiting unions" where women do not live with their partners or have any legal ties to them. Motherhood is important, and about 75% of Caribbean women have children; on the average they have 4.5 children by the end of their childbearing years. Around two-thirds of births take place outside legal marriage (Brydon & Chant, 1989).

Women have more status if they have a permanent male partner and they generally prefer to be married. First, marriage is considered the proper condition for parenthood. Second, discrimination against women in the labor market gives men access to better paying jobs that provide greater family financial security. Although Caribbean women appear to have greater economic and social freedom than do women in other parts of the developing world, they still have secondary status in family and society (Brydon & Chant, 1989).

North Africa and the Middle East

These two regions are treated together because of their geographical proximity and cultural similarities. Islam in particular has been a powerful force affecting women's roles.

Gender roles are extremely segregated. Women and men have limited contact and women are frequently secluded through physical separation and the wearing of long concealing garments (seclusion is called *purdah*). Such control over mobility and appearance is imposed to enforce women's sexual modesty and to prevent women from creating irrational, overpowering sexual desires in men that divert attention from Allah (Brydon & Chant, 1989). Women's labor force participation in the Middle East and North Africa is the lowest in the world (Townsend & Momsen, 1987).

Marriage is expected and only a very few women are not married by age 30. Between 25% and 50% are married by age 19. Polygamy with up to four wives is permitted and practiced, provided that the husband treats all his wives equally. Polygamy is an important determinant of female subordination and male privilege. Women often see their co-wives as rivals, which prevents the development of female solidarity. Also, the husband is able to fulfill his sexual appetite without forming strong conjugal bonds with individual women (Brydon & Chant, 1989).

Inequality within marriage is legally sanctioned. Men can expect a wife's total fidelity, obedience, domestic labor, breast-feeding of his children, and deference to his relatives. A woman can expect financial support, equal treatment with other wives, and permission to visit her relatives and to dispose of her own possessions as she pleases. She cannot demand fidelity, obedience, or respect for her relatives (Brydon & Chant, 1989).

Deference toward the husband's relatives is a key characteristic of Islamic family life. Filial rather than conjugal ties are emphasized. Mothers play a major role in their sons' mate selection and later influence the marital relationship in significant ways. Newlyweds often live with the husband's family. The couple's intimacy is inhibited by close contact with the husband's parents, a lack of time together to develop common interests, and parental supervision of the couple's activities. Mothers-in-law act to "drive a wedge" between the wife and her spouse by burdening young women with domestic chores and interfering with the marital relationship to prevent the development of love and companionship (Brydon & Chant 1989, p. 27; Mernissi, 1985).

Women are under pressure to bear sons and fertility is high as women attempt to have the desired number of male children. On average, women in the region give birth to at least six children. Infertility or failure to bear sons frequently serves as grounds for men to divorce their wives. Divorced women find it difficult to remarry because they are not virgins, and women often return to live with their fathers or brothers, who are charged with guarding women's honor. Children often are assigned to the custody of their legal father, the man to whom the mother was married at the time of the child's birth, even though he may not be the biological father. When a father is considered unfit, children are assigned to the mother's custody, although the father is still obligated to provide for the food, clothing, shelter, and education of his offspring (Brydon & Chant, 1989).

Clearly, sexual control of women is a fundamental aspect of Islamic society as manifested in early marriage of young women, *purdah*, in-law supervision, and divorce. Another method of control that is not a Muslim institution but is condoned in these societies is "female circumcision," which was discussed in the section on health. Like women in other world regions, women in the Middle East and North Africa are expected to be wives and mothers. More than other women, however, fulfillment of these roles is enforced through legal, social, and religious systems that control women's physical mobility, emotional intimacy, and sexual activity (Brydon & Chant, 1989).

Sub-Saharan Africa

Sub-Saharan Africa includes those nations bordering the southern edge of the Sahara Desert and transverses the continent across an area so large that it is divided into regions known as West, Central, East, and South Africa. In general, Africa's population continues to be rural and agricultural production serves as the economic base in most states (Brydon & Chant, 1989). Small farms are the typical production system in sub-Saharan Africa, and the changes described in detail in the earlier section on small farm production are characteristic of this region.

There is considerable diversity in kinship systems continentwide that affects gender roles. In many parts of West Africa, women have preserved matrifocal traditions and live with their female kin. In other areas, polygamous extended households are common. In some southern African countries, large numbers of women head their families due to the migration of men to mines and cities for jobs and high divorce rates in parts of West and East Africa. It seems that the nuclear, patriarchal family is *not* the norm in Africa. Indeed, a smaller proportion of African women legally marry than in other regions, although common law marriages are typical and accepted (Brydon & Chant, 1989).

Whether or not a woman lives with a man, birthrates are high through-out Africa, ranging from four to six in a handful of countries, but on aver-age women have more than six children for whom they are responsible. Thus, despite relative autonomy, African women face a number of pressures, often without the resources to alleviate difficulties in providing for their families' basic needs (Brydon & Chant, 1989).

South Asia

The South Asian region includes India, Nepal, Pakistan, Bangladesh, and Sri Lanka. The regional urban population has increased dramatically in the past 20 to 30 years, but most people live in rural areas and depend on agriculture for their livelihoods.

The wide range of religious beliefs in South Asia, including Buddhism, Hinduism, Islam, and others, influences these countries' cultures. The focus here is on India, Sri Lanka, and Nepal, with an emphasis on Hindu influ-ences on women's family roles (Brydon & Chant, 1989).

According to the Hindu religion, women have little or no worth due to their position in the caste structure, which assigns status at birth. Certain behaviors and occupations are prescribed for each group as a condition for being rewarded in a later life. Although some castes are regarded as unpure or unclean, women of all castes are seen as inferior in that they are more unclean than men. This concern about women's uncleanliness pervades both the spiritual and the routine aspects of life. For instance, women are not allowed to become religious scholars or to participate in religious ceremo-nies (as with Islam and various Christian and Jewish sects). They are segre-gated during menstruation and childbirth because these are considered key sources of pollution (Brydon & Chant, 1989).

According to Hinduism, women should always come under the jurisdic-tion of a man and should be completely devoted to him in marriage and in widowhood. Under the dowry system, a girl's parents must pay an agreed-on sum to the groom's family, but demands for payments to keep the wife often increase over time, reflecting women's status as dispensable and easily replaced. When the bride's family cannot afford to meet the required payments, brides may be murdered by their in-laws or commit suicide due to continued physi-cal and verbal abuse. Although the dowry system is a criminal offense, little official action is taken to legally or physically protect women (Brydon & Chant, 1989).

Widowed women are considered unclean (i.e., contaminated by death) and their lives are severely restricted. In continuing devotion to their hus-bands, widows are supposed to refrain from adorning themselves and to sacrifice all pleasure. Widows are permitted to remarry in India, providing a religious ceremony is not performed. Remarriage of widows is illegal in Nepal (Brydon & Chant, 1989).

The South Asian family is patriarchal and extended. Marriages are usually arranged, and brides must be virgins. The common nuptial age for women in 1980 was 9; more than half of girls ages 15 to 19 have been officially married in India, Nepal, and Bangladesh. Motherhood, particularly of boys, is a primary goal. South Asian women have on the average four to six children (Brydon & Chant, 1989).

Southeast Asia

The Philippines, mainland Southeast Asia, and the Indonesian islands are included in this region. The diversity of religions, cultures, and economies in the region are due in part to a varied colonial history, with some countries experiencing greater degrees of colonial control than others.

In addition, the level of industrialization varies. Some mainland countries and the Philippines have undergone a considerable degree of industrialization associated with the development of an export-manufacturing sector. Multinational firms have relocated assembly operations to tariff-free production zones in these countries. Their preference for hiring female labor results in some of the highest female employment rates in the Third World (Brydon & Chant, 1989).

As in other regions, religion is a prominent part of the culture and plays a major role in relegating women to a subordinate status. Buddhism and Islam are most common, with other major world religions scattered in different areas. One of these not previously mentioned is Confucianism, which teaches that women are inferior to men and must defer to their husbands at all times. A woman's place is considered to be in the home. The cultural ideal is a patrilocal joint family with several generations and married couples living in one household. Only the socialist countries have taken major steps to improve the status of women at home and in the labor force by, for example, outlawing polygamy and eliminating bridewealth payments (Brydon & Chant, 1989).

Despite the acceptance of women's labor force participation and associated older age at marriage, women's primary responsibility is to home and family. On average, women give birth to between four and six children, which is comparable to several other world regions with a lesser degree of industrialization. Even when women move into the labor force they are employed in highly exploitative positions as, for example, poorly remunerated factory labor or prostitution. Thus, women in Southeast Asia face similar problems to those in other world regions (Brydon & Chant, 1989).

EMPOWERING WOMEN

In this chapter, I explored the similarity and diversity of women's lives in the major regions of the Third World. We found that preference is given to men and boys in the distribution and control of three critical social and human resources: education, employment, and health. Women have lower educational achievement and receive relatively little encouragement to attend school. They are responsible for most of the work that gets done in the home and in factories, markets, and fields but are relegated to low-paying jobs or marginal work in the informal sector. Despite the importance of reproduction to Third World cultures, women and girls are deprived of an adequate, nutritious food supply with measurable negative effects on their own health and the health and survival rates of their offspring. Finally, they suffer the tragic consequences of female circumcision that impair their physical and psychological health.

We also discovered that gender stratification systems structure relationships between men and women within households. This inequality is exacerbated by the stratification of societies based on race, ethnicity, and class. I have taken the position that women have been marginalized in the process of colonialism and capitalist expansion into rural and urban systems of production.

Cultural practices and social institutions, particularly religion and the family, are also powerful forces shaping women's lives. Culture and society often perpetuate traditional stereotypes about men's and women's roles and sanction women's secondary status in society and family (Acosta-Belén & Bose, 1990; Brydon & Chant, 1989). Men are primarily defined by religious and cultural traditions as economic providers and community leaders. First and foremost, a woman's duty is to be a mother, domestic caretaker, and deferent wife. Early age at marriage and high fertility thrust women into these roles, often as adolescents. As a result of potent cultural, social, and economic forces, women are excluded from positions of authority in the home, workplace, religious institutions, and government.

In short, women have fewer economic and human capital resources than do men and have more family and work responsibilities. Women's workday has lengthened and their workload has increased. Families are being split apart in efforts to make ends meet, while women are expected to hold them together. Given these fairly grim circumstances, what is the future for Third World women?

Scholars believe that Third World women's lives must be *decolonialized* if they are to gain access to health, an adequate income, and basic necessities (Acosta-Belén & Bose, 1990). Many argue that *empowerment* is critical to this process. At its most basic level, empowerment for women means having or gaining greater control over their lives so that they achieve greater equity in society and their relationships (see Balswick & Balswick, Chapter 13, this volume, for more on empowerment in marriage). Empowerment refers to "the broadening of choices, the expansion of options and alternatives available to women in determining the course of events which will shape their own lives and determine their own destinies" (Everett, 1989, p. 3). In large part, this may depend on women's ability to gain and control valuable social resources (Coltrane, 1992).

Empowerment is developed through education by improving women's literacy rate and enrollment in primary and secondary schools. Empowerment is promoted in the workplace with assurances of gainful employment, but also through recognition of the value of women's contributions to production with domestic work, child care, and subsistence agriculture. Gaining access to social and health care services that assist women in supporting their families may also empower women (Blumberg, 1989).

In industrialized nations, women's empowerment has been pursued by organizing women to work for women's rights and full participation in the public sphere (Johnson-Odim, 1991). For instance, as women's labor force participation has increased, so have efforts to equalize women's and men's salaries for comparable work, to free women from sexual harassment in the workplace, and to establish national parental leave policies and other family-supportive acts that enable parents to be productive workers. In addition, there have been major campaigns to increase the number of women in governance by electing women to public office or appointing them to political leadership positions.

In contrast, gender discrimination is not the primary focus of women's movements in the Third World (Enloe, 1989; Johnson-Odim, 1991). Many lower-income and less educated women from traditional cultures feel that First World feminism is irrelevant to their needs. They generally feel more comfortable in organizing to address specific problems in their communities and pressuring governments for changes that have to do with family survival (Acosta-Belén & Bose, 1990).

Examples from the Third World suggest that women's social actions are often motivated by their desire to improve the quality of their family's lives (Nash, 1990; Safa, 1990). Women want their rights as wives and mothers to be affirmed as a legitimate basis for incorporation as full participants in the public world and use their domestic role to give them strength and legitimacy in making demands of the state (Safa, 1990). Often women have organized simply to survive (Enloe, 1989; Nash, 1990; Safa, 1990). For women who head families, their employment may be the sole source of economic support for their children. Similarly, married working-class urban women often depend on their albeit poorly paid work to feed, clothe, and house their families (Enloe, 1989).

In urban areas of Latin America, women have demanded running water, electricity, and transportation for the squatter settlements in which most poor women live. Women have also been at the forefront of demands for programs to provide health services and day care (Safa, 1990). In Brazil and other Latin American countries, the Catholic church's ecclesiastical communities have organized women into "mother clubs" to provide food, sewing classes, and other traditional domestic tasks at the grass-roots level. Women have also started communal kitchens to cope with severe economic crises by buying and preparing food for the neighborhood. Such groups are based on women's traditional roles but also provide an organizational base from which women could challenge the existing social order (Safa, 1990).

Rural women have also organized to protect the natural resources on which they depend. For example, in India, the "Chipko" movement demonstrates women's collective power to preserve natural resources they needed for family survival (Dankelman & Davidson, 1988). British colonization of India and its majestic forests in the late 19th century and the continued commercial exploitation in this century resulted in large-scale forest destruction, massive erosion due to overcutting, and poverty for those who depended on the diverse forest resources for productivity. Because women are responsible for meeting their families basic needs for food and water, women have concretely and vividly experienced a reduced ability to access food, fertilizer, fuel, and water for drinking and irrigation that has quite literally endangered human survival (Shiva, 1989).

In the 1970s, women in the Himalayan mountain regions started the Chipko movement to protect their forests from continued commercial extraction and to protect threatened life-giving resources. The Chipko movement mobilized women throughout the hill regions for a ban on commercial exploitation. Women encircled, guarded, or embraced living trees to save them from logger's saws and axes and to preserve their communities' rights to utilize local forest products, even when these actions could cost women their lives. ("Chipko" means to hug.)

Women's interest was in preserving the forests for renewable food and water resources for family use. As 50-year-old activist Hima Devi spread the message to save the trees, she said, "I have come to you with [the women's] message. Stop cutting trees. There are no trees even for birds to perch on. Birds flock to our crops and eat them. What will we eat? The firewood is disappearing: how will we cook?" (Shiva, 1989, p. 75).

Because more than 300 villages were threatened by landslides and severe erosion, women responded forcefully, launching public information campaigns, protests, and appealing directly to forest contractors to suspend logging. As a result, in 1980, the government established a 15-year ban on green tree felling in some areas. Since then, the movement has spread and generated pressure for a broader natural resource policy sensitive to the needs of people and their environment (Rodda, 1993). (See the following example.)

"In 1973, a woman grazing her cows spotted a few persons with axes in their hands; she whistled and collected all her companions who surrounded the contractor's men and said 'This forest is our mother, when there is a crisis of food, we come here to collect grass and dry fruits to feed our children. We dig out herbs and collect mushrooms from this forest. You cannot touch these trees'. . . . [In] small groups they formed vigilance parties to keep an eye on the axemen till the government was forced to set up a committee, which recommended a 10-year ban on commercial green-filling in the . . . catchment." (Shiva, 1989, p. 74.)

These examples illustrate that in many countries and communities, women's actions have resulted in greater visibility for human needs. As Safa (1990) states, "By politicizing the private sphere, women have redefined rather than rejected their domestic role" (p. 367). In doing so, women are transforming their work and family lives to do away with gender, race, and class oppressions that have so long subordinated the world's women (Safa, 1990).

Such actions are not without their costs for families, however. Men may resist women's participation in organizations that take them away from their family responsibilities. In such cases, women may be torn between taking needed action to preserve their income and access to resources—for their families as well as their own rights—and responding to their spouse's demands and social pressure to conform to traditional roles. (See the following example.)

"The morning of September 19, 1985, Mexico City experienced one of North America's worst earthquakes. . . . For [many factory] . . . seamstresses, the earthquake marked a political and personal turning point. An estimated 800 small garment factories . . . were destroyed . . . killing over 1,000 garment workers and leaving another 40,000 without jobs.

"Women who were just arriving at work as the quake shook Mexico City stood looking at the rubble that an hour before had been their source of livelihood. . . . Many of them were single mothers and their families depended on their wages. But their first thought was of those women, already at work at 7:00 A.M., who were trapped inside flattened buildings. . . . Within a day . . . soldiers began to pull away piles of cement [with a crane] so that owners could retrieve their machinery. Employees . . . watched with mounting horror and indignation as their bosses and the soldiers chose to rescue sewing machines before women. . . .

"Some women . . . block[ed] the trucks that were about to carry off the owners' precious machines. Several dozen women decided that they would have to stay at the site overnight to prevent the army trucks from moving and thus the owners from leaving . . . without [paying employees]. . . .

"In the months that followed . . . garment workers . . . kept up their road-block and vigil until the government pushed the owners to pay compensation for lost wages. . . . They created . . . the September 19th Garment Workers Union [that by] 1987 had gained worker's support . . . in twelve factories. . . . But [there was] pressure from the outside [from government, garment companies, and teenage thugs who were sent to the factories to throw stones at women activists]. Some [men] prohibited their wives and companions from taking part in [union] activities. . . .

"The . . . women discussed ways to lessen their partners' and families' resistance to their spending so much time away from home. . . . At first women felt . . . they had to choose either to end their participation in the new union or to leave their male partners. . . . Such a choice had to be challenged, or it would have severely restricted the union's potential membership and made it hard to gain an audience in factories not yet organized. So members chose to try to make children and partners feel like participants in union activities. Setting up a child-care center at . . . head-quarters was intended to relieve some of the tensions that were mounting between union work, factory work, and family responsibilities. . . . [A]s the Mexican garment workers have demonstrated, any success in altering managerial and political policies will require taking up sensitive questions about home life. . . ." (Enloe, 1989, pp. 169–176. Berkeley: University of California Press. Copyright 1989 by Cynthia Enloe. Reprinted by permission.)

These examples indicate that Third World women are taking action to improve their living conditions, protect precious natural resources, and ensure their legal rights to an income. Third World women are changing their lives at the institutional level by organizing their neighborhoods or mobilizing women in nearby villages, placing demands on governments, and challenging unjust corporate policies. In so doing, they are also changing their self-concept and their family lives. They are both working for their families *and* changing traditional gender roles within their families, possibly altering the gender stratification system through their personal power and motivation (Balswick & Balswick, Chapter 13, this volume; Fenstermaker, West, & Zimmerman, 1991).

NOTES

1. The definition of economic activity used here is based on the recommendation of the International Labor Organization and includes all work for pay or in anticipation of profit, such as all production and processing of agricultural products, whether for the market, for barter, or for home consumption. It still excludes unpaid housework and the care of family members (United Nations, 1991a).

2. It is difficult to measure the extent of difference because of the limited availability of comparable income data across Third World nations (e.g., for Latin

America and the Caribbean) and the segregated nature of the labor force (United Nations, 1991a).

REFERENCES

Acosta-Belén, E., & Bose, C. (1990). From structural subordination to empowerment: Women and development in Third World contexts. *Gender and Society*, 4, 299–320.

Agarwal, B. (1985). Women and technological change in agriculture: The Asian and African experience. In I. Ahmed (Ed.), *Technology and rural women: Conceptual and empirical issues* (pp. 67–114). London: Allen & Unwin.

Arzipe, L., & Aranda, J. (1986). Women workers in the strawberry agribusiness in Mexico. In E. Leacock & H. Safa (Eds.), *Women's work* (pp. 174–193). South Hadley, MA: Bergin & Garvey.

Baber, K. M., & Allen, K. R. (1992). *Women and families: Feminist reconstructions.* New York: Guilford Press.

Blumberg, R. L. (1988). Income under female versus male control. *Journal of Family Issues*, 9, 51–84.

Blumberg, R. L. (1989). *Making the case for the gender variable: Women and the wealth and well-being of nations.* Washington, DC: U.S. Agency for Women in Development.

Brydon, L., & Chant, S. (1989). *Women in the Third World.* New Brunswick, NJ: Rutgers University Press.

Burja, J. M. (1986). Urging women to redouble their efforts . . . Class, gender, and capitalist transformation in Africa. In C. Robertson & I. Berger (Eds.), *Women and class in Africa* (pp. 117–140). New York: Africana.

Chafetz, J. S. (1988). The gender division of labor and the reproduction of female disadvantage. *Journal of Family Issues*, 9, 108–131.

Cloud, K. (1985). Women's productivity in agricultural systems: Considerations for project design. In C. Overholt, M. B. Anderson, K. Cloud, & J. E. Austin (Eds.), *Gender roles in development projects* (pp. 17–56). West Hartford, CT: Kumarian Press.

Cock, J. (1988). Trapped workers: The case of domestic servants in South Africa. In S. B. Stichter & J. L. Parpart (Eds.), *Patriarchy and class* (pp. 205–220). Boulder, CO: Westview Press.

Coltrane, S. (1992). The micropolitics of gender in nonindustrial societies. *Gender and Society*, 6, 86–107.

Dankelman, I., & Davidson, J. (1988). *Women and environment in the Third World.* London: Earthscan.

Deere, C. D., Antrobus, P., Bolles, L., Melendez, E., Phillips, P., Rivera, M., & Safa, H. (1990). *In the shadows of the sun.* Boulder, CO: Westview Press.

Dixon-Meuller, R. (1985). *Women's work in Third World agriculture.* Geneva: International Labor Organization.

Ellis, P. (1986). *Women of the Caribbean.* London: Zed Press.

Enloe, C. (1989). *Bananas, beaches, and bases.* Berkeley: University of California Press.

Etienne, M., & Leacock, E. (1980). Women and colonization. New York: Praeger.

Everett, J. (1989). *The global empowerment of women.* Washington, DC: Association for Women in Development.

Fenstermaker, S., West, C., & Zimmerman, D. H. (1991). Gender inequality: New conceptual terrain. In R. L. Blumberg (Ed.), *Gender, family, and economy* (pp. 289–307). Newbury Park, CA: Sage.

Finch, J. (1992). Women work harder than men. *Cultural Survival Quarterly, 16,* 44–46.

Flora, C. B. (1988). Public policy and women in agricultural production: A comparative and historical analysis. In W. G. Haney & J. B. Knowles (Eds.), *Women and farming* (pp. 265–280). Boulder, CO: Westview Press.

Friedman, S. A. (1992, July-September). Girls' education: From childhood to womanhood. *First Call for Children, 3,* 13, 15.

Fuentes, A., & Ehrenreich, B. (1983). *Women in the global factory.* Boston: South End Press.

Gailey, C. W. (1992). Keeping kinship alive. *Cultural Survival Quarterly, 16,* 47–49.

Gisbert, M. E., Painter, M., & Quiton, M. (1992). Women's work in areas of high male out-migration. *Development Anthropology Network, 10*(2), 3–10.

Grant, J. (1992). *The state of the world's children 1992.* Oxford, England: Oxford University Press.

Huber, J. (1988). A theory of family, economy, and gender. *Journal of Family Issues, 9,* 9–26.

Jacobson, J. (1993). Closing the gender gap in development. In L. R. Brown & Associates, *The state of the world 1993: A Worldwatch Institute report on progress toward a sustainable society* (pp. 61–79). New York: W. W. Norton.

Jacquette, J. (1985). Women, population, and food: An overview of the issues. In J. Mouson & M. Kalb (Eds.), *Women as food producers in developing countries* (pp. 1–10). Los Angeles: UCLA African Studies Center.

Johnson-Odim, C. (1991). Common themes, different contexts: Third World women and feminism. In C. T. Mohanty, A. Russo, & L. Torres (Eds.), *Third World women and the politics of feminism* (pp. 314–327). Bloomington: Indiana University Press.

Jones, C. (1986). Intra-household bargaining in response to the introduction of new crops: A case study from North Cameroon. In J. L. Moock (Ed.), *Understanding Africa's rural households and farming systems* (pp. 105–123). Boulder, CO: Westview Press.

Kim, S. (1992). Industrial soldiers. *Cultural Survival Quarterly, 16,* 54–56.

Lightfoot-Klein, H. (1992). *A woman's odyssey into Africa.* Binghampton, NY: Harrington Park Press.

Mermel, A., & Simons, J. (1991). *Women and world development.* Washington, DC: OEF International.

Mernissi, F. (1985). *Beyond the veil: Male–female dynamics in modern Muslim society.* London: Al Saqui Books.

Nash, J. (1990). Latin American women in the world capitalist crisis. *Gender and Society, 4,* 338–353.

Overholt, C., Anderson, M. B., Cloud, K., & Austin, J. E. (1985). Women in development: A framework for project analysis. In C. Overholt, M. B. Anderson,

K. Cloud, & J. E. Austin (Eds.), *Gender roles in development projects* (pp. 3–16). West Hartford, CT: Kumarian Press.

Rodda, A. (1993). *Women and the environment.* London: Zed.

Rogers, B. (1980). *The domestication of women.* London: Routledge.

Rudolf, G. (1992). When servants could always go home. *Cultural Survival Quarterly, 16*, 28–30.

Safa, H. (1990). Women's social movements in Latin America. *Gender and Society, 4*, 338–353.

Saito, K. A., & Weidemann, C. J. (1990). *Agricultural extension for women farmers in Africa.* Washington, D.C.: The World Bank.

Shiva, V. (1989). *Staying alive.* London: Zed Books.

Stephen, L. (1992). Marketing ethnicity. *Cultural Survival Quarterly, 16*, 25–27.

Townsend, J., & Momsen, J. H. (1987). Towards a geography of gender in developing market economies. In J. Momsen & J. Townsend (Eds.), *Geography of gender in the Third World* (pp. 27–81). London: Hutchinson.

UNICEF. (1992, April–June). Focus sharpens on structural impediments to women's gains. *First Call for Children 3*, 1–2.

United Nations. (1991a). *The world's women 1970–1990.* New York: Author.

United Nations. (1991b). *Women: Challenges to the year 2000.* New York: Author.

Villareal, M. (1992). Yo no soy nada. *Cultural Survival Quarterly, 16*, 31–33.

Vickers, J. (1991). *Women and the Third World economic crisis.* London: Zed Books.

CHAPTER TWELVE

Household Division of Labor in Industrial Societies

LINDA L. HAAS

This chapter describes how families in industrial societies divide responsibility for the work that must be done to support their families. Of particular interest is how this work is allocated on the basis of gender and how this gender-based division of labor is related to the status of women and men in society.

The focus here is on three types of work prevalent in industrial societies: breadwinning, housework, and child care.

1. Unlike agricultural subsistence economies, in industrial societies most of the products and many of the services that families need must be purchased, including food, clothing, consumer goods, and leisure activities. *Breadwinning* involves the responsibility of wage earning outside the household. This earned income is essential for family survival and comfort.

2. *Housework* is the work that must be done to keep family members fed, clean, and comfortable and to keep the home in good order. It includes cooking, dishwashing, shopping, housecleaning, laundry, and clothing care.

3. In order for families to reproduce themselves, children must be born and cared for. The practical aspects of *child care* include feeding, washing, and arranging for substitute care. Children also need love, security, guidance, and instruction in order to develop self-respect and the skills necessary to get along in society. Play and parent–child interaction thus become important for nurturing the attributes desired in a given society.

This chapter focuses on these three types of activities because they take up most of family members' time and because they have received the most attention from researchers. Other types of work performed by families include house and lawn maintenance, care of dependent elderly family members, maintenance of kin relations, financial management, and securing the family's position in the larger social community.

In industrial societies, the responsibilities of breadwinning, housework, and child care have traditionally been assigned to individuals on the basis of their gender. Men are regarded as more responsible for breadwinning, whereas women are considered more responsible for housework and child care. Either sex might cross over gender boundaries, but such behavior is often viewed as unusual because these behaviors tend to be assigned to one gender. When individuals do cross over gender boundaries, they tend to be regarded as deviant or as "helping out" the person who is really responsible. For example, women who are employed outside the home are seen as supporting husbands' income earning or working for "extras." Families can find alternative ways of getting housework or child care done, for example, by hiring help or involving children, but under these circumstances women tend to maintain a supervisory role.

Women, especially wives and mothers, have entered the labor force in dramatic numbers in the past few decades. This development has the potential to influence attitudes about gender roles, as well as the actual division of labor for breadwinning, housework, and child care. This chapter shows, however, that the notion that men and women ought to assume distinctive social roles within the family remains strong.

This chapter discusses the following topics:

1. How the household division of labor in industrial societies became gender based.
2. How the household division of labor is organized in various contemporary industrial societies.
3. Why some societies have developed a more egalitarian approach to the division of labor than others.
4. What future trends can be foreseen in the household division of labor in industrial societies.

HOW THE HOUSEHOLD DIVISION OF LABOR BECAME GENDER BASED

Historical Perspectives

Anthropological evidence suggests that a gender-based division of labor in human societies has always existed. Yet before industrialization (i.e., the development of capitalism and market economies), there was no universal pattern for the division of labor that *always* assigned one task to women and one task to men, which we might expect if the division of labor had some basis in biological sex differences. For example, in some societies women were the ones who grew crops, whereas in others it was the men. Before industrialization, men were not exclusively responsible for production of goods and services needed for the family's survival; indeed, research suggests that women's activities probably provided a large share of food (Brown, 1970). Aronoff and Crano's (1975) study of 862 nonindustrial societies found that worldwide, women contributed 44% of the food.

In preindustrial societies, women's work was not confined to the home. They gathered herbs, roots, fruits, and seeds, tended and harvested crops, fetched firewood and water, and raised small livestock (Stephens, 1963). They were often involved in economic exchanges outside the household as they sold or bartered surplus products of their labor to outsiders. The "housework" that women did was qualitatively and quantitatively different from that done by women in industrialized countries today. Food preparation involved butchering, curing meats, and grinding grains, not just cooking. Clothing care involved tanning hides, spinning, weaving, and garment construction, not just laundry. Women tended to be held more responsible for house cleaning and child care. But these latter activities took up a small portion of their time and were considered less important and less worthy of effort, compared to women's other chores (Crano & Aronoff, 1978; Newland, 1980). Dwellings were small and simply furnished, and high standards of cleanliness were not maintained. Children were regarded as little adults who did not require constant adult attention; the care of the youngest was often left to older siblings. Each of the parents was responsible for the moral upbringing and skills training of same-sex children.

Impact of Industrialization

Industrialization led to a dramatic redefinition of men's and women's household roles. As factories began manufacturing goods once produced in the home, family members were drawn into wage labor. Many of the first factory workers were women. Eventually, as factory work came to be seen less as a peripheral activity and more as the mainstay of the new economy, men wanted to gain control over this new source of cash income, power, and prestige (Jackson, 1992). A powerful set of beliefs, "the doctrine of separate spheres," arose to justify men's monopolization of waged work. This doctrine maintained that men were naturally more suited for wage labor in the public sphere outside the home, while women were by nature more suited to perform housework and child care in the private sphere. Men would provide income for women and children so that goods and services previously produced outside the home could be purchased; women, in turn, would care for men's personal needs, the house, and children. Although labor was divided along gender lines, men's and women's activities were viewed as complementary in that they supported similar ends, the survival and economic advancement of the household unit. The resulting gender differences in power and economic social status were not discussed.

The belief in natural differences and the desirability of complementary roles of women and men became first entrenched in the middle class, where families could survive on the pay of a single wage earner. Eventually this ideology shaped the aspirations (if not the reality) of the working class as well. Trade union leaders, politicians, clergy, educators, writers, physicians, politicians, and even female social reformers promoted this belief. Some of these groups had vested interests in men having privileged access to cash income and women remaining subordinate to men; others believed devoutly in women and men having different biological capacities and divine missions.

In accordance with the idea that men were to be family breadwinners, men had greater access to jobs that would provide cash income essential to obtain the necessities of urban life. Women were supposed to concentrate on doing unpaid work within the home. The character of this work was substantially different from what it was like before industrialization. Many of the tasks women had spent so much time on before industrialization, such as food production and processing, and making clothes, were not needed because these items could be purchased. Instead, women were supposed to devote themselves to housework, which "as a distinctive form of labor emerges only with industrialization" (Ferree, 1991, p. 111). Dwellings, furnishings, and wardrobes became more elaborate, and women spent more time maintaining them. Standards for cleanliness escalated; domestic scientists warned women that they had to eliminate germs to preserve their family's health. In time, new products and machines were invented for women to use to maintain their homes and possessions in even better condition (e.g., washing machines and vacuum cleaners). The amount of time women spent on housework increased dramatically.

Standards for child care changed even more, which shaped women's new social identities in important ways. Childhood came to be viewed by clergy, psychologists, and physicians as the most crucial stage in the development of the individual. Children were seen as needing special protection, education, and nurturing in order to develop normally. Mothers were regarded as the ideal parents to do this because religion and popular opinion maintained that they were more moral, spiritual, and tender than were men (Rotundo, 1985). The joys of motherhood were promoted from pulpits and in the mass media, and motherhood began to represent "the greatest achievement of a woman's life, the sole true means of self-realization" (Oakley, 1974, p. 186). Women's time spent with children increased dramatically, and women's personal and social identities became tied up with being mothers. Children's need for full-time care by mothers was used to justify women's exclusion from the paid labor market.

It is important to note that the doctrine of separate spheres did not succeed in excluding women entirely from wage labor. For example, in 1900, one-fourth of U.S. women worked for pay outside the home; in France, nearly one-third did (Lewis, 1992). Other women worked for pay at home—taking in boarders, sewing, and doing laundry—in a hidden labor market not counted by demographers of the day (Bose, 1987). Many (but not all) women who worked for pay were single, poor, minority, or immigrant women whose families could not afford to conform to the dominant middle-class ideal advocating women as full-time housewives and mothers. Employers benefited from these women's need for work by using them as a low-paid labor force.

Recent Developments

In nearly all industrial societies, women's entrance into the labor market has dramatically increased in the past two to three decades. More wives and mothers have been drawn into the labor market from all social classes. Mothers of young children who previously did not enter the labor force until their children were of school age have entered the labor market in record numbers. One typical example is Canada: In 1970 less than half of women in the primary childbearing and childrearing years (ages 25–34) were in the paid labor force; by 1988, almost three-fourths were (Sorrentino, 1990). Women are now a highly visible part of the paid labor force in industrial societies, composing between one-third and one-half of the labor market.

There are several reasons for this change. Smaller family sizes and higher educational attainment made women more eligible for employment. But most of women's increased participation in the labor market has been due to societies' needs for cheap labor, especially in the growing service sector of the economy, and to families' needs for additional income. In the United States, for example, one-fourth of the jobs in 1988 were in the service sector, up from 14% in 1961 (Howe & Parks, 1989). The increase in service jobs has helped to encourage women to enter the labor market; these jobs are also often regarded as more consonant with women's traditional responsibilities for nurturing and service.

In many industrial societies, a decline in real earnings since the 1970s has made two incomes crucial for the maintenance of the family's standard of living. This decline seems to be associated with the elimination (or removal to developing countries) of many formerly well-paying manufacturing jobs and the development of a two-tier wage system that offers lower wages and slower pay increases to new entrants in the labor market. In the United States, for example, by the late 1980s, one-third of white men ages 20–34 had incomes below the official poverty level, up from one-fourth in the mid-1960s. African American men's wages have decreased even more, with over half earning wages below poverty level in 1987 (Wilkie, 1991). With women providing between one-fourth and one-third of family income in most industrial societies, their contribution to the household's economy is considerable.

Women have also entered the labor market to enjoy the benefits of economic independence, such as more control over resources, more say in family decision making, and less vulnerability to economic misfortune after divorce (Newland, 1980). In many countries, a strong feminist movement has helped women realize the advantages of earning their own income.

Despite the increasing employment of wives and mothers, women's opportunities for highly paid work remain limited. Their wages in comparison to men's have not risen to any significant extent, although slight improvements are noticeable in some countries (Willborn, 1991). Women's low wage potential and segregation in the lower-status areas of the labor market keep them economically dependent on men, who remain, for the most part, their families' primary breadwinners. Being a good family breadwinner is the surest route for men to achieve recognition as good husbands, fathers, and citizens. Women are still evaluated according to their performance as housekeepers and mothers. (Television commercials provide a good example of this.) Yet this unpaid family work lacks social recognition as work. It is seen as something women do because they love their families or as something they want to do in their leisure time (Thompson & Walker, 1991). Women must arrange their participation in the paid labor market around their families' needs, whereas men are able to devote themselves to their jobs and careers without having to be concerned about their spouses' occupational involvement or child care (Gerson, 1985).

In summary, industrialization resulted in men being assigned the most visibly productive and highly valued responsibility in the family, namely, breadwinning, while women were assigned to housework and child care, redefined to encompass more activities with a different set of standards than previously existed. Women's job opportunities were limited because women were considered less suitable laborers than were men and were held responsible for home and children. This same division of labor exists to a greater or lesser extent in all contemporary industrial societies. However, important differences exist not only in the way breadwinning, housework, and child care are assigned and performed as responsibilities but also in terms of the directions societies are taking in this regard.

CROSS-NATIONAL VARIATIONS
IN THE HOUSEHOLD DIVISION OF LABOR

Industrial societies can be divided into different types, based on the extent to which the society promotes gender equality in the family. For the purposes of this chapter, three types of societies are distinguished: *traditional, transi-*

tional, and *egalitarian.* The specific criteria used to determine whether a society falls in one group or another are as follows:

1. *Shared breadwinning.* This concerns the extent to which women, including mothers of young children, are income providers for their families. To be income providers, women must be employed outside the home for pay, and society must support women's employment through legislation. For breadwinning to be shared by men and women, women's wage work must be defined as contributing money for the family's basic needs and women must be as obligated as men to be financial providers for their families (Haas, 1986).

2. *Shared family work.* This concerns the extent to which women and men share the work of caring for family members and their living quarters. The most common measure of sharing housework and child care is comparing how much time each spouse spends on them. Because spending time in household labor does not necessarily mean a person is involved in the planning and administration of it, it is also desirable to know to what extent men and women share equally in the overall responsibility for housework and child care.

3. *Blending of public and private spheres.* Blending of public and private spheres exists when working parents of both sexes prioritize family and work roles to an equal degree, and when both have easy and affordable access to and are expected to take advantage of programs designed to help them combine breadwinning, housework, and child care responsibilities (e.g., parental leave, child care, time off for sick children, part-time work, and flexible work scheduling). Blending is also evident when the standards of work and career advancement are no longer based on the assumption that a worker has no family responsibilities. There would also be signs that unpaid family work is as socially valued as paid employment. For example, wage replacement programs would exist for people who do unpaid family work (e.g., stay home to care for children), as well as assurances that such time will not hurt them later in terms of job security, advancement, seniority, and retirement benefits.

Using these criteria, societies are labeled "traditional" if available research evidence suggests that they meet none of the above criteria, "transitional" if they are beginning to meet one or more, and "egalitarian" if they meet all three. It is, in fact, difficult to classify societies according to the criteria because the data on societies are incomplete; often, little research has been done or made available to an international audience. At other times, the information provided on different societies is not comparable. For example, international statistics about women's labor force participation involve different definitions of "participation," age ranges, and base years. Survey data on the household division of labor for individual couples are even more difficult to compare cross-nationally because researchers employ different methods with various degrees of sophistication. To minimize potential bias in assigning countries to one group over another, I found it helpful to look closely at the government and workplace policies in existence as proxies for cultural definitions of men's and women's roles. I also examined the results of some other comparative analyses of gender roles in contemporary industrial societies to see whether they were in general agreement with my findings (e.g., Boh et al., 1989; Lewis, 1992; Stafford & Sundström, 1991; Statistiska Centralbyrån, 1992). Below are descriptions of some societies that fit each type.

Traditional Societies

Traditional industrial societies are characterized by a rather strict gender-based division of household labor, with the man being responsible for bread-winning and the woman (even if employed for pay) having primary responsibility for home and children. Work life and social policy are structured to perpetuate this division of domestic labor. The following societies appear to fit into this category: Japan, Ireland, Greece, Spain, Italy, Great Britain, the Netherlands, Belgium, Germany, and the United States. In this section, I discuss three of these societies: Japan, Great Britain, and the United States.

Japan

Historically, Japan was a strongly patriarchal society, where men exercised direct control over the lives of their wives and children and expected absolute obedience and respect from family members. After World War II, however, more democratic ideals emerged. Laws granted women more authority in marriage and over children (Ishii-Kuntz, 1993). More recently, Japanese women's opportunities for employment have become protected by law (Hendry, 1989).

Despite these trends, the division of labor in Japanese households generally remains quite traditional. As part of their education, Japanese girls take special courses to prepare them to become good wives and mothers, and they are not expected to go as far in school as are boys (Hendry, 1989). Japanese wives' household duties include housework, financial management, care of elderly relatives, and close attention to children, especially supervision of their schooling.

More than 60% of Japanese wives are in the labor force, and most women expect to be in the labor force sometime during their life (Hendry, 1989). However, they expect to curtail their employment while they have children. Japanese women are significantly less likely than U.S. women to think that women can handle both home and career and more likely to think that marriage problems would arise if the wife were employed (Engel, 1988).

When women are in the labor market, they tend to hold jobs that have less security and status than men's, especially if they work for large corporations (Hendry, 1989). Women's regular pay averages 58% of men's, which is lower than in most other industrial societies (Willborn, 1991). Employers do not usually grant women the extra "family allowances," which men get because they are considered breadwinners (Hayashi, 1991). There are some programs for working mothers, but the benefits tend to be more limited than those provided in other countries. For example, Japanese women have access to only 14 weeks of maternity leave paid at 60% of regular wages (Trzcinski, 1992). They must rely on relatives for child care, because of the lack of day-care facilities (Hendry, 1989). Women's tendency to quit work while children are young causes them to lose job opportunities and to receive lower wages when they return to a labor market that rewards continuous service (Ishii-Kuntz, 1993).

Men's jobs, on the other hand, typically require considerable overtime hours, and they have no regular access to parental benefits. Although some observers have concluded that men's devotion to work has contributed greatly to Japan's financial success, it has meant that fathers are absent from their children's lives, leaving domestic work and nurturance to wives. One national survey found that fathers spent 3 minutes a day on weekdays and 19 minutes per day on weekends on child-care activities. A cross-national study found that 37% of Japanese children never interacted with their fathers (even to eat meals together), compared to 15% of U.S. children and 20% of German children. Absence does not make fathers weak parents, however. Fathers remain psychologically present through the daily talk of Japanese mothers, who continually affirm to children that fathers are the authority figures and breadwinners and thus at the center of the family. Research shows that children approve of their fathers' heavy involvement in work outside the home and name their fathers as the real boss in the family. A six-nation study showed that Japanese children respected their mothers much less than do children in other societies, which illustrates Japanese society's devaluation of women's unpaid family role (Ishii-Kuntz, 1993).

Gender roles in Japan are by no means static. Japanese attitudes have become more egalitarian over time, as women have become more interested in having greater educational and occupational opportunities and more power in the larger society (Hendry, 1989). Recent legislation also promises to improve Japanese women's job opportunities. Protective laws barring women from certain jobs were dropped and sex-specific job advertising was made illegal. The same legislation, however, encourages companies to establish a two-track employment system, one for managers who can expect relocation, job rotation, and long hours and one for support workers. Such a system will likely institutionalize gender segregation, although it will also give Japanese women a greater chance to work for the larger corporations (Hill, 1991).

Until recently, the Japanese have exhibited little interest in changing the division of labor for unpaid work in the home, with Japanese women expressing much less interest in this than U.S. women (Suzuki, 1991). Findings from a 1988 national survey of married people suggest that things may be changing (Rindfuss, Liao, & Tsuya, 1992). Three-fourths of respondents agreed that "it is a good thing for men to work in the kitchen at home." Men's extreme absorption in paid work will be difficult to break because work organizations (as well as families) are structured on this model. Some small initiatives have begun, however. The Japanese government has recently expressed concern over the negative impact of father absence on children. Some male public employees in a Tokyo suburb were granted parental leave, and in other cities special programs about childrearing have been instituted for fathers (Ishii-Kuntz, 1993).

Great Britain

Britain has a long history of restricting the employment rights of wives and mothers. Historically, men were defined as family breadwinners, and women's employment was assumed to be detrimental to children. Not until the 1970s did British women gain some legal employment rights and access to benefits that would make it easier for them to be working mothers (e.g., maternity leave). This coincided with women entering the labor force in ever greater numbers. For example, in 1970 only 29% of British women (ages 15–64) were in paid employment, compared to 64% in 1990 (Statistiska Centralbyrån, 1992).

Most of the jobs women entered, however, were low status and low paid. A large number of wives (44%, compared to France's average of 22%) are also in part-time jobs. This part-time work tends to involve less than 20 hours a week and be associated with few fringe benefits (Lewis, 1992). Moreover, British mothers of young children are unlikely to be in the labor force and have the lowest labor force participation rate in Western Europe. In 1988, only 37% of British mothers with children under age 3 were in the labor force, compared to 86% in Sweden (Sorrentino, 1990).

There is a general lack of social policies designed to promote mothers' employment. Paid maternity leave lasts only 18 weeks, and not all women are eligible. Day care for children under age 3 is virtually nonexistent (Brannen, 1992; Lewis, 1992). Only a few companies provide any leave for dependent care (Wolcott, 1991).

Taking time out for childbearing and childrearing has more serious economic effects on women than in other countries. British women forgo 50%

of lifetime earnings when they have children, compared to French and Swedish women, who forgo 10% or less. Women's limited job opportunities and the lack of support services for working parents perpetuate their segregation into the low-paid sector of the labor market, which means that they remain dependent on men to be their families' main breadwinners (Lewis, 1992). No progress in British women's wage rates was made in the 1980s. Women's income in comparison to men's stayed around 68–69% throughout the decade (Statistiska Centralbyrån, 1992).

Brannen's (1992) study offers interesting findings on mothers who returned to full-time employment after childbirth, something only about 17% of British women do. The women tended to be professional women who earned high incomes. The money they brought in averaged about 40% of total household income and was used to pay for essentials. The vast majority of women said that men and women should share equally in family work, but almost none of them practiced this arrangement. The women still defined their husbands as the family breadwinners. Husbands earned more and expressed greater interest and commitment to paid employment. Wives were also more concerned about maintaining emotional closeness in the marriage than they were in demanding that their husbands do an equal share of housework and child care. In Britain, extreme emphasis is placed on the importance of full-time motherhood for children's healthy development, and the majority of British men and women disapprove of mothers of small children working outside the home (Alwin, Brown, & Scott, 1992). To compensate for not being there full time, these women spent as much time with children as possible, and women tended to remain primarily responsible for child care, possibly to relieve feelings of guilt.

The research on dual-career couples in Britain suggests that the traditional division of labor will be difficult to change. High unemployment and economic recession make it very difficult for women to advance in the labor market. Women's rights to maternity leave have already been reduced, making Britain the only society in which women are losing such privileges rather than gaining them (Brannen, 1992).

The United States

The last traditional society to be examined is the United States. Despite a strong feminist movement, the division of labor in the family in the United States can still be classified as traditional. Some of the same patterns already mentioned for Japan and Great Britain apply.

Women in the United States have entered the labor force in record numbers during the last three decades. Nevertheless, their employment opportunities remain inferior to men's. Women have much less access to prestigious, well-paid jobs, and those traditionally available to women are low paid in comparison to men's jobs requiring similar skill levels. Although women's average pay levels have gradually risen in recent years, they still receive only 70% of men's wages. The relatively disadvantaged status of women in the labor force reinforces the male-as-breadwinner ideal.

As in Britain and Japan, U.S. women remain much more responsible for housework and child care than do their husbands, and the unpaid family work they do is not highly valued by society. One study found that among full-time working couples, U.S. men's proportion of housework and child-care tasks was 20% (Wright, Shire, Hwang, Dolan, & Baxter, 1992). The amount of time men spend in domestic work does not vary by their wives' employment status. Their absolute amount of time spent in household work has not increased much, even in dual-earner families. Men's *relative* share of domestic work has risen, but only because working women spend less time doing domestic work (Shelton, 1990). When men are involved in unpaid family work, they tend to take on tasks with more discretion (e.g., household repairs), clear boundaries (e.g., mowing), more leisure (e.g, playing with children), and less time commitment (e.g., drying dishes) (Gunter & Gunter, 1990). A belief in the importance of mothering for children's development seems to be as entrenched in the United States as it is in the other two countries (Alwin et al., 1992), which helps to support and rationalize the unequal division of household labor. As in Britain, women tend not to express dissatisfaction with the unequal division of work in the home (Gunter & Gunter, 1990).

Another similiarity is that the U.S. government has made little effort to develop social policies to help working parents. When it comes to public subsidies for child care, maternity leave, and parental leave, the United States usually appears at the bottom of the list of industrialized countries (e.g., Trzcinski, 1992). The few leave policies that do exist are gender neutral, but in practice only women are encouraged to take advantage of them (especially since they are usually unpaid). The idea that work should be restructured to allow both men and women opportunities to develop relationships with children has not been seriously considered.

Although the United States is basically similar to Japan and Britain, it does appear to be somewhat less traditional on several counts. Moreover, it appears to be making progress toward moving out of the traditional category altogether and becoming a society under transition to a more egalitarian model of gender roles.

The first reason for this is that U.S. women, especially mothers, have been more involved in the labor force than in Japan and Great Britain. These women tend to work full time. Almost three-fourths of U.S. women ages 25–34 are in the labor force, compared to two-thirds of British women and half of Japanese women (Sorrentino, 1990). Women in the United States, through their full-time employment and more continuous attachment to the labor market, have the potential of defining themselves as co-providers in their families to an extent not possible in Japan and Great Britain. One study found that half of U.S. working couples say the responsibility for breadwinning is shared equally by husband and wife (Perry-Jenkins & Crouter, 1990).

Another respect in which the United States appears to be ahead of Japan and Great Britain is in men sharing responsibility for domestic work. One study found that U.S. women spent 2.3 times more hours in household work than did men, compared to British women spending 2.8 times (Haavio-Mannila, Liljeström, & Sokolowka, 1985). Americans also seem more interested in an egalitarian family life. A 1990 national poll found that 57% of adults preferred a marriage in which both spouses have jobs and share responsibility for children and home care; this number was up from 48% in 1977 (DeStefano & Colasanto, 1990). Substantial interest has been shown in changing the role of the father to be more nurturing and caring, and studies show that many fathers regret not having developed a closer relationship with their children (LaRossa, 1988).

The U.S. government seems to be changing its attitudes toward working parents, as witnessed by the recent passage of a child-care bill and national family leave legislation. U.S. companies seem increasingly aware that it is in their economic interest to help workers combine employment and family roles. Some 4,300 companies are known to provide some type of help with child care for their employees, ranging from information and referral services to on-site child care (Wolcott, 1991).

It seems likely that the United States will experience some redefinition of gender roles in the near future. Recent changes in the political climate in the United States favor women's concerns and support dual-earner life-styles. The number of women elected to government office rose dramatically in the last election (1992), and most of the new female officeholders seem inclined to push for social policies to encourage gender equality.

Transitional Societies

I turn now to a description of two transitional societies, Russia and France. Other societies that seem to fall in this category include all other former state socialist societies in the former Soviet Union and Eastern Europe, as well as China, Israel, Canada, Australia, and Norway. In transitional societies, substantial efforts have been made to implement a national policy to encourage women to assume an active breadwinning role. Considerable resources have also been devoted to services to help working mothers, such as maternity leave and day care. These societies, however, fall short of being considered egalitarian because they have not made much attempt to promote men's greater participation in unpaid family work and because the motivations behind programs that improve women's employment opportunities have usually had little to do with the promotion of gender equality.

Russia

The Past

Russia is unique in the length of its official commitment to the concept of women's equality, one of the goals of the Bolshevik Revolution in 1917. Soviet policy was based on the premise that gender equality depended on women taking their place besides men in the paid labor market. Accordingly, Russian women gained legal rights unheard of in the rest of Western Europe and the United States, including the right to work and to receive equal pay (Broschart, 1992). Policymakers promised to shift unpaid family work to the public sphere, through the establishment of child-care facilities, public laundries, and communal dining halls (Goldman, 1991). Interest in women's participation in the paid labor market was not just based on an ideological commitment to women's equality. Russia badly needed women as labor power because of a strong push for economic expansion and industrialization.

By 1940, millions of Russian women had joined the labor market, making up almost 40% of all industrial workers. World War II brought on an even greater demand for female labor power, as a way to compensate for heavy casualties among the men. At one point, there were only 59 men to every 100 Russian women in the 35–59 age group, and almost one-third of households were headed by women (Lapidus, 1988).

Yet the promised public services that would relieve women of unpaid family work (with the exception of some child care) never materialized on a wide scale (Goldman, 1991). Moreover, a decision was made to emphasize heavy industry and construction, rather than developing light industry and the service sector. This meant that the kind of consumer products that would make unpaid family work easier were not produced (Lapidus, 1988).

After first downplaying the importance of the family as an important institution in the new society, authorities concluded that strong family relationships were necessary for social stability, economic productivity, and population growth (Lapidus, 1988). New emphasis was placed on women's family roles to help bolster family stability. The women's section of the Communist Party was disbanded, and organizations to promote women's interests were outlawed, making it difficult for women to influence social policy development (Goldman, 1991).

The 1960s were characterized by continued labor shortages. To encourage even more women to enter employment, more day-care places were created and women's wages and pension benefits were improved. At the same time, general wages were too low for most families to live on one income, forcing many women into the labor market (Lapidus, 1988). Consumer shortages continued to be common, and women spent long hours waiting in lines to purchase food and other necessities. At home, they had to take care of domestic work without the help of refrigerators, washing machines, and hot water. Because of the poor quality of day-care facilities (with overcrowding, poor sanitation, and inferior food), children often became sick and women were forced to miss work (Goldman, 1991). To reduce their heavy domestic burdens, women began to have fewer children. By the mid-1970s, the birth rate in the two largest cities, Moscow and Leningrad, stood at 1.69 and 1.55 children per woman (Lapidus, 1988). Concerned about declining family sizes and labor shortages, policymakers tried to encourage larger families in the 1970s by lengthening paid pregnancy and maternity leaves, but without success.

The Present

Despite the Soviet emphasis on women's employment rights, Russian women have always occupied a distinctly inferior position to men in the labor market. In some respects, gender segregation in the labor market seems to be less than in other industrialized countries: One-fourth of managers are women, women are a majority of skilled technicians and physicians, and women can be found in great numbers in nontraditional blue-collar fields such as construction and mining, compared to the West (Broschart, 1992). On the other hand, Russian women dominate the same fields as women do in other industrial countries (e.g., clerical work, health care, and teaching). Many typically female jobs in Russia are much worse in quality than in other countries because most of the unskilled physical jobs in urban areas and manual agricultural jobs have been assigned to women (Broschart, 1992; Goldman, 1991).

Gender segregation in the labor market in Russia, as in other industrial countries, is associated with women earning less wages. In general, Russian women make 60–70% of what men do because they dominate the low-paying sectors of the economy. Blue-collar workers have historically earned more than white-collar workers, which keeps women who are employed in technical and professional jobs from making much headway (Lapidus, 1988). But sex segregation in the labor market is not the only reason why women earn less. Women's responsibility for housework and child care forces them to pick more convenient and less demanding jobs and leaves them less time for additional training and education (Broschart, 1992). One study showed that at age 20, Russian women earned 85% of what men earn, but by age 30 after having children they earned only 70% (Goldman, 1991).

By 1985, women made up 51% of the labor force. Almost all (90%) were employed full time for pay. Nearly all (97%) Russian women in the prime childrearing years, ages 25–44, were in the labor force, compared to 66% of U.S. women and 59% of British women (Broschart, 1992). The original Bolshevik goal of women's full entrance into the labor market was reached.

But women's dual responsibilities for employment and family work caused problems. Working women had poorer health, higher absenteeism, and lower productivity than did men. The birthrate remained very low and the divorce rate very high. It became clear from social science research that women were working much harder than men. Studies found that women did 18 to 21 more hours of household work per week than men in dual-earner households, and that men had 50% more leisure time (Goldman, 1991; Lapidus, 1988).

When *glasnost* and *perestroika* took hold, debate was started about appropriate remedies for the "woman problem." The following solutions were considered: Move women into less difficult jobs to protect their health, increase the supply of consumer goods and services (refrigerators, mass transit, public laundries), and increase the length of maternity leave. Making men more responsible for housework and child care and granting women greater access to more highly paid jobs were not considered (Lapidus, 1988).

The Future

The debate continues now, as the economy and political system are in the process of being restructured toward a free-market, democratic system. Freed from traditional Communist constraints against free speech, women are able for the first time to participate in an open debate on the issues of concern to them (Broschart, 1992). After years of difficult physical labor, long lines, no washing machines, and sending their children to bad day-care centers, many women are demanding an easier life, including much longer maternity leaves and more part-time jobs. They want more time for themselves and better care for their children (Goldman, 1991). A desire for more involvement of men in family work is not often mentioned by Russian women. Most women assume that there are important personality and biological differences between the sexes that lead to women being more likely to prioritize family over work roles. Yet women do not want to leave the labor market entirely. Most want to be employed for economic independence and personal satisfaction. Some 80% say they would stay in the labor force even if their husbands earned much more (Broschart, 1992).

Russian women are currently in a weak position to press for employment rights, as the economy is in a shambles. Indeed, as work organizations close down or become privatized and as the government seeks to save money on social programs, women are more likely than men to become unemployed (Moghadam, 1992). Women in some other formerly Communist societies are losing access to maternity leaves and day care. Gender equality is not the most pressing issue for the new Russian government, particularly because the issue of women's equality tends to be associated with now outmoded Communist ideology and rhetoric.

The policies and programs now being suggested by many Russian women and policymakers, along with rising female unemployment, seem likely to reintroduce the traditional doctrine of separate spheres into Russia. If women have difficulty keeping jobs, it will be easy to define Russian men as family breadwinners once again. Reducing women's paid work hours does not promise to increase equality between the sexes. Previous shifts from a 6-hour day to a 5-hour day in Russia and an experiment with reducing the work hours of women factory workers both found that the disparity between women's and men's work in the home grew. By being more available, women took on more domestic tasks, and men gained more leisure time (Lapidus, 1988). Protecting women's health by restricting their entrance into certain jobs will likely lead to women occupying an even smaller part of the labor market. Increasing the length of maternity leave will give employers an excuse not to hire women in certain jobs, and a longer period out of the labor market can hurt women's productivity. Only time will tell if Russian women's increased freedom to organize and speak out about their situation will reinforce or undermine traditional gender roles in the family.

France

Until the 1960s, French tradition demanded that the man be the family breadwinner and the woman be responsible for home and child care. Until 1964, the law made the husband the financial and moral head of the family and put him formally in charge of all major decisions about children (Laubier, 1990). In spite of the law, French women have been involved in the labor force in large numbers for a long time. As early as 1866, 30% of all French women were employed for pay, many in family-owned businesses and in agricultural labor. No real attempts were made to push women out of the labor market. French men did not feel that their masculinity was threatened by having a working wife, in contrast to the way British men have felt (Lewis, 1992).

French women entered the labor force in increasing numbers beginning in the 1960s, as elsewhere in the industrial world. French women are likely to have a continuous attachment to the work force, independent of whether or not they have children. Ten times as many French women as British women work continuously through the childbearing and childrearing years (Crompton, Hantrais, & Walters, 1990). In recent studies, 60% of French women with children under age 2 were employed, compared to 37% in Great Britain (Sorrentino, 1990). French women are also more likely to work full-time than are women in Great Britain (Lewis, 1992).

Programs to help women balance employment and motherhood were established early in France, starting with paid maternity leave in 1913. In the 1930s, women could receive a substantial allowance to stay home and care for children as a substitute for foregone earnings. At the same time, Britain denied mothers access to unemployment benefits (Lewis, 1992).

In the 1970s, strong laws were established to discourage sex discrimination and sex segregation of workplaces. French women enjoy relatively high wages compared to women in Britain or the United States, earning 81% of male wages in 1990 (Statistiska Centralbyrån, 1992). Maternity leaves were established, granting 90% of French women 16 weeks off with 84% pay for the first child and longer periods for later children. Parents receive tax credits for child-care expenses. The supply and quality of child-care facilities were improved to a level now considered to be among the best in Europe (Lewis, 1992; Stafford & Sundström, 1991).

Yet these policies were not based on the premise that women should be family breadwinners, in contrast to Russia and, as we shall see, Sweden. Women have been given the choice whether to work and can count on support for whatever choice they make. In reality, the way benefits and taxes are formulated, one-earner families are somewhat better off, and highly paid professional women are encouraged to work part time, despite the rhetoric about free choice (Lewis, 1992). Policies also have developed much more out of concern for children's welfare than out of interest in creating equality between men and women. Programs such as maternity leave and day care are justified in terms of how they benefit children and provide encouragement to French couples to have children (Lewis, 1992).

Some interest has been shown in France in men participating more in child care. Research shows that French fathers are increasing their participation in the daily care of babies and young children and that French men's attitudes toward sharing child care are becoming more liberal over time (Laubier, 1990). French fathers are allowed to take unpaid time off from work to care for children (Stafford & Sundström, 1991).

No progress seems evident, however, when it comes to French men sharing housework. One study found that married men do less housework after they get married than they do when they are single. When they participate in domestic work, French men prefer cooking rather than cleaning or shopping (Laubier, 1990). One researcher who interviewed dual-career couples found that French men did less housework than British men (Hantrais, 1990). This same study found that French professional women want support from the government and the opportunity to hire paid help so that they can better manage the double role of mother and professional; they are not especially interested in equally sharing household responsibilities with their spouse. Beliefs about the importance of mothers for children remain strong (Lewis, 1992).

The future of French gender roles is uncertain. There is a tendency for the French government to reduce benefits to working parents by denying these benefits to the more highly paid workers as a way to improve the conditions of low-income families and to reduce social expenditures (Lewis, 1992). This might discourage some women from being employed, especially during the childrearing years. Changes in the structure of the labor market have reduced the supply of full-time jobs in women's traditional areas, although part-time working women in France still receive excellent benefits. There is also no indication that the government or the general public is pushing for an ideological shift, to hold men and women equally accountable for breadwinning, child care, and housework.

Egalitarian Societies

Egalitarian societies, the last category to be considered, manifest equal sharing of breadwinning, housework, and child care by men and women. In these societies, the social importance of unpaid family work is recognized and and the division between private and public spheres of social life is eliminated. There are no societies that fully fit in this category, but one country, Sweden, has made very serious efforts toward these goals. Denmark and Finland could also be considered in this category, but both lag considerably behind Sweden.

Sweden's Gender Policy

Gender equality has been a goal of social policy in Sweden since the late 1960s. Gender equality is defined as women and men having "the same rights, obligations, and possibilities to have a job which gives them economic independence, to care for children and home, and to participate in political, union, and other activities in society" (Statistiska Centralbyrån, 1992, p. 5). This policy was outlined first in a publication prepared for the United Nations in 1968. It has continuously been included in the official programs of all trade unions, political parties, and government agencies.

The government's most recent plan for equality (1988–1993) called for workplaces to develop strategies to eliminate job segregation and pay differences, reorganize work life so that both sexes can combine parenthood and employment, and give women more access to power and responsibility in work life. A 1992 employment law made employers responsible for helping both sexes to combine parenthood and employment. A 1992 campaign by the department of social welfare encouraged more fathers to stay home to care for small babies. (The cabinet minister in charge of the department has himself stayed home 1 month on parental leave.)

These efforts are only the latest in a long series of programs and laws that have been developed in Sweden to help bring about gender equality (see Haas, 1992). A majority of these programs and laws aimed to improve women's employment opportunities so that they would become family breadwinners on an equal level with men. Compared to women in other societies, Swedish women have had unusual access to educational opportunities and job training. Women entered the labor market because of plentiful job opportunities (especially in the public and service sectors), high wages (the result of union efforts to lessen class differences by raising the wages of the lowest-paid workers), and a tax system that taxes their incomes separately from their spouses.

The Swedish government has also been active in providing a high level of support services and programs for working parents, which has helped women maintain a continuous attachment to the labor force. These include heavily subsidized public child care of high quality, 1 year of parental leave at 90% pay, 60 days off with 80% pay to care for sick children or to visit children at day care or school, and the right to reduce the workday to 6 hours or the workweek to 4 days in order to care for children.

Many programs encourage men to be more active in family life. Both sexes have to take courses in child care in school. Men's participation in prenatal classes, parent education programs, and delivery is almost mandatory. Fathers get 10 days off with 90% pay at childbirth to take charge of the household while mothers recuperate from childbirth and to get to know their babies. Men are given the same access as mothers to parental leave after childbirth, days off with pay to care for sick children, and reduced work hours.

Reasons for Sweden's Policy

Why has Sweden developed such a radical approach to gender relations in comparison to other countries? Interest in equality is closely related to and influenced by deep-rooted social values and the nature of political culture in Sweden.

One important Swedish value that relates to interest in gender equality is productivity. A large part of policymakers' interest in women's labor force participation in Sweden is due to their desire to boost society's productivity and to meet Sweden's need for labor power, which was particularly pressing in the 1970s and 1980s. This labor shortage led to a recognition of the importance of women's labor power and the development of specific programs designed to enhance women's lifetime attachment. However, there is an ideological component as well. Working at a job is seen as good and important for an individual to do, apart from its economic benefits (Sandqvist, 1992). Full employment is seen as a measure of the society's success, and this means women need to be in the labor force (Jonung & Persson, 1990).

Another important social value is children's welfare, a concern that has been strong since the worldwide economic depression of the 1930s, when the Swedish birthrate dropped to below replacement levels. Swedish children are seen as benefiting from having two parents who enjoy economic independence and the opportunity to seek personal fulfillment outside the home and from the economic security of being in a two-earner household. Having close relations with fathers who are involved in their daily care is also considered necessary for children's healthy development. Day care is seen as a positive way for children to learn intellectual, social, and emotional skills. It is considered appropriate that workplaces have to adjust to the needs of children by allowing parents time off to care for them. This is an interesting contrast to the situation in traditional societies such as Great Britain or the United States, where children's welfare is used as a rationale for excluding women from employment and encouraging their full-time absorption in child care. Swedish policies have been notably successful in improving the climate for having children. After many decades of a birthrate below replacement level, Sweden's birthrate is now one of the highest in Western Europe, and researchers have found that social policy has contributed to the upswing (Stafford & Sundström, 1991).

A third Swedish value that explains why gender equality has become a popular goal is pragmatism, the valuing of cooperation and broad-based political solutions over confrontation and conflict. Gender equality fits well with the Swedish ideals of fairness and general equality (Sandqvist, 1992). Gender equality is defined in a nonthreatening way; power differences and conflict between men and women are not highlighted and both sexes are regarded as benefiting from its realization. The legislation that supports the goal is phrased in a gender-neutral fashion, offering individuals opportunities to change gender roles without demanding or mandating such change (Eduards, 1991). The ideal of cooperation also is evident in the way Swedish women have chosen to press for change. Activists tend to involve themselves in established political institutions (i.e., the political parties) rather than developing new organizations. For women, this has led to their being unusually successful in achieving political office. Currently, one-third of the members of the Parliament are women, and the same proportion is found in the Cabinet. No other society has such a high representation of women at the top level of government.

Sweden's Success

How successful has Sweden been in eliminating the traditional division of labor for breadwinning, housework, and child care? The general answer is "somewhat successful." When it comes to breadwinning, Swedish women are almost as likely to be in the labor force as men, having the highest labor force participation rate of women of all industrial societies except for former state socialist societies. For example, in 1988, 91% of women ages 25 to 54 were in the labor force, compared to 95% of Swedish men. Having young children has little effect on women's paid employment, with 86% of mothers of preschool-age children being employed (Persson, 1990). One study of new parents found that the vast majority believed that the breadwinning responsibility should be shared equally by mothers and fathers (Haas, 1993). Swedish women earn about one-third of family income, which appears to be higher than women earn in most other societies.

Swedish women do not earn more money in comparison to men because large numbers work part time (around 43%). Many jobs in the public and service sectors were established as part-time jobs to attract women to the labor force, and women have taken more advantage of legislation that allows parents to work part time until their children reach school age. Unlike in Britain, where women also tend to work part time, Swedish women tend to work longer hours (30), receive prorated benefits, and have more job security. There is a slight tendency for fathers of young children to also reduce their work hours in Sweden, while in the rest of the world fathers are notable for increasing their work hours (Sandqvist, 1992).

Women's contribution to family income is also reduced because of wage differences between the sexes. Yet here again, Sweden ranks at the top of all industrial societies in terms of how successful it has been in reducing the gender pay gap. In 1990, Swedish women's hourly wages averaged 89% of men's. In 1960, the figure was 72% (Jonung & Persson, 1990).

Some of the pay gap is due to differences in the types of jobs men and women hold. Sweden has one of the most sex-segregated labor markets in the industrial world. Few occupations have a ratio of 40 men to 60 women, and half of all Swedish workers are at workplaces that are occupied by only one sex. Women hold few of the top positions in any field. The Swedish government has made several attempts to break down gender segregation through laws, special demonstration projects, subsidies to employers that hire equal numbers, and changes in education to encourage girls to consider nontraditional jobs. In some professional areas (e.g., law and medicine), these efforts have been successful, but in technical fields and management less success has been realized. Some researchers have speculated that Swedish women are less motivated to seek nontraditional jobs because there are few wage differences between traditionally female and male jobs. Swedish women also seem to reject the notion that traditionally male jobs are more worthwhile to have (Sandqvist, 1992).

Studies have been conducted on the participation of Swedish men in housework and child care. As early as 1981, the vast majority of Swedish men agreed that men's roles should be changed to make them equally responsible for home and children. In spite of the widespread acceptance of egalitarian ideology, Swedish men do not do 50% of the work. One national time-use study found that men's household work hours were 36% of all the hours the couple spent (Flood & Klevmarken, 1990). Child care is more shared, and for older children (ages 8–12) each parent contributes half of the couple's hours spent in child care (Jonung & Persson, 1990).

Nevertheless, one study of new parents found that only one-fourth of couples share equal responsibility for the youngest children (under 2). Fathers in these families tend to participate more in emotional care-giving tasks (e.g., playing) than they do in physical caretaking (e.g., feeding). Noninteractive domestic work associated with child care (e.g., laundry) is shared least of all (Haas, 1993). Research shows that Swedish men have been doing more housework and child care over time (since 1957, when the first measurements were taken), both relative to women and in an absolute sense. Their levels of participation appear higher than those for men in other societies. When men's and women's labor market and household work hours are totaled, Swedish men and women work the same number of hours, whereas in other societies men have noticeably more leisure. Swedish men are not equal partners in the home, but they come closer than do men in other industrial societies.

Swedish fathers take advantage of programs to assist working parents with child care, but not to the same degree as do mothers. In 1991, nearly half of all Swedish men took parental leave after childbirth to care for their child alone while the child's mother returned to work. (Nearly all take the 10 days off immediately after childbirth.) Only a few other countries (generally in Scandinavia) grant paid parental leave to fathers, but none of them comes close to having as many fathers take leave. Still, Swedish fathers take a small proportion of the parental leave available, with those who take leave using only about 1½ months of the year-long period available to a couple. Fathers also take about one-third of the days to care for sick children (Haas, 1993).

Swedish social policies help to break down the distinction between public and private spheres. Employers do not have complete control over the work lives of their employees because legislation grants workers rights to stay home with children at frequent intervals. Many leave benefits are directly tied to employment because compensation levels are determined by pay levels. Taxes on employers' payrolls help to pay for these programs. These practices give the impression that unpaid family work, particularly child care, is a valued social activity for which one should be fairly compensated. The time parents spend at home with children is also credited to seniority and retirement benefits (Jonung & Persson, 1990).

Sweden's Future

Several current developments in Sweden make continued progress toward gender equality questionable. The election of a conservative government in 1991 and a severe economic recession in 1992 led to significant changes in social policy. A rising level of unemployment has hit hardest those industries in which men dominate (e.g., the building and auto industries), but public-sector jobs, where women dominate, are also being eliminated. To balance the budget and move toward a more conservative social agenda, the new government has reduced or eliminated many social services, and individuals are being asked to make more out-of-pocket payments for services (e.g., home help for the elderly and day care). Although it is possible that rising unemployment and an increase in the amount of unpaid family work might induce men to become more involved in domestic labor, it would be easy to fall back to tradition and have women resume greater responsibility for these activities.

One positive sign should be mentioned. In response to the conservative political climate, Swedish feminists have lately become much more active in pressing for the complete elimination of gender inequality. Some new feminist organizations have arisen, including a women's political party, a group of women politicians organizing across party lines, and a group of trade union women organizing across union boundaries. Women's studies scholars provide a theoretical basis for this movement. They object to the valuing of productivity over reproduction and the public sphere over the private, and they point out how men's better position in production and the public sphere helps to strengthen their social power. They would like to see work life restructured to maximize family well-being and gender equality, by instituting a 6-hour workday for all workers, for example. They believe that change can only come when women get into positions of power and challenge men's norms (Eduards, 1991; Hirdman, 1990). This new movement may or may not be successful in pushing Sweden toward becoming a more egalitarian society. It does, however, suggest that the most important barriers to gender equality are being discussed and challenged.

WHY SOME SOCIETIES ARE
MORE EGALITARIAN THAN OTHERS

The descriptions of the six societies above show that each society approaches the issue of the household division of labor somewhat differently, depending on social values, economic circumstances, and political priorities. Although each society is unique in the way it comes to define men's and women's roles, the information provided can be used to develop hypotheses concerning why some societies are more egalitarian than others.

We have seen that all the industrial societies featured have experienced and been affected by the entry of women into the labor force during the past few decades. Some societies, however, seem to notice and appreciate this development more than do others. Information on the nontraditional societies suggests that women's labor force participation will lead to a redefinition of who is responsible for breadwinning, as well as an interest in support programs for working parents and men sharing domestic work, when women's work involvement is defined as being essential for the society's economic growth and/or individual families' economic survival.

The birthrate drops in all industrial societies with the advent of birth control and a lessened need for family laborers. Some industrial societies, however, seem to become more concerned about this development than others, usually in connection with productivity issues, and seek to develop social policies that would encourage people to have more children. Societies that both recognize the importance of women's labor power and are concerned about the birthrate are more likely to develop policies that support women in their roles as workers and parents. Such policies enable women to participate in breadwinning throughout their childbearing and childrearing years. When women maintain a continued presence in the work force, their earning potential increases and it becomes less obvious that they should always be the ones to shoulder the burden of domestic chores. Men then become more likely to share family responsibilities, starting with child care.

Since industrialization, a cult of motherhood has existed that portrays children as needing their mother's full-time attention and considers mothers as being fulfilled only through parenting activities. Although all industrial societies subscribe to this ideology to some degree, we have seen that societies that are less permeated by the cult of motherhood are more likely to develop in an egalitarian direction.

Industrialization also brought increased concern for the welfare of children, who were not as highly regarded in the past due to high childhood mortality rates, little understanding of children's emotional and cognitive development, and preoccupation with economic survival. Societies that show the greatest amount of concern for children tend to support mothers' working by providing services such as parental leave and day care. These same societies also show more interest in fathers developing close relations with children.

Another hypothesis concerns women's power. Industrialization helped to consolidate men's power over women by giving them greater access to the more valued public sphere and opportunities to make money. Although all industrial societies have extended more political rights to women over the years (starting with the vote), in most cases women still have little access to formal power in government or at the workplace. When women have access to power positions, issues of gender equality are more likely to be raised and appropriate social policies developed.

Finally, it is clear from the information provided here that societies differ in the extent to which government policy is regarded as an appropriate instrument for bringing about social change. In some societies, the government has tried to stay out of the business of encouraging changes in gender roles, partly because government is not looked upon favorably by either feminists or conservatives as trustworthy or wise. Societies that accept the state as fundamentally benevolent seem better able to establish new structures and expectations for family roles.

FUTURE TRENDS

Both as a fact and as an ideal, the division of labor that assigned wage labor to men and unpaid family work to women is breaking down in industrial societies. Women are in the labor force to stay, and they increasingly maintain an attachment to work even during their childbearing and childrearing years. Yet women are not yet able to share equally in the responsibility for providing family income because of the persistence of traditional attitudes, labor market discrimination, the structure of male-dominated work organizations, and their husbands' lack of interest and participation in domestic work. We have on our hands what sociologist Arlie Hochschild (1989) calls a stalled revolution. Some governments and workplaces reinforce this stalled revolution by developing policies that make it easier for women to balance employment with primary responsibility for housework and child care. Not much progress has been made in recognizing that men's employment should also be responsive to family life. Where such recognition has occurred, as in Sweden, men's greater participation in family life tends merely to be encouraged, not mandated or expected.

The poor economic conditions that exist currently in industrial societies seem likely to impede further progress toward equality, as women's jobs and support services for working parents are being cut back. When economic conditions improve, we can expect progress toward egalitarianism to resume. Moreover, women are becoming more active in demanding that their concerns be addressed in policymaking. Many industrial societies described here might become more likely to respond to women's concerns because they are in a state of political, economic, and social transition. The breakdown of tradition might pave the way for the development of societies that value caring and productivity to equal degrees.

REFERENCES

Alwin, D., Brown, M., & Scott, J. (1992). The separation of work and family: Attitudes toward women's labour force participation in Germany, Great Britain and the United States. *European Sociological Review, 8*, 13–36.

Aronoff, J., & Crano,W. D. (1975). A re-examination of the cross-cultural principle of task segregation and sex-role differentiation in the family. *American Sociological Review, 40*, 12–20.

Boh, K., Bak, M., Clason, C., Pankratova, M., Qvortrup, J., Sgritta, G., & Waerness, K. (1989). *Changing patterns of European family life: A comparative analysis of 14 European countries.* London: Routledge.

Bose, C. (1987). Dual spheres. In B. Hess & M. Ferree (Eds.), *Analyzing gender* (pp. 267–285). Newbury Park, CA: Sage.

Brannen, J. (1992). Money, marriage and motherhood: Dual earner households after maternity leave. In S. Arber & N. Gilbert (Eds.), *Women and working lives* (pp. 54–70). London: Macmillan.

Broschart, K. (1992). Women under glasnost: An analysis of "women's place" in contemporary Soviet society. In S. Arber & N. Gilbert (Eds.), *Women and working lives* (pp. 118–127). London: Macmillan.

Brown, J. (1970). A note on the division of labor by sex. *American Anthropologist, 72*, 1073–1078.

Crano, W. D., & Aronoff, J. (1978). A cross-cultural study of expressive and instrumental role complementarity in the family. *American Sociological Review, 43*, 463–471.

Crompton, R., Hantrais, L., & Walters, P. (1990). Gender relations and employment. *British Journal of Sociology, 41*(3), 329–349.

DeStefano, L., & Colsanto, D. (1990, February). Unlike 1975, today most Americans think men have it better. *The Gallup Poll Monthly*, pp. 25–36.

Eduards, M. (1991). The Swedish gender model: Productivity, pragmatism and paternalism. *West European Politics, 14*, 166–181.

Engel, J. (1988). Japanese and American housewives' attitudes toward the employment of women. In E. Goldsmith (Ed.), *Work and family: Theory, research and applications* (pp. 363–372). Corte Madera, CA: Select Press.

Ferree, M. (1991). Feminism and family research. In A. Booth (Ed.), *Contemporary families* (pp. 103–121). Minneapolis: National Council on Family Relations.

Flood, L., & Klevmarken, A. (1990). Tidsanvändningen i Sverige 1984 [Time use in Sweden in 1984]. In C. Jonung & I. Persson (Eds.), *Kvinnors roll i ekonomin* [*Women's role in the economy*] (pp. 87–152). Stockholm: Finansdepartementet.

Gerson, K. (1985). *Hard choices: How women decide about work, career, and motherhood.* Berkeley: University of California Press.

Goldman, W. (1991). A "non-antagonistic" contradiction? The wages and unwaged labor of Soviet women. *Gender and History, 3*, 337–344.

Gunter, N., & Gunter, B. (1990). Domestic division of labor among working couples. *Psychology of Women Quarterly, 14*, 355–370.

Haas, L. (1986). Wives' orientations toward breadwinning in Sweden and the United States. *Journal of Family Issues, 7*, 358–381.

Haas, L. (1992). *Equal parenthood and social policy: A study of parental leave in Sweden.* Albany: State University of New York Press.

Haas, L. (1993). Nurturing fathers and working mothers: Changing gender roles in Sweden. In J. Hood (Ed.), *Men, work and family* (pp. 238–261). Newbury Park, CA: Sage.

Haavio-Mannila, E., Liljeström, R., & Sokolowka, M. (1985). The state, the family, and the position of women in the Nordic countries and Poland. In R. Alapuro, M. Alestalo, E. Haavio-Mannila, & R. Väyrynen (Eds.), *Small states in comparative perspective* (pp. 69–90). Oslo: Norwegian University Press.

Hantrais, L. (1990). *Managing professional and family life: A comparative study of British and French women.* Aldershot, England: Dartmouth.

Hayashi, H. (1991). Legal issues in Japan on the wages of womenorkers. *International Review of Comparative Public Policy, 3,* 243–260.

Hendry, J. (1989). *Understanding Japanese society.* London: Routledge.

Hill, M. A. (1991). Women's relative wages in postwar Japan. *International Review of Comparative Public Policy, 3,* 243–260.

Hirdman, Y. (1990). Genussystemet [The gender system]. In Maktutredningen [National Commission on Power] (Ed.), *Demokrati och makt i Sverige [Democracy and power in Sweden]* (pp. 73–166). Stockholm: Statens Offentliga Utredningar.

Hochschild, A. (1989). *The second shift.* New York: Viking.

Howe, W. J., & Parks, W. (1989). Labor market completes sixth year of expansion in 1988. *Monthly Labor Review, 110,* 3–12.

Ishii-Kuntz, M. (1993). The Japanese father: Work demands and family roles. In J. Hood (Ed.), *Men, work and family* (pp. 45–67). Newbury Park, CA: Sage.

Jackson, S. (1992). Towards a historical sociology of housework. *Women's Studies International Forum, 15,* 153–172.

Jonung, C., & Persson, I. (1990). Hushållsproduktion, marknadsproduktion och jämställdhet [Household production, market production and equality]. In C. Jonung & I. Persson (Eds.), *Kvinnors roll i ekonomin [Women's role in the economy]*. Stockholm: Finansdepartementet.

Lapidus, G. (1988). The interaction of women's work and family roles in the U.S.S.R. *Women and work, 2,* 87–121.

LaRossa, R. (1988). Fatherhood and social change. *Family Relations, 37,* 451–457.

Laubier, C. (1990). *The condition of women in France: 1945 to the present.* London: Routledge.

Lewis, J. (1992). Gender and the development of welfare regimes. *Journal of European Social Policy, 2,* 139–173.

Moghadam, V. (1992). Gender and restructuring: A global perspective. In V. Moghadam (Ed.), *Privatization and democratization in central and eastern Europe and the Soviet Union: The gender dimension* (pp. 9–23). Helsinki: World Institute for Development Economics Research of the United Nations University.

Newland, K. (1980). *Women, men and the division of labor* (Worldwatch Paper No. 37). Washington, DC: Worldwatch Institute.

Oakley, A. (1974). *Woman's work.* New York: Vintage.

Perry-Jenkins, M., & Crouter, A. (1990). Men's provider role attitudes. *Journal of Family Issues, 11,* 136–156.

Persson, I. (1990). The third dimension: Equal status between Swedish women and men. In I. Persson (Ed.), *Generating equality in the welfare state: The Swedish experience* (pp. 223–244). Oslo: Norwegian University Press.

Rindfuss, R. R., Liao, T., & Tsuya, N. (1992). Contact with parents in Japan: Effects of opinions toward gender and intergenerational roles. *Journal of Marriage and the Family, 54*, 812–822.

Rotundo, E. A. (1985). American fatherhood: A historical perspective. *American Behavioral Scientist, 29*, 7–25.

Sandqvist, K. (1992). Sweden's sex-role scheme and commitment to gender equality. In S. Lewis, D. Izraeli, & H. Hootman (Eds.), *Dual-earner families* (pp. 80–98). London: Sage.

Shelton, B. (1990). The distribution of household tasks: Does wife's employment status make a difference? *Journal of Family Issues, 11*, 115–135.

Sorrentino, C. (1990). The changing family in international perspective. *Monthly Labor Review, 113*(3), 41–58.

Stafford, F., & Sundström, M. (1991). *Labor force participation, fertility and public policy: Sweden compared to 20 other OECD countries.* Unpublished manuscript, Center for Research on Working Life, Stockholm.

Statistiska Centralbyrån. (1992). *Om kvinnor och män i Sverige och EG [Women and men in Sweden and the European Community].* Stockholm: Central Bureau of Statistics.

Stephens, W. (1963). *The family in cross-cultural perspective.* New York: Holt, Rinehart & Winston.

Suzuki, A. (1991). Egalitarian sex role attitudes: Scale development and comparison of American and Japanese women. *Sex Roles, 24*, 245–259.

Thompson, L., & Walker, A. (1991). Gender in families. In A. Booth (Ed.), *Contemporary families* (pp. 76–102). Minneapolis: National Council on Family Relations.

Trzcinski, E. (1992). *Maternity and parental leave: A historical and cross-national comparison of arguments concerning the role of government policy towards work, caring for children, and families.* Unpublished manuscript, Department of Consumer Economics, Cornell University.

Wilkie, J. R. (1991). The decline in men's labor force participation and income and the changing structure of family economic support. *Journal of Marriage and the Family, 53*, 111–122.

Willborn, S. (1991). Economic and legal perspectives on women's wages in six countries: An overview. *International Review of Comparative Public Policy, 3*, 1–17.

Wolcott, I. (1991). *Work and family: Employers' views.* Melbourne: Australian Institute of Family Studies.

Wright, E., Shire, K., Hwang, S., Dolan, M., & Baxter, J. (1992). The non-effects of class on the gender division of labor in the home: A comparative study of Sweden and the United States. *Gender and Society, 6*, 252–282.

CHAPTER THIRTEEN

Gender Relations
and Marital Power

JACK O. BALSWICK
JUDITH K. BALSWICK

Power, or the ability to influence another person, is a significant dimension in all human relationships, including marriage. The marital relationship is profoundly affected by power and how it is defined in a particular society. Yet we often overlook the power dimension in marriage because it tends to be exerted through authority and persuasion rather than through rules and force. Also, in Western societies marriage is romanticized, which may lead us to reject the notion that one partner would seek to control or influence the other.

Marital power is the relative ability of either spouse to influence the other. Technically speaking, power is the *capacity to influence* rather than the actual exercise of that capacity. A marital partner may have a powerful influence, for example, but choose not to exercise that power. Spouses who are personally powerful do not need to take dramatic action to demonstrate their power. A wife's simple requests or a husband's subtle glance will evoke a respectful response.

In the last two decades, five major reviews of the literature on family power have been written by family sociologists (Safilios-Rothschild, 1970; Cromwell & Olson, 1975; Scanzoni, 1979; McDonald, 1980; Szinovacz, 1987). The persistent scholarly interest in marital power indicates its importance to family studies. Furthermore, changes in gender roles worldwide have brought increased attention to the fact that misuse of power is a primary source of inequality in conjugal relationships.

In this chapter, we set out to acquaint the student with the study of marital power. Because power in marriage can be conceptualized in different ways, our first task is to define contrasting types of marital power. Next we describe marital power in cultural and historical context, looking at how power has traditionally been viewed in family studies. Then we offer a feminist critique of models of marital power and use the example of violence against women to demonstrate the importance of new perspectives. In the final sections, we present the empowerment model as a radical alternative to understanding marital power.

DEFINING TYPES OF MARITAL POWER

When comparing marital power from one culture to the next, we must be careful to understand marital power from the cultural context in which it is embedded. Specifically, attention needs to be given to the way marital power is *legitimized, ascribed,* and *implemented* within a particular culture. Failure to be sensitive to the cultural context of marital power puts us at risk of misunderstanding marital power from an ethnocentric view. People from Western cultures, for example, may assume that wives in traditionally patriarchal societies are totally powerless. In fact, wives in these cultures may enjoy considerable power within a specific arena, such as making economic decisions for the household.

Legitimization of Power: Authority versus Dominance

One of the most important, although potentially problematic, ways to differentiate power is to gauge whether it is legitimate power. Simply put, legitimate power is *authority* and illegitimate power is *dominance.* The marital partner whose power is based on the authority bestowed by social norms possesses legitimate authority. Legitimate power in marriage is often defined on the basis of resources valued by society, such as education; religious sanctions granting authority to certain individuals or groups; or material wealth in the form of money, land, animals, or goods.

We must emphasize that legitimate power is not evenly or equitably distributed in society. People will have greater or lesser access to resources due to their position in the social structure. Usually, class, race, and gender privilege some and deprive others. Social structures do not just privilege men, however; they privilege wealthy men from majority ethnic or religious groups.

The distinction between legitimate and illegitimate power becomes problematic because legitimate power also can be used as justification to dominate others. *Purdah* in the Middle East, clitoridectomies in Africa, widow burning in India, and marital rape and spousal violence in the United States are examples of abusive acts against women which have been sanctioned by their respective societies. With an increased awareness of violence against women in many parts of the world, a global standard condemning the use of physical force against women is essential. The process of adapting a critical versus cultural relativistic understanding of marital power is discussed in the concluding section of this chapter.

Unlike legitimate power, dominance can be defined as an attempt to control others in ways that are not sanctioned by society. Therefore, dominance is illegitimate power. In societies that refuse to condone physical force as a way to control a spouse, the abuser will be punished and/or restrained. In fact, in Western societies, having to face a jail sentence for abusive behavior is the one factor that seems to be most effective in deterring potential perpetrators from abusing their marital partners. The fact that the threat of forced restraint is needed to control abusive spouses may mean that there is a subtle (nonlegal) sanction of violence against women, or at least that it is tolerated due to the acceptance of misogynist beliefs in these cultures.

As indicated earlier, power is based not only on societal sanctions but on resources that are valued by a society. Resources include much more than fame and fortune and encompass personal and emotional qualities such as self-esteem, confidence, nurturing ability, and interpersonal skills. The value of personal resources is defined by a society. In the United States, for example, the personal qualities traditionally associated with masculinity—aggressiveness, independence, and competitiveness—are highly valued. Those associated with femininity—nurturance, interpersonal and empathic skills, and emotional expressiveness—are devalued.

Those who have both normative power and personal power are in an extremely influential position. They have the weight of society behind them in their business, social, and personal transactions. Yet, when people lack material and personal resources, they will attempt to influence others, often in an indirect way. Men and women differ, however, in the ways they attempt to indirectly influence others.

Men who are devalued due to their lack of prestige and wealth may be desperate to claim authority in some ways that define them as valuable in their culture. In the absence of material and personal resources and legitimate authority, it may be especially tempting for some men to resort to intimidation and/or brute force in an effort to influence others. In his book *Power through Intimidation,* Ringer (1979) claimed that although individuals may not possess many skills and resources, they can gain power through intimidation tactics. Much of Ringer's book consists of clever tricks that will enhance a person's position of power. Manipulation is considered the way of gaining a "one-up" position while simultaneously putting another in the "one-down" place of powerlessness. The message comes through loud and clear: The only avenue for men who lack material or personal resources is to use such indirect means of gaining control.

Women who lack power are more likely to become depressed, to give in, or to use other means of gaining influence, such as pretending to be weak and dependent or manipulating a spouse. Sadly, both husbands and wives who lack respect for themselves or their spouse resort to force and dominance on one hand or intimidation and manipulation on the other in order to be in control. Spouses who respect themselves and each other are influential without such methods of intimidation.

Ascribed versus Achieved Power

Ascribed power is closely related to the concept of legitimate power. This power is not earned but merely comes with the status or position a person has been given in society. In most societies, the husband has *ascribed* power and everyone expects that he automatically has more authority simply because he is the husband.

Cross-cultural comparisons reveal that agricultural societies are more likely than hunter–gatherer and industrial societies to assign husbands legitimate marital power on the basis of gender rather than on the respect and authority they have earned (Whyte, 1978). In contrast, especially in modern industrial societies, *resources* are an important basis of marital power. Being a husband does not automatically guarantee legitimate power within the household. The essential factor is whether the husband's resources are valued by his partner, whether it be the ability to earn money or to be an effective parent. Thus, marital power is based on a partner's *achieved* status rather than on the particular position he/she holds. Power is gained by contributing personal resources to those who need and value what they have to give. Marital power comes out of respect others have for the one who possesses these resources.

It is important to acknowledge that in rural societies, even though a man is deemed powerful because of his esteemed position, he is also required to prove his worth by fulfilling the expectations that accompany that position. In order to maintain credibility, he needs to fulfill such *obligations* as earning a living, sending his children to school, providing dowries and brideprices, and paying for his children's weddings. When he fails to meet the requirements of the position, it seems reasonable to speculate that power is likely to be withdrawn.

Orchestrative Power and Implementative Power

Another way of conceptualizing power is to distinguish between orchestrative power and implementative power (Safilios-Rothschild, 1970). Orchestrative power is using one's position to delegate power to others. Implementative power involves carrying out the task that has been delegated by the one in power. If the implementer fails to do the job, the orchestrator steps in to straighten things out or to help the implementer to do it correctly.

An outsider who spends time observing the patriarchal family system in conservative Christian families may be struck by the fact that many family decisions are made by the wife. The fact is, she is implementing what has been delegated to her to do by her husband. Although she is in charge of the household, is highly responsible for task administration, and looks quite powerful, the husband claims final authority in decision making. For example, the wife may make many decisions about routine household purchases such as groceries and clothes, but major purchases are still under the husband's control.

Asian societies that are based on a strong Confucian ideology ascribe the male as the ultimate authority at both the state and family levels. It is believed that men should devote themselves to learning and scholarship rather than preoccupy or contaminate themselves with mundane concerns like budgeting and spending money (Brydon & Chant, 1989). Thus, the wife is usually in charge of the family budget and makes most of the economic decisions for the family. Although the husband is the head of the family, the wife is in charge of domestic life, implementing the practical matters of family living. The roles are clearly defined and well organized so that spouses know exactly what to expect. In both these examples, the husband has orchestrative power and the wife has implementive power.

In this section, we have discussed how marital power can differ in the way in which it is legitimized, ascribed, and implemented in a given culture. Although all types of power can be observed in all societies, various cultures differ in what types of power are legitimized. We have also seen that social structural influences of a particular society profoundly affect how power is conceptualized, sanctioned, and played out in relationships. With this understanding, we are prepared to consider marital power in cultural and historical context.

MARITAL POWER IN CULTURAL AND HISTORICAL CONTEXT

Some 30 years ago, Goode (1964) pointed out that the worldwide change from agrarian to industrial societies has been associated with a change from extended to conjugal family systems. He predicted that this change will be accompanied by a decline in traditional *patriarchal* norms and an emergence in *egalitarian* patterns. In response, two models of marital power were proposed by researchers. Blood and Wolfe (1960) suggested a *resource* model of marital power, whereas Brickman (1974) and Scanzoni (1979), promoted a *social exchange* model, both of which we discuss here. In addition, we summarize the *traditional patriarchal model*, which is a dominant model in most nonindustrial societies.

After presenting these three models, we offer a feminist critique of power and gender roles in marriage. Based on the arguments that find that these models fail to challenge a self-interested conceptualization of power, we introduce the empowerment model of power in marriage as a hopeful alternative. As the models are presented, we invite you to critically examine the ability of each model to conceptualize marital power in a multicultural context.

The Traditional Patriarchal Model of Marital Power

The traditional patriarchal model is based on the assumption that *power in marriage is ascribed to the husband because he occupies the position of husband/father in the marriage.* Cultural ideological justifications of this model are usually anchored in the sacred authority of religious beliefs and rituals. Whether the religious system be theistic, pantheistic, or animistic, there is a belief that ultimate moral authority justifies male authority. Relevant here is Chafetz's (1991) theory of how female disadvantage in the gender division of labor is perpetuated. She stated, "To the extent women perceive that they choose the roles they play, the system of gender stratification is substantially bolstered because of its apparent legitimacy. Most women do not feel that their domestic and child-rearing responsibilities . . . result from male power. Rather, they define them as their natural, God-given, or desired labors" (p. 90).

In their book *The War over the Family*, Berger and Berger (1983) defended the traditional division of gender roles on pragmatic functional grounds. They argued that this family type is most successful in rearing children to compete in modern society. The Bergers argued that when both marital partners work outside the home, there will be an accompanying decline in a family's capacity to socialize children capable of succeeding in the modern world. They asserted that where husbands and wives specialized in complementary tasks, the result would be the development of "strong character" in children (Berger & Berger, 1983, p. 111). In essence, they reasoned that when one spouse works outside the home, the other is "liberated" to spend the amount of time needed to nurture children toward the independence, self-assertiveness, and self-confidence that allow them to succeed in a competitive world.

In some of the extreme cultural versions of the traditional patriarchal model, the husband has dictatorial rule. In religious fundamentalism, whether it be Islam, Hindu, Confucian, Jewish, or Christian, the father is placed just below God in a chain of command that extends downward to the mother and then to the children. The husband/father has absolute power over his wife and children. Children are to submit to both father and mother, the wife is to submit to her husband, and the husband is to submit to God/Allah. When the husband takes his commitment to God seriously, the cultural version of male authority resembles a benevolent dictatorship. For example, a version of the patriarchal model in Christianity argues that the husband should be head of his wife as Christ was head of the church by assuming the role of a *suffering servant*. The authority remains with the husband, but he is expected to assume the responsibility and decision-making power in the best interest of his family, whom he serves as a fulfillment of his duty to God (Hawley, 1994).

The Resource Theory of Marital Power

Blood and Wolfe's (1960) book *Husbands and Wives* explained marital power in U.S. marriages in terms of *resource theory*. They believed that as marriages changed from a clear division of labor between spouses to one in which marital tasks could be allocated to either partner, the power to make decisions would be determined by spousal resources. This would be the new bargaining tool for negotiation between spouses, for marital power would be based on status that comes from resources held by each of them in their marriages.

Research on marriages in Western societies yielded support for the idea that high-status husbands have more power in the home. However, comparative research was less than conclusive. Buric and Zecevic's (1967) study of marriages in Yugoslavia and Safilios-Rothschild's (1976) study of marriages in Greece found the exact opposite—that low-status husbands had more relative marital power than did high-status husbands.

Rodman (1972) attempted to explain the apparent contradiction by proposing a *theory of resources in cultural context*. According to Rodman, marital systems can be conceptualized along a continuum ranging from *patriarchy* to *modified patriarchy* to *transitional equalitarian* and finally to *full egalitarian*. As Rodman described it, resource theory will explain very little in the two extremes—patriarchy and full egalitarian marital systems. In each, the norms are so strong and clear that there will be very little variation in their marital power structures. He argued that in transitional marital systems, however, resources will prove to be important in influencing the relative power of husband and wife.

In a review of relevant comparative studies, Lee (1987) concluded that there is only moderate support for the theory of resources in cultural context. He offered three concluding statements:

First, neither resource theory nor the theory of resources in cultural context provides a sufficient explanation of the distribution of conjugal power.
. . . Second, the effects of modernization and cultural change on the bases
and distribution of marital power have probably been seriously overrated
in recent research and theory. . . . Finally, in a related view, cultural change
may affect the way in which power is distributed between spouses without changing the overall balance of power. (pp. 72–73)

Lee did not determine resource theory to be inaccurate, but he found it
to be an incomplete model of marital power. Specifically, he believed that it
fails to emphasize the *ideological context* within which decisions are made
within marital relationships. It is the ideological context that defines for each
spouse the potential value of the resources they possess. As Blumstein and
Schwartz (1991) pointed out, even when women have a substantial amount
of resources, "they have been normatively inhibited from using it in a powerful way" (p. 262).

In *Gender, Family, and Economy: The Triple Overlap*, Blumberg (1991a)
examined the link between marital resources and ideological context. In this
collection of articles, marital power is viewed as a function of gender-based
control of resources at the family and societal levels and cultural ideology.
Therefore, if resource theory is to be used to explain marital power, it will
need to be inclusive enough to consider the nature of gender control at all
levels—marital, family, extended family, community, and societal—as well
as the ideological context at each of these levels. Commenting on this theory
of gender stratification, Coleman (1991) stated, "While our model has roots
in resource theory, its grounding in stratification theory enlarges it to consider a number of critical factors that early resource theory overlooked"
(p. 252).

The Democratic Exchange Model of Marital Power

The democratic exchange model assumes the importance of resources but
also focuses on the process of power as part of the marital unit. Power in the
democratic exchange model can best be understood by examining three components: *the basis of power, the processes of power,* and *the outcome of
power*. The power basis consists of resources, power processes consist of
interaction, and power outcome has to do with who makes the important
decisions. *The process and outcome of power are determined by each partner using his/her resources to negotiate and bargain for what each needs in
the relationship.*

According to this model, marital power is best understood as a balance
between the democratic ideal in which each spouse is given equal power and

a practical reality in which each partner can use differing resources with which to bargain and negotiate for power. A resource is any personal quality or possession that is valued by the other. Whereas a couple might assume that they each have equal power, if they resort to using their resources as a means of controlling the other, the relationship is probably not equal.

The democratic exchange model presumes that women can be equal to men and exert as much influence in the relationship; each spouse is supposed to be heard and have equal input into the decision-making process. Evidence from Western societies has suggested that employed wives have more marital power and decision-making ability than do women in non-Western cultures. However, evidence from household studies using economic decision-making models applied cross-culturally has led us to question whether this is always the case. Where ideological norms of patriarchy are strong and limit women's access to economic resources, it is difficult for a wife to convert personal resources into marital power (Lee, 1987). The issue of marital power within the democratic exchange model is even more problematic when power is based on ascription rather than achievement.

In Korea, for example, research found that the wives who work outside of the home actually *lost* power in the marital relationship (Balswick, 1981). Because wives in Korean culture already had the responsibility and authority to spend the family's money, they gained little personal power from increased financial resources. In addition, employed wives *lost* the nurturant power status they had before they left the home. After a day at work, the traditional Korean husband liked to be showered with caring gestures. Because these nurturing resources were greatly valued by the husband, his working wife was put in a difficult situation. He did not value her financial contribution to the home and she lost influence with her husband when she no longer carried out the roles as nurturer.

From a multicultural perspective, we need to understand the personal qualities that are valued in a particular culture rather than remain preoccupied with economics. Some couples may be fairly equal in power—not because both are contributing in equal proportions economically to the marriage but because affection and nurturance are highly valued resources that are appreciated and given powerful status in that marital system. At the same time, we must weigh the increasing evidence that questions whether emotional and economic resources are truly equal in their influence on marital power.

For women in all cultures, the lack of economic power is a barrier to becoming a more powerful force in marriage and in society. However, the gains women receive when they become part of the employed work force may be partially offset by a deterioration in their traditional nurturing power base in the home. As money becomes the source of power, spousal involvement by either the husband or the wife within the home can be devalued. When both spouses value status achieved in the workplace as well as in the homeplace and equally share in both places, they will gain individual and marital power. Writing on the politics of caring argues that assuming women are caregivers further excludes them from power and men from sharing responsibilities at home.

MODELS OF MARITAL POWER
AND THE FEMINIST PERSPECTIVE

In an extensive review article on family power, Szinovacz (1987) surmised that the most fervent criticisms of marital power research come from feminist scholars. In her *Journal of Marriage and the Family* decade review article, Ferree (1990) also used a feminist theoretical perspective to critique previous research on marital power.

Feminist scholars have argued that research on marital power has failed to take into account the aspects of social structure that reinforce men's privilege within the marital relationship. Ferree (1990) pointed out that feminists agree that "male dominance within families is part of a wider system of male power, is neither natural nor inevitable, and occurs at women's cost" (p. 867). She recommended that a gender perspective should be used that identifies the issue of domination as central to power relationships. According to this approach, gender is "a lifelong process of situated behavior that both reflects and reproduces a structure of differentiation and control in which men have material and ideological advantages" (p. 870).

An additional criticism of the marital power literature has been the lack of attention to social influences on power in marital relationships (Ferree, 1990). Feminists have argued that well-established religious, educational, economic, and political ideological structures are used to justify suppression and control of women. For example, Ferguson (1984) suggested that human history can best be understood in terms of three semiautonomous systems of human domination—class, race/ethnicity, and sex/gender. As the dominant group begins to use power, reification takes place. When applied to traditional gender relationships, this means that the justification of male dominance comes to be an accepted part of societal ideology. Women, as the subordinate group, are no longer considered to be suppressed but rather are subject to the rule of the more powerful because of presumed inequality in abilities.

Feminists have been especially critical of those who unquestionably accept a social exchange model. Given the competitively based capitalistic economic system of Western industrial societies, it is not surprising that the dominant way in which power is viewed within these marital systems is in terms of a self-centered social exchange. We should not even be surprised by the sociological preoccupation with a social exchange perspective in trying to make sense of marital power. However, feminists have urged that the time has come to realize the debilitating view that our theories of power place on our perception of how power is used in marital and family relationships. As Szinovacz (1987) suggested, "To avoid interpretations which 'eternalize' present societal constraints, we may further profit from in-depth analyses of couples or families who have themselves at least to some extent transcended these constrictions" (p. 682).

We concur with feminist theory that there is something fundamentally wrong with the way power is conceptualized in some contemporary marital and family theories. Resource and social exchange theories may be useful because they explain the way marital partners *usually* utilize power. However, the social exchange model will be in danger of reification if it is seen as the *normative* or the ideal way for power to operate in marriages. Such a view places a limitation on the development of a more constructive use of marital power.

In challenging models of structural inequality and exploitation, a feminist perspective is more consonant with an empowering model of marital power. When feminists criticize patriarchy as self-serving, they are implicitly suggesting that the basis of marital relationships should be one of mutual empowerment. From a feminist perspective, the goal in marriage must be equality. This will only be accomplished when nonoppressive structures are replaced by egalitarian ones.

By identifying the destructive ways in which power can be used to suppress and control, feminist theory can be a springboard from which to develop an empowerment model of marriage. Such a model is needed in order to transcend racism, classism, and sexism as they continue to have oppressive effects on society and family life. Due to their dependent status, children are most directly effected by the way power is used in the family. We turn next to a consideration of the detrimental effects of sexism on children.

Marital Power and the Welfare of Children

Recent cross-cultural research dramatically demonstrated the relationship between marital power and the welfare of children. In general, when women rather than men are in control of at least some resources, these resources will be used more for the welfare of children than for personal pleasure (Blumberg, 1991b). This seems to be true in a number of cultures around the world.

In her study of 20 villages in South India, Mencher (1988) found that women contributed a significantly higher proportion of their earnings to the welfare of the family than men. She reported that men typically held back about 30% of their earnings for such personal pleasures as "sitting in tea-shops, eating food and drinking toddy or *arrack* with friends, and having a clean white shirt for special occasions" (p. 100; quoted in Blumberg, 1991b, p. 103). Women in all villages held back less than 10% for themselves. Even more striking was Mencher's finding that during economic hard times, women contributed a *higher* proportion of their earnings to their families' welfare while men contributed *less*.

In a study of 33 marriages in Mexico City in which spouses claimed to pool their income, Roldan (1988) found that whereas wives contributed 100% of their earnings, husbands held back 25% of theirs. Wives' resentment of their husbands' retention of this personal allowance for themselves was the major source of marital disputes.

There is also evidence that more of a mother's than a father's income goes toward obtaining food for their children. In a study of the poorest of the poor in southern India, Kumar (1978) found that as mothers' income increased, the level of child nutrition rose correspondingly, whereas an increase in fathers' income did not result in an increase in the level of child nutrition. Also noteworthy is Guyer's (1988) research on how men and women in Cameroon spend the income they gain from farming. On average, rural Cameroon women spent 67% of their crop-cash income on family food supplies, whereas men spent only 33% of their income on family food. In a study of 187 children living in rural Ghana, Tripp (1981) reported that the strongest predictor of the nutritional status of children was the amount of money earned by their mother. A similar discrepancy between women's and men's contribution to child nutrition was found among rural families in Belize. Whereas women's income benefited child nutrition, a good proportion of men's income was spent on such personal pleasures as drink, travel, and purchase of female companionship (Stavrakis & Marshall, 1978, cited in Blumberg, 1991a).

In considering the evidence on how income is used differently under female versus male control, Blumberg (1991b) concluded that "wherever women have any structural obligation as providers, income (or food crops) under their control seem to translate more fully and more directly to family sustenance and child nutrition" (p. 108).

There is some evidence that children benefit most when marital power and parental involvement in their lives is approximately equal. Children who have been co-parented (i.e., fathers are equally involved with mothers in the care of their children) reap the benefits in their journey toward social and psychological maturity.

In *Parenting Together: Men and Women Sharing the Care of Their Children*, Ehrensaft (1990) reported that when co-parented children were compared to non-co-parented children, they (1) had a more secure sense of basic trust, (2) more successfully adapted to brief separations from the mother, (3) had closer relationships to both mother and father, (4) developed better social discrimination skills, such as discerning who could better meet their needs, (5) displayed greater creativity and moral development, (6) had less animosity toward the other gender, (7) were better able to develop strong friendship bonds with opposite gender children, and (8) displayed fantasies of sustained connectedness.

Contrary to this modern version of co-parenting, parents in traditional societies have primarily been involved with children of their own gender; that is, fathers with sons and mothers with daughters. As a host of writings on the contemporary men's movement have pointed out, the process whereby older men initiate boys into adulthood has been completely eviscerated in modern society (Balswick, 1992; Garfinkel, 1985; Osherson, 1986). The specific benefits of co-parenting to boys will be given in our concluding section. We turn now to a consideration of the relationship between marital power and violence against women.

THE EMERGENT WORLDWIDE RECOGNITION OF VIOLENCE AGAINST WOMEN

The extensiveness of marital violence has been documented by Levinson (1993) in a study based on a sample of 90 small-scale societies selected from the Human Relations Area Files. Levinson reported that wife beating, the most common form of family violence around the world, occurred at least occasionally in 85% of societies. It occurred in virtually all households in 19% of societies, in a majority of households in 30% of societies, and in a minority of households in 38% of societies.

Wife beating was sanctioned around the world for three main reasons. First, in 17 societies wife beating was accepted as punishment for adultery or when a husband was *suspicious* that his wife was adulterous. Second, in 15 societies a husband was given the right to beat his wife as long as he had a good reason, such as believing that his wife was not treating him with respect or was not performing her duties properly. Third, in the majority of societies in which wife beating occurred (39), a husband had the right to beat his wife "for any reason or for no reason at all" (Levinson, 1993, p. 265).

The emergence of feminist theory invites us to identify such acts of physical abuse of one spouse by the other as undesirable to marriage and as acts of violence in any cultural system. In the name of cultural relativism, some may seek to normalize marital violence by showing that it is sanctioned by the wider cultural system of which the marital system is a part. The lesson to be learned from feminist and other so-called value-laden theories, is that so-called value-free theories of marital power must be challenged.

Anthropologists have documented the practice of female circumcision in African cultures as an integral part of centuries-old cultural traditions. Alice Walker's (1992) book *Possessing the Secret of Joy* can serve as an example for social scientists of the need to challenge such culturally supported sexism in marriage. In her best-selling novel, Walker strongly condemns this practice for what it is—genital mutilation—by documenting the severe traumatic effect that desexualization has had on millions of African women. If social scientists, in the name of value neutrality, fail to condemn such practices, they indirectly condone this destructive gender-based misuse of power in marital systems.

Cross-culturally, there seems to be an inverse relationship between how powerful a spouse is and how active and even "disruptive" the spouse must be in order to influence his/her partner. A powerful spouse is influential without having to assert power directly, whereas a less powerful spouse will aggressively make demands to control a partner. The husband who rants and raves, screams and yells, or bullies and badgers is communicating a *lack* of culturally prescribed power. Although wives can also be abusive, they usually disrupt in manipulative rather than violent ways. A wife who appears weak and frail can control her partner by withholding favors, feigning sickness, or appearing to be helpless.

From a multicultural perspective, the relationship between power and marital violence is a husband's feelings of *relative deprivation*. This means there is a greater likelihood of marital violence in marriages in which husbands lack personal power but live within a society that expects them to be powerful. We expect that marital violence will be least where husbands possess personal power and live in a society that values equality.

In equalitarian marriages, husbands are content with equal sharing of power and mutual decision making with their spouse. In patriarchal systems, the husband whose wife is equally powerful may resort to drastic means to gain more power in the relationship. A powerful husband in a patriarchal system can influence his wife without resorting to marital violence. Therefore an act of marital violence is a sign that the husband wants to control his wife but in reality has little personal clout or power over her.

Although it has seldom been a part of the literature on marital power, there is a radical alternative to the control model of marital power. This is the empowerment model, which we will consider next.

THE EMPOWERMENT MODEL: A RADICAL ALTERNATIVE

Most of the research on the use of marital power has focused on how each spouse tries to influence or control the behavior of the other. The underlying assumption is that when one spouse is more powerful, the other partner is less powerful. It follows, then, that the person with more resources has the more powerful position in the marital dyad.

The empowerment model, in contrast, purports that each spouse can use personal resources to move the other from a position of weakness to one of strength. Empowering is not merely one spouse yielding to the wishes of the other. It does not involve giving up one's power to empower others. Rather, *empowering is the active and intentional process of each spouse developing and affirming power in the other.* Each spouse is encouraged to reach full personal potential. Empowerment is an interactive process in which each desires that the other become all that he/she can be. Each believes in the other and uses personal resources to build the other up. This mutually empowering process leads to interdependence in the best sense of the word (Balswick & Balswick, 1987, 1990).

The empowerment model also allows us to focus on autonomy instead of control "over" something or someone. The greater the degree of empowerment in a marriage, the greater the sense of autonomy by each spouse. If marriages are structured so as to encourage each spouse to use his/her respective power for the other, spousal autonomy, as well as mutual respect and interdependence, will result.

Empowerment and Limited Supply Theory

The concept of empowerment makes no sense within a theoretical framework that perceives power as a commodity that comes in limited supply. The operationalization of power within social exchange theory, for example, is based on the view that there are a maximum number of power units available in any relationship. *Quid pro quo* (i.e., I get something when I give something) is considered an equal exchange where two people keep a 50/50 account record.

According to the empowerment model, power is available to both partners in *unlimited* amounts. Each has 100 units and does not work toward keeping an equal balance. Rather, each spouse desires that the other be 100% powerful because it benefits and strengthens the relationship. Empowered partners live in a relationship of mutual and reciprocal empowerment of each other. The increase of power is interactive, as the power of one spouse increases the potential for empowerment in the other; in the process, *each* spouse must expand and extend toward growth and greater potential. It is not a simple or nonconflictual process, but the end product is satisfying because both spouses have equally grappled with personal and relational issues that develop character and integrity. Personal power becomes the cutting edge of growth for an empowering marriage.

CONCLUSION

In this chapter we have examined traditional approaches to the study of marital power. Using cross-cultural examples and a feminist perspective, we have found the existing work in this area severely lacking. We have seen that traditional models of marital power share the assumption that partners will use power to *control* their spouses. These models do not take into account the social forces that structure gender roles so that men almost always control more resources, have greater prestige, and are dominant in their marital relationships.

We presented the empowerment model as a bridge to multicultural understanding because it changes how people of various cultures can learn to view marital power. We are challenged to utilize this model in an attempt to understand the dynamics of marital power in our own and other societies. By seeing marital power through a new lens, we can hope not only to gain a new understanding of marital power but to be drawn toward empowering marital relationships as an ideal. This chapter concludes by suggesting the societal changes that are needed to achieve marital empowerment.

Marital empowerment will only be possible when a societal ideological structure allows both men and women equal access to all valued resources of power. This means that men are affirmed and awarded power for their nurturing resources just as women are affirmed and awarded power for their earning resources. Although most models of marital power have concentrated on resources within the family, we believe that it is equally important to have access to resources in the wider social structure.

Social structures that predispose people to seek to control rather than to empower must be challenged. We propose that *in societies in which women are kept in a one-down position, boys and girls will grow up considering it normative for men to control and women to be controlled.* To break this pattern, children need to be co-parented in a home in which the marital-empowerment model is the norm.

Szinovacz (1987) described power as a potential for shaping a person's identity and self-concept. This shaping of another's self-image is interpreted as an attempt by the actor to impose his/her own subjective realities on the other. One way to develop an individual's self-concept is not to direct the person what to *be* but to tell that person who and what he/she *is*. This has to do with acknowledging the potential in another and believing in that person to grow and develop to his/her full potential.

The close ties with mother *and* father are the means of valuing all the competencies of living for both males and females. In a culture in which parenting is primarily done by mothers, women have the continual advantage of being socialized toward altruism, nurturing, and attachment behaviors. These qualities contribute to becoming empowerers. If boys are never allowed to develop the very traits that lead to empowerment, they will continue to perpetuate domination and control.

Therefore, boys as well as girls need to connect closely with mothers and *fathers* through sustained activities of care and attachment, as well as through differentiation and strong self-concept. These are qualities that promote their capacity to be empowering persons. Characteristics from both father and mother that serve to empower rather than to control will enable children to carry on a new way of thinking and acting out marital power when they are adults.

Recent evidence of the effects of co-parenting on boys has important implications for the future of marital power. Boys from co-parented homes (1) develop strong bonds of friendship with opposite gender children, (2) display higher empathy skills, (3) expect both genders to be affectionate and nurturing and protest when they see distant fathers portrayed on television or when either gender is "left out" of parenting or career, (4) defend and push for gender equality and envision their family type as optimal, and (5) express their desire to be a father when they grow up (Ehrensaft, 1990). When boys and girls are socialized with these qualities, it can be expected that when they marry, they will be psychologically prepared to enter into an equalitarian, empowering marital relationship.

REFERENCES

Balswick, J. O. (1981). Strong men and virtuous women: Changing male and female roles in Korea. *Transactions of the Royal Asiatic Society, 56*, 27–35.

Balswick, J. O. (1992). *Men at the crossroads: Beyond traditional roles and modern options*. Downers Grove, IL: Inter Varsity Press.

Balswick, J. O., & Balswick J. K. (1987). A theological basis for family relationships. *Journal of Psychology and Christianity, 6*, 37–49.

Balswick, J. O., & Balswick, J. K. (1990). *The family*. Grand Rapids, MI: Baker Books.

Berger, B., & Berger, P. (1983). *The war over the family: Capturing the middle ground*. Garden City, NY: Anchor Press.

Blood, R. O., Jr., & Wolfe, D. M. (1960). *Husbands and wives: The dynamics of married living*. New York: Free Press.

Blumberg, R. L. (1991a). Introduction: The "triple overlap" of gender stratification, economy, and the family. In R. L. Blumberg (Ed.), *Gender, family, and economy: The triple overlap* (pp. 7–34). Newbury Park, CA: Sage.

Blumberg, R. L. (1991b). Income under female versus male control. In R. L. Blumberg (Ed.), *Gender, family, and economy: The triple overlap* (pp. 97–127). Newbury Park, CA: Sage.

Blumstein, P., & Schwartz, P. (1991). Money and ideology: Their impact on power and the division of household labor. In R. L. Blumberg (Ed.), *Gender, family, and economy: The triple overlap* (pp. 261–288). Newbury Park, CA: Sage.

Brickman, P. (1974). *Social conflict.* Lexington, MA: Heath.

Brydon, L., & Chant, S. (1989). *Women in the Third World.* New Brunswick, NJ: Rutgers University Press.

Buric, O., & Zecevic, A. (1967). Family authority, marital satisfaction, and the social network in Yugoslavia. *Journal of Marriage and the Family, 29,* 325–326.

Chafetz, J. (1991). The gender division of labor and the reproduction of female disadvantage: Toward an integrated theory. In R. L. Blumberg (Ed.), *Gender, family, and economy: The triple overlap* (pp. 74–96). Newbury Park, CA: Sage.

Coleman, M. (1991). The division of household labor: Suggestions for future empirical consideration and theoretical development. In R. L. Blumberg (Ed.), *Gender, family, and economy: The triple overlap* (pp. 245–260). Newbury Park, CA: Sage.

Cromwell, R. E., & Olson, D. H. (Eds.). (1975). *Power in families.* New York: Halstead Press.

Ehrensaft, D. (1990). *Parenting together: Men and women sharing the care of their children.* Chicago: University of Illinois Press.

Ferguson, A. (1984). On conceiving motherhood and sexuality: A feminist materialist approach. In J. Treblicot (Ed.), *Mothering: Essays in feminist theory.* Totowa, NJ: Rowman & Allanheld.

Ferree, M. M. (1990). Beyond separate spheres: Feminism and family research. *Journal of Marriage and the Family, 52,* 866–884.

Garfinkel, P. (1985). *In a man's world: Father, son, brother, friend, and other roles men play.* New York: W. W. Norton.

Goode, W. G. (1964). *The family.* Englewood Cliffs, NJ: Prentice Hall.

Guyer, J. (1988). Dynamic approaches to domestic budgeting: Cases and methods from Africa. In D. Dwyer & J. Bruce (Eds.), *A home divided: Women and income in the Third World* (pp. 161–172). Palo Alto, CA: Stanford University Press.

Hawley, J. S. (Ed.). (1994). *Fundamentalism and gender.* New York: Oxford University Press.

Kumar, S. (1978). *Roles of the household economy in child nutrition at low incomes: A case study in Kerala* (Occasional Paper No. 95). Ithaca, NY: Cornell University, Department of Agricultural Economics.

Lee, G. (1987). Comparative perspectives. In M. Sussman & S. Steinmetz (Eds.), *Handbook of marriage and the family* (pp. 59–80). New York: Plenum Press.

Levinson, D. (1993). Family violence in cross-cultural perspective. In L. Tepperman & S. Wilson (Ed.), *Next of kin: An international reader on changing families* (pp. 260–274). Englewood Cliffs, NJ: Prentice Hall.

McDonald, G. (1980). Family power. The assessment of a decade of theory and research, 1970–1979. *Journal of Marriage and the Family, 42,* 841–854.

Mencher, J. (1988). Women's work and poverty: Women's contribution to household maintenance in South India. In D. Dwyer & J. Bruce (Eds.), *A home divided: Women and income in the Third World.* Palo Alto, CA: Stanford University Press.

Osherson, S. (1986). *Finding our fathers: The unfinished business of manhood.* New York: Free Press.

Ringer, R. (1979). *Winning through intimidation.* New York: Fawcett.

Rodman, H. (1972). Marital power and the theory of resources in cultural context. *Journal of Comparative Family Studies, 3*, 50–69.

Roldan, M. (1988). Renegotiating the marital contract: Intrahousehold patterns of money allocation and women's subordination among domestic outworkers in Mexico City. In D. Dwyer & J. Bruce (Eds.), *A home divided: Women and income in the Third World.* Palo Alto, CA: Stanford University Press.

Safilios-Rothschild, C. (1970). The study of family power structure: A review 1960–1969. *Journal of Marriage and the Family, 32*, 539–552.

Safilios-Rothschild, C. (1976). A comparison of power structure and marital satisfaction in urban Greek and French families. *Journal of Marriage and the Family, 29*, 345–352.

Scanzoni, J. (1979). Social process and power in families. In W. Burr, R. Hill, F. Nye, & I. Reiss (Eds.), *Contemporary theories about the family* (Vol. 1, pp. 295–316). New York: Free Press.

Szinovacz, M. (1987). Family power. In M. Sussman & S. Steinmetz (Eds.), *Handbook of marriage and the family* (pp. 651–693). New York: Plenum Press.

Tripp, R. (1981). Farmers and traders: Some economic determinants of nutritional status in Northern Ghana. *Journal of Tropical Pediatrics, 27*, 15–22.

Walker, A. (1992). *Possessing the secret of joy.* Orlando, FL: Harcourt Brace Jovanovich.

Whyte, M. K. (1978). *The status of women in preindustrial societies.* Princeton, NJ: Princeton University Press.

PART FIVE

SOCIAL INEQUALITY IN THE CONTEMPORARY WORLD

Courtesy Bron B. Ingoldsby.

Introduction

Part V examines dimensions of social inequality not explicitly covered in other parts of the text—race, ethnicity, and class. This approach is based on the concept of social stratification, that is, the structure of society according to certain social characteristics. Social stratification gives some groups greater access to resources such as income or political influence—and therefore greater power—than others have. Most societies are structured by race, ethnicity, class, caste, and gender, such that resources and power are concentrated among majority racial and ethnic groups, the wealthy, higher castes, and men. The social inequality created by stratification systems can have profound effects on family life.

Part IV discussed gender inequality—how societies are structured on the basis of gender. Those chapters demonstrated that gender stratification has resulted in women's subordination worldwide. Part V looks more closely at the impacts of inequalities of race and class on families.

In Chapter 14, "Looking Back, Looking Forward: African American Families in Sociohistorical Perspective," Norma J. Burgess provides a compelling overview of the history of African American families and the continuing impact of the experiences of slavery, reconstruction, and the civil rights movement on family structure, interactions, and relationships with the larger kin group and community. In addition, she analyzes the biases inherent in U.S. family and social policies and the consequences for African American families. She urges readers to challenge the prejudiced assumptions of early research on African American families that have had a lasting impact on scholarship and public policy and to adopt new ways of thinking about black family life.

In Chapter 15, "Poverty and Patriarchy in Latin America," Bron B. Ingoldsby focuses on the economic deprivation common in the Hispanic world and its relationship to patriarchal abuse in the family. A theory for understanding *machismo* is developed, and the social problems of abandoned children and marital violence are examined. The chapter suggests that "familism," which is also associated with this culture, is a positive alternative to *machismo*.

319

In Chapter 16, "Public Policy and Poverty: A Framework for Analysis," Rosalie Huisinga Norem and Suzanna Smith present an overview of poverty in the Third World and the United States and ask how we can begin to intervene to ameliorate the situation. They suggest that public policy can have a powerful effect on improving family health and well-being for the world's poor. They offer a framework for analyzing policy interventions at various systems levels to assist in policy planning. They close by suggesting the policy implications of issues raised in this text.

CHAPTER FOURTEEN

Looking Back, Looking Forward: African American Families in Sociohistorical Perspective

NORMA J. BURGESS

It is difficult to understand what African American families are like today without having a perspective on past family structures, especially as they relate to the roles, functions, and responsibilities members usually carry out within the family unit. This chapter focuses on historical factors that have affected family functioning, including enslavement, emancipation and migration, and early social policies. Further, the impact of these historical processes on contemporary family phenomena is examined, including the recent issues of marriageability, decisions to delay marriage or to never marry, and the timing of parenthood.

A sociohistorical perspective on African Americans and their families provides one means to examine the aspects of black family life that have impacted contemporary attitudes and beliefs about these families. This chapter demonstrates that the history and social conditions of African Americans in the United States have affected a number of phenomena such as family structure (whether a family is headed by two parents, a single female-headed, a single male-headed, or extended kin), underemployment (due to inadequate job skills and inequality of opportunities), discrimination (based on race and gender), and family formation (the timing of family formation and the availability of marriage partners).

LOOKING BACK

Past studies of African American families have suffered from ahistoricism and have not taken into account the impact of experiences prior to the emancipation on contemporary family structure and functioning (Oyebade, 1990). Sociologist Walter Allen (1978) identified the basic approaches that have been used to examine African American families as the cultural equivalent, cultural deviant, and cultural variant models. The culturally deviant model, which is generally characterized by ethnocentric biases, was popularized in the 1960s and culminated in what has commonly become known as the *Moynihan Report* (Moynihan, 1965). Moynihan used census data and a white middle-class model of family structure as a measure of family stability. Because a larger proportion of families in the African American community did not fit the two-parent ideal, the black family itself was viewed as deviant and therefore by definition was assumed to be pathological (Allen, 1978).

The early writings of E. Franklin Frazier (1939/1966) were used to support the idea that the matriarchal family was the norm in African American communities. Much of Frazier's writing and thinking developed out of his association with prominent members of the Chicago School of sociology who also believed African Americans lacked a culture of their own and therefore should be taught a new culture and life-style more in keeping with Western ideology (Gutman, 1975; Platt, 1991). Frazier's (1939/1966) conclusion that "the maternal family organization, a heritage from slavery . . . continued on a fairly large scale" (quoted in Gutman, 1976, p. 633) rested more on opinion than on historical evidence (Platt, 1991). Frazier's work, however, undeniably set the tone for how African American families have been viewed from a scholarly perspective since the early 1900s.

Frazier's arguments about the matriarchal structure of the African American family gained widespread acceptance during the 1900s and eventually culminated in the 1960s with Moynihan's interpretation of black families as a "tangle of pathology." Drawing on Frazier's previous work, Moynihan concluded that the deterioration of the family—that is, a disproportionate number of female-headed households—was a root cause of the "pathological" nature of the black family.

As a result of such thinking, public policies were developed based on the belief that African Americans had no culture and were not able to function in society as other families with "stronger" cultural roots. The *historical* presence of the female-headed family form, both in the African American family of orientation and in independent households, was rarely discussed. From this perspective, female-headed families were one structural adaptation to environmental circumstances (e.g., male–female ratios creating an excess of black women), and cultural norms (e.g., greater community acceptance of female-headed families) (Burgess, 1994). As students of the family, it is our responsibility to examine writings that present alternative views and contribute to our understanding of the current dilemmas contemporary African American families regularly encounter. Thus, this discussion begins with an acknowledgment that the history of Africans in the United States begins in Africa.

From Africa to the United States

Not all Africans came to the United States as slaves. Some came as explorers and adventurers, some came as freemen before the beginning of slavery, and some came as indentured servants who eventually earned their freedom. Thus, African American families varied greatly in legal, economic, and social status. Many free and freed black families were headed by entrepreneurs, professional artisans, landowners, and businessmen. This small but important elite contrasted with the majority of blacks who had to maintain themselves under conditions of economic deprivation and social disruption (McAdoo & Terborg-Penn, 1985; Sudarkasa, 1981).

The majority of persons who were purchased from Africa for purposes of enslavement came from the West or Central regions of the continent (i.e., present-day Nigeria and surrounding countries) (Asante & Mattson, 1992). Members of numerous ethnic groups and tribes with various familial formation patterns, rituals, and class statuses were sold together. Subjected to blatant disregard for their past social standing in their countries of origin, these slaves' common bond in early America was the painful inability to be free and the likelihood of experiencing similar maltreatment by the slave owner.

The disparity in African tribal/regional origins and the dissimilarity of language and customs have often been cited as primary sources of communication difficulty among enslaved persons and may have contributed to the annihilation of some African family patterns during slavery. However, both Levine (1977) and Herskovits (1958/1990) noted that similar attitudes toward family, such as caring for the old and the young, were present among various African groups and helped to ensure continuity within the group.

Contrary to popular belief, slave traders made no deliberate attempt to separate slaves who had the same ethnic background and language. Thus, these traders unwittingly guaranteed continuity of the African cultural heritage during the middle passage and after the slaves arrived in the New World. The slaves and their descendants underwent common experiences sufficient to enable them to cooperate in fashioning new customs, traditions, and even languages that reflected their African background (Mulira, 1990). This shared nationalism enabled the Africans in the United States to create recognizably African patterns wherever they lived (Holloway, 1990; Herskovits, 1958/1990). Adaptations were made to their particular circumstance in conjunction with the recognition that in some instances, lack of conformity meant death.

Unlike other ethnic and racial groups that migrated to the United States for religious or economic reasons during the same period, the enslavement process, its consequences, and surrounding circumstances provided a different but commonly shared beginning for the majority of African Americans. However, the history of their subordinate status, racism, and discrimination are often left out of contemporary explanations for structural conditions including unemployment, underemployment, low education, and poverty. In this chapter, I further explore the continued impacts of slavery on the African American family experience.

Enslavement: Family Structure and Functioning

The majority of families of African descent living in the United States in the 1700s and 1800s were characterized by two-parent households. Through his studies of plantation records, historian Herbert Gutman (1976) observed the common presence of the nuclear family among enslaved Africans. Although Gutman's work was based on ethnocentric, a priori assumptions about family structures, the results emerged as "proof" that the nuclear family existed and were used to dispute the Frazierian premise that mother-dominated families characterized early African American family life. Gutman (1976) and Degler (1980) argued confidently that the model of family development adopted by most slaves was nuclear in form and resembled that of their owners, including the custom of soliciting permission for courtship and eventual marriage. Because African Americans were often sold apart at the discretion of the slave owners, other family forms were present, although not to the same degree.

Slave parents lived in continual fear of losing their children to sickness or the selling block. One child recalled how her mother had saved her:

> My mother often hid us all in the woods, to prevent master selling us. When we wanted water, she sought for it in any hole or puddle formed by falling trees or otherwise. It was often full of tadpoles and insects. She strained it, and gave it round to each of us in the hollow of her hand. For food, she gathered berries in the woods, got potatoes, raw corn (etc). After a time, the master would send word to her to come in, promising he would not sell us. (Sterling, 1984, pp. 58–59)

The mother–child dyad, rather than the husband–wife bond, was central to family life and children did not require the presence of a father to be "legitimate" in the eyes of the community. To ensure safety for children born to single mothers during the enslavement period, community members played an important role in childrearing. Most single mothers during that time, whether widowed, never married, or once married, did not live alone (Billingsley, 1968). "Fictive" kin, other mothers, grandmothers, and community members adapted an African-type extended kinship system to provide support in the place of absent or ineffective fathers (Collins, 1990). In cases in which parents were sold to other landowners, it was commonplace for other adults in the slave community to assume care-giving functions (Gutman, 1976; Collins, 1990). Such inherent strengths enabled enslaved families to survive the worst of hardships (Surdarkasa, 1981).

Few scholars will argue that enslavement did not have a detrimental impact on the black family. Indeed, the tragic occurrences of the first 100 years of adaptation to conditions of slavery may have had long-term effects on the family, including earlier ages of coitus, childbearing, and household formation. In some African communities, natural spacing techniques such as breast-feeding and polygamous unions had allowed women to postpone childbearing for several years after a birth. However, because the emphases in the United States shifted away from African family formation patterns and toward increased economic production and human reproduction, enslaved African women began parenting at earlier ages and had greater numbers of children than did their mothers. Thus, slavery impacted not only household size and composition but also the physical health of mothers and children.

Because men, women, and children were treated as property, they could be sold at any time (Staples & Johnson, 1993). In contrast to traditional marriage vows theoretically adhered to by the early settlers, marriages between Africans in the United States received little respect or support from slave owners. Enslaved persons were required to obtain permission from their owners to marry, even though such marriages were not legally recognized. Marriage between enslaved individuals did not guarantee the union's permanency. Slave masters terminated more than one-third of the marriages; about one-half of slave marriages ended by death of a spouse, and only about one-tenth ended by mutual consent or desertion (Degler, 1980).

The cruel conditions of slavery, its rigid working system, and its rules against any African tradition that threatened the slave system guaranteed the destruction of many African political, social, and economic institutions. Many artistic skills were also lost because the new slave system provided no leisure time to engage in such activities. Despite these disruptions, remnants of prior family forms and culture (i.e., Africanisms) have continued to be evident among African American families well into the 20th century. For example, although the slaves were forced to abandon outward material representations of their culture, they preserved the inward, nonmaterial aspects, such as religion and magic; these have been the most retained of African customs and beliefs.

Indeed, the new world experiences of African Americans encouraged them to maintain ties to their African past. This unspoken association with a rich cultural heritage enabled them to survive and to create a meaningful existence in a world in which they were not welcomed beyond their performance as workers (Amott & Matthaei, 1991). They adapted to environmental changes and social upheavals by relying on familiar traditions and practices. Music played an important role in this process. Although specific African songs and ways eventually disappeared from the culture of African Americans, new ones were created in the traditional style, using African vocabulary and idiom, or in an alternative style that combined African and non-African resources.

In short, misinterpretations and ethnocentric assumptions about family formation and structure formed the basis of prejudicial ideas about African American families. As discussed later in this chapter, these particular beliefs went well beyond the enslavement period, however, emerging later as the minimal guidelines for many of the social policies affecting the lives of African Americans (Burgess & Horton, 1993).

The Emancipation and Reconstruction

As discussed previously, historical evidence (Gutman, 1976) has made clear that the vast majority of African American families were headed by both parents and has contradicted the view that slavery "destroyed" the black family. One major conclusion is that the slave family was undeniably stronger than previous documentation suggested. The complete destruction of the family is unlikely. Rather, it is far more likely that theories and conceptual frameworks used to examine early families were flawed. Clearly, alternative family forms in the black community were important to preserving families and their traditions during enslavement.

During the emancipation and reconstruction period of 1865 through 1898, significant changes occurred in the lives of African Americans. They began to own farms and to develop banking systems, stores, and churches. Some literacy was achieved and in the 1890s, black agricultural colleges were formed, such as Alcorn State University and the Tuskeegee Institute.

Fathers who had been sold away prior to the emancipation later reestablished relationships with other family members. This evidence contradicts Frazier's earlier portrait of former slaves wandering from place to place following reconstruction. After slavery, an abrupt rise in two-parent households occurred in formerly slave-holding states, as fathers rejoined their families and couples established their own legal unions (Ricketts, 1989). Nevertheless, economic recovery and associated benefits after emancipation and reconstruction were short-lived, as we will see in the following sections (Amott & Matthaei, 1991).

The Great Migration and Its Aftermath

Between 1910 and 1930, families were weary from years of struggle against economic and social exploitation in the South, including denial of the right to vote, unequal educational opportunities, discrimination in public places, and legal injustices. More than one million African Americans migrated North during those years in families and as individuals (Amott & Matthaei, 1991). The indomitable spirit of the black family inherited from slavery and reconstruction was reflected in the families that migrated from the rural South to Chicago and other northern cities during the 1920s in search of new opportunities. One description summarizes their experience:

> Often squeezed into shabby and segregated neighborhoods, these Black men and women endured and prevailed over hardships to gain a better life. Employers still placed immigrant Europeans above African Americans on the job hierarchy, kept Blacks in menial positions, and subjected them to frequent layoffs. Many Blacks found jobs, developed businesses and took care of their children under the most trying conditions. Contrary to some views, the Great Migration and subsequent urbanization did not destroy the Black family. ("From the Ebony Files," 1993, p. 138)

In many ways, African American families were culturally distinct because they emphasized reliance on each other for survival rather than an individualistic approach to success. Black families often received support from African American institutions such as churches and community groups; these organizations were a mainstay for families, providing assistance and enabling self-sufficiency. As social policies were developed after the Depression, however, these supports were seldom recognized and were rarely included in government plans to promote economic progress among African Americans.

From their inception, the social services system of the pre-1940s did not consider the important role of community-based social institutions within the African American community. For example, the white "breadwinner" model assumed that all husbands could provide basic needs within families. But such an approach rested on the availability of steady, paid work for men and did not take into account black men's lower wages and economic and racial injustices in a society that made it impossible for men to support their families on a single wage (Woody, 1992). Although black fathers were able-bodied, many did not earn sufficient wages or maintain steady employment to provide for their families. Jewell (1988) suggested that early policies and social programs indirectly encouraged father-absent families among African American households. Public assistance requirements prohibited men's participation in formal living arrangements with their families. Many men temporarily changed residences to meet the stringent requirements set by public assistance agencies. This trend has continued into contemporary families as well.

Policy analysts followed one type of family model theoretically, the middle-class nuclear family, but they did not acknowledge the gap between actual and perceived occurrences of the traditional two-parent families, even among the European American population, and based their policy recommendations on these biased assumptions (Jewell, 1988). In the contemporary United States, however, individual legislators and governmental bodies are gradually recognizing the need for changes in the understanding of African American families so that policies are more consistent with actual varieties in family structures.

The Civil Rights Era

Many African Americans recognized the opportunity for change made possible by World War II. Painfully aware of the disparity between democratic ideals and practice in the United States, African Americans organized to use this international crisis to further their demands for equality at home. Many saw this period as providing opportunities, through civil demonstrations and legal action, "to persuade, embarrass, compel and shame our government and our nation . . . into a more enlightened attitude toward a tenth of its people" (Dalfiume, 1968, pp. 96–97).

The first 20 years after World War II were an era of challenge to discriminatory barriers to African American participation. As the civil rights movement grew and African American community organizations accelerated their campaigns, an increasing number of judicial, presidential, and congressional decisions, orders, and legislation aimed at dismantling barriers to African American participation appeared. Some important dates (Jaynes & Williams, 1989, pp. 63–64) are noted here:

- 1948: President Truman, in Executive Order 9981, directs the U.S. Armed Forces to institute equal opportunity and treatment among the races.
- 1954: The Supreme Court, in *Brown v. Board of Education of Topeka*, rules against segregation of blacks and whites in public schools.
- 1955: President Eisenhower, in Executive Order 1059, establishes the President's Committee on Government Employment Policy to fight discrimination in employment (replacing the Fair Employment Practices Committee established by President Truman in 1948).
- 1955: The Interstate Commerce Commission issues an order banning segregation of passengers on trains and buses used in interstate travel.
- 1957: The Civil Rights Act creates a six-member presidential commission to investigate allegations of the denial of citizen's voting rights.

- 1960: The Civil Rights Act strengthens the investigatory powers of the 1957 Civil Rights Commission.
- 1961: The Justice Department moves against discrimination in airport facilities under the provisions of the Federal Airport Act and against discrimination in bus terminals under the Interstate Commerce Commission Act.
- 1962: President Kennedy, in Executive Order 11063, bars discrimination in federally assisted housing.
- 1964: The Civil Rights Act prohibits discrimination in public accommodations and employment.
- 1965: The Voting Rights Act suspends literacy tests and sends federal examiners into many localities to protect the rights of black voters.
- 1968: Fair housing legislation outlaws discrimination in the sale or rental of housing.

Few of these laws led to the immediate implementation of their stated objectives. Many efforts were expended to see that the initial goals of the laws were reached. Fair housing laws continue to be challenged with illegal practices of "redlining" (i.e., applying differential financial qualifying rules for home loans resulting in exclusion from certain neighborhoods or more stringent credit requirements disproportionately by race). Opportunities for employment have not reached full equity. A disproportionate number of workers remain unemployed and underemployed, while jobs in semiskilled occupations, where many African Americans have earned middle-class wages, continue to erode (Woody, 1992). Consequently, ensuring economic stability and keeping families together has become an ever-present challenge for many black communities.

LOOKING FORWARD

Contemporary African American Families

Like most U.S. families today, only a small percentage of African American families fall into the "traditional" nuclear household—a couple living together with the husband as sole provider and mother caring for children at home. Family composition has changed significantly for African Americans. In 1970, married couples accounted for 68% of African American family households. Another 28% were maintained by women with no husbands present, and the remaining 4% were maintained by men with no wife present. The 1980s was the first period during which the number of female-headed households outnumbered married-couple households (Billingsley, 1992).

Nearly 25% of African American women will remain unmarried for various reasons. These include lower ratios of black marriageable males (those with steady employment) to females and structurally based economic instability among African American males, including unsteady employment and low-wage occupations (Horton & Burgess, 1992; Woody, 1992). In addition, the movement of jobs out of the United States and the decline in demand for semiskilled workers are important factors in men's decisions to marry and to start families. Other social factors, including disproportionately higher levels of homicides in African American communities and encounters with the legal system, may ultimately affect the number of males who are marriageable. Perhaps an examination of factors leading to these misfortunes as they reach epidemic levels would provide a better understanding of the marriageability issue.

African American families of the 1990s experience a unique array of social situations that directly affect family functioning and well-being. As discussed previously, for decades most households have been headed either by two parents or by women. Regardless of headship, extended family members have assisted with the care and rearing of children.

Media attention directed toward contemporary African Americans focuses consistently on the rise in female-headed households. In large part, this rise may be attributed to the decline in employment among African American males in the 1980s (Woody, 1992). Financial strain often forces women to live with men who are barely self-sufficient or else without a male as a permanent member of the household. As a result, many mothers choose to live alone with their children, even though this may mean living in poverty. Often, relatives provide a high level of emotional support and a subsistence level of financial assistance. This dependence on familial support makes it difficult for women to escape from poverty. On the other hand, some mothers point out the positive aspects of single parenting as well—a view rarely voiced in the media:

> Black single mothers and their families have something to offer us all. By daily demonstrating that they can survive and succeed without marriage, that they may even be better off without it, they challenge the basic patriarchal ideal. My children and other children of black single mothers are better people because they do not have to live in families where violence, sexual abuse, and emotional estrangement are the daily, hidden reality. They are not burdened by violent sexist nightmares that block their strength and sensibilities at the core of where they live. They know that fathers and mothers are only men and women, not infallible tyrants or gods. They have choices and a voice. In a society where men are taught to dominate and women to follow, we all have a lot to overcome in learning to build relationships, with each other and with our children, based on love and justice. For many Black single mothers, this is what the struggle is about. (Omolade, 1986)

Currently, most African American single parents are adults, not teenagers. African American women, like all U.S. women, are marrying later and making choices to become single parents (Cherlin, 1992). Woody (1992) noted that the decline of employment among African American males during the 1980s coincided with the decline in marriage rates. Many African American women have not given up on the marriage ideal (Billingsley, 1992). However, marriage and parenting within African American communities are taking on new meaning in that marital status does not necessarily precede parental status. The timing of family development within communities may have changed over time as many families have adapted to their environment.

The Community

African American communities can be subdivided into several categories based on income, education, and occupation. Billingsley (1992) classified them into (1) the nonworking poor, where no family member has a permanent attachment to the work force; (2) the working poor, those who work but earn income at or below poverty level; (3) the nonpoor working class, unskilled and semiskilled workers with earnings above the poverty line; (4) the middle class, primarily skilled and professional workers with family income above the median for all families; and (5) a small black upper class of families with high incomes and substantial wealth as well as social and economic influence. Changes in recent decades have also resulted in an expanding group of black nonworking poor, that is, those living at poverty level (13% in 1969, 21% in 1983, and 18% in 1986). At the other extreme, the upper class, which is composed of families whose median income was $50,000 and above, has expanded (5% of all families in 1969, 6% in 1983, 9% in 1986, and 14% by 1990).

Blackwell (1985) portrayed the African American community as a social system, sharing norms, values, sentiments, and expectations. The community is diverse, with members being held together by adherence to commonly shared values and goals. As prosperous African Americans move out of their old neighborhoods, they leave behind important sources of cohesion and culture. Yet essential components of the original community, such as kin, religious organizations, and some small businesses such as beauty and barber shops, provide a sense of place for transplanted African Americans, as well as services not often found in suburbia.

Equally important to a continued sense of identity is the common thread that consistently pricks the consciousness of African Americans—the color of their skin. Despite the upward mobility of some African Americans, race remains a significant issue. Suburban, upwardly mobile African Americans are frequently targeted and taunted because of their dual status in America.

They are members of two worlds and adjust to each accordingly. The hidden rage felt by these African Americans because of their skin color has been the forum of *Newsweek*, *Ebony*, and professional journals such as *Social Forces*. Benjamin (1991, p. xix) and DuBois (1903/1990, p. 3) discussed the color line as a dominant issue in the "twilight of the twentieth century" and noted that it would continue to be a significant factor in the lives of African Americans because of their dual status in society. The level of discrimination and discomfort due to race is one that consistently ties African Americans at all socioeconomic levels to the community of origin.

Future Trends in African American Families

African American families may be characterized by determination and struggle. Various societal conditions ultimately will affect future adjustments in family structure. Trends in male–female sex ratios, underemployment, and unemployment are all issues that will have continued impact on African American family structures. These conditions will affect African American women's decision not to marry in greater numbers than in the past (Horton & Burgess, 1992). Female-headed households are likely to represent a significant proportion of African American family structures, along with married-couple families.

African American families have not been immune to the social problems that plague other families, including disproportionate levels of violence (e.g., homicide), drug abuse, and health-related issues. However, there is little indication to suggest that the African American family will deteriorate or weaken, whether defined by traditional or nontraditional family norms. Support strategies, such as the greater use of fictive kin and nonrelatives, will continue to fill a significant void because of ineffective social policies. Indeed, policies designed to "strengthen" family structures among African Americans have not taken full advantage of resources already present within the community, such as churches and community groups.

What is critical for students of the family is the continued challenge to be objective, to explore personal values, and to be willing to examine varying ways of looking at this important topic. I suspect that there will never be complete agreement on any explanation or family perspective. In some cases, the ethnocentric bias of middle-class norms combined with lack of concrete evidence due to limited research has provided sufficient rationale to continue to assume that the nuclear family exists in large numbers in the population. The challenge to the student is to go beyond these biases and critically examine relevant information and analyze it carefully. This approach requires the important step of new and innovative research and theory. A critical approach is necessary because so much of what have learned about African

American families from scholarly sources, combined with stereotyped images in the popular media, has been inaccurate at best. Recent scholarly works are currently providing the stimulus for careful study of one of our most populous groups. We must meet the challenge to become enlightened.

ACKNOWLEDGMENT

Work on this chapter began while the author was a fellow at the Center for Research on Women, Memphis State University. Grateful acknowledgment goes to the National Science Foundation for its support in the Postdoctoral Fellowship Program. Neither the Center nor the Foundation bears responsibility for the content herein.

REFERENCES

Allen, W. (1978). Of Black family life. *Journal of Marriage and the Family, 40,* 117–129.

Amott, T. L., & Matthaei, J. A. (1991). *Race, gender, and work: A multicultural history of women in the United States.* Boston: South End Press.

Asante, M. K., & Mattson, M. T. (1992). *Historical and cultural atlas of African Americans.* New York: Macmillan.

Benjamin, L. (1991). *The Black elite: Facing the color line in the twilight of the twentieth century.* Chicago: Nelson Hall.

Billingsley, A. (1968). *Black families in white America.* Englewood Cliffs, NJ: Prentice Hall.

Billingsley, A. (1992). *Climbing Jacob's ladder: The enduring legacy of African American families.* New York: Simon & Schuster.

Blackwell, J. (1985). *The Black community: Diversity and unity.* New York: Dodd, Mead.

Burgess, N. J., & Horton, H. D. (1993). African American women and work: A socio-historical perspective. *Journal of Family History, 18,* 53–63.

Burgess, N. J. (1994). Female-headed households in African American families: A sociohistorical perspective. In B. Dickerson (Ed.), *Female-headed households: African American women's perspectives.* Newbury Park, CA: Sage.

Cherlin, A. J. (1992). *Marriage, divorce, remarriage.* Cambridge: Harvard University Press.

Collins, P. H. (1990). *Black feminist thought: Knowledge, consciousness and the politics of empowerment.* Boston: Unwin Hyman.

Dalfiume, R. M. (1968, June). The forgotten years of the Negro revolution. *Journal of American History, 55,* 90–106.

Degler, C. N. (1980). *At odds: Women and the family in America from the revolution to the present.* New York: Oxford University Press.

DuBois, W. E. B. (1990). *The souls of black folk.* New York: Vintage. (Original work published 1903)

Frazier, E. F. (1966). *The Negro family in the United States.* Chicago: University of Chicago Press. (Original work published 1939)

From the Ebony Files. (1993, August). *Ebony Magazine,* p. 3.

Gutman, H. (1975). Persistent myths about the Afro-American family. *Journal of Interdisciplinary History, 6,* 181–210.

Gutman, H. (1976). *The Black family in slavery and freedom: 1750–1925.* New York: Pantheon.

Herskovits, M. J. (1990). *The myth of the Negro past.* Boston: Beacon Press. (Original work published 1958)

Holloway, J. E. (1990). *Africanisms in American culture.* Bloomington: Indiana University Press.

Horton, H. D., & Burgess, N. J. (1992, Spring). Where are the Black men? Regional differences in the pool of marriageable Black males in the United States. *National Journal of Sociology, 6*(1), 3–20.

Jaynes, G. D., & Williams, R. M. (1989). *A common destiny: Blacks and American society.* Washington, DC: National Academy Press.

Jewell, K. S. (1988). *Survival of the Black family: The institutional impact of U.S. social policy.* New York: Praeger.

Levine, L. (1977). *Black culture and Black consciousness.* New York: Oxford University Press.

McAdoo, H. P., & Terborg-Penn, R. (1985). Historical trends in perspectives of Afro-American families. *Trends in History, 3*(3/4), 97–111.

Moynihan, D. P. (1965). *The Negro family: The case for national action.* Washington, DC: U.S. Government Printing Office.

Mulira, J. G. (1990). The case of voodoo in New Orleans. In J. E. Holloway (Ed.), *Africanisms in American culture* (pp. 34–68). Bloomington: Indiana University Press.

Omolade, B. (1986). *It's a family affair: The real lives of Black single mothers.* New York: Kitchen Table Women of Color Press.

Oyebade, B. (1990). African studies and the Afrocentric paradigm: A critique. *Journal of Black Studies, 21*(4), 233–238.

Platt, A. M. (1991). *E. Franklin Frazier reconsidered.* New Brunswick, NJ: Rutgers University Press.

Ricketts, E. (1989). The origin of Black female-headed families. *Focus,* pp. 32–36.

Staples, R., & Johnson. L. B. (1993). *Black families at the crossroads: Challenges and prospects.* San Francisco: Jossey-Bass.

Sterling, D. (1984). *We are your sisters: Black women in the nineteenth century.* New York: W. W. Norton.

Sudarkasa, N. (1981). African and Afro American family structure: A comparison. *The Black Scholar, 12,* 37–60.

Woody, B. (1992). *Black women in the workplace: Impacts of structural change in the economy.* New York: Greenwood Press.

CHAPTER FIFTEEN

Poverty and Patriarchy in Latin America

BRON B. INGOLDSBY

It is not possible to make accurate generalizations about an area as large and diverse as Latin America. There are, of course, many different kinds of Latin Americans. However, this chapter will provide some background on family life in the Hispanic world, drawing mainly on the research done in a few key countries such as Mexico and Colombia, and with special focus on how the struggle for economic survival affects that life. It has been reported that 40% of families in Latin America have insufficient income for essential needs, and that another 28% can be categorized as "working poor" (David, 1987). In 1980, 41% of the population was under age 14. Population growth in the Western Hemisphere, and Latin America in particular, has exceeded that of the "Old World" for some time (Stycos, 1968). With this trend continuing, poverty is the way of life for most Hispanic children.

Drawing on census data, Chaney (1984) gives us the following snapshot: In looking at 20 different countries, the most common minimum age for marriage for females is 14. Colombia and Mexico have declared 18 to be the minimum age for marriage for both sexes, but the other countries range from 12 to 16 for females, and 14 to 16 for males. Other research indicates that the average age of marriage for women is about 18, and that these young brides will average more than five children in the course of their married lives (Balakrishnan, 1976).

Chaney also points out that childrearing is still the highest social status available to women. Because of the costs involved, many of the poor cannot afford to marry, and legal divorce is usually difficult to attain. Thirty percent of households are female-headed (similar to households in the United States) and the typical household has 3.5 to 5.3 members.

Especially among the lower classes, consensual unions may significantly outnumber formal marriages. For instance, among poor blacks in Venezuela, 57% of couples are not married, in spite of the influence of Catholicism. These families tend to be matrifocal (mother-centered) and characterized by early motherhood, migration, and poverty (Pollak-Eltz, 1975).

In fact, migration appears to be an important variable for understanding the Hispanic family. Males often migrate to the United States or other places in search of work in order to support their families (Wiest, 1983). This allows the family to live better but puts strains on the relationship. Wives rarely have affairs because if their husbands were to find out, they could beat or abandon their wives. Even though the mother is responsible for the children, the usually absent father is the final decision maker. This pattern holds in Mexico, where patriarchal notions make it difficult for women to support themselves (Chant, 1993).

In other subcultures, such as the black caribs of Guatemala (González, 1983), women change companions fairly frequently in search of economic support. They have also discovered that they can provide for themselves as well as their migrating menfolk can and, as a result, are less likely to look up to males as leaders than they used to.

When the Spaniards came to the Americas, they worked hard to impose their family ideals on the indigenous populations. That ideal was a patriarchal, monogamous, nuclear family (Muñoz, 1983). Before this pressure, there was significant variety among local peoples, including polygyny, cousin marriages, extended clans, and the more familiar patriarchal power and strict separation of tasks by sex (Boremanse, 1983).

Ignorance often goes with poverty, and one example of this is in the area of health. Anesthesia is often avoided in childbirth, as many Mexicans believe that the mother must endure pain in order to be a "real mother." This has nothing to do with the pros and cons of natural childbirth but is related to the biblical idea of women bringing forth children in sorrow. Some attribute miscarriages, and other problems, to *susto*, which means a terrible fright. Even when their health is in danger, some women will avoid birth control because their main purpose in life is to reproduce. Having children is proof of the husband's virility, and using birth control might tempt the wife to have affairs (Haffner, 1992).

So, what is the "typical" Latin American family like? Some research (Ingoldsby, 1980) indicates that psychological intimacy is not as highly valued as it is in the United States. In comparing couples from the United States and Colombia, it was found that high-satisfaction marriages in the United States were correlated with a high level of emotional expressiveness between spouses. This was not true for the Colombian couples, however. Their satisfaction was predicted by having a similar level of expressiveness, be it high, medium, or low. Also, Colombian women and men are equally likely to say what they feel and are at the same level as U.S. males, whereas U.S. females are significantly more expressive as a group than are their male counterparts.

This pattern appears similar to the preindustrial United States, where the marital focus was on agreement between spouses and task completion. As more women in Latin America enter the labor force, it may be that marriages will shift from traditional to more companionate, as has occurred in the United States, where the emphasis is on emotional sharing.

In looking at the literature on Hispanic families, two general types are described. The first, called familism, is the cultural ideal and it describes a close, loving, and religious family. The second type is a result of *machismo*, which is an abuse of patriarchy due in large part to poverty.

FAMILISM

Familism places the family ahead of individual interests and development. It includes many responsibilities and obligations to immediate family members and other kin, including godparents. Extended family often live in close proximity to each other, with many often sharing the same dwelling. It is common for adult children to supplement their parents' income. In many ways, the Hispanic family helps and supports its members to a degree far beyond that found in individualistically oriented Anglo families.

Kephart and Jedlicka (1991) claim that a large majority of Mexican American young people comply with parental rules in the following areas: (1) dating and marriage within their ethnic and religious group, (2) having parental approval and some supervision of dating, and (3) complete abstinence from sexual intercourse before marriage. American-born Hispanics are less likely to insist on the tradition of chaperoning their daughters on their dates, and it is not known how well the children adhere to the no-sex rule. Nevertheless, a positive picture of Latin American family life is painted that includes lower mental illness and divorce rates, greater personal happiness, and a secure feeling about aging.

MACHISMO

Two principal characteristics appear in the study of *machismo*. The first is aggressiveness. Each *macho* must show that he is masculine, strong, and physically powerful. Differences, verbal or physical abuse, or challenges must be met with fists or other weapons. The true *macho* should not be afraid of anything, and he should be capable of drinking great quantities of liquor without necessarily getting drunk (Giraldo, 1972).

The other major characteristic of *machismo* is hypersexuality. The impotent and homosexual are scoffed at—the culturally preferred goal is the conquest of women, and the more the better. To take advantage of a young woman sexually is cause for pride and prestige, not blame. In fact, some men commit adultery just to prove to themselves that they can do it. Except for the wife and a mistress, long-term affectionate relationships should not exist. Sexual conquest is to satisfy male vanity. Indeed, one's potency must be known by others, which leads to bragging and storytelling. A married man should have a mistress in addition to casual encounters. His relationship with his wife is that of an aloof lord–protector. The woman loves but the man conquers— this lack of emotion is part of the superiority of the male (Giraldo, 1972).

Most women also believe in male superiority (Stycos, 1955), and they want their men to be strong and to protect them. According to the dominant cultural stereotype, a man must protect his female relatives from other men because they should be virgins when they marry. Knowing that other men are like himself, the *macho* is very jealous and, as a result, allows his wife few liberties.

The theme of sexual promiscuity and the forces behind it are elucidated in *The People of Aritama* by Gerardo and Alicia Reichel-Dolmatoff (1961). Their anthropological work investigates life in a Colombian village and has the following to say about *machismo*:

> This system of concubinage and short-term monogamous or polygamous unions, already established in the past century, continues today in the same form and is practiced ... by almost all inhabitants of the village. Even among the upper-class placeros who are married as Catholics, there is not a single man who has not at least one illegitimate child from such an ex- tramarital union. Of course, there are some men with rather monogamous inclinations but they are openly ridiculed by all. Sometimes their economic situation obliges them to be monogamous, but the local prestige system does not permit it and other men would call them cowards and weak- lings, and put into doubt their virility. Quite often a man then establishes such extramarital relations only so as not to lose face with his friends and to demonstrate his maleness. (p. 146)

In summary, *machismo* may be defined as "the cult of virility, the chief characteristics of which are exaggerated aggressiveness and intransigence in male-to-male interpersonal relationships and arrogance and sexual aggres- sion in male-to-female relations" (Stevens, 1973, p. 315).

The Biological Model

We will now look at two theories for explaining *machismo*, and then try to integrate them. The first is the biological model.

It is well established that males everywhere tend to be more aggressive than are females. This is one of the few clear differences between the sexes and it appears to have a genetic base (Maccoby & Jacklin, 1974). The male sex hormones, particularly testosterone, seem to be the source of male aggressive behavior, which is one of the two basic characteristics of *machismo*.

The modern theory of sociobiology offers a parsimonious (meaning simple but complete) explanation for *macho* behavior (Wilson, 1975). According to sociobiology, much of animal, and perhaps human, behavior is influenced by the drive for our genes to reproduce themselves. In this refinement of Darwin's basic theory, it is not the survival of the species that motivates behavior but the survival of each individual's own genes. In this unconscious drive for "reproductive success," males may adopt one of two strategies.

The first, which is called the "tournament strategy," is common to most mammals. In it, males fight with each other to control, and therefore to be able to inseminate, as many different females as possible (DeVore, 1979). This neatly explains both *macho* aggressiveness—fighting with other males— and nonexclusive sexual activity—trying to impregnate as many different females as possible so as to enhance one's reproductive success and therefore ensure the survival of one's genes.

The other approach, which is common to the bird kingdom, is "pair-bonding," or "male parental investment." Among species or conditions where the survival of offspring is greatly enhanced if the father stays around to help, we find that males will mate, and stay with, just one female as this results in greater long-run reproductive success. One presumes that females of all species would be pair-bonders by nature, because they gain no reproductive benefits by having many mates but do gain if one remains to help protect and provide for her and her offspring.

DeVore cites evidence indicating that in many societies, human males, like other primates, have tended to be tournament strategists, fighting with other men (homicide, war) in order to control and therefore reproduce with the women. Note, also, that research consistently finds higher rates of non-marital sex for men than for women. This higher interest in sexual variety is institutionalized as well in the many polygynous societies. The *machos* of the world, therefore, are the tournament strategists, and other males are monogamous pair-bonders (Ingoldsby, 1986). Figure 15.1 illustrates this biological model.

The Psychological Model

That *machismo* is an expression of an inferiority complex runs through most of the explanations to be found in the literature. It is, in fact, the most generally accepted theory.

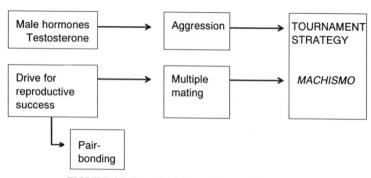

FIGURE 15.1. The biological model for *machismo.*

Most studies on *machismo* are restricted to the lower classes, where it is easier to collect data (Kinzer, 1973). The upper classes are considered less likely to exhibit *machismo* (Stycos, 1965). As research in the United States shows, the lower the social class, the more authoritarian the family. Comparing research from Mexico, Puerto Rico, England, and the United States, Rainwater (1964) found that lower-class males from all areas suffer from job insecurity and compensate for their feelings of inferiority by exaggerating their masculinity and subordinating women.

Machismo may be due to feelings of inferiority, which men try to hide by acting superior. This superior act is accomplished by avoiding feminine traits and emphasizing strong masculine ones. Ramos (1951) and Stycos (1965) both concur that an inferiority complex is the basis of *machismo.*

Adler (1949) found the origins of feelings of inferiority in the experiences of early childhood. Examining childrearing practices should prove illuminating in that case. Many writings of Lewis (e.g., 1959, 1960, 1961) and Stycos (1965) reveal that Latin fathers show a lack of affection toward their sons. The emphasis in the relationship is on respect—characterized by separation, distance, and fear of the father as the domestic legislator whose punishments are really something to be afraid of.

Lewis (1960) cites an example in which one son said of his father: The boys had to pay room and board at home, which was humiliating; he wanted them to be exactly as he was; they could have no opinions of their own, nor could they come to him for counsel. The boys were to grow up to be tough and self-sufficient, while the girls received affection. Lewis (1960, p. 59) reported: "Most children are subdued and inhibited in the presence of their father and remain so well into adulthood."

Giraldo (1972) has developed a circular model to explain the continuation of *machismo* across generations. Father–son relations and childrearing practices and education create inferiority feelings in the boy. These are compensated for by the psychological mechanism of acting superior by way of the cultural institution of *machismo*. This compensation produces cultural traits that are conducive to the father–son relationship and childrearing practices referred to earlier, thus creating the inferiority complex in a new generation, and so on. *Machismo*, then, is a cultural trait to satisfy the psychological need resulting from the inferiority complex in men. The culture provides the way to its satisfaction, looking for feelings of superiority and transmitting them down the generations.

Female Support of *Machismo*

A major support for *machismo*, which deserves separate consideration, is the woman's role in Latin American society. Her role is such that men can carry out their own *macho* roles. Women are submissive and dependent and can even endure physical punishment from men; thus, they can be dominated. They are sexually passive, to be conquered. The cult of virginity—staying virgin and being indifferent to sex until marriage—gives the men female relatives to protect and makes them feel even more *macho* when they do succeed in seduction. Indeed, can there be a *macho* without a virgin to seduce, an inferior to protect, a submissive to dominate, other men to protect one's sisters from? Can males feel *macho* without childrearing practices for boys that create and enlarge sexual differences, making the males feel superior (Giraldo, 1972)?

Stevens (1973) discusses the other side of *machismo*, which she calls *marianismo*. This term refers to the concept that women are semidivine, spiritually and morally superior to men. Her construct refers mainly to the *mestizo* middle class and is principally a division of labor along sex lines due to the existence of certain ideal characteristics for the members of each sex.

Male dominance is, according to this, a myth, in part perpetuated by the women themselves because it preserves their way of life, which has certain advantages for them. Women learn that they must cater to their father's whims and that they are less important than are their brothers. However, they also learn that their mother is venerated and respected by all male family members.

For this sainthood, women must have many children, which also satisfies the *macho* need for offspring. Grown children provide homage for the mother, who socialized her children to believe the pervasive myth of male dominance and female submissiveness. Yet the behavior of the women belies acceptance of this standard for dependent-like behaviors. Women can—if they are subtle—engage in men's activities, which gives them a greater variety of roles than the men have. This system depends on being able to continue to exploit the poorer indigenous members of the society as domestic servants.

Summary

In summary, poor family relations and low income lead to feelings of inferiority (although there is evidence that *machismo* exists among the middle and upper classes as well). In addition, males are taught that they are superior, and they act out this superiority with aggressive and sexually exploitative behaviors. This combination of feeling inferior and acting superior is *machismo*, which leads to a repetition of the same factors that caused it in the next generation. Drawing on the information found in the literature, a flow chart (Figure 15.2) emerges that represents the development and continued existence of the *machismo* construct (Ingoldsby, 1991b).

Can these two viewpoints be reconciled? It is generally understood today that few behaviors or traits can be explained from a totally genetic or environmental viewpoint. Most are a combination, where biology predisposes or sets limits and environment or culture realizes or shapes that potential.

Assuming innate tendencies toward aggressive behavior and sexual variety in males, culture could serve as a "screen," pushing men toward or away from *machismo* (Figure 15.3). With this model, a male's natural inclinations can be exaggerated toward *machismo* if his life situation leads to low self-esteem and if he lives in a culture in which women reward traditional masculine behavior. If, on the other hand, those inclinations are deflected by a positive sense of self—so that there is no need to prove oneself in the arena or the bedroom—and by female refusal to reward *macho* behavior (e.g., no sex before marriage and a female equality movement), the man is more likely to embrace pair-bonding, which is similar to the familism concept. Although these conclusions come from research on the Hispanic family, it is clear that they would apply to any society, because our biology is essentially the same.

For humans, of course, biology is not total destiny. A man's natural predisposition may be to follow other primates with the *macho* tournament strategy, but he can be socialized toward male parental investment. If this is true, the incidence of *machismo* will be less where men are prosperous (self-esteem) and women are liberated (equality). The establishment of a large and

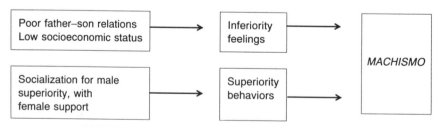

FIGURE 15.2.   The psychological model for *machismo*.

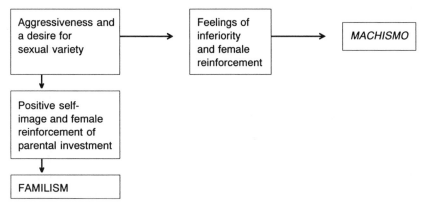

FIGURE 15.3.   The development of *machismo*.

secure middle class, along with principles of equal rights, may be necessary for a shift away from patriarchal patterns.

So far, I have discussed the two prevailing views on the Latin American family. No doubt, they are both correct to some extent, defining different families in a diverse society. My feeling is that familism represents the traditional ideal, still adhered to by many families. Research, however, supports the evidence that *machismo* is also a common style. One of the most negative outcomes of the *macho* family is its treatment of unwanted children, an area that has received some public media attention in recent years.

STREET CHILDREN

Young children living on their own in the streets is a widespread problem throughout Latin America. The United Nations International Children's Emergency Fund (UNICEF) estimates that there are more than 40 million children surviving on their own without parental supervision. Aptekar (1990) claims that this is not as tragic and threatening a claim as it sounds. His research indicates that the children are not so much abandoned as they are encouraged into early independence. This is a natural consequence of poor, matrifocal family life. Most writers have seen it in a more negative light, however.

In one study by Velasco (1992), in which 104 street boys in Guayaquil, Ecuador, were interviewed, the following profile emerged. They ranged in age from 8 to 18, with 13 the most common age (31% were age 13, 15% were age 12, and 15% were age 14). The large majority, 62%, had been on the street for less than 2 years, and on average they had a third-grade education. Over half of these boys had seen their parents within the last year. This is supportive of most research which indicates that these boys are not lost in the sense of not knowing where their home and family is. In order to survive, each boy has one or two "jobs." Selling and begging are common, but shining shoes was the work most often mentioned (38.5%). Another 19% identified themselves as "artists," with about half of them acting like a clown for money and the others being comics or singers. Few admitted to being thieves, although they are feared by the community, especially for violence and stealing car parts. They typically stay within a certain part of town and sleep on the sidewalks or even in the sewers to avoid harassment by adults. That they form their own little communities is exemplified by the fact that four-fifths of them go by nicknames given to them by their comrades.

The Colombian term for runaway or abandoned children who live on their own and on the street is "gamine." There are 5,000 gamines in Bogotá, the capital of Colombia, alone. They are mostly boys (there are girls as well, but they have received less attention by researchers and the media) and they live in small groups, controlling a territory where they sleep at night under cartons or sheets of plastic. They work hard each day to survive by begging or stealing (Bikel, 1979). In a country with no real social welfare program, this is a significant concern.

Becoming a Gamine

There are different types of gamines, and a boy may sometimes progress from one category to the next.

1. *The pregamine:* This boy still lives at home, but his mother works and is seldom there, so after school he spends his time on the street, occasionally staying away from home for 2 or 3 days at a time.
2. *The neighborhood gamine:* This boy lives in the street but has not left the general area of his home and may visit his family from time to time.
3. *The street gamine:* This is the true gamine who has left his home and is learning to live by stealing.
4. *The predelinquent:* These are older boys, who, after about age 14, will become either marginal unskilled workers (selling lottery tickets, etc.) or part of organized crime—stealing with other boys and/or drug using and sales, careers they carry with them into adulthood (de Nícolo, Iremarco, Castrellon, & Marino, 1981).

Why They Leave Home

But why do the boys leave their homes? There are many suggested possibilities: lack of love at home, child abuse, neglect of basic needs due to parental unemployment, too much free time and television, pornography, escaping overwork by parents for the freedom of the streets, and so on. There may be some truth in all these ideas, but parental rejection appears to be the chief cause, and the family dynamic is based on the stress of economic poverty. As de Nícolo (1987) says, "Due to poverty it is impossible to hold the family together."

The predominant pattern resulting in a gamine appears to be as follows: A young man moves from the country to the city in search of a better life. He does not find it—the Colombian economy is structured so that unemployment is consistently and extremely high, creating widespread poverty. He does fall in love with a young lady and they get married. The husband cannot find work, becomes depressed, acts irresponsibly, and eventually leaves his wife and children. They can have sex but they cannot eat (de Nícolo, 1987).

Another man moves in with the children's mother. This "stepfather" (informally so, as divorce and remarriage are rare in Colombia) is not interested in the fruit of a previous union and pushes the boys away, generally when they are 8–12 years old. Almost half (47%) of all street urchins have stepfathers. The child feels rejected and leaves for the street. The mother, for fear of her new husband, does not try to bring her sons back (Bikel, 1979).

Examples of Abuse

The following interview (Bikel, 1979) with some gamine children illustrates the pattern of rejection and abuse:

Daniel, how old are you? Twelve.
Umberto? Fourteen.
Enrique? I was just nine.
Daniel, when did you leave your house? Four years ago.
Why? Because my stepfather beat me a lot. He came home drunk and threw me in the well because my mother complained that we didn't obey her.
Umberto, what was life like in your house? My father liked to drink, so he spent everything he earned on drinks. And he fought a lot with my mother. Then one day my mother told him to leave the house, so he left. We never saw him again. Then one night my mother refused to give me food. She said I could sleep, but she refused to give me food, so I had to leave.
Enrique, why did you leave your house? Because my father beat me a lot.
And your mother? No. She was as helpless as we were. My father worked in the police.
And you don't miss your mother? Yes, I miss her. I miss my mother.
And your father? No. Him no. But my mother, yes.

Ernesto, how old are you? Twelve.
Why did you leave your house? Because my mother and brothers beat me.
Why did they beat you? Because they didn't love me.
How do you like living in the streets? I don't.
How do you live? I am ashamed to say.
Tell us. I beg with the other kids, and we steal.
Does your mother worry about you? She? No.

To summarize, unemployment leads to poverty and desertion, which results in child abuse and neglect, which creates the gamines. Once again, similar conditions can result in abandoned children in any culture of poverty, not just in Latin America.

A Rehabilitation Program

Father Javier de Nícolo is an Italian Catholic priest who has spent most of his life working with the disadvantaged youth of Colombia. Over the past 15 years he has developed a government-supported program for helping the street children. Recognizing that the gamines value their freedom and fear the juvenile detention centers, Father de Nícolo has developed a series of houses that offer acceptance and freedom of choice (Ingoldsby, 1991a).

First, he visits groups of street children and invites them to a downtown building called El Patio. They may come and go there as they please and receive meals, medical attention, and a bath. Close by is another house called Liberia. They may spend the night in a real bed there but must abide by certain rules for the privilege: no drugs or weapons permitted.

The next stage is Bosconia, a true orphanage with meals and dormitories plus educational and vocational training. Finally, for those who desire it and will make the effort, there is La Florida, a self-contained farm, school, living quarters, and metal mechanics workshop. It is estimated that de Nícolo's organization has rehabilitated over 1,000 street urchins (Segundo, 1983).

Father de Nícolo estimates that the average age for leaving home used to be about 10, but now it is about 8. If he does not get to them by the time they turn 14 or 15, it is generally too late to help them. The biggest problem for rehabilitation is the drug trade: first marijuana and now cocaine. The boys become both addicts and pushers, making a lot of money and needing a lot to support their habit.

Casa Las Niñas

When I interviewed Father de Nícolo, he was visiting a home that he ran for girl gamines, called Casa Las Niñas (The Girls' House). There were 75 girls living there, ranging in age from 5 to 15. This is the only facility of its kind in Bogotá for girls, as they are less likely to leave bad home situations for the streets.

Half of those who do are escaping sexual abuse by their "stepfather." They generally leave when they are 10–12 years of age. Tragically, the most likely survival path for girl gamines is prostitution. Girls are less likely to run away as the street life is more dangerous for them, and parents are less likely to turn them away as they are generally more useful around the house, performing domestic tasks, than are the boys.

As with the boys, the girls are responsible for maintaining their home. With adult guidance, they literally make their own furniture, meals, and so on. The facility was clean and impressive. Most impressive, however, were the girls themselves. They left their school rooms when Father de Nícolo brought me out to meet them. They swarmed around him in obvious adoration. He is the only positive male role model and father figure they have and they reciprocate the love he has for them.

At about age 16, Father de Nícolo must send the children out on their own. Although he now spends most of his time looking for employment opportunities for his gamines, they are essentially being returned to the economic structure that created them. The odds are that as adults, they will recreate the poverty-to-abuse cycle leading to more gamines.

FAMILY VIOLENCE

Spouse and child abuse are characteristics of family life that received very little attention in the United States before 1970. Even though violence does not fit our notion of what home life should be, we have since realized that it is often a common aspect. Leading researchers in this area have concluded that family violence is more common in male-dominant marriages and in societies that condone violence in general. Another predictor is the privacy of the conjugal family, which could predispose Western societies to violence, though it is widespread throughout the world (Strauss, 1977). Studies on domestic violence in Oceania (Counts, 1990) attribute it to patrilocal residence and brideprice. Paying for a wife and controlling her environment increase cultural support for male dominance. In one study of 90 different societies, wife beating was found to occur at least occasionally in 84.5% of them (Levinson, 1989).

The serious problem and pervasiveness of family violence in the United States has received considerable attention in recent years. For instance, public polls have indicated that one-fifth of all spouses approve of a man slapping his wife under certain circumstances. More assaults and murders are committed within the family than in any other context. In fact, one-third of all women killed are victims of their husband or boyfriend, and a woman is more likely to kill her husband than she is anyone else (Wells, 1991).

Wife abuse is consistently mentioned as commonplace in traditional Hispanic families. In one study (Straus & Smith, 1989), almost one-fourth of Latino couples experience violence in their relationship; a rate over 50% higher than it was for Anglo couples. This may not be surprising when we realize that the characteristics of *machismo* are some of the same ones mentioned in studies of spouse abuse. One is alcohol. Estimates vary from 40% to 95% of all wife-beating situations being ones in which the husband has been drinking. Another is male dominance, or the man's right to force compliance to his wishes within his family. The last is low self-esteem, often related to financial problems. All these predictors of spouse abuse are aspects of being a macho male (Ingoldsby & Ingoldsby, 1981).

CONCLUSION

The culture of poverty and the rejection by men of children not their own provide the context and tragic results of *machismo*. In fact, it may be that it is poverty that is breaking down the personal dignity necessary for traditional familism and replacing it with the excesses of *machismo*. There is evidence, however, of movement toward what Western clinicians would describe as a more functional, or healthy, family.

A survey of 71 married women in Panama (Stinnett, Knaub, O'Neal, & Walters, 1983) revealed fairly egalitarian beliefs concerning marriage. Large majorities believed that (1) women should have an equal quality education as men, (2) women should receive equal pay for equal work, (3) women are just as intelligent as men, (4) women are just as capable of making important decisions as are men, and (5) a wife should express her opinions even if her husband does not ask for them, and she should voice her disagreements with him.

On the other hand, most agreed that the husband is the head of the family, that the wife must obey her husband, and that the woman's place is in the home (even though 77% of the sample worked outside the home). This indicates a "separate but equal" attitude compatible with the familism construct.

Finally, Hispanic families that rate themselves as "strong" and have a high level of marital satisfaction emphasize the companionate psychological variables over the traditional ones. Casas, Stinnett, Williams, DeFrain, and Lee (1984) collected data from nine Latin American countries using Stinnett's Family Strengths Inventory. Results were virtually identical to studies conducted in the United States.

The most important factors for maintaining a happy family life were (1) love and affection, (2) family togetherness, (3) understanding and acceptance, (4) mutual respect and appreciation, (5) communication/relationship skills, and (6) religion. Wives emphasized love and affection more than husbands did, and husbands were more likely than wives to mention the importance of religion.

There is evidence that a growing number of Latin American families value love and affection in the husband–wife and parent–child relationships more than they do the traditional authority–submissiveness approach. All this bodes well for familism, which avoids not only the abuses of patriarchy but the possible disengagement of Western individualism as well.

REFERENCES

Adler, A. (1949). *Social interest: A challenge to mankind*. London: Faber & Faber.

Aptekar, L. (1990). How ethnic differences within a culture influence child rearing: The case of Colombian street children. *Journal of Comparative Family Studies, 21*(1), 67–79.

Balakrishnan, R. (1976). Determinants of female age at marriage in rural and semiurban areas of four Latin American countries. *Journal of Comparative Family Studies, 7*(2), 167–173.

Bikel, O. (1979) *World: Bogotá, one day*. [Transcript of PBS program produced by WGBH Boston].

Boremanse, D. (1983). A comparative study of the family lives of the northern and southern Lacandan Mayas of Chiapas (Mexico). *Journal of Comparative Family Studies, 14*(2), 183–202.

Casas, C., Stinnett, N., Williams, R., DeFrain, J., & Lee, P. (1984). Identifying family strengths in Latin American families. *Family Perspective, 18*(1), 11–17.

Chaney, E. (1984). Marital status and living arrangements. In *Women of the world: Latin America and the Caribbean* (pp. 99–132). Washington, DC: U.S. Bureau of the Census.

Chant, S. (1993). Family structure and female labor in Querétaro, Mexico. In L. Tepperman & S. Wilson (Eds.), *Next of kin* (pp. 205–210). Englewood Cliffs, NJ: Prentice Hall.

Counts, D. A. (1990). Domestic violence in Oceania: Conclusion. *Pacific Studies, 13*(3), 225–254.

David, P. (1987). Children in despair: The Latin American experience. *Journal of Comparative Family Studies, 18*(2), 327–337.

de Nícolo, J. (1987). [Personal interview]. Bogotá, Colombia.

de Nícolo, J., Irenarco, A., Castrellon, C., & Marino, G. (1981). *Musarañas*. Bogotá, Colombia: Industria Continental Gráfica.

DeVore, I. (1979). *Sociobiology*. Paper presented at the National Council on Family Relations, Boston.

De Vos, S. (1993). Latin American households in comparative perspective. In L. Tepperman & S. Wilson (Eds.), *Next of kin* (pp. 38–43). Englewood Cliffs, NJ: Prentice Hall.

Giraldo, O. (1972). El machismo como fenómeno psicocultural. *Revista Latinoamericana de Psicología 4*(3), 295–309.

González, N. (1983). Changing sex roles among the garifuna (black carib) and their implications for the family. *Journal of Comparative Family Studies, 14*(2), 203–213.

Haffner, L. (1992). Translation is not enough: Interpreting in a medical setting. *Western Journal of Medicine, 157*(3), 255–259.

Ingoldsby, B. (1980). Emotional expressiveness and marital satisfaction: A cross-cultural analysis. *Journal of Comparative Family Studies, 11*(4), 501–515.

Ingoldsby, B. (1986, September). Theory of the development of machismo. *Resources in Education.* (ERIC Document Reproduction Service No. ED 268399)

Ingoldsby, B. (1991a). Street children and family life. *Family Science Review, 4*(2), 73–77.

Ingoldsby, B. (1991b). The Latin American family: Familism vs. machismo. *Journal of Comparative Family Studies, 22,* 57–61.

Ingoldsby, B., & Ingoldsby, V. (1981). The macho male and wife beating. In J. Budke (Ed.), *Proceedings of the Ohio Council on Family Relations Annual Convention* (pp. 48–51). Columbus: Ohio Council on Family Relations.

Kephart W., & Jedlicka, D. (1991). *The family, society, and the individual* (7th ed.). New York: HarperCollins.

Kinzer, N. (1973). Priests, machos and babies: Or, Latin American women and the Manichaean heresy. *Journal of Marriage and the Family, 35,* 300–311.

Levinson, D. (1989). *Family violence in cross-cultural perspective.* Newbury Park, CA: Sage.

Lewis, O. (1959). *Five families.* New York: New American Library.

Lewis, O. (1960). *Tepozlan.* New York: Holt, Rinehart & Winston.

Lewis, O. (1961). *The children of Sanchez.* New York: Vintage.

Maccoby, E., & Jacklin, C. (1974). *The psychology of sex differences.* Stanford, CA: Stanford University Press.

Muñoz, J. (1983). Changes in the family structure of the Pokaman of Petapa, Guatemala in the first half of the 16th century. *Journal of Comparative Family Studies, 14*(2), 215–227.

Pollak-Eltz, A. (1975). Household composition and mating patterns among lower-class Venezuelans. *International Journal of Sociology of the Family, 5*(1), 85–95.

Rainwater, L. (1964). Marital sexuality in four cultures of poverty. *Journal of Marriage and the Family, 4,* 457–466.

Ramos, S. (1951). *El perfil del hombre y la cultura en México.* Buenos Aires.

Reichel-Dolmatoff, G., & Reichel-Dolmatoff, A. (1961). *The people of Aritama.* Chicago: University of Chicago Press.

Segundo, C. (1983, March–April). Priest's faith reclaims Bogota's urchins. *Americas,* pp. 8–23.

Stevens, E. (1973). The prospects for a women's liberation movement in Latin America. *Journal of Marriage and the Family, 35,* 313–321.

Stinnett, N., Knaub, P., O'Neal, S., & Walters, J. (1983). Perceptions of Panamanian women concerning the roles of women. *Journal of Comparative Family Studies, 14*(2), 273–282.

Straus, M. (1977). Societal morphogenesis and intrafamily violence in cross-cultural perspective. *Annals of the New York Academy of Sciences, 285,* 719–730.

Straus, M., & Smith, C. (1989). Violence in Hispanic families in the United States:

Incidence rates and structural interpretations. In M. Straus & R. Gelles (Eds.), *Physical violence in American families: Risk factors and adaptations to violence in 8,145 families.* New York: Transaction Books.

Stycos, J. (1955). *Family and fertility in Puerto Rico, A study of the lower income group.* New York: Columbia University Press.

Stycos, J. (1965). Female employment and fertility in Lima, Peru. *Milbank Fund Quarterly, 43,* 42–54.

Stycos, J. (1968). *Human fertility in Latin America: Sociological perspectives.* Ithaca NY: Cornell University Press.

Velasco, P. (1992). Unpublished study. [Interview with street boys in Guayaquil, Ecuador].

Wells, J. (1991). *Choices in marriage and family.* San Diego: Collegiate Press.

Wiest, R. (1983). Male migration, machismo, and conjugal roles: Implications for fertility control in a Mexican municipio. *Journal of Comparative Family Studies, 14*(2), 167–181.

Wilson, E. (1975). *Sociobiology: The new synthesis.* Cambridge: Harvard University Press.

CHAPTER SIXTEEN

Public Policy and Poverty: A Framework for Analysis

ROSALIE HUISINGA NOREM
SUZANNA SMITH

Several chapters in this book discuss the unequal distribution of wealth, other resources, and power within families and societies (Smith, Chapter 11; Haas, Chapter 12; Balswick & Balswick, Chapter 13; Burgess, Chapter 14; Ingoldsby, Chapter 15). Despite worldwide diversity of cultures, histories, economic systems, and family forms, this pattern is consistent. Across societies, inequities are structured on the basis of social characteristics, particularly gender, class, caste, race, ethnicity, age, and location in the global system. The result is that some individuals or social groups have greater control over a society's resources and greater power or influence over other people.

Often, the product of these social and economic inequities is poverty. Those groups that have the least access to resources such as land, material goods, education, wages, and decision-making authority—women and minorities—are also most likely to be poor.

Some of the authors of this text have called for personal and social change that would result in greater equality and would improve the daily lives and opportunities of women and minorities. Balswick and Balswick (Chapter 13) proposed an empowerment model that would equalize women's and men's power in marriage and lay the groundwork for a social ideology supporting these relationships. Smith (Chapter 11) advised that women's empowerment in society and family is a necessary condition for improving women's lives. Ingoldsby (Chapter 15) suggested that programs that build young men's sense of inner worth could help reduce men's domination and abuse of women in intimate relationships.

Haas (Chapter 12) discussed various social policies that create or restrain opportunities for women to participate equally in industrialized societies. Smith (Chapter 11) reported that international economic policies have detrimental effects on Third World women and suggested that access to important social resources be improved. Burgess (Chapter 14) argued that discriminatory social policies must be corrected to create conditions whereby African Americans can attain adequate employment opportunities in the United States. Smith (Chapter 1) summarized feminist and human ecology theories, which call for actions to alleviate the suffering of subordinated or disadvantaged people. Certainly there is a recognized need for social changes that will improve the lives of the disadvantaged. Yet these are complex problems to understand, let alone to feel confident to do something about. What could we possibly do to begin to alleviate these problems?

In this chapter, we examine the manifestation of social inequality in poverty and suggest that social policy plays a critical role in improving the lives of poor families. We begin by defining poverty and discussing its prevalence in the Third World and the United States. We then respond to previous calls for social change presented in this book by introducing social policy as an essential step in ameliorating poverty and reducing social inequalities. Because there is an extensive literature on family policy in the United States, Europe, and Scandinavia (Aldous, 1990; Kamerman & Kahn, 1988; Levitan, 1990; Zimmerman, 1992), we do not review those policies and programs. A comprehensive review of family policy in the Third World is beyond the scope of this chapter.

Much of our focus is on the development of a model that allows us to conceptualize the social problems in holistic ways and to formulate appropriate policy interventions. We do introduce a framework for policy analysis that enables us to examine poverty and other social issues, the types and levels of policy that pertain to the issue, and potential points of intervention in various social systems. We then illustrate how such a framework could be applied to poverty and related social concerns.

WHAT IS POVERTY AND WHO IS AFFECTED?

Poverty Defined

Poverty is defined as "insufficient resources for an 'adequate' standard of living" (Levitan, 1990, p. 1). To operationalize this definition, the United States has developed a standard, numerical definition of poverty based on the cost of an economy food plan and family size (Levitan, 1990). Unrelated individuals and families (defined as two or more persons related by birth, marriage, or adoption and residing together) are classified as below or above poverty using a numerical index. Thus, poverty rates reflect different consumption requirements of families based on their size and composition (U.S.

Bureau of the Census, 1992). Similarly, other countries (e.g., those in Latin America) have fixed a poverty line based on some estimate of a low-cost, nutritionally adequate basket of common food items (Berg, Hunter, & Lenaghan, 1993).

A number of scholars have questioned the utility and accuracy of a poverty index. They have pointed out that it is difficult to determine a level of income needed to meet a minimally acceptable standard of living because of considerable variation in social wealth, local economic conditions, available informal support, and perceptions of wealth and poverty (Levitan, 1990; Rural Sociological Society, 1993).

In this chapter, we adopt a general definition of poverty rather than referring to an absolute poverty index. A person or family is considered poor if their total earnings from various assets, such as land, capital, and labor, do not allow them to obtain a minimum nutritionally adequate diet and other essential nonfood requirements. This means that in rural areas, poverty is concentrated in households that are landless or have insufficient land or wages. In urban areas, the poor hold unstable, low-paying jobs, usually in the informal sector (United Nations, 1993).

Poverty in the Third World

Poverty is concentrated in Third World countries. Three-fourths of the world's poor live in South Asia and East Asia. This poor population comprises over half (57%) of the population of these regions. Sub-Saharan Africa has the second largest number of people in poverty: Fifty percent of the population live below poverty. In Latin America and the Caribbean, poverty affects 20% of the population (United Nations, 1993).

Of the Third World's poor, about 60% are considered extremely poor. They are barely able to meet their nutritional needs, which in turn makes them vulnerable to disease and weakens their working capacity.

According to the United Nations (1993), poverty increased in the past decade in Africa and Latin America. It decreased in Asia, which can primarily be attributed to improvements in China.

In Latin America, decades of rapid economic growth that had alleviated poverty in the 1970s ended in the 1980s. In 1970, 40% of households were in poverty; at the beginning of the 1980s, 35% lived in poverty; and at the end of the decade, 37% of households and 44% of the population were in poverty.[1] In Latin America, poverty increased mainly in urban areas due to a rise in urban unemployment, a decline in real wages, and the loss of social services that gave the "borderline" poor access to education, housing, and health care. The share of households in poverty in rural areas was stable or decreased. Nevertheless, most of the extremely poor lived in rural areas.

KING ALFRED'S COLLEGE LIBRARY

The available data on Africa are more limited and the patterns less consistent than for Latin America, so it is difficult to provide accurate figures for the entire continent. Some countries have grown rapidly and poverty has fallen, whereas for others poverty has increased. Nevertheless, it is common for poverty rates to be 35% or higher, even where countries' economies are expanding.

In Africa, poverty is the result of rapid population growth, which has increased pressure on limited arable land. Poverty is also the consequence of reduced agricultural yields and output, which have failed to keep pace with the increasing population. In addition, poverty is due to declines in social services, drought, wars, and pest infestations. Finally, poverty is also attributed to failed economic development policies emphasizing industrialization at the expense of agricultural investments.

In South and East Asia, previous progress in alleviating poverty in the region held during the 1980s, although some countries experienced at least short-term increases (e.g., Thailand and China). In many countries, the proportion of the population living in poverty declined from 50–70% to about 20–30%.

These improvements are due to increased employment opportunities in fast-growing economies that give the poor access to employment or some type of remuneration. In some countries, rural development programs have expanded employment in rural areas or introduced new technologies that raised agricultural output, which has had a marked effect on reducing poverty. Also, lower fertility has reduced population pressure on land resources and decreased the number of children dependent on economically active adults in a household.

Third World Women and Poverty

Much of the burden of Third World poverty falls on women. They usually carry more of the workload, are less educated, and have fewer opportunities to engage in remunerative activities. They lack access to health care, social services, credit, inputs, and improved technologies that would enhance their productivity and earning capacity (United Nations, 1993). Because children depend on their mothers for basic needs, children also carry the poverty burden.

Women in poor households are often worse off than men due to gender-based differences in the distribution of resources in the household. For instance, there are *poor women* in families in which the total household income or consumption level is *above* the poverty line. However, there are also *nonpoor men* living in households *below* the poverty line (Jacobson, 1993).

These factors are tied together in ways that make it difficult for many women to avoid or to escape poverty. Low literacy levels limit women's employment opportunities. Women's participation in rural development programs might help them to increase agricultural products or to generate an income, but they are often hampered by a lack of time and energy. Heavy workloads and household responsibilities requiring 15–16 hours a day or more of labor during peak agricultural periods take a physical and mental toll.

The increase in female-headed households is also associated with poverty. About one-third of Third World households are headed by women. In some regions (e.g., rural Africa and urban Latin America), the figure is closer to half. A large proportion are unskilled, illiterate, unemployed, or landless. Their lack of access to resources and the absence of other productive adult family members make it extremely difficult to provide adequately for their households (see Smith, Chapter 11).

Women's poverty places their children in jeopardy. Women are responsible for food production in most of the Third World, producing more than half the food in all developing countries and as much as three-fourths in Africa. Women account for approximately 90% of the time that goes into food processing and preparation after harvest as they prepare raw agricultural products for family consumption and market sale. Women are the primary collectors of fuel and water for cooking; the availability of these resources has a major impact on women's ability to prepare nutritionally adequate meals for their families (United Nations, 1993).

Economic recession and the introduction of structural adjustment programs have also contributed to women's impoverishment. As the public has less disposable income available, demands for goods have decreased, thereby reducing women's income from market sales. Women's income from formal-sector employment has also fallen due to the elimination of jobs, cutbacks in hours, reduced wages, and declines in real earnings. The result for women is decreased earnings, which force them to put more time into income-generating activities and other measures that stretch the household budget to meet subsistence needs. This often means purchasing or growing foods that are easier and faster to prepare but have less nutritional value, cutting back on the number of meals prepared, or shifting production from food to cash crops. The poorest, landless women are often forced to sell their labor to farmers for a meager wage that may or may not meet their families' subsistence needs.

In short, women's health, nutrition, and education have decreased along with the rest of society. However, women in particular have been adversely affected, especially in the countries experiencing the most serious economic problems (United Nations, 1993).

Governments around the world use policy in their efforts to resolve or alleviate the problems of households in poverty. If the goal of a policy is directed at changing things for families, we would probably call it family policy. Thus, family policy may include responses to issues such as fertility, education, health, nutrition, shelter, sanitation, and income.

Governments and institutions do make policy specifically directed at families, but it is important to remember that almost *any* policy has a potential impact on families. There is, therefore, a distinction between family policy and the impact of other policies on families. Even a policy about fertility may have a macroeconomic goal rather than a family goal, although it certainly affects families. There has been fairly extensive research on family policy in many countries, but much less attention has been given to the potential and actual impact of other policies on families. In this chapter, we illustrate one model for analyzing the policy process so that such impacts may be assessed.

Poverty in the United States

The poverty level in the United States has varied over the last few decades but has increased substantially since the late 1970s. In 1960, 22% of the population lived in poverty, whereas by 1969, 12% were classified as poor. Improvements in the last part of that decade have been attributed to the increased availability of jobs and associated declines in unemployment, an increase in real family income, and an increase in special federal programs to reduce the ranks of the poor. Some additional headway was made in the 1970s, and the poverty rate hovered at 11–12% (Levitan, 1990; O'Hare, 1989).

The picture changed after 1978 (O'Hare, 1989). Between 1978 and 1983, more than 10 million Americans were added to the poverty rosters, a 44% increase that resulted in a poverty rate of 15% of the U.S. population (O'Hare, 1989). These changes reflected dramatic increases in unemployment and declines in median family income from 1978 to 1982. Even during the prolonged recovery period of the 1980s, the poverty rate stayed at about 13%, which was higher than any recovery year since the 1960s (Levitan, 1990; O'Hare, 1989). In 1991, the poverty rate for all people was 13.5% and 12% for families (U.S. Bureau of the Census, 1992, 1993).

There has been an increase in persistent poverty, which lasts over a long period of time, compared to episodic poverty, which occurs in spells (Kelly & Ramsey, 1991; Korbin, 1992). Persistent poverty is not evenly distributed among population subgroups. Generally, whites and two-parent families experience transitory poverty, while blacks and children born into poor families face poverty that endures for years (Levitan, 1990).

Much of the recent increase in poverty is due to the difficulty that younger workers have in finding steady and reasonably well-paid jobs (O'Hare, 1989). The number of people looking for jobs has increased, while the number of jobs has declined due to mechanization, automation, and the restructuring of the economy from an industrial base to a service base (O'Hare, 1988; Schorr, 1992). Since 1973, average earnings have stagnated and the declining value of wages relative to inflation has kept many individuals from earning more than a poverty income.

Even those who get a job are not guaranteed an adequate income (Levitan, 1990). About two-thirds of *poor* families with children have at least one wage earner (Korbin, 1992). In 1990, most of the households in poor married-couple families (56%) worked at least part time. Also, about 45% of poor female householders with no husband present were employed. Thus, even though a large proportion of the poor work, some combination of low wages, spells of unemployment, part-time hours, lack of benefits, and large families keeps them in poverty. For the nonworking poor, retirement, illness, and family responsibilities are the most common reasons given for not working (Lamison-White, 1992; Levitan, 1990; Schorr, 1992).

The Face of U.S. Poverty

The incidence of poverty is related to household type, sex, race, age, education, and place of residence. The largest concentration of poverty is in female-headed households. Although this group makes up around a fifth of the U.S. population, female-headed households make up half of poor families (Levitan, 1990; United Nations, 1993). In 1990, the poverty rate for these household types was 33%, compared to 6% for married-couple families (Lamison-White, 1992). Families headed by women are more than five times as likely to be poor as are other families. Single mothers are particularly vulnerable to poverty because only one adult is available to provide an income; wages for women tend to be lower; the parent lacks marketable skills or education and therefore cannot locate steady, well-paid employment; and divorced or separated mothers fail to receive child support from the absent parent (Levitan, 1990; O'Hare, 1989).

Generally there is a higher concentration of poverty among women, indicating an association between gender and poverty that has popularized the term "feminization of poverty" (O'Hare, 1989; Pearce, 1979). Not only has the proportion of female-headed households increased, but women outlive men, creating a large number of widows with meager retirement incomes (O'Hare, 1989).

Poverty rates are higher among minority populations. In 1991, 33% of African Americans and 28% of Hispanics were poor, compared to 11% of whites. The poverty rate for African American families was 30%, for Hispanics it was 26.5%, and for whites it was 9% (U.S. Bureau of the Census, 1992). This means that these minority groups are two or three times as likely to be poor as are whites (Levitan, 1990; O'Hare, 1989).

Regarding age-related poverty rates, there is good news for older adults as a group and bad news for children (O'Hare, 1989). The poverty rate for the elderly (65 and older), which has historically been among the highest in the country, plunged in the last three decades to around 12%. This decline is due to more generous, inflation-proof social security benefits and the growth of private pensions (Levitan, 1990; O'Hare, 1989). Without these benefits, 55% of the elderly would have been poor in 1983 (O'Hare, 1989). In addition, a high proportion of the elderly are concentrated just above the poverty threshold, representing the largest concentration of "near poor" in the country (Lamison-White, 1992). Furthermore, whereas 10% of whites 65 and older live in poverty, this is true for 34% of older African Americans and 21% of older Hispanics (U.S. Bureau of the Census, 1993).

Children now represent the largest single group living below the poverty line (Korbin, 1992). In 1991, 21% of all children were poor. The youngest children are most likely to be poor—23% of children under age 6 live in poverty (U.S. Bureau of the Census, 1993). In large part, children's poverty is tied to the increase in female-headed households (Lichter & Eggebeen, 1992). Children in single-parent families are six times more likely to be poor than those in two-parent families (Levitan, 1990; O'Hare, 1989). As discussed earlier, poor economic conditions and reductions in social programs often make it difficult for female-headed households to rise above the poverty level.

Child poverty is alarmingly high among ethnic groups. In 1990, African American child poverty rates were nearly 50%, and approximately 40% of Hispanic children lived in poverty (Korbin, 1992; U.S. Bureau of the Census, 1993). Child poverty rates are even higher in ethnic families headed by women—63% of African American children and 64% of Hispanic children in single-mother families live in poverty, compared to 42% of children in comparable white households (Korbin, 1992). If we look only at children under age 6, these rates are even higher—69% for African American children, 72% for Hispanic children, and 49% for white children in single-mother households (U.S. Bureau of the Census, 1992). Because people tend to remain poor longer than in the past, poverty is not an isolated event but an ongoing condition of children's lives (Garbarino, 1992). However, African American children are more likely to experience persistent poverty, whereas event-driven poverty is more common among whites (Korbin, 1992).

Poverty is also associated with lower educational attainment. Adults with less than 12 years of education are five times more likely than those with a college education to be poor (Lamison-White, 1992; Levitan, 1990).

Poverty rates in nonmetropolitan areas are higher than in metropolitan areas (16% compared to 12% in 1990). This is due to the outmigration of a younger and better-educated work force from rural areas, the decline in jobs and rising unemployment and underemployment rates, slow economic growth, and falling incomes in nonmetropolitan communities (Dudenhefer, 1994; O'Hare, 1988).

Poverty rates for central cities are generally higher (19%) than those for all other residential areas due to a growing number of poor in these areas and a large exodus of middle-class and wealthier residents (Lamison-White, 1992; O'Hare, 1989; Rural Sociological Society, 1993). These changes have weakened community institutions that formerly buffered economic hardship (Kelly & Ramsey, 1992). If we look at specific population groups, including female-headed households, married-couple families, unrelated individuals (living alone or with nonrelatives), blacks, whites, and the elderly, we find that rural poverty is higher than poverty in metropolitan areas as a whole. Poverty rates for these subgroups residing in rural areas and central cities are about the same, except for blacks and unrelated individuals, who were more likely to live in poverty in nonmetropolitan areas than in central cities (Rural Sociological Society, 1993).

The United States and the International Context

When U.S. poverty rates are compared to those in other industrialized nations, the United States performs poorly. Results of a study of six developed nations indicated that the incidence of poverty in the United States was higher than in Canada, the United Kingdom, West Germany, and Sweden, and lower only than Australia. The United States also led all countries in child poverty (Korbin, 1992; Levitan, 1990).

Further evidence can be found in comparisons of infant mortality rates (IMR) for economically developed countries. Between 1950 and 1985, the IMR ranking of the United States among 20 industrialized nations fell from sixth place to a tie for last. In 1988, the U.S. IMR ranked 19th in the world (Korbin, 1992). When the U.S. black IMR was compared with other nations' rates, its rank was 28. A black child born in Georgia or South Carolina was more likely to die than one born in Czechoslovakia (Rosenbaum, 1992).

One reason for the exacerbated rates of poverty and child poverty in the United States compared to those for other industrialized nations is that low income is closely tied to access to services. In some other countries, all poor families with children receive some income support and are eligible for basic services such as prenatal care and well-child care regardless of income level. However, more than one-fourth of poor U.S. families do not receive any assistance and therefore are unable to afford services (Levitan, 1990).

Compared to the poorest of nations in the Third World, the United States fares well when it comes to the proportion of its citizens living in poverty. For example, the IMR (possibly the most important indicator of the health and well-being of a nation's population) in Angola of 170 per 1,000 live births absolutely overshadows the U.S. rate of 11 per 1,000 (Korbin, 1992; Grant, 1993). In addition, recall that poverty is concentrated in the Third World and poverty rates in many countries are 35% or higher.

Nevertheless, we also noted similarities between the Third World and the United States. Poverty can be attributed to economic downturns that have touched all parts of the globe and have resulted in higher unemployment and declines in real wages. Reductions in social services have moved some families into poverty and have made it increasingly difficult for the poor to meet their basic needs.

In the United States and the Third World, poverty is disproportionately concentrated among women and children due to inequities in social structures that limit women's access to resources. Persons living in female-headed households are particularly vulnerable to poverty. Generally, those who are poorly educated, of minority status, and rural residents are also more likely to be poor than better-educated, majority, and urban dwellers.

Although studies of the demography of poverty isolate descriptors such as sex, age, ethnic status, and rural–urban residence to develop comparisons, in the real world these characteristics overlap. Falling into more than one structural category—such as being a poor woman of color—creates a double or triple burden of gender, race, and class discrimination. Furthermore, those whose profiles are constructed from several categories are particularly likely to experience poverty over long periods. Thus, when we describe the "face" of poverty, we are likely to see those who are at a considerable disadvantage in the social structure. They experience increased vulnerability to social and economic conditions that limit life options, harm their physical and mental health, and have negative outcomes for their children's development.

Yet it is also true that families have resources that enable them to modify the negative impacts of poverty. For instance, as Burgess explained in Chapter 14, informal social support systems in the African American community often make it possible for poor women to meet their subsistence needs. In our discussion of Third World women and poverty, we pointed out that women have responded to unfavorable economic conditions by increasing their work hours and adjusting their meal preparation patterns. It is true that families do adjust in order to survive, but clearly families and children with few resources suffer. Under poverty conditions families cannot do well. Parenting is extremely difficult, health and productivity are compromised, and child development outcomes are poor (Garbarino, 1992; Kelly & Ramsey, 1992; Rural Sociological Society, 1993).

The Ecology of Poverty

Thus far, we have discussed macrolevel contributors to poverty status, including changing economic opportunities, job quality, and structurally defined characteristics such as gender and ethnicity. We have also pointed out that these macroconditions create poverty conditions at the microlevel and have an impact on families and children (Rural Sociological Society, 1993). For instance, being poor is strongly associated with children's academic failure and learning disabilities (Garbarino, 1992; Grant, 1993). Thus, economic cycles, household survival strategies, and family processes are *interdependent*. An understanding of how the macro and micro relate—that is, how the macrocontext affects families and how they respond—is essential for analyzing poverty (Rural Sociological Society, 1993).

We concur with others that social policies and associated services "stand at the nexus of the macro/micro interface" (Rural Sociological Society, 1993, p. 231). Although public policies often are initiated at the national level, to understand their impact on families we need to study how policies are implemented by local institutions and how they affect the household. This is where communities and families interface with public policies and we can begin to alleviate poverty.

The implication of analyzing the macro–micro interface is that a micro-approach that is designed to provide resources to individuals or families will not in and of itself ameliorate poverty. This is because the way that economic and government policies are arranged *produces* "candidates for poverty" who are constantly swimming against the policy tide simply to stay afloat (Schorr, 1992, p. 335). If we want to reduce the number of people in poverty, we have to do something about our policies.

Furthermore, because poor families tend to experience multiple problems (Levitan, 1990), we cannot expect a policy aimed at one problem to improve the situation if other problems are not also addressed (Schorr, 1992). For example, providing job training to welfare recipients to enhance income-earning opportunities will do little to remove them from public assistance if child care is not available; if living in poor and dangerous neighborhoods limits women's movement, undermines their self-esteem, and creates fear for their children; and if reasonably well-paying jobs are not available in nearby communities. In the following section, we look more closely at how we can better understand the macro–micro interface and develop appropriate interventions.

PUBLIC POLICY, POVERTY, AND HOUSEHOLDS

As discussed previously, poverty is a product of social and economic inequities that exist in and between various systems. Policy *connects* the social-cultural (macro) and family (micro) ecosystems. Policy is set and carried out by social and economic institutions and reflects cultural constructions such as laws, values, and norms. Policy also defines what alternatives are available to families and influences the adaptations they make to the environment.

We have constructed a model that identifies specific systems that are part of the policy process, including, from the broadest to the most specific, cultural, political, legal/juridical, institutional, community, small group, and family and household systems (see Figure 16.1).

We can use the model presented in Figure 16.1 to analyze how poverty occurs at any level. For example, we can map the geography of neighborhoods or villages to identify "pockets" of poverty around certain geographically specific areas (e.g., eroded hillsides surrounding shantytowns). We can examine poverty within the household to determine how valuable resources are distributed to women, men, and children.

This intersystem analysis also allows us to look at how various systems levels ameliorate or reinforce poverty at other levels. For example, at the political level, government policies defining the poverty level determine the earnings that make an individual or family eligible for programs offered by institutions (e.g., Medicaid and Aid to Families with Dependent Children).

This brings us to the question of how policy and poverty are linked. We propose that this takes place at the household level, where macrolevel policies and microlevel family processes interface. Here, we begin to define the relationship between policies and households, particularly those households that are at or below the poverty level.

As we think about households, poverty, and policy, we enter a complex maze of various types of policies and numerous interlinking levels of systems. It is possible, however, to set parameters to understand the policy process

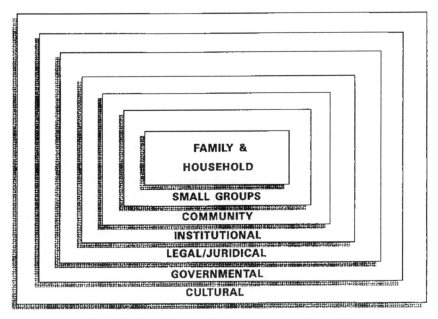

FIGURE 16.1. A framework for intersystem policy analysis.

and the direct linkages between various types of policies and people's lives. This analytical framework helps us to understand these linkages and their impact on households. But first we must first know a bit more about policy.

Types and Levels of Policies

A policy is a plan or set of guidelines that determines decisions and actions. We typically think of policies as set by governments, and many are. However, institutions, agencies, schools, and businesses all have policies. In fact, households and individuals usually have policies about certain things. We hear people make statements such as, "It is my policy to pay all my credit charges at the end of each month." Or, "Our family has a policy that you must call home if you are going to be more than 30 minutes late." Sometimes we might call these "rules," but the idea is that they regulate or govern actions.

Policy functions at different levels, *from the macrolevel to a very micro-level*. These different levels are linked together because their policies influence each other. The intersystem model presented in Figure 16.1 is helpful in identifying linkages between and among various levels of policies. Such linkages become important in analyzing the impact of policy on families and households and understanding relationships between policy and poverty.

A simple illustration of such linkages between levels of policy is the previous example of a family's policy about being late. Individual members of that family will develop or adapt their personal policies about time because of the family's rule or policy. It is this type of linkage we are talking about when we look at more complex policy issues throughout this chapter.

In addition to being concerned about levels of policy, we must be clear about the types of policies we are discussing. We may be interested in economic policy, family policy, educational policy, health policy, and so on. Often, in a more formal sense, if the word "policy" is used without modifiers, the assumption is made that we are talking about macroeconomic policy. Examples include policies that regulate currency valuation, debt levels, public expenditures, and revenue. Macroeconomic policies are set by international institutions and governments and structure a macropolicy environment or context in which *other* types of policies function. The International Monetary Fund (IMF) is a key player in macroeconomic policy. Currency valuation and commodity pricing (components of structural adjustment) are two related types of policies influenced by the IMF.

It may seem like a distant link between international macroeconomic policies and the resulting impact on families and households. The link is difficult to measure, but there is both research-based and anecdotal information that can help us understand what some of the linkages might be. One example serves to illustrate:

> In a slum area of the capital [of Zambia], Lusaka, I met a young woman called Florence. Prior to the debt crisis, she would have been regarded as one of the better-off. Now she is one of the new strata, the *nouveaux pauvres* [new poor], and she was close to breaking point. For four years, prices of basic foods had been rising rapidly and it had become more and more difficult to survive on her husband's salary as a junior clerk in a government office.
>
> Her two children became prone to diseases and in November the smallest developed an acute respiratory infection. The doctor prescribed a course of medicine but the clinic had run out of the drug because the government could only afford enough foreign exchange to import one-seventh of the country's requirements of essential drugs. She managed to find a chemist's shop which could sell her the medicines she needed, but at an exorbitant black market price. The family's food allowances for the week went in a stroke; she had to borrow. . . .
>
> A week later her husband came home with the news that, due to the IMF austerity programme introduced to rescue the economy, the price of maize meal, the staple food was going to double. (John Clark [OXFAM/ UK], at a UN/NGO Workshop in Oxford, September 1987)

(See Gladwin, 1993, for a summary of the research on the impact of structural adjustment policies on women and their children.)

In addition to macroeconomic policies, governments also set, usually at the national level, *sectoral policies* about education, health, social services, agriculture, natural resource use and conservation, housing, and so on. These policies function within the macropolicy context and, if planning is effective, serve as supplementary implementation mechanisms for macropolicies. For example, structural adjustment (a macroeconomic policy), is likely to involve the privatization of a country's public health care system. In order for privatization to occur, it will also be necessary to change policies related to health (sectoral policies).

This approach to policy analysis is based on concepts from systems theories that identify the connections and mutual influences between various subsystems (see Smith, Chapter 1, for a summary of systems theories). As a general rule, if policies at different levels are "nested" or linked, the less inclusive levels may have policies that are more restrictive than the more inclusive levels but may not have policies that are less restrictive. For example, in the United States, a national policy influences policies at the state level. States may not have policies that directly conflict with national policy—or if they do, there may be a penalty. Presently, the U.S. national policy on speed limits on secondary highways is 55 miles per hour. States that do not comply with this policy are not eligible for federal aid for highway construction and maintenance.

Another example is the age of marriage without parental consent. If this is regulated at the national level in a country, a region or state or city may require an older age for marriage without consent but not allow a younger age. The national policy is more inclusive.

Policies are sometimes linked to legislation and are the operational or applied *guidelines* for fulfilling legal requirements. In other instances, policies are regulatory. Legislation may provide regulatory power to government ministries, agencies, or institutions. If so, policy has the *authority of law*. Of course, there are many complexities in the relationships between legislation and policy and many differences among and within countries.

Points of Policy Intervention

This analytical framework helps us to specify points for policy intervention at each system level. Generally, the *cultural level* is not targeted for policy intervention. Culture affects other systems by shaping values and norms related to poverty and wealth, stereotypes about the poor and the rich, and moral judgments about how to deal with poverty problems. Culture is a dynamic system that changes with historical, demographic, economic, and social developments. Nevertheless, culture changes slowly, which makes it a poor target for intervention intended to ameliorate the immediate problems in peoples lives. We must, however, remember that all other levels of systems function within a cultural context.

Policy intervention often takes place at the *political or governmental level*, which may have a vested interest in the status quo and does not represent all stakeholders. The *legal/juridical level* of system is important in policy analysis and implementation. It is through the legal system that policy is interpreted and adjudicated. The *institutional level* of system may control the access of groups and individuals to resources and usually implements policy. It is often a target for policy intervention. We can think of the *community level* of system as a local gatekeeper, with influence on cultural change, and therefore an important target for and source of information about policy issues. Small groups within a community are also an important information source and target. They can help to identify the needs for policy changes and guide policy interventions. At the *family and household level*, policymakers can influence family outcomes and decision making through the kinds of policies enacted and implemented, but the policies *of* families also change as part of their decision-making process.

Later in this chapter, we detail the impact of policies at these various levels and how important these policies are in understanding poverty. First, however, let us look at the policy process.

The Policy Process

The development and implementation of policy is an iterative process. Policy analysis can occur at all stages in the process and should inform subsequent actions. The process outlined in Table 16.1 illustrates the steps taken to develop and implement a policy.

The first step is to define an issue. On a microlevel, for example, if a business or an agency is having problems with employees arriving at and leaving the work site at irregular hours, management will probably establish a policy about working hours. In order to do so, management moves to the second step and examines policy alternatives to address the issue. This means *evaluating the tools* for obtaining information about the issue and *formulating policy alternatives*. How does management know there are problems? Management may, for example, gather information about irregular hours from anecdotal evidence, supervisors' reports, client complaints, or other sources. Policy alternatives could range from setting strict work hours to a flexible but specified schedule for each worker, which would make sure key positions were always staffed at the busiest times.

The third stage in the policy process is to make policy choices. *Choice-making criteria* must be established and *trade-offs between objectives analyzed*. One choice may meet management objectives but be less acceptable to employees, or vice versa.

Once a choice is made, the fourth step, policy implementation, takes place. *Implementation procedures* must be formulated. Perhaps management decided to allow employees to have flexible hours as long as they worked 8 hours each day, 5 days a week, and were at work during the key hours of

---

TABLE 16.1.   The Policy Process

1. *Define issue*
2. *Examine policy alternatives to address issue*
   2.1. Evaluate tools
   2.2. Formulate policy alternatives
3. *Make policy choices*
   3.1. Formulate choice-making criteria
   3.2. Analyze policy trade-offs between objectives
4. *Policy implementation*
   4.1. Formulate implementation procedures
   4.2. Evaluate implementation impacts
5. *Monitoring and evaluation*
6. *What went wrong?*
   What went right? throughout process

Note. Adapted from K. Baum (personal communication, April 14, 1994).

9:30 A.M. to 4:30 P.M. Procedures would have to be developed to make sure necessary functions were being performed at all times during the business day and to schedule each employee's hours. Then an *evaluation of the impact* of the changes resulting from the intervention would need to be conducted.

Monitoring and evaluation of the policy and its implementation occur as a final phase of the first cycle of the policy process. Assessment of *what went wrong and what went right at all phases of the process* begins an iteration that may lead back to any earlier phase, including the definition of the issue.

Before we analyze the policy process, note that establishing a policy does not automatically make changes happen. Programs must be developed that implement that policy. For example, policies that set as a goal the employment of single mothers who are receiving public assistance may establish supportive programs, such as child care and job training, so that women are able to locate and retain adequately paying jobs.

Conversely, programs often are developed without coordinating policies. For instance, groups or individuals in a community may set up certain programs such as food for homeless families without a municipal or community policy to develop such programs. These programs may or may not work effectively. Either way, they are single efforts not linked through a policy-level approach to resolving problems of the homeless. In this chapter, we are discussing a process that would link both policies and programs. The process we describe rarely flows neatly, but it can if policymakers have issue-related policy actions as their goal.

It also important to understand that the policy process provides for the careful integration of research as a basis for policy decisions. Systematically collected research data, whether drawn from an existing data set or gathered for the purpose of informing the policy or program, are important in all policy research. Research data identify new policy issues and are key to formulating logical policy and program alternatives. Choices should be made and trade-offs evaluated through the careful analysis and understanding of such information.

As implementation proceeds, special studies may be needed to assess impact and determine what adaptation in policies or programs needs to be made. Sometimes, implementation may be initiated on a "pilot study" basis before extensive changes are made. Analysis of the impact of policies is a key element throughout the process to evaluate whether the desired goal has been achieved.

Analyzing the Policy Process

So far we have looked at three elements: poverty, levels and types of policies, and the policy process. In order to analyze the policy process and the relationships between poverty and policy, we need to put these dimensions of the policy process together.

Using Table 16.1 as a model, let us examine a hypothetical problem and policy intervention. First, we must identify the type of policy we want to analyze. Suppose, for the sake of example, we are particularly concerned about high rates of chronic health problems and associated high costs of treatment among poor families. Thus we decide to analyze health policy. Next we would ask which levels of policy are critical to understanding the impact of health policy on poor households. Our example will look at the community, institutional, and national government levels. In our hypothetical community, there are no public hospitals, publicly supported clinics, or health care centers. There are also few businesses employing more than 50 people, so few residents of the community have employer-paid health insurance. This is a country and state that do not mandate publicly supported health care.

What is the impact of this situation on the poor? Poor families are differentially affected because they cannot pay for their own health care. Financial assistance (e.g., Medicaid) is limited in terms of what services will be paid for, and the community does not provide any subsidy to assist poor families. Children may not receive adequate preventive or remedial services. Elderly family members may not be able to purchase needed medication. These are the issues in our example. Keep in mind that in a real situation, the definition of the issue would undoubtedly be more complex.

The second step is to examine policy alternatives. What are the tools available to do this? Examples include figures on expenditures for per-unit health care, the number of private facilities and health care professionals, the community tax base, and the level of giving through private funds such as foundations that might be tapped. Also, it will be useful to get information about what similar communities are doing to provide health services. Once such information is collected, we can begin to look at policy alternatives.

Are there any alternatives at the community level? Again, for sake of example, let us think of two options. One used by many small communities is to pass a bond to build or support public facilities. Perhaps the community could explore the possibility of publicly supporting services purchased from private health care providers. These become policy interventions because a community decides to take action to solve a problem. Community guidelines for action are modified; community policy is changed.

In our example, the next level is the institutional level. In this case, we can focus on at least two types of institutions, business and health care. The tools for analysis include some of the same ones we used at the community level, cost of health care and number of facilities. In addition, we would want to know the cost of various group health insurance plans and how much employers were willing to pay in terms of employee benefits. Some possible alternatives might include employee-paid group health insurance available through employers and extension of partial benefits to hourly or part-time employees. Health care institutions should examine care costs to see whether profits could support some public health care services.

As these policy alternatives at different levels are identified, we move quickly to the third step in the policy process, making policy choices. Formulating choice-making criteria and analyzing policy trade-offs are perhaps the most critical part of this analysis process. Will our hypothetical community make its choices on criteria designed to maximize health care for poor households or on criteria designed to keep the cost of private health care down? There are many trade-offs either way. There will be "winners" and "losers" regardless of choices.

Therein lies a universal problem for policymakers. Are the criteria for choice based on maximum benefit for the larger community or society at the expense of the disadvantaged? Or, does the larger community pay a price to benefit those in poverty? As this is written, in mid-1994, our example of health care policy is being widely debated at the national level in the United States. The criteria for policy choice making and the perceived policy trade-offs are the basis for the debate.

This brings us to the fourth step, policy implementation. Choices can be made but the selected actions must be taken. If a community decides to implement a policy to provide community-based public health care, how will this be done? Will existing groups in the community take the responsibility? Will there be a need for new institutional structures? If so, how will they be instituted, maintained, and supported? What impact will implementation efforts have on the community and its households? For example, do we see a reduction in preventable childhood disease, infant mortality, or chronic illness? Does the price per unit of health care go down? How do particularly vulnerable groups—women, children, minorities, and the elderly—respond?

The possible answers to such questions—that is, what would be considered success or failure—must be thought through carefully before policy implementation. Then the outcomes must be monitored and evaluated throughout the process, as indicated by step 5 in the policy process. Step 6 reminds us that policy analysis means constantly asking "What went wrong?" and "What went right?" This is essential if we are to make progress in designing and implementing the best possible policy alternatives at all levels to respond to the needs of poor households. Indeed, the same analysis process we have used here to think about policy and poverty can be used to guide policy decisions and to consider their potential impact on all households and families. You may wish to create your own hypothetical example to test this process.

A POLICY ANALYSIS EXAMPLE

We can follow the policy analysis process through a specific example in the country of Guatemala. In January 1991, a national conference was held in Guatemala to bring together leading policymakers to focus on the policy issue of girls' education and the role it plays in the economic and social development of a country. Policy alternatives were examined through the use of several important sources of information, or evaluation tools.

Based on information gathered from various Guatemalan data sources, the following generalizations were made (First National Conference, 1991).

1. There is a strong relationship between girls' education and country indicators of education, health, employment, and family welfare.
2. There is a strong inverse relationship between women's primary education and age at first marriage, fertility rates, and infant mortality.
3. Investment in girls' education has a long-term, positive impact on family income and well-being.
4. There is an inverse relationship between family income and rural residence and level of girls' education.

In addition to the Guatemalan-specific data, more general information about girls education was also considered. For example, most country statistics show that women's education is a critical factor in increasing women's level of employment and the number of women participating in a country's economic development. Studies also indicate an improvement in children's health and nutritional status when women earn and control a higher portion of the household's income. An examination of data supporting the above statements and a discussion of how education for girls is linked to other indicators of improved quality of life for families (e.g., health, nutrition, and income) led policymakers to formulate policy alternatives to improve girls' education.

Policy choices were identified at various systems levels, as illustrated in Table 16.2. At the national government level, a *national emergency plan for the education of girls* was proposed. The president of the republic later declared girls' education in Guatemala a national emergency. At the institutional level, public and private institutions convened to form a national *multisectoral commission* entrusted with developing a plan. This commission is making more detailed policy choices and examining choice-making criteria. The conference declared that, among other things, "the educational system must be flexible and oriented toward an education that is practical and useful for work and daily life, and that programs must be directed primarily toward girls" (First National Conference, 1991, p. 57). This declara-

TABLE 16.2. Analysis of Policy Process—Policy Issue: Enhanced Quality of Life of Families/Households in Guatemala

The policy process	Family/household level	Small-group level	Community level	Institutional level	Legal/juridical level	National/state government level
1. Define issue	Girls are responsible for domestic and agricultural work. Family poverty is a factor in whether or not girls stay in school. By age 15 there is only 1 girl for every 2 boys enrolled in primary school in rural areas.	Guatemala is the only country in the region where the majority of women are not literate.	Little importance has traditionally been placed on girls' education.	Girls do not receive an equitable portion of educational resources.		There is a strong relationship between girls' education and social and economic development.
2. Examine policy alternatives						
2.1. Evaluate tools	School location, hours, and programs influence girls' enrollment.	Female teachers act as role models.	Community-based program to change perceptions of education for girls will be implemented.	Schools must have flexible, practical programs including curricula that eliminate gender and ethnic discrimination.	All children must have the right to an education.	Education for girls and boys is a national priority.
2.2. Formulate policy alternatives	Provide all families with easy access to schools. Books, and other resources will be made available.	Train and recruit female teachers in all fields at all levels.	Interventions will be made at the community level to promote a positive image of educating girls and the subsequent benefit to families.	Programs and curricula will be evaluated and modified accordingly.	There will be no legal barriers to girls' education.	A national emergency is declared for girls' education.
3. Make policy choices						
3.1. Formulate choice-making criteria	Assess long-term benefit versus short-term cost.	Same (there may be additional specific trade-offs).	Same.	Same.	Same.	Same.

372

3.2. Analyze policy trade-offs	Other services to families may have fewer resources.	Changes may challenge status quo.	Community norms may be changed.	Changes are necessary in private and public institutions, some other program priorities may be changed, institutional structures and internal policies may change.	Resources may be diverted from other programs.
4. Policy implementation					
4.1. Formulate implementation procedures	Make sure families know which educational resources are available.	Involve local groups such as church groups, and cooperatives. All communities have existing groups—make sure the active ones are included.	Assess existing educational facilities and resources in communities, and identify needs.	Work through inter-institutional commission.	Allocate resources and maintain public support.
4.2. Evaluate implementation impacts	Record number of families contacted.	Record number of groups that participated. Assess follow-up provisions.	Completed assessment data.	More specific policy guidance from commission's working.	Resources made available and public support elicited and maintained.
5. Monitoring and evaluation					
6. What went wrong? What went right?					

tion is one of the choice-making criteria for more specific policy actions. In this example, conference participants analyzed policy trade-offs and decided that the costs for the country as a whole were lower over the long term if girls' education was a top priority.

The first two steps in policy implementation were the declaration of a national emergency and establishment of the commission. As further implementation steps are taken, monitoring and evaluation plans will be developed. Obviously, over the long term, indicators will include an improvement in children's health and nutrition, improved economic well-being of families, increased age of first marriage, and lower fertility rates. What went wrong and what went right can be addressed in the shorter term by examining school enrollment and literacy statistics.

Table 16.2 puts this analysis in a framework that shows how the various levels relate to one another. The specific examples within the levels of the framework are, to an extent, hypothetical; they are not the exact interventions made in Guatemala since the process is still under way. Note that the table shows that not all levels are always involved. In this case, no legal constraints were initially identified, so no implementation steps are identified at that level.

Of course, using this analysis in a real situation would result in a much more extensive listing of alternatives. Also, a more complete analysis that included steps 5 and 6 would be possible with a longer-term perspective.

This example illustrates how a policy issue can be examined not only within various levels but in terms of its potential impact *across sectors*. The analysis focuses on the *linkages* between education, health, nutrition, income, and overall social and economic development. The broad-ranging potential impact of changing educational policy is almost overwhelming. Whereas the issue could have been defined as simply related to school enrollment and have had a much more limited effect, in this case the policy addressed the interlinking aspects of a defined social issue, with potentially powerful results for girls and families. This example is illustrative of the policy process that might be used to develop integrated policies to address other social problems.

CONCLUSION

In this chapter we described trends in poverty for families in the Third World and the United States and the characteristics of those who seem to be particularly vulnerable to poverty. Our findings reinforced what previous chapters suggested regarding the organization of inequality: Poverty is structured on the basis of gender, race/ethnicity, marital status, age, and rural/urban residence.

Poverty is usually discussed as either a macro- or microlevel phenomenon, but an accurate analysis of the impact of poverty on families and appropriate strategies for intervention depend on an understanding of the *interface* between these levels. We proposed that *policy* connects macro- and microsystems, linking macrolevel processes (e.g., economic recessions) and microlevel family processes (e.g., preventive health practices). Policies influence the alternatives families have available and select as they make adaptations to the environment.

We presented a model that identifies specific and multiple systems that affect families and therefore must be part of the policy process. We analyzed the use of the policy process at various systems levels to ameliorate family poverty and contributing social conditions.

Various chapters in this text discussed other, difficult areas of family life that could be improved through proper national and sectoral policies. Although the framework presented here was applied specifically to poverty, it can also be used to assist in planning other types of interventions. For example, the framework could be used to analyze the problem of abandoned street children in Latin America (Ingoldsby, Chapter 15). Using the policy planning process, we could propose alternative interventions, (e.g., school programs and job-creation programs for low-skilled workers) and evaluate their success in alleviating not only poverty but abuse in family relationships. We could also use the model as a comparative framework for planning policy interventions. For example, we might identify long-term care of the elderly as a social problem and examine the various approaches used by other societies to deal with this problem at the family, community, and institutional level (see Meredith & Abbott, Chapter 10, for an example from China).

Unfortunately, there are certain aspects of the policy process we have not been able to address at length. We have emphasized macrolevel societal responses rather than microlevel family processes and outcomes. Other writers (Eshleman, 1994; Scanzoni, 1983) include a focus on a "mesolevel" as an alternative between the microlevel and macrolevel, a conceptualization that is implicit in the model we presented but which requires further elaboration.

Additional work needs to be done to clarify the transaction between family- or household-level characteristics and processes and policies and programs. In particular, future work should examine variations in family needs and policy impact depending on family life-cycle stage; family composition, including gender, age, and marital structure; and ethnic patterns of support. For example, policies and related programs could be strategically designed to supply resources at critical junctures in the family life cycle, particularly during childbearing and young adulthood when poor families are vulnerable to dissolution and financial hardship and have difficulty providing guidance to their children (Aldous & Hill, 1969).

Policies can enable families to better meet their needs when family responsibilities are at a maximum if the policies take into account the following: stage of the family life cycle, the needs and resources of poor families, cultural and ethnic patterns of support, household marital structure (e.g., female-headed or married-couple), the responsibilities of women for caring for children and elderly parents, and gender and age differences within the household that affect access to and distribution of resources (see, e.g., Aldous & Hill, 1969; Burgess, Chapter 14, this volume; Mattesich & Hill, 1987). Clearly, it will be no small task to further refine the model and carry out related research to examine the impact of policy at the family level. In the meantime, however, this chapter represents a start toward that goal.

In summary, we have presented poverty as one social problem that is both created and ameliorated at various systems levels. We have proposed a framework that allows us to conceptualize poverty in reference to the multiple systems that impact families and to determine the potential points of intervention that will allow us to alleviate poverty and other social problems.

NOTE

1. The discrepancy between the two poverty estimates, one for Latin America and one for the Caribbean and Latin America, can be attributed to methodological differences in definitions of poverty. In the first instance, for the purpose of estimating poverty across world regions, poverty was defined as a yearly income of $370 or less. In the second case, country-specific poverty lines, not a universal cutoff point, were established for specific Latin American economies, and the population living below those lines was identified. The regional figure represents an aggregation of the results for individual countries (United Nations, 1993).

REFERENCES

Aldous, J. (1990). The impact of workplace family policies [Special issue]. *Journal of Family Issues, 11*.

Aldous, J., & Hill, R. (1969). Breaking the poverty cycle: Strategic points for intervention. *Social Work, 14*(3), 3–12.

Berg, E., Hunter, G., & Lenaghan, T. (1993). *Structural adjustment and the poor in the 1980s: Trends and social conditions in Latin America and Africa.* Bethesda, MD: DAI.

Dudenhefer, P. (1994). Poverty in the rural United States. *The Rural Sociologist, 14*(1), 4–25.

Eshleman, J. R. (1994). *The family* (7th ed.). Boston: Allyn & Bacon.

First National Conference. (1991, January). *Educating girls: Achieving the development of Guatemala.* Guatemala City, Guatemala.

Garbarino, J. (1992). The meaning of poverty in the world of children. *American Behavioral Scientist, 35*, 220–237.

Gladwin, C. (1993). Women and structural adjustment in a global economy. In R. S. Gallin, A. Ferguson, & J. Harper (Eds.), *The women and international development annual* (Vol. 3, pp. 87–112). Boulder, CO: Westview Press.

Grant, J. P. (1993). *The state of the world's children 1993.* Oxford, England: Oxford University Press.

Jacobson, J. L. (1993). Closing gender gap in development. In L. R. Brown (Ed.), *State of the world 1993* (pp. 61–79). New York: W. W. Norton.

Kamerman, S. B., & Kahn, A. J. (1988). Social policy and children in the United States and Europe. In J. T. Palmer, T. Smeeding, & B. B. Torrey (Eds.), *The vulnerable* (pp. 351–381). Washington, DC: Urban Institute Press.

Kelly, R. R., & Ramsey, S. H. (1991). Poverty, children, and public policies: The need for diversity in programs and research. *Journal of Family Issues, 12,* 388–403.

Korbin, J. E. (1992). Child poverty in the United States. *American Behavioral Scientist, 35,* 213–219.

Lamison-White, L. (1992). *Income, poverty, and wealth in the United States: A chartbook* (U.S. Bureau of the Census Current Population Reports, Series P-60, No. 179). Washington, DC: U.S. Government Printing Office.

Levitan, S. A. (1990). *Programs in aid of the poor* (6th ed.). Baltimore: Johns Hopkins University Press.

Lichter, D. T., & Eggebeen, D. J. (1992). Child poverty and the changing family. *Rural Sociology, 57,* 151–172.

O'Hare, W. P. (1988, July). The rise of poverty in rural America. *Population trends and public policy* (Occasional Papers Series No. 15). Washington, DC: Population Reference Bureau.

O'Hare, W. P. (1989). Poverty in America: Trends and new patterns. *Population Bulletin, 40*(3), 1–45.

Pearce, D. (1979). Women, work, and welfare: The feminization of poverty. In K. Feinstein (Ed.), *Working women and families* (pp. 103–123). Beverly Hills, CA: Sage.

Rosenbaum, S. (1992). Child health and poor children. *American Behavioral Scientist, 35,* 257–289.

Rural Sociological Society. (1993). *Persistent poverty in rural America.* Boulder, CO: Westview Press.

Scanzoni, J. (1983). *Shaping tomorrow's family: Theory and policy for the 21st century.* Beverly Hills, CA: Sage.

Schorr, A. L. (1992). Ending poverty: The children's hour. *American Behavioral Scientist, 35,* 322–339.

United Nations. (1993). *Report on the world social situation 1993.* New York: Author.

U.S. Bureau of the Census. (1992). *Statistical abstract of the United States 1992.* Washington, DC: U.S. Government Printing Office.

U.S. Bureau of the Census. (1993). *Statistical abstract of the United States 1993.* Washington, DC: U.S. Government Printing Office.

Zimmerman, S. (1992). *Family policies and family well-being.* Newbury Park, CA: Sage.

STUDENT EXERCISE BANK,
EXERCISE GUIDELINES
FOR THE INSTRUCTOR,
AND APPENDIX

Courtesy Robert Thorpe.

Student Exercise Bank

This collection of exercises is designed to develop students' awareness of their own perspectives on the major topics included in the text. These activities are organized according to the book's major sections: Foundations of Comparative Family Studies, Family Variation, Family Development, Gender and Family Relations, and Social Inequality in the Contemporary World. The instructor will lead students through these activities at the appropriate time in the term.

PART I: FOUNDATIONS OF COMPARATIVE FAMILY STUDIES

Exercise 1: The Arias Family

The following exercise is designed to help you better understand the concepts presented in Chapter 1. You will analyze one family's situation using the perspective of selected family theories. This exercise demonstrates how theoretical perspectives shape the way we think about and study families. Read the following case. Then follow the instructions for the exercise after the case.

José and Ramona Arias live in a rural area of Costa Rica. They are 43 and 39, respectively, and have been married for 21 years. They live in the same village in which they were born; both of their extended families live nearby. The couple has four children: Christina, age 16; Maria, 14; Lilianna, 11; and Frederico, 9. After finishing primary school, Christina began working in a packing shed at a nearby pineapple plantation, but she still lives at home. The three youngest children are in school. José tends to favor Frederico and is exceedingly proud to have a son.

The Arias family earns a living from agricultural production, primarily from coffee and tobacco. Almost all their products are destined for foreign markets.

José employs a few men who assist him in his fields year-round. During peak times of the production cycle, José hires a few day laborers looking for some kind of work.

Ramona does not work in the fields at all, but she does prepare food for the laborers. She also handles all the household and child-care duties. Although José loves his wife and children, his time with them is limited to evening meals and church on Sunday. During the week he frequents a café where he socializes with his men friends.

Ramona considers José a good husband because he provides for the family and spends time with them whenever he can. As far as she knows, he does not cheat on her. The family has been able to make a better living than their parents did, and Ramona credits this to José's good business sense and frugality. Indeed, José constantly reminds Ramona of the need to conserve money and resources. A few times, when he believed that she was spending money "frivolously," José hit Ramona and angrily demanded that she be more careful with "his" money. At these times, Ramona turns to prayer, asking God's forgiveness for both José and herself.

Recently, the family has had another type of crisis to cope with, Christina's pregnancy. Although several of Christina's friends became pregnant, Ramona and José did not expect this of their daughter. They have told no one, not their parents, friends, or priest, about this situation.

José did confront the young man's parents, telling them how irresponsible and disrespectful their son Ernesto is. They were apologetic but said, "After all, what can we do? What is done, is done." José wondered bitterly what he could have expected from those people. Ernesto's father works on the plantation, makes little money, and spends it all on beer. José knows little about the mother—he and Ramona rarely see her in church. They have heard that she sometimes works as a domestic for the plantation managers. José never approved of Christina seeing Ernesto.

Now Ernesto refuses to take any responsibility for the child. He plans to move to the city to look for work and a more exciting life than the one here in the village. José angrily confronted Ernesto, accusing him of taking advantage of Christina. José tried to force the young man to marry her, to no avail. Since then, Ernesto has not been seen near the house or anywhere Christina normally spends time. José has been cold and distant from his daughter.

Ramona urges her husband to control his temper and tries to soothe Christina's feelings of fear, hurt, and rejection. Ramona expects that when the baby comes she will have responsibility for child care while Christina returns to her work at the plantation. Ramona considers this her duty as a mother and grandmother, as well as her destiny, like the women in the generations before and after her. However, Ramona vows to insist that the younger girls go on to high school or some other training so they can find other opportunities outside this village and its traditions.

Instructions for the Case Study Analysis

Analyze the case using two of the following theoretical frameworks.

Structural–functionalism
Family systems
Human ecology
Family development
Symbolic interactionism
Exchange
Feminism
Phenomenology

To conduct your analysis, answer the questions below.

1. What aspects of the Arias family's life does the theory tell you to focus on? For example, if you were using symbolic interactionism, the theory would guide you to examine the meanings individuals gave to their interactions.
2. How do the aspects of family life defined by the theory emerge in the Arias family? For example, if you are using structural–functionalism, you would focus on the husband's and wife's instrumental and expressive roles.
3. What aspects of this family's life is the theory *unable* to address? For example, exchange would not focus your attention on the emotional dynamics of the family's interactions.
4. Which one of the two theories you chose does the better job of representing this family, in your opinion? Why?

Exercise 2: Comparative Family Research Study

This exercise is designed to help students apply the concepts covered in Chapters 1 and 3. Students select a theoretical framework and conduct a comparative research study of (1) intergenerational relationships or (2) gender roles. To conduct your study, follow the steps listed below:

1. Read the descriptions of the two topics and the research questions. Select a topic for your project.
2. Follow your instructor's directions for completing the research project.

Topic One: Intergenerational Relationships

There has been tremendous growth of the world's elderly population and the number of elderly is expected to continue growing rapidly into the next century. The fastest growth of the elderly population is in the Third World. Nearly 60% of the world's elderly live in developing countries. This proportion is expected to increase to 72% by 2020 (Torrey, Kinsella, & Taeuber, 1987).

As longevity has increased, so has the number of living generations in families. Now three, four, and five generations of family members may be living. These "intergenerational relationships" can be an important dimension of family life. For many families throughout the world, grandparents—and especially grandmothers—provide help with child care and household finances when needed (Brubaker, 1990).

Recent research has called attention to possible ethnic, racial, or cultural differences in grandparents' roles. For example, in African American families in the United States, elderly adults occupy a highly respected and significant position and often interact regularly with grandchildren. They are more likely than European Americans to live in three-generation households and to provide considerable emotional and instrumental aid to adult children and grandchildren (Taylor, Chatters, & Jackson, 1993; Taylor, Chatters, Tucker, & Lewis, 1990).

Other research shows that in many cultures, the elderly traditionally hold a place of prestige and authority. However, in countries undergoing rapid urbanization and industrialization, there may be tension between younger and older generations as "traditional" and "modern" value systems come into conflict (Chaney, 1990). Similarly, for some immigrant young people who want to assimilate into U.S. culture, grandparents may be a source of embarrassment for their "old-fashioned" (i.e., traditional) beliefs and practices (Vega, 1990).

Research Questions

The purpose of this project is to compare intergenerational relationships in different cultures. You may choose one of two options: (1) Select two countries in the world for a library research project, *or* (2) conduct a case study of a minority or immigrant family in the United States (e.g., Asian/Asian American, Native American, African American, or Hispanic).

Option A: Library Research on Two Countries. Use library materials to review the literature on grandparents'/elderly roles in two countries. One country should have a growing elderly population (e.g., Japan) or a history of reverence for older adults (e.g., China). Answer the following questions.

1. What are the traditional roles of grandparents in both cultures. What are the differences between grandmothers' and grandfathers' roles and degree of involvement with grandchildren?
2. How has the grandparent role changed in both countries in the past 10–20 years? Why have these changes occurred (e.g., high mobility of younger generations or changing value systems)?
3. How have the changes you identified in items 2 and 3 above affected intergenerational relationships between older and middle, and older and younger generations?

Option B: Case Study of Minority or Immigrant Population in the United States. This option gives you hands-on research experience. Before you begin your study, familiarize yourself with the research literature on immigrant families or the minority population you selected. This knowledge is important background before you begin.

Conduct a case study of intergenerational relationships in one minority/immigrant family in the United States. Interview family members from the older, middle, and younger generations. Find the answers to the following questions.

1. What is the traditional role of grandparents in the family's country of origin? What are the differences between grandmothers' and grandfathers' roles and degree of involvement with grandchildren?
2. How is the grandparent role in the United States similar to or different from the role the grandparent(s) in your study would traditionally play in their country of origin?
3. How does each generation feel about its relationships? What are the sources of tension? What would each generation change about its relationships if it could?

Topic Two: Gender Roles

Women worldwide have certain things in common. They are almost always responsible for the fundamental aspects of family life, including child care, family health, and household care and management (Brydon & Chant, 1989; Thompson & Walker, 1989).

Women differ in their degree of participation in labor force activities. This depends on a number of opportunities and constraints, such as available employment; women's level of education and training; their family income; societal, family, and personal attitudes toward women's employment and family roles; religious doctrines and cultural traditions; and child-care or elder-care responsibilities. Decision making within families also varies.

In some cultures or classes, men are the primary decision makers, whereas in others husbands and wives share some decisions (Brydon & Chant, 1989).

Women from agriculturally based economies are less likely than their sisters from industrial nations to be employed in wage-earning jobs outside the home (United Nations, 1991). However, most women have ways of earning some cash for household expenditures, such as market sales of homegrown vegetables, contracting with export companies to produce handmade crafts or selling these at roadside markets to tourists, or doing piecework in their homes—sewing parts of garments for later assembly and market sales.

In many families in industrialized as well as developing nations, traditional gender roles are changing. This often creates tension in families, as men and women struggle to negotiate and to redefine their family responsibilities while meeting their individual needs and aspirations.

Research Questions

The purpose of this exercise is to compare women's and men's work and family responsibilities in different cultures. You may choose one of two options: (1) Conduct a case study of one family not of U.S. origin, *or* (2) design a research study of gender roles in two countries in two different world regions. For *either* option, answer the questions that follow.

Option A: Case Study of a Family. This option gives you hands-on research experience. Before you begin your study, familiarize yourself with the research literature on gender roles in the country or countries and world region you plan to study. Identify one family not of U.S. origin and interview both the husband and the wife.

Option B: Research Proposal. This option allows you to plan a research project to learn more about gender roles in a country or countries. This will involve identifying a study sample, collecting data, and overcoming problems you might encounter as you attempt to answer the questions below. Work with your instructor to plan this project.

1. What are the family responsibilities of husbands and wives from the country or countries you selected for study? What are the religious, economic, and social roots of gender roles in family and employment? (Note that in some countries there may be differences among ethnic groups and these should be identified.)
2. How are these men and women involved in income-generating activities within or outside the home?

3. Who (husband, wife, or both) is responsible for decisions about household tasks? Household expenditures? Children's health or activities? Women's income-generating activities and men's income-generating activities?
4. Are husbands' and wives' traditional responsibilities and attitudes toward men's and women's roles changing?

References and Suggested Readings

Women-Headed Households

Brydon, L., & Chant, S. (1989). *Women in the Third World.* New Brunswick, NJ: Rutgers University Press.

Crummet, M. (1987). Rural women and migration in Latin America: Research findings and future directions. In C. D. Deere & M. Leon de Leal (Eds.), *Rural women and state policy: Feminist perspectives on Latin American agricultural development* (pp. 239–260). Boulder, CO: Westview Press.

Palmer, I. (1985). *The impact of male out-migration on women in farming.* West Hartford, CT: Kumarian Press.

Richards, L., & Schmiege, C. (1993). Problems and strengths of single-parent families: Implications for practice and policy. *Family Relations, 42,* 277–285.

Intergenerational Relationships

Brubaker, T. (1990). Families in later life: A burgeoning research area. *Journal of Marriage and the Family, 52,* 993–1014.

Chaney, E. (1990). *Empowering older women: Cross cultural views.* Washington, DC: American Association of Retired Persons.

Taylor, R., Chatters, L., & Jackson, J. (1993). A profile of family relations among three generations of black families. *Family Relations, 42,* 323–332.

Taylor, R., Chatters, L., Tucker, M. B., & Lewis, E. (1990). Black families. *Journal of Marriage and the Family, 52,* 993–1015.

Torrey, B., Kinsella, K., & Taeuber, C. (1987). *An aging world* (International Population Reports Series P-95, No. 78). Washington, DC: U.S. Bureau of the Census.

Vega, W. (1990). Hispanic families in the 1980s: A decade of research. *Journal of Marriage and the Family, 52,* 1015–1024.

Gender Roles

Brydon, L., & Chant, S. (1989). *Women in the Third World.* New Brunswick, NJ: Rutgers University Press.

Thompson, L., & Walker, A. (1989). Women and men in marriage, work, and parenthood. *Journal of Marriage and the Family, 51,* 845–872.

United Nations. (1991). *The world's women.* New York: Author.

PART II: FAMILY VARIATION

Exercise 3: World Diversity

In this exercise you will get a glimpse of the world's diversity. Then you will have a chance to explore your own understanding of diversity. Wait for your instructor's directions. Then read the information below.

- Eighty-five percent of world population growth between 1950 and 1987 took place in developing countries. By the year 2020, another 3 billion people are projected to be added to the world population; 93% of them will live in the Third World.

- About 40% of the population of Third World countries is under age 15. In industrialized countries the rate is 22%. The young age structure of the Third World is the result of high birth rates and reductions in infant mortality.

- Third World metropolitan areas are expected to become the most populous in the world. By the year 2000, 17 of 20 top metropolitan areas are projected to be in the Third World. Whereas five U.S. cities were among the world's most populous areas in 1950, only two will remain on the list by the year 2000.

- Racial and ethnic minorities now account for 20% of the U.S. population. This proportion will rise to nearly one-third by 2030.

- African Americans are still the dominant minority group in the United States, but Hispanics are the fastest-growing segment of the minority population. By 2030, African American and Hispanic groups will be about equal in size.

- By the year 2000, almost one-third of school-age children in the United States will be from minority populations. In Los Angeles, 80 different languages are spoken in the schools.

- Early settlers in the United States were of white, European ancestry, but today this group accounts for only 11% of immigrants. In contrast, 38% of legal immigrants come from Latin America and the Caribbean and 40% come from Asia.

- Over 70% of recent immigrants to the United States settle in six states: California, New York, Texas, Florida, New Jersey, and Illinois. Immigrants are concentrated in the major metropolitan areas of these states.

- Asian American families tend to have incomes above the national norm, whereas African American and Hispanic family incomes are below the norm. In part, these differences reflect differences in educational attainment. Asian Americans are more likely than other groups, including non-Hispanic whites, to finish college. Asian Americans are prepared to advance economically by getting professional and managerial jobs.

- Most of the U.S. poor do not live in urban ghettos. Poverty is more common in medium- and small-size communities and rural areas.

• The demographic composition of the U.S. poor has changed in the past 30 years. Whereas the elderly used to have the highest poverty rates, now persons living in female-headed households, including children, are at greater risk of being poor.

[*Sources*: De Vita, C. J. (1989). *America in the 21st century: A demographic review*. Washington, DC: Population Reference Bureau; Merrick, T. W. (1989). *America in the 21st century: A global perspective*. Washington, DC: Population Reference Bureau.]

Discussion Questions

On one page, write your answers to the following questions.

1. Did you know all this before? What did you learn?
2. Are there some statements you find troubling? Which ones? Why?
3. What challenges do these demographic changes pose for U.S. society? For our world?
4. What challenges to your beliefs do these changes pose?

On a second page, write your answers to the following questions:

5. Describe your own approach to cultural diversity by selecting one of the following statements that best describes you: (1) you believe that stereotypes are grounded in fact and do not care much about changing them; (2) you are aware that cultural biases toward people exist but do not mean to harm anyone and do not try to change yourself or others; (3) you try to take action to fight stereotyping and cultural biases.
6. Are you satisfied with your approach to cultural diversity? What would you like to change? How might you begin to change?

Exercise 4: The Ethnic Genogram

Can you trace your family to its country or countries of origin? In this exercise, you will attempt to do so. Here are the procedures you should follow.

1. Draw a genogram of your family, starting with yourself at the bottom. Trace only upward through parents, parents of parents, etc. Do not show siblings in any generation. Use gender symbols for all family members, including yourself (triangles for males; circles for females).

2. Include the branches upward (backward through the generations) until you reach a person who emigrated from another country. If different

branches emigrated during different generations, the "tree" will have different "heights" at spots. As another example, if all eight of your great-grandparents came to the United States during their lifetime, the top of your tree will have eight branches at the top and the top will be flat.

3. For each person at the top of your genogram, indicate above his/her gender symbol the country from which the person came. If you are not absolutely sure, put a question mark after the country. If you have no idea what the country was, just put a question mark at the top. You may know the region (e.g., Caribbean) or continent but not the specific country. Include this information if it applies, but be as specific as you can.

4. If you have no idea which generation came to the United States, use dotted lines at the top of the applicable branches and try to estimate how many additional generations are involved before reaching an immigrant.

5. If a person came from another English-speaking country outside Great Britain (including England, Scotland, or Wales) or Ireland, note the name of that country (e.g., Canada, etc.) but continue the branch upward until you reach a country in Great Britain (England, Scotland, Wales) or Ireland, or a country that is not English speaking.

6. Some people may have moved twice or more between different countries during their lifetime. Ignore this, and show only the *last* country before coming to the United States. You can make an exception to this if residence in the intermediate country did not last long. For example, if a person was born in Spain and spent only two years in Mexico when she was a young adult before coming to the United States, the most important thing is that she came from Spain.

7. In some cases, branches may terminate at the top with "Native American." Of course, if these could be traced back further, they might show that an ancestor came across the Bering Strait thousands of years ago. Ignore this, but indicate the tribal affiliation of the Native American ancestor if you know it.

8. Some of you will have complicated genograms if a person was raised for a significant period by a stepparent or was adopted. Note this if necessary, but trace using whatever information you have about blood relations and add to it whatever you know about the other kinds of relationships.

9. Work out your genogram in a preliminary version until you complete it. Then, redraw it *neatly* and turn in only the neat version, making sure it is easy to read.

10. If there are some peculiar circumstances in the case of your family, describe them in a few sentences at the bottom of your genogram. For example, you might note that a particular ancestor traveled to the United States on the *Mayflower* or on a slave ship. Also, you should indicate if a person was a racial minority group member in his/her country of origin. For example, a caucasian might have come from Kenya or Japan, so this should be men-

tioned if it applies. The point is, countries by themselves may not tell the whole story of your ethnic heritage, so you may need to clarify this.

[*Source*: This exercise was provided by David Klein, Department of Sociology, University of Notre Dame.]

PART III: FAMILY DEVELOPMENT

Exercise 5: Mate Selection

The purpose of this exercise is to help you to see how your own marriage could be if you lived in another culture. Write a one-page paper answering the questions presented in each of the following scenarios.

1. If your parents were to select your spouse for you, what kind of person would they choose? How would their choice fit with your personal preferences? Consider such issues as race, religion, social class, compatibility, and physical attraction. Also, what kind of dowry or brideprice could your parents afford to pay? How would this affect their selection of a spouse for you?
2. Assume that the sororate or levirate is practiced where you live. If you have a same-sex sibling or cousin who has been married or seriously involved with someone, imagine what it would be like if that person died and you had to marry his/her spouse. How well would the two of you get along?
3. Now assume that you live in a culture in which it is mandated that you marry a cross-cousin. For males, that would be the daughters of your mother's brothers and the daughters of your father's sisters. For females, it would be your father's sisters' sons and your mother's brothers' sons. List those people by name and indicate how happily you think that you could live together.

Exercise 6: Family Development

This exercise is designed to help you explore how your life cycle, or expected life cycle, differs from those of some other cultures. Figure 1 is a chart illustrating how the family life cycle can vary depending on the culture in which one lives. Type A depicts the traditional process in the United States, where people generally date in the teen years, formally marry in their 20s, rear a family, experience a period without children at home, and finally experience a postretirement time, some of which may be spent alone after the death of

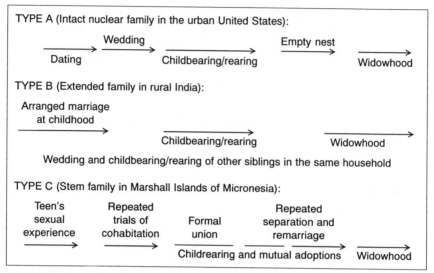

FIGURE 1. Examples of family life cycles in different cultures. From Wen-Shing and Jing (1991). Copyright 1991 by The Haworth Press. Reprinted by permission.

a spouse. Types B and C indicate patterns common to other places. Note how some of the stages vary in length and how others do not occur at all and/or are replaced by new and different stages.

Compare your own life cycle to these patterns by writing a short paper answering the following questions.

1. Chart how you think your own family life cycle will be if you do not make a commitment to a partner, or how your life cycle has been if you have established a committed relationship.
2. Add explanatory comments on how your family life cycle differs from or is similar to Type A, as well as Types B and C of other cultures. Draw from the alternatives provided and create what would be, for you, an ideal life cycle.

[*Source:* Wen-Shing, T., & Jing, H. (1991). *Culture and family: Problems and therapy* (p. 45). New York: Haworth Press.]

PART IV: GENDER AND FAMILY RELATIONS

Exercise 7: The Meaning of Dirt

The following is an excerpt from *Dave Barry's Guide to Marriage and/or Sex.* Barry is a syndicated columnist for the *Miami Herald.*

The major issue facing a man and a woman who decide to live together is: Dirt. Men and women do not feel the same way about dirt at all. Men and women don't even *see* dirt the same way. Women, for some hormonal reason, can see individual dirt molecules, whereas men tend not to notice them until they join together into clumps large enough to support commercial agriculture. There are exceptions, but over 85 percent of all males are legally classifiable as Cleaning Impaired.

This can lead to serious problems in a relationship. Let's say a couple has decided to divide up the housework absolutely even-steven. Now when it's the woman's turn to clean, say the bathroom, she will go in there and actually clean it. The man, on the other hand, when it's his turn, will look around and, because he is incapable of seeing the dirt, will figure nothing major is called for, so he'll maybe flush the toilet and let it go at that. Then the woman will say: "Why didn't you clean the bathroom? It's *filthy*!" And the man, whose concept of filthy comes from the men's rooms in bars, where you frequently see bacteria the size of cocker spaniels frisking around, will have no idea what she's talking about.

So what happens in most relationships, is, the man learns to go through the motions of cleaning. Ask him to clean a room, and he'll squirt Windex around seemingly at random, then run the vacuum cleaner over the carpet, totally oblivious to the question of whether or not it's picking up any dirt.

I have a writer friend, Clint Collins, who once proposed that, as a quick touch-up measure, you could cut a piece of two-by four the same width as the vacuum cleaner and drag it across the carpet to produce those little parallel tracks, which as far as Clint could tell were the major result of vacuuming. (Clint was also unaware for the first 10 or 15 years of his marriage that vacuum cleaners had little bags in them; he speculated that the dirt went through the electric cord and into the wall.)

[*Source*: Barry, D. (1987). *Dave Barry's guide to marriage and/or sex* (pp. 14–16). Copyright 1987 by Dave Barry. Reprinted by permission of Rodale Press, Inc., Emmaus, PA.]

Discussion Exercise

Think about and be prepared to discuss the following:

1. Do men and women really have such different attitudes about dirt, and do they have sharp differences in standards of cleanliness more generally?
2. If such differences exist, what really causes them? Are hormonal differences responsible, or is something else responsible?
3. Are differences in cleanliness standards liable to erupt into important arguments during a marriage (or even before)? When such arguments occur, how are they likely to be resolved? Will men "cheat" to please their partners, as Barry suggests?

4. Generally speaking, we are rewarded by others for doing things that have visible and measurable results. To what extent are women less rewarded for their accomplishments than men because women are assigned tasks without visible and measurable results?

Exercise 8: Characteristics of a Neotraditional Partner

Many men claim to be "liberated." They agree with the recent "women's movement" and support the recent changes in values and practices that promote equality in marriages or close relationships.

Most of these men really have qualified views about changing gender roles. They are not strictly traditional, but they are not fully equalitarian either. Hence, we may call them neotraditional, indicating that they are "caught in the middle" between the older ways and the newer ones.

Instructions to the Student

Complete the checklist below to determine whether you can be considered a neotraditional man or woman. Then follow your instructor's directions for the rest of the exercise.

personal endorsement of

CHARACTERISTICS OF THE NEOTRADITIONAL MAN	NEOTRADITIONAL CHARACTERISTICS	
	MAN: This is true for me	WOMAN: This is what I expect from a partner
1. THE HELPER: He "helps" with housework if his partner asks, but he does not initiate it, nor does he take full responsibility for any aspect of the work.	☐	☐
2. SKILL DEFICIENCY: He often needs to be told how and when to do housework. He is clumsy and forgets easily.	☐	☐
3. ENJOYMENT/VISIBILITY BIAS: He sometimes volunteers for the more enjoyable and "cleaner" household tasks, as well as those with visible results (e.g., cooking or playing with the children and taking them places).	☐	☐

4. AUTONOMIC EQUALITARIANISM: He agrees to do 50% of the housework, but only the "masculine" half (yard care, building and repairing items, keeping track of money, etc.). ☐ ☐

5. SOCIALIZATION BIAS: He believes each spouse should do the housework each "likes" to do and knows how to do. ☐ ☐

6. THE FLEXIBLE JOB: He may have a job that "permits" him to spend meaningful time with his family. ☐ ☐

7. AVAILABILITY BIAS: He believes that whoever has "more time available" should do particular household tasks. ☐ ☐

8. LEISURE BIAS: He schedules his housework around his recreational activities, whereas his wife is expected to schedule her recreation around her housework. ☐ ☐

9. THE GOOD FATHER: He loves his children and would do "anything" for them, except when they are troublesome (have runny noses or dirty diapers, are crying, etc.). ☐ ☐

10. THE GOOD PROVIDER: He believes his wife should work outside the home for pay "if she wants to," but only as long as she makes less money than he does. If he has a "career," it is acceptable for her to have one too, but her "career" should not be as demanding as his. ☐ ☐

11. HIS VS. HER JOB PRIORITIES: If his wife works outside the home for pay, her job should be rewarding, but she should be willing to quit or change if his job requires him to change. So, for example, he believes the family should move to another location if it is important for his career advancement, and his wife should be willing to go along. If her job requires such a move, however, she should adjust her occupation and not hinder his—"for the good of the family." ☐ ☐

12. THE DEVELOPMENTAL HANDICAP: He
believes his wife should be able to work
outside the home for pay, except when
the children are young. He may believe
that young children need a parent
around 100% of the time. Because his
occupation is viewed as more important
than hers, the wife is the one who should
stay home with young children. She can
go back to work after the children are
in school.   □   □

13. THE NANNY SYNDROME: If he believes in
formal or informal child care provided
by someone outside the nuclear family,
it is preferable that it be used on a part-
time basis. If child-care services are hired,
it is preferable that they be provided by a
female relative or by women who are
professionals, and at the lowest possible
cost.   □   □

14. THE HETEROSEXUAL DOUBLE STANDARD: He
expects his wife to do everything possible
to remain physically attractive and
youthful, and to sometimes initiate
sexual advances. She should not
have a sexually provocative
appearance in public, however, and
should not encourage other men to
"come on"to her. It is more acceptable to him to"flirt" with other
women, but he should also resist
their advances. He sees nothing
wrong with "going to lunch occasionally" with female colleagues
at work. After all, he has more
female colleagues than he used to,
and mingling is a part of effective
business. His wife, however, should
not "make a habit" of going out with
her male colleagues.   □   □

15. THE "LUCKY" NEOTRADITIONALIST HUSBAND:
He is married to a neotraditional wife,
someone who agrees with all the ideas
listed above.   □   □

Implications of Being a Neotraditional Partner

Following are the characteristics of the neotraditional partner with a description of the consequences of each approach for the man, woman, or relationship. Look over the features that best described you or your relationships. What have you learned about your expectations? Is there anything you would like to change?

1. THE HELPER: He "helps" with housework if his partner asks, but he does not initiate it, nor does he take full responsibility for any aspect of the work. *The rhetoric of "helping" maintains the husband in a secondary role regarding housework, and gives the impression that he is making things easier for his wife.*

2. SKILL DEFICIENCY: He often needs to be told how and when to do housework. He is clumsy and forgets easily. *His partner ends up doing most of the work and all the organizing.*

3. ENJOYMENT/VISIBILITY BIAS: He sometimes volunteers for the more enjoyable and "cleaner" household tasks, as well as those with visible results. *He has more fun and experiences less stress and fatigue.*

4. AUTONOMIC EQUALITARIANISM: He agrees to do 50% of the housework, but only the "masculine" half. *Because his portion tends to be outside work while his wife's portion tends to be inside work, his portion is more occasional whereas hers is more repetitive. As a result, his "half" seldom adds up to as much time spent as her "half" does. For example, he will gladly cook a meal on an open campfire in the woods or the barbecue at home, but he will not prepare "regular" meals in the kitchen. He will gladly mow the lawn—once a week for a few months—but will not do the housework.*

5. SOCIALIZATION BIAS: He believes each spouse should do the housework each "likes" to do and knows how to do. *He assumes that household skills are learned during childhood and cannot be learned (at least not by men) after a person gets married. He ignores the fact that women are socialized during childhood to "like" housework and to know how to do it much better than men.*

6. THE FLEXIBLE JOB: He may have a job that "permits" him to spend meaningful time with his family. *The key, however, is that the job requirements dictate his family obligations, not the other way around.*

7. AVAILABILITY BIAS: He believes that whoever has "more time available" should do particular household tasks. *He conveniently ignores the fact that his wife will have more available time than he does because the extrafamilial demands on his time are viewed as more important than his wife's extrafamilial demands.*

8. LEISURE BIAS: He schedules his housework around his recreational activities, whereas his wife is expected to schedule her recreation around her

housework. *He has more fun whereas she has less time for leisure and personal interests.*

9. THE GOOD FATHER: He loves his children and would do "anything" for them, except when they are troublesome. *Women must always be available for their children and husbands.*

10. THE GOOD PROVIDER: He believes his wife should work outside the home for pay "if she wants to," but only as long as she makes less money than he does. If he has a "career," it is acceptable for her to have one, too, but her "career" should not be as demanding as his. *She should not "have to" work because this would make him feel like an inadequate provider. Her income is viewed as "supplemental," to be used for luxuries the family otherwise could live without. This deprives her of opportunities for advancement, self-improvement, and a sense of accomplishment.*

11. HIS VS. HER JOB PRIORITIES: If his wife works outside the home for pay, her job should be rewarding, but she should be willing to quit or change if his job requires him to change. *Children learn that the man is the primary breadwinner whose career interests matter more.*

12. THE DEVELOPMENTAL HANDICAP: He believes his wife should be able to work outside the home for pay, except when the children are young. Because his occupation is viewed as more important than hers, the wife is the one who should stay home until after the children are in school. *He conveniently forgets how long this gap is and how much it would interfere with her occupation. If children enter school at age 5, having two children 2 years apart keeps his wife out of the labor force for 7 consecutive years. Having five children 5 years apart keeps her at home for 25 consecutive years. Because he knows that it is unfair to expect his wife to stay at home with the kids for several years or decades, he may favor her finding a part-time job until the youngest child is 6 or even 12 years old. This means lower pay, fewer fringe benefits, and fewer opportunities for advancement.*

13. THE NANNY SYNDROME: Formal or informal child care provided by someone outside the nuclear family, if used, should be on a part-time basis, preferably by a female relative or by women who are professionals, and at the lowest possible cost. *This implies that his wife (but not he) has a part-time occupation. The implication is that even if his own wife cannot provide 100% of the child care, some other woman will pick up the slack, but her care is not highly valued.*

14. THE HETEROSEXUAL DOUBLE STANDARD: He expects his wife to do everything possible to remain physically attractive and youthful. He expects her to limit her interactions with other men. It is more acceptable for him to "flirt" with other women and to spend time alone with them. *Ironically, recent public attention to sexual harassment in the workplace may increase the husband's concern about his wife's vulnerable situation, but it may do little to encourage him to reassess his own behavior toward women in the workplace.*

15. THE "LUCKY" NEOTRADITIONALIST HUSBAND: He is married to a neo-traditional wife, someone who agrees with all the ideas listed above. *What are the benefits for these couples? What are the costs, for example, for the woman's individual growth?*

PART V: SOCIAL INEQUALITY
IN THE CONTEMPORARY WORLD

Exercise 9: The Story of Eduardo and Lana

This course is designed to help you learn about families of diverse cultural backgrounds. The information presented is intended to develop your aware-ness of and empathy for families and individuals with experiences quite dif-ferent from your own. In the process, you may have learned to appreciate differences among families of various cultures or discovered biases you may have toward people who are not like yourself. The following exercise is de-signed to help you explore your changing attitudes. Read the following story and then wait for your instructor's directions.

Imagine that you are Eduardo or Lana—Eduardo if you are a man, Lana if you are a woman. Recently you have emigrated illegally to the United States from El Salvador with your mother, Doña Maria, your grandmother, Doña Margarita, and your four brothers and sisters.

You came to the United States because there was nothing left for your family in your country. Your father divorced your mother a few years ago and moved from the village to San Salvador. He said he would send money but he did not. No one in the village has heard from him and you fear he may be dead. Your family's farm has been ruined by war.

Your mother wanted you to have a chance at a better life. She took all her savings and paid them to a man you did not know to help you make it to the Mexican border. You hated having to sneak across the border. You were frightened and knew it was wrong. Your mother worries constantly about being caught now, and you feel an underlying tension almost all the time at home. But what choice did you have?

Your mother wants you to go to school, but she depends on you to help her, so there is no time. Your mother does not have any education. She works as a maid and because she cannot make much money, she works two jobs. She does not get any help from the government because she is afraid of being caught. But she works so hard that a lot falls on you at home. You help your mother with the younger children. (If Lana,) you do almost all the house-work. (If Eduardo,) you go from house to house asking people if they need yardwork done, garbage hauled, or windows washed to try to make some extra money. You spend time listening to your grandmother—she is very sad and cries a lot.

You know a little English from listening to the radio. You sometimes go to the university library and try to read the papers. You like being around the college students and hope that someday you will also be able to get an education. Usually you go to the library late in the evening, when your mother has come home and the younger children are fed, bathed, and in bed. This is the only time of day you really have to yourself, and sometimes you stay up late just to read and think. Tonight at the library, right before closing, you notice that a student seems to have left some papers behind—no one is around and the papers are laying loose on the table next to you. You decide to read them to see what this student is learning, and to see if you might want to try to return the papers to him/her.

Exercise 10: Awareness of Difference

In this exercise you will be asked to reflect on ways you may have changed (or not changed) in your approach to cultural diversity. Your instructor will give you directions for completing this exercise.

Exercise Guidelines
for the Instructor

The exercises included in this "bank" are designed to develop students' awareness of their own perspectives on the major topics included in the text. These activities are organized according to the book's major sections: Foundations of Comparative Family Studies, Family Variation, Family Development, Gender and Family Relations, and Social Inequality in the Contemporary World. The instructor assigns students the activities at an appropriate and convenient time during the term. The instructor may choose to use a few or all of the exercises. The instructor will need to clarify and modify instructions to meet students' particular needs, select a grading strategy, and decide how to lead discussion. Instructions for using all the exercises are described below.

PART I: FOUNDATIONS OF COMPARATIVE
FAMILY STUDIES

Exercise 1: The Arias Family

The exercise is designed to demonstrate that theories focus our attention on certain aspects of family life and not on others. Students analyze a family situation using concepts from two family theories covered in Chapter 1. The application to a particular family is intended to help students see that even abstract concepts have utility in describing family life. At the end of the case study, students are given the four questions listed below to answer in essay format. The instructor will need to review the questions, set limits on length, and develop the grading criteria.

1. What aspects of the Arias family's life does the theory tell you to focus on? For example, if you were using symbolic interactionism, the

theory would guide you to examine the meanings individuals gave to their interactions.

2. How do the aspects of family life defined by the theory emerge in the Arias family? For example, if you are using structural–functionalism, you would focus on the husband's and wife's instrumental and expressive roles.

3. What aspects of this family's life is the theory *unable* to address? For example, exchange would not focus your attention on the emotional dynamics of the family's interactions.

4. Which one of the two theories you chose does the better job of representing this family, in your opinion? Why?

Exercise 2: Comparative Family Research Study

In this exercise, students apply selected theoretical concepts (Chapter 1) and research methods or concepts (Chapter 3) to a study of intergenerational relationships *or* gender roles. Students may choose to do a literature review, case study, or research proposal. Detailed directions for assigning this exercise to students follow. The instructor may wish to substitute other guidelines depending on the class level, time, and student needs.

1. Read and select a research topic.
2. Select a theoretical foundation from Chapter 1.
3. Decide what method to use to conduct the project:
   a. Library literature review;
   b. Case study; or
   c. Original research proposal.
4. Read the articles suggested at the end of each topic, others located in the library, and those suggested by the instructor.
5. Carry out the research project as directed by the instructor.
6. Write a report of the study findings according to the following directions:
   a. Describe the topic selected for the research project.
   b. Summarize the theory used to guide the research.
   c. Describe the questions the research tried to answer, including all or some of the questions provided in the instructions and others suggested by the theory.
   d. Describe how the study was done.

The instructor will need to provide additional instructions for reporting results. The level of detail required will vary, but the following guidelines are suggested:

1. Describe the countries or cultures studied. Describe what is known about the topic for that country/culture based on the literature review.
2. Describe the study sample.
   a. Identify the number and types of people included in the sample.
      - For library research, describe the number of cases included in each of the studies cited.
      - For the case study for Topic One, describe the number of family members of each generation who were interviewed.
      - For the original research study for Topic Two, identify the number of men and women that will be selected for the sample.
3. If the case study method was used, describe the research procedures, including:
   a. How people were located for the case study; and
   b. The questions that were asked in the interviews.
4. If the original research project was planned, describe the research methods proposed, including:
   a. How the sample will be located;
   b. How many men and women will be sampled;
   c. How the data will be collected (i.e., through face-to-face in-depth interviews, mail surveys, and/or observations of interactions or time use); and
   d. What problems might be expected in carrying out the study.
5. What type of comparative research did the student conduct, according to Chapter 3?
6. What are the strengths and weaknesses of the student's study based on Lee's explanation of:
   a. Sample size;
   b. Representativeness;
   c. Generalizability; and
   d. Use of theory to explain study results.

PART II: FAMILY VARIATION

Exercise 3: World Diversity

This is the first of three exercises that are tied together and require some additional preparation and instruction: "World Diversity," "The Story of Eduardo and Lana," and "Awareness of Difference." The information presented in these exercises is designed to develop students' awareness of the unequal distribution of resources and power worldwide; to support empathy for the families and individuals who are particularly vulnerable to poverty, poor health, discrimination, and oppression; and to increase students' awareness of their own attitudes toward people who are different from themselves. Additional instructions for leading these exercises follow.

The "World Diversity" exercise should be used early in the coverage of Part II. Follow this format for leading the exercise:

1. Read the exercise aloud as students read the copy in their text.
2. Ask students to write an immediate response (no discussion).
3. Collect the students' papers and keep them for the Part V exercises on "The Story of Eduardo and Lana" and "Awareness of Difference."
4. Lead a discussion about students' reactions to the reading.

[*Source:* The "World Diversity" exercise is based on Mollenkott, V. R. (1991). Awareness of diversity: A classroom exercise. *Transformations,* 2(1), 15–18. The instructor will probably find it useful to read this article before leading the activities.]

Exercise 4: The Ethnic Genogram

This exercise asks students to uncover the diverse ethnic roots of their families of origin by developing their family ethnic genogram. After students complete their individual journey through their family histories, the instructor can shift the focus of the exercise from the personal to the societal level by following the instructions given below for analyzing and discussing the exercise. Note that these instructions give thorough directions for a detailed exercise. However, one or two parts of the exercise may be selected and used or the entire exercise may be modified, depending on students' needs and available class time.

Table 1 lists the major countries of origin for most U.S. immigrants between 1820 and 1990. As indicated at the bottom of the table, two-thirds (66%) of the total 57.6 million immigrants came from these places. The far left column presents the total number of immigrants, in millions, for each country. The second column shows the *percentage* of the total of immigrants between 1820 and 1990 represented by each country. The third column lists the country and, in parentheses, the peak years of emigration for that nation. In the far right column are the numbers for a coding scheme that will be explained under Coding and Preparation for Class Discussion.

About one-third of immigrants to the United States in the 170-year period covered by the census came from *other* countries. Table 2 lists those countries of origin, organized by world regions. The totals at the bottom of this table incorporate the countries in Table 1 (e.g., Northwest Europe includes Great Britain and Ireland), as well as the "other" countries with the *largest* number of immigrants. Note that because there is a large residual cat-

TABLE 1.   Major Countries of Origin, 1820–1990 (in Millions)

Millions	% of total	Country of origin	Code
7.1	12	Germany (1846–1893, 1959–1957)	(1)
6.1	11	Ireland (1847–1924, 1960s)	(2)
5.3	9	Italy (1887–1924, 1960s)	(3)
5.1	9	Great Britain (colonial, 1849–1924)	(4)
4.2	7	Canada (1880–1884, 1909–1930)	(5)
3.6	7	Mexico (1920–1929, since 1954)	(6)
3.4	6	U.S.S.R. (pre-Soviet: 1891–1914)	(7)
2.7	5	West Indies (since 1960)	(8)
	a	Cuba	(9)
	a	Dominican Republic	(10)
	a	Jamaica	(11)
	a	Haiti	(12)
	a	Other West Indies	(13)
37.5	66	*Subtotal*	

*a*Less than 1%.

egory of countries with smaller numbers of immigrants that could not be easily classified, the totals for the country categories do not add up to the total for each world region. The "other" category listed under each world region is for coding purposes only and does not represent a residual category established by the census. The last column lists the coding scheme for these regions and countries.

Coding and Preparation for Class Discussion

To prepare for class discussion, collect, score, and tabulate students' genograms as explained below. Fill out the blank Tables 1, 2, and 3 at the end of the "Exercise Guidelines" with the results. These tables can be duplicated and made into transparencies.

1. Code the country of origin for the persons at the top of each student's genogram. For example, if the individual came from Germany, he/she would be coded "1"; if from Ireland, he/she would be coded "2"; and so on. Note that the general category "West Indies" is broken down by country in the region, so that the specific country of origin can be coded when known.
2. If students' ancestors came from countries not listed in Table 1, they would fall into regional or "other" categories listed in Table 2. To identify those origins, follow the codes in the far right column of Table 2. Recall that the countries listed represent the largest immigrant populations from these world regions. Some students' ances-

TABLE 2. Other Origins and Regional Totals, 1820–1990 (in Millions)

Millions	% of total	Region and country of origin	Code
1.4		Sweden (est.) (1880–1914)	(20)
0.8		France (est.) (colonial, 1881–1893, 1903–1914)	(21)
0.8		Norway (est.) (1880–1914)	(22)
2.1		Other Northwest Europe (Netherlands, Belgium, Luxembourg, Switzerland, Denmark, Finland, Iceland)	(23)
15.3	27	**Northwest Europe** (includes Ireland, Great Britain)	
2.7		Austria (est.) (1846–1893, 1950s)	(30)
1.7		Hungary (est.) (1881–1914)	(31)
1.7		Czechoslovakia (est.) (1881–1914)	(32)
0.6		Poland (1891–1892, 1921–24)	(33)
0.5		Yugoslavia (est.) (1881–1914)	(34)
		Other Central Europe	(35)
12.3	21	**Central Europe** (includes Germany)	
0.3		El Salvador (est.) (since 1980)	(40)
0.3		Colombia (est.) (since 1980)	(41)
0.8		Other Central and South America	(42)
12.2	21	**Americas** (includes Canada, Mexico, West Indies, Latin America)	
0.6		Spain (est.) (colonial, 1903–1921)	(50)
0.6		Greece (est.) (1966–1980)	(51)
0.3		Portugal (est.)	(52)
		Other Southern Europe	(53)
6.8	12	**Southern Europe** (includes Italy)	
1.0		China (1854, 1869–1883, since 1970)	(60)
1.0		Philippines (since 1966)	(61)
0.7		Korea (since 1970)	(62)
0.7		Vietnam (est.) (since 1970)	(63)
0.5		Japan (1900–1908, since 1952)	(64)
0.5		India (since 1966)	(65)
0.3		Iran (est.) (since 1980)	(66)
0.3		Turkey (1910–1914)	(67)
1.0		Other Asia (Cambodia, Hong Kong, Laos, Thailand, Pakistan, etc.)	(68)
6.0	10	**Asia**	
0.3		Romania (est.)	(70)
0.2		Bulgaria (est.)	(71)
		Other Eastern Europe	(72)
4.0	7	**Eastern Europe** (includes former U.S.S.R.)	
0.4	1	**Africa** (17th and 18th centuries, since 1970)	(80)
0.1		Australia	(90)
0.1		Other (New Zealand, etc.)	(91)
0.2	0.3	**Pacific Islands** (1946–1947, 1966–1970)	
0.4	0.01	**All Other** (unrecorded at the time of immigration)	(100)
		Native American	(200)

tors may have come from countries not listed. Code them "Other Asia," "Other Eastern Europe," and so on.

3. The category "All Other" is countries of unrecorded origin at the time of immigration. The category "Native American" was added to this chart to enable the instructor to count students of this origin.

4. If the country of origin is unknown (indicated by a "?" on the student's chart), code that individual "300."

5. Prepare worksheets of the tables you have filled out. Count the total number of *students* (not immigrants on the genogram) listing at least one branch of the genogram from a region and/or particular country. For example, count the number of students who identified one or more ancestors from Great Britain. Enter the raw data in column 4 of Tables 1 and 2 (under *n* for Great Britain and Northwest Europe, respectively).

6. Calculate the percentage of total students with ancestors from each region and/or country of origin. For example, if 10 of 100 students said a relative at the top of their genogram emigrated from Africa, enter 10% in the last column of Table 2 for Africa.

7. Now you are ready to complete Table 3. Take all students who said their first ancestors were unknowns ("?"), calculate the number and percentage of students coded 300 and enter those results in the last two columns of Table 3.

8. Go back to the original charts and count the number of students indicating that all of their ancestors (all final branches) come from a single country. Enter the number and percentage of students in the second and third columns of Table 3. Note some of the most common examples.

9. For each student, code the number of generations since the first relatives emigrated. For example, if the student's ancestor was his/her great-grandfather, code the student "4" for the fourth generation. Then sum all students whose first ancestors fell into each generational category, enter these figures, and calculate the percentage of students for each category. Enter these results in the second and third columns.

Class Discussion

Report your findings to the class. Lead a discussion of the following questions and points.

1. How well do the class data conform to the general U.S. immigration picture? Does the distribution of students' ancestors' country of origin roughly parallel U.S. immigration patterns? That is, did most

students' ancestors come from Germany, Italy, Great Britain, and Ireland? (Note that tabulations are based on sums of one or more branches, not all branches. Thus, this picture is simpler than it would be if all branches were taken into account.)

2. What other countries/regions are represented by a large number of students (Table 2)? For example, classes in Texas, Florida, and California may have a large percentage of ancestors from Mexico or Central America.

3. Looking at Table 3, how common is it to *not* know the countries from which students' ancestors emigrated? This may be particularly true of African American students. What does it mean for all originating branches to have come from the same country?

4. How many generations did most students go back to find an emigrating ancestor? Students' responses are likely to be concentrated under category 4 (coded "55") since so much emigration from Europe occurred in the middle and later 19th century.

[*Source*: David Klein, Department of Sociology, University of Notre Dame. Data compiled from U.S. Bureau of the Census. (1976). *Historical statistics of the United States, colonial times to 1970*. Washington, DC: U.S. Government Printing Office; U.S. Bureau of the Census. (1992). *Statistical abstract of the United States*. Washington, DC: U.S. Government Printing Office.]

PART III: FAMILY DEVELOPMENT

Exercise 5: Mate Selection

This exercise asks students to apply the concepts presented in the chapter on mate selection (Chapter 7) to their own decisions about a marital partner. Students are asked to write a one-page paper answering the questions listed in their section of the text.

Exercise 6: Family Development

The family development exercise depicts examples of variations in life-cycle patterns in different cultures and asks students to compare their own life cycles with those of other cultures. This exercise also helps students recognize how their choices and preferences are affected by their own cultural background. Students are asked to write a short paper answering questions listed in their section of the text.

PART IV: GENDER AND FAMILY RELATIONS

Exercise 7: The Meaning of Dirt

Students read the humorous passage, "The Meaning of Dirt," in their section of the text. They are asked to think about and prepare to answer the questions listed in their section of the text. These questions address differences between men and women in attitudes toward cleanliness and the sources of these differences in biology or society. The exercise is intended to challenge stereotypes by helping students (and instructors) recognize and laugh at their assumptions and behaviors.

Exercise 8: Characteristics of a Neotraditional Partner

This exercise is designed to help students recognize their own expectations regarding gender roles in close relationships. Students are presented with a checklist of "neotraditional" characteristics of men and women and are asked to indicate whether their own behavior fits the neotraditional pattern.

The instructor should plan the following activities for this exercise:

1. Ask students to complete the checklist.
2. Divide students into pairs of men and women. Ask them to exchange answer sheets and discuss similarities and differences in their responses. Then have them imagine they are committed partners in real life. What would these similarities or differences in expectations of themselves and their partner mean for their relationship? Ask the couple to imagine they live in Sweden. How might their answers differ? What implications would this have for their relationship?
3. Ask couples to prepare a short written or verbal report on the experience of this exercise. These may be presented during a class session or turned in for grading.

PART V: SOCIAL INEQUALITY
IN THE CONTEMPORARY WORLD

Exercise 9: The Story of Eduardo and Lana

The readings and activities of the course culminate in the last activities under Part V. In the first exercise in the section, "The Story of Eduardo and Lana," students are asked to evaluate themselves through the eyes of someone from the Third World who has "met" them for the first time. This is done by asking students to look at their responses to Exercise 3, "World Diversity," from Eduardo's or Lana's viewpoint.

For this exercise, the instructor guides the class through an exercise of the imagination and a discussion of what they learned. To conduct the activity, follow these directions:

1. Ask students to close their eyes to participate in an exercise of the imagination. Ask the women to imagine that they are Lana; the men that they are Eduardo.
2. Read "The Story of Eduardo and Lana" aloud with the class.
3. Following the reading, return *page one* of each student's written responses to the exercise on "World Diversity."
4. Ask students to read their reaction papers through the eyes of Eduardo or Lana and to write, from Eduardo's or Lana's perspective, whether the students' reactions would indicate that the students would be desirable candidates for friendship, and why or why not. In other words, students "evaluate their own responses through the eyes of someone from a less privileged background" (Mollenkott, 1991, p. 17).
5. Ask students to respond to Eduardo or Lana in their own words, telling Eduardo or Lana how the students feel about the judgments Eduardo and Lana made about them. In other words, the students are asked to respond to the evaluation made by their Third World counterpart.
6. Discuss their reactions, if you wish, or collect student papers.

Exercise 10: Awareness of Difference

The last exercise asks students to reflect on how they have changed over the course of the semester in their approach to cultural diversity. This exercise may be conducted in class session after "The Story of Eduardo and Lana" exercise, or it may be given as a final homework assignment for collection and/or discussion at the last class or exam period. To conduct the activity, follow these directions:

1. Distribute page two of students' response to the "World Diversity" exercise in which they selected one of the following statements that best described them: (a) you believe that stereotypes are grounded in fact and do not care much about changing them; (b) you are aware that cultural biases toward people exist but do not mean to harm anyone and do not try to change yourself or others; (c) you try to take action to fight stereotyping and cultural biases.

2. Ask students to write a one-page discussion of the following questions.
   a. Select the answer (a, b, or c) that best describes you now.
   b. Is this response different from the one you selected at the beginning of the course? How have you changed (or not changed) over the duration of the course?
   c. If you feel you have changed, give two examples of how your behavior is different from the way it was at the beginning of the course (e.g., you try to get to know people from other cultures or you avoid making derogatory remarks about women or ethnic or racial groups).

The instructor may wish to obtain the Diversity Awareness Profile by Karen Grote (1991) for this exercise. The Profile is designed to assist individuals in becoming aware of their biases against people who are different and the ways in which they discriminate against or judge others. The Profile provides a self-rating scale of the individual's typical behavior (e.g., challenge others on derogatory comments) that measures the degree to which the person ignores, accepts, or takes action against biases toward people who are different (contact Pfeiffer & Company, 8517 Production Avenue, San Diego, CA 92121).

TABLES FOR GENOGRAM EXERCISE

TABLE 1.   Major Countries of Origin, 1820–1990 (in Millions)

Millions	% of total	Country of origin	Students with at least one branch	
			n	%
7.1	12	Germany (1846–1893, 1959–1957)		
6.1	11	Ireland (1847–1924, 1960s)		
5.3	9	Italy (1887–1924, 1960s)		
5.1	9	Great Britain (colonial, 1849–1924)		
4.2	7	Canada (1880–1884, 1909–1930)		
3.6	7	Mexico (1920–1929, since 1954)		
3.4	6	U.S.S.R. (pre-Soviet: 1891–1914)		
2.7	5	West Indies (since 1960)		
	[a]	Cuba		
	[a]	Dominican Republic		
	[a]	Jamaica		
	[a]	Haiti		
	[a]	Other West Indies		
37.5	66	*Subtotal*		

[a]Less than 1%.

TABLE 2. Other Origins and Regional Totals, 1820–1990 (in Millions)

Millions	% of total	Region and country of origin	Students with at least one branch n	%
1.4		Sweden (est.) (1880–1914)		
0.8		France (est.) (colonial, 1881–1893, 1903–1914)		
0.8		Norway (est.) (1880–1914)		
2.1		Other Northwest Europe (Netherlands, Belgium, Luxembourg, Switzerland, Denmark, Finland, Iceland)		
15.3	27	**Northwest Europe** (includes Ireland, Great Britain)		
2.7		Austria (est.) (1846–1893, 1950s)		
1.7		Hungary (est.) (1881–1914)		
1.7		Czechoslovakia (est.) (1881–1914)		
0.6		Poland (1891–1892, 1921–1924)		
0.5		Yugoslavia (est.) (1881–1914)		
		Other Central Europe		
12.3	21	**Central Europe** (includes Germany)		
0.3		El Salvador (est.) (since 1980)		
0.3		Colombia (est.) (since 1980)		
0.8		Other Central and South America		
12.2	21	**Americas** (includes Canada, Mexico, West Indies, Latin America)		
0.6		Spain (est.) (colonial, 1903–1921)		
0.6		Greece (est.) (1966–1980)		
0.3		Portugal (est.)		
		Other Southern Europe		
6.8	12	**Southern Europe** (includes Italy)		
1.0		China (1854, 1869–1883, since 1970)		
1.0		Philippines (since 1966)		
0.7		Korea (since 1970)		
0.7		Vietnam (est.) (since 1970)		
0.5		Japan (1900–1908, since 1952)		
0.5		India (since 1966)		
0.3		Iran (est.) (since 1980)		
0.3		Turkey (1910–1914)		
1.0		Other Asia (Cambodia, Hong Kong, Laos, Thailand, Pakistan, etc.)		
6.0	10	**Asia**		
0.3		Romania (est.)		
0.2		Bulgaria (est.)		
		Other Eastern Europe		
4.0	7	**Eastern Europe** (includes former U.S.S.R.)		
0.4	1	**Africa** (17th and 18th centuries, since 1970)		
0.1		Australia		
0.1		Other (New Zealand, etc.)		
0.2	0.3	**Pacific Islands** (1946–1947, 1966–1970)		
0.4	0.01	**All Other** (unrecorded at the time of immigration)		
		Native American		

TABLE 3. Branch and Generational History

Branches and generations	Students	
	n	%
One or more missing branches (origin unknown)		
All branches from a single country		
Most common examples:		
At least one branch indicating generations since migration		
1 student emigrated		
2 parents emigrated		
3 grandparents emigrated		
4 great-grandparents emigrated		
5 great-great-grandparents emigrated		
6 great-great-great-grandparents emigrated		
7 or more generations emigrated		

Appendix

The two tables included in this Appendix provide detailed information about worldwide diversity in family formation, dissolution, and living conditions. This allows for country comparisons on different demographic, social, and economic indicators. The tables are useful for illustrating overall differences in family life on a country or regional basis, as well as for supplementing some of the information presented in the text.

SELECTED INTERNATIONAL COMPARISONS

Table A.1 presents information for selected countries that represent all regions of the world and two-thirds of the world's population. The data include total fertility rates, life expectancy, total marriage rates, teen marriage rates, household/family size, and births to unmarried women. Table A.1 also provides data on per capita consumption (a rough indicator of personal wealth), female labor force participation, agricultural employment, persons per room of dwelling (an indicator of crowding), infant mortality rates, and literacy rates. At the bottom of the table are the countries that score highest and lowest on each indicator.

The contrasts between First World nations such as the United States and Canada and Third World nations such as Zaire and Mexico are particularly striking. For example, we generally observe lower fertility, longer life expectancy, smaller household/family sizes, and lower infant mortality among industrialized nations, reflecting their relatively better economic and health care conditions. The reader may also wish to select certain indicators for country-by-country comparisons or to examine differences and similarities among First World and Third World nations.

Looking more closely at how the United States compares to other nations, we see that it is at or near the top, numerically speaking, on a number of indicators. The United States scores high on life expectancy, marriage rate, monetary compensation, female employment rate, dwelling space, and literacy. Family size is relatively small, the economy is not based on agricultural employment, and infant mortality is low. For other indicators, the United States is intermediate. Total fertility is 2.0,

TABLE A.1.   Selected Cross-National Comparisons

	Total fertility rate[a]	Male/female life expectancy	Crude marriage rate	Percentage of marriages to teen women	Household (H) or family (F) size	Percentage of of births to unmarried women
Australia	1.9	73/80	7.0	6.9	F3.1	20.0
Brazil	3.2	64/69	6.7	32.0	F4.2	—
Canada	1.7	73/80	7.2	5.7	F3.1	16.2
People's Republic of China	2.2	68/71	8.5	—	H4.3	28.2
France	1.8	73/81	4.9	4.2	H2.7	15.5
West Germany	—	72/79	6.9	6.5	F2.7	—
India	3.7	58/59	—	—	H5.5	—
Indonesia	3.7	56/59	8.8	—	H4.9	—
Iran	6.5	64/65	6.8	—	H5.1	6.3
Italy	1.4	73/80	5.4	18.7	F3.2	1.0
Japan	1.6	76/82	5.8	3.4	F5.4	27.5
Mexico	3.2	68/74	7.1	40.7	H5.0	—
Nigeria	6.6	51/54	—	—	H5.0	5.0
Poland	2.1	69/76	6.7	19.9	F3.6	13.5
Russia	1.9	64/74	9.4	27.4	H3.2	47.0
Sweden	2.0	74/80	4.7	2.2	H2.2	27.9
United Kingdom	1.8	72/78	6.8	7.6	H2.7	23.4
United States	2.0	72/79	9.4	11.8	F2.6	23.4
Zaire	6.1	52/56	—	—	H6.0	—
Worldwide high	Rwanda (8.0)	Japan (see above)	U.S. Virgin Is. (18.0)	Guatemala (41.5)	H Marshall Is. (8.7) F W. Samoa (7.8)	San Tome and Principe (90.0)
Worldwide low	Monaco (1.2)	Sierra Leone (43.0)	Botswana (1.5)	U.S. Virgin Is. (1.0)	H Monaco (2.2) F Denmark (1.8)	Egypt (0.0)

which is exactly at the replacement level. Births to teenage women and unmarried women are either much more common or much less common in a few other countries.

We can also look at a few indicators to get a picture of the overall position of women in these countries. One might argue that high total fertility is a burden on women. Low female literacy and employment may signal discrimination against women in education and the labor force. Looking at how the United States fares on these measures, we observe that it, along with other industrialized nations, comes out relatively well. The "worst" places to be a woman, according to these indicators, are Iran and Mexico, although a full accounting would probably add many other countries to this list.

It is important to note, however, that these data must be interpreted in the context of the particular country's cultural and economic systems and methods of conceptualizing and measuring various activities. For example, low levels of women's employment in agricultural economies (e.g., Zaire) do not accurately reflect women's high participation in productive activities that are vital to subsistence living. Iran's low level of women's labor force participation is indicative of cultural prescriptions limiting women's movement outside the home but does not reflect their considerable contributions to household production. A high percentage of births to unmarried

Private consumption expenditure per capita, 1990 (U.S. $)	Females age 15–64 employed	Percentage of economy agricultural	Persons per room of dwelling[b]	Infant mortality (rate per 1,000 births)	Percentage of males/ females over 15 literate
10,150	41.2	5.3	0.6	10	99/99
740	29.7	23.3	0.9	86	82/81
12,960	46.2	3.5	0.5	9	96/96
160	49.2	71.0	1.8(37)	44	87/68
12,650	36.7	5.1	0.7(77)	10	99/99
12,720	39.2	3.2	0.5(86)	11	100/100
270	21.9	66.4	2.6	148	62/34
320	34.0	54.7	1.7(59)	117	86/70
4,750	5.5	25.0	1.8(60)	155	65/43
11,750	30.3	7.9	0.8(85)	12	98/96
13,650	42.0	6.6	0.7(90)	8	100/100
1,990	13.6	22.0	1.5	68	90/85
140	20.9	43.1	3.0	173	54/32
900	43.2	27.8	1.1(56)	19	99/98
4,860	47.9	12.5	—	27	—
13,730	50.1	3.1	0.6	7	100/100
10,860	42.6	2.0	0.6	11	100/100
14,630	44.2	2.9	0.5(147)	12	96/95
200	27.5	67.5	—	161	84/61
Switzerland (19,050)	Cayman Is. (59.8)	Burundi (92.9)	Djibouti (6.9)	Afghanistan (318)	Several (100/100)
Somalia (17)	Gaza Strip (1.0)	Macau (0.2)	United States (see above)	Sweden (see above)	Ethiopia (9.3/0.5)

Note. Compiled and provided courtesy David Klein, from U.S. Bureau of the Census (1992) and Encyclopedia Britannica (1993). Dates are not strictly comparable, but almost all are for years since 1986. The 19 countries in the table represent all parts of the world and two-thirds of the world's total population.
[a]The average number of children that would be born per woman if all childbearing women lived to the end of their childbearing years and bore children at each age at the average rate for that age.
[b]The numbers in parentheses indicate the average size dwelling space in square meters, where available.

women may be interpreted differently in Sweden, which has extensive social welfare programs to support parents, than it is in countries in which nonmarital births might place women in economic jeopardy. Thus, it is important to interpret these figures relative to a particular social and economic context.

SELECTED COMPARISONS OF INDUSTRIALIZED NATIONS

Most of the world's economically developed countries have maintained sufficiently reliable information about their populations so that changes over time in a few family-relevant characteristics can be displayed. Table A.2 presents information about household structure (in terms of married couple families), marriage and divorce rates, and births to unmarried women for the major industrialized nations. We can examine similarities in trends across nations as well as differences among them, such as percent of births to unmarried women (e.g., compare Sweden and Japan).

TABLE A.2.   Selected Cross-National Comparisons: 1960–1990

	Percentage of households married couple with children under 18	Marriage rate per 1,000 population of ages 15–64	Divorce rate per 1,000 married women	Percentage of births to unmarried women
United States				
1960	44	14	9	5
1970	40	17	15	11
1980	31	16	23	18
1989	27	15	21	27
Canada				
1961	51	12	2	4
1971	47	14	6	10
1981	36	12	11	13
1986	32	11	13	23
Japan				
1960	49	15	4	1
1970	45	14	4	1
1980	43	10	5	1
1990	33	8	5	1
Denmark				
1960	—	12	6	8
1976	24	12	8	11
1983	23	8	11	33
1989	20	9	14	46
France				
1960	—	11	3	6
1968	44	12	3	7
1982	40	10	6	11
1989	36	8	8	28
Netherlands				
1961	55	13	2	1
1971	52	15	3	2
1981	44	10	8	4
1989	35	9	8	11
Sweden				
1960	36	10	5	11
1970	30	8	7	18
1980	25	7	11	40
1990	20	20[a]	12	52
United Kingdom				
1961	38	12	3	5
1971	34	14	5	8
1981	31	12	12	12
1989	26	11	12	27
West Germany				
1960	44	14	4	6
1970	42	12	5	6
1980	37	9	6	8
1989	31	9	9	11

[a]The increase in 1990 was due to a change in inheritance laws that caused many cohabiting to marry.

Looking at how the United States scores, we see that it is intermediate with respect to the percentage of married-couple households with children. France is highest and Denmark is lowest. The U.S. marriage and divorce rates tend to be quite high relative to the other eight countries included. The United States also is at an intermediate level for births to unmarried women. This phenomenon is relatively uncommon in the Netherlands and West Germany and rare in Japan. It is prevalent in the Scandinavian countries, where there is greater social acceptance of nonmarital cohabitation and births.

Nevertheless, the trends over time are similar for all nine countries. Married-couple families with children and the marriage rate are declining, whereas divorce and nonmarital births are increasing. Thus, the changes away from "traditional" family structure and formation are not confined to the United States.

REFERENCES

Encyclopedia Britannica. (1993). *1993 Britannica book of the year*. Chicago: Author.

U.S. Bureau of the Census. (1992). *Statistical abstract of the United States 1992*. Washington, DC: U.S. Government Printing Office.

Index

feminist view of, 24, 25
functions of, 9, 11, 84–87, 90
heterosexual nuclear; *see* Nuclear
  family
hierarchies in, 7, 18
in industrialized versus Third World
  countries, 5, 6
life-cycle stages, 15, 375, 376, 392
modern, 53–56
and origin theories, 87–89
polygamous, 84; *see also* Polyandry;
  Polygynandry; Polygyny
same-sex, 101
single-parent; *see* Single parenthood
and social change, 10, 15, 16
structure, 90
theory, 7, 8
types of, 100, 101
Family development theory, 15–17,
  30
Family ecology theory, 13–15
Family planning, 6, 217
Family Strengths Inventory, 348
Family systems theory, 11–17, 30
Family work, 268–293
Fatherhood, 313
  in African American enslavement,
    326
  in Japan, 276, 277
  and child care, 285, 288, 292
  and *machismo*, 340, 342
  in polyandry, 125, 130, 131
  in United States, 280
Female circumcision, 242, 243, 257,
  260, 298, 310
Femininity, devaluation of, 299
Feminism, 19
  and family diversity, 24
  and origin of family, 88
  rejection of in Third World, 261
  in Sweden, 291
  types of, 23
Feminist theory, 22–26, 31, 243, 353;
  see also Feminism
  of marital power, 306, 307, 309
Fertility rates, 6, 241, 242, 257,
  355
Fertility symbols, 153–155

Filial piety, 215–217, 222, 228, 229
  and funeral ceremonies, 226, 227
Finland, 237
Foot binding, 223
Forests, preservation of, 262, 263
France
  cultural changes in, 195, 237
  divorce rate in, 195, 196
  maternity leave in, 285
  working women in, 272, 277, 284–
    286
Functional requisites, 9

Gamines, 344–347
  rehabilitation of, 346, 347
Gender, 22, 24, 25, 306
Gender roles, 10, 11, 87, 190, 260,
  269, 302, 312
  in agricultural societies, 247, 248
  changing, 197, 264
  in China, 214
  economic function of, 86
  and government intervention, 293
  and household division of labor,
    233, 268–293
  historical perspective on, 269,
    270
  in Islamic society, 256
  in Japan, 276, 277
  and job loss, 18
  in Latin America, 254
  origin of, 88, 89
  socialization to, 23, 251, 260, 312
  in Sweden, 288
  in urban employment, 250, 251
Gender stratification, 243–245, 253,
  260, 264, 302, 304
  and colonialism, 246, 260
  and race/class discrimination, 244,
    245, 260
  in Third World employment,
    247–253
Ghana
  child welfare in, 308
  divorce in, 206
Great Britain; *see* United Kingdom

KING ALFRED'S COLLEGE
LIBRARY